EUROPEAN AND US
CONSTITUTIONALISM

European constitutionalism is not merely an intra-European phenomenon but it can also be compared to other major forms of constitutionalism. Over the past decade or so issues have emerged which seem to
indicate that European constitutional theory and practice is becoming
aware that it has developed certain rules and possesses certain characteristics which distinguish it from US constitutionalism and vice versa. This
book explores whether such differences can be found in the five areas of
'freedom of speech', 'human dignity', 'duty to protect', 'adjudication'
and 'democracy and international influences'. The authors of this book
are constitutional scholars from Europe and the United States as well as
from other constitutional states, such as Canada, Israel, Japan, Peru and
South Africa.

GEORG NOLTE is Professor of Law at the University of Munich. From 1999
until 2004 he was Professor of Law at the University of Göttingen and in
2003–4 he was a Visiting Fellow at All Souls College, Oxford.

EUROPEAN AND US CONSTITUTIONALISM

Edited by

GEORG NOLTE

CAMBRIDGE
UNIVERSITY PRESS

CAMBRIDGE UNIVERSITY PRESS
Cambridge, New York, Melbourne, Madrid, Cape Town, Singapore, São Paulo

CAMBRIDGE UNIVERSITY PRESS
The Edinburgh Building, Cambridge CB2 2RU, UK
Published in the United States of America by Cambridge University Press, New York

www.cambridge.org
Information on this title: www.cambridge.org/9780521854016

First published 2005

Printed in the United Kingdom at the University Press, Cambridge

A catalogue record for this book is available from the British Library

ISBN-13 978-0-521-85401-6 hardback
ISBN-10 0-521-85401-6 hardback

CONTENTS

v

This book is the fruit of an intense collaboration between the European Commission for Democracy through Law (the 'Venice Commission') and academia. The Venice Commission is the Council of Europe's advisory body on constitutional matters. Established in 1990, the Commission has played a leading role in the adoption of constitutions that conform to the standards of Europe's constitutional heritage. It contributes to the dissemination of the European constitutional heritage while continuing to provide 'constitutional first-aid' to individual states. The Venice Commission also plays a role in crisis management and conflict prevention through constitution building and advice.

The Venice Commission is composed of independent experts. The members are senior academics, particularly in the fields of constitutional or international law, supreme or constitutional court judges or members of national parliaments. Acting on the Commission in their individual capacity, the members are appointed for four years by the participating countries. All Council of Europe member states are members of the Venice Commission; in addition, Kyrgyzstan joined the commission in 2004. Argentina, Canada, the Holy See, Israel, Japan, Kazakhstan, the Republic of Korea, Mexico, the United States and Uruguay are observers. South Africa has a special cooperation status similar to that of the observers. The European Commission and OSCE/ODIHR participate in the plenary sessions of the Commission.

The work of the European Commission for Democracy through Law aims at upholding the three underlying principles of Europe's constitutional heritage: democracy, human rights and the rule of law which represent the cornerstones of the Council of Europe. Accordingly, the Commission works in the four key areas of constitutional assistance, elections and referendums, cooperation with constitutional courts, and transnational studies, reports and seminars.

In May 2003, the Commission organized a seminar in Göttingen, Germany, on 'European and American Constitutionalism'. This seminar was held in collaboration with the Institute of International Law, University of Göttingen, and Yale Law School. In addition to the Council of Europe, the Volkswagen Foundation provided generous funding. After the conference all speakers revised and completed their papers in the light of the discussions in Göttingen.

Many people deserve to be thanked for their contributions. Apart from the authors, these are Professors Jeffrey Jowell, University College London, and Jed Rubenfeld, Yale Law School, for their support during the preparatory phase of the conference; Ms Caroline Martin and Ms Caroline Godard from the Council of Europe for all their organisational work; Ms Anna-Jule Arnhold, Mr Helmut Aust, Ms Nina Naske, and Mr Florian Prill, all University of Göttingen, for patiently and diligently checking the footnotes and putting them into the correct format; Ms Roslyn Fuller, University of Göttingen, for enthusiastically and professionally dealing with all the language aspects of the text; and, finally, as ever, Ms Christiane Becker, University of Göttingen, for being the friendly, competent and determined manager of the whole enterprise.

Georg Nolte

PART I

Introduction

European and US constitutionalism: comparing essential elements

GEORG NOLTE

Until the end of the Cold War comparative constitutional lawyers and political scientists tended to emphasise the common ground within the North Atlantic region.[1] Today, some even speak of a 'European-Atlantic constitutional state'.[2] This view was and is perfectly legitimate. It was not only the radically different socialist understanding of law which made western constitutional theories and practices appear to be so similar. This similarity is also firmly grounded in the cross-fertilising constitutional developments between Western Europe and North America which have taken place before and since the eighteenth century.

The end of the socialist systems in Eastern Europe and increasing 'globalisation', however, may bring about a change of emphasis from the similarities to the differences between the constitutionalisms in the United States and Europe. Over the past few years issues have emerged which seem to indicate that European constitutional theory and practice is becoming aware that it has developed certain rules and possesses certain properties which are characteristically different from US constitutionalism and vice versa. This new perspective, or rather such a change in emphasis, is likely to be reinforced by political developments which expose discrepancies in the evaluation of fundamental questions between the majority of Europeans on the one hand and the majority of Americans on the other.[3]

---

[1] See e.g. Klaus Stern, *Grundideen europäisch-amerikanischer Verfassungsstaatlichkeit* (Berlin: de Gruyter, 1984).

[2] Thomas Giegerich, 'Verfassungsgerichtliche Kontrolle der auswärtigen Gewalt im europäisch-atlantischen Verfassungsstaat: Vergleichende Bestandsaufnahme mit Ausblick auf die neuen Demokratien in Mittel- und Osteuropa' (1997) 57 *Zeitschrift für ausländisches öffentliches Recht und Völkerrecht*, 405–564.

[3] Robert Kagan, *Of Paradise and Power* (New York: Knopf, 2003).

This book was conceived before the drama of the latest Iraq crisis unfolded. That crisis has had profound repercussions on transatlantic and intra-European political relationships. It has obviously gone beyond disputes about international law. But has it also reached the level of constitutional law? It is true that weapons of mass destruction and Iraq as such have little to do with constitutionalism. The approaches of how to deal with such threats, however, may well be somehow connected to more fundamental questions of the respective political identities. This is where the area of constitutionalism begins.

I. European constitutionalism?

Constitutionalism is about the fundamental rules and the identity, or better the self-understanding (*Selbstverständnis*), of any particular political community.[4] In different ways, the self-understanding of both the European states and Europe on the one hand, and the United States on the other, has become somewhat insecure over the past few years. The question is therefore whether this insecurity has affected the most fundamental areas of political self-understanding, the respective constitutionalisms, and whether a new relationship between Europe and the United States is emerging in this respect. In exploring this question the political context cannot be disregarded. At the same time, however, one should not lose one's sense of proportion. Constitutional law concerns the deepest layers of the respective legal systems and political identities. Those layers cannot be changed easily even by major international developments.

But does comparing 'European and US constitutionalism' at all make sense? Is it not an exercise in comparing apples to oranges? European constitutionalism mostly appears to be a distinctly intra-European phenomenon.[5] This is true even though reference to US constitutionalism

---

[4] Michel Rosenfeld (ed.), *Constitutionalism, Identity, Difference and Legitimacy* (Durham: Duke University Press, 1994); on constitutionalism generally see also Charles Howard MacIlwain, *Constitutionalism* (Ithaca: Cornell University Press, 1947); Larry Alexander (ed.), *Constitutionalism* (Cambridge: Cambridge University Press, 1998).

[5] *Cf.* Joseph H. H. Weiler and Marlene Wind (eds.), *European Constitutionalism Beyond the State* (Cambridge: Cambridge University Press, 2003); Koen Lenaerts and Piet van Nuffel, *Constitutional Law of the European Union* (London: Sweet and Maxwell, 1999); Denis Blanchard, *La Constitutionnalisation de l'Union européenne* (Rennes: Apogée, 2001); Renaud Dehousse (ed.), *Une Constitution pour l'Europe?* (Paris: Presses de Sciences Po, 2002); Paul Magnette (ed.), *La Constitution de l'Europe* (2nd edn, Bruxelles: Editions de l'Université de Bruxelles, 2002).

is frequently made in the intra-European debate.[6] One hesitates to compare the term European constitutionalism to US constitutionalism. Traditionally, US constitutionalism is still compared to French or German or other national constitutional systems.[7] The reason for this is obvious since the US, French and German constitutional systems, with their respective characteristic judicial practice and cultures of interpretation – their constitutionalism – concern the same object: the rules concerning the working of an independent and self-governing political community of human beings and their fundamental rights. 'European constitutionalism', on the other hand, seems to embody something which is both more removed from 'the people' and more vague than national constitutional law.

The development of European integration, however, has started to make these clear-cut differences disappear. This is not only because a European entity is developing which more closely resembles a state. It is also because the European states themselves and their characteristic constitutionalisms are being transformed by the process of European integration. This is visible most clearly in the jurisprudence of the European Courts in Strasbourg and Luxembourg. The jurisprudence of the European Court of Human Rights necessarily influences and harmonises national human rights jurisprudence. To a lesser extent, similar developments are taking place in the area of state organisation.[8] These developments seem to justify posing the question of whether a

---

[6] Anne Peters, Anne Peters, *Elemente einer Theorie der Verfassung Europas* (Berlin: Duncker and Humblot, 2001), pp. 96 et seq.; Armin von Bogdandy (ed.), *Europäisches Verfassungsrecht* (Berlin: Springer, 2003), at pp. 60, 75, 99, 646, 932; also Ulrich Everling, 'Die Europäische Union im Spannungsfeld von gemeinschaftlicher und nationaler Politik und Rechtsordnung,' in ibid., p. 852 and Paul Kirchhof, 'Die rechtliche struktur der Europäische Union als Staatenverbund,' in ibid., p. 907; Michel Rosenfeld, 'La Convention européenne et l'œuvre des constituants américains' (2003) 13 *Cités*, 47–55.

[7] Vicki C. Jackson and Mark Tushnet, *Comparative Constitutional Law* (New York: Foundation Press, 1999); Donald P. Kommers, 'Can German Constitutionalism Serve as a Model for the United States?' (1998) 58 *Zeitschrift für ausländisches öffentliches Recht und Völkerrecht*, 787–98; Elizabeth Zoller, 'Les Horizons de la souveraineté – l'ésprit de la constitution hier et aujourd'hui – des usages de la Constitution en France et aux États Unis' (2002) 1 *Esprit*, 99–107.

[8] The consultative practice of the European Commission for Democracy through Law, the so-called Venice Commission of the Council of Europe, is an important, though sometimes overlooked, resource for identifying the European constitutional heritage in the area of democracy and rule of law, which includes separation of powers, see www.venice.coe.int.

distinct 'European constitutionalism' is beginning to emerge.[9] Asking this question correctly, however, requires not only determining the *genus* of this constitutionalism, as it is currently undertaken in the intra-European debate, but also the *differentiae specificae*, which have so far been somewhat neglected.

Trying to determine identity by looking for characteristic differences is, however, a delicate enterprise. Much depends on what is being looked at. Even if characteristic differences between a European constitutionalism and US constitutionalism could be found, this would not automatically mean that Europe would already possess its 'own' characteristic constitutionalist traits. It is equally possible that Europe and its member states share any characteristic differences vis-à-vis the United States with other non-European constitutional states. This is why the comparison cannot be limited to European and US constitutionalism strictly speaking. There must also be a *tertium comparationis*. This *tertium* cannot be the rest of the world but must rather be other constitutional states.[10] For this reason a number of commentators from such other constitutional states, such as Canada, Israel, Japan, Peru and South Africa have been invited to contribute to this book. Perhaps these *tertia comparationis* lead to the conclusion that it is not so much Europe which is developing a more distinctive constitutional identity, but rather that it is the United States which is once and here again an exception.

II. The choice of topics

The choice of topics for this book deserves to be explained. The first consideration is a limitation to the most fundamental aspects of constitutionalism. A second consideration is that any topic must be apt to provide meaningful comparison between Europe and the United States. While it should be fairly obvious that the topics chosen do satisfy these criteria, it may be less clear why other important areas have been left out. Freedom of religion and the relationship between church and state, for

---

[9] Paul P. Craig, 'Constitutions, Constitutionalism, and the European Union' *European Law Journal* (2001) 7, 125–50; Renaud Dehousse, 'Un nouveau constitutionnalisme?' in Dehousse, *Constitution pour l'Europe?*, above, note 5, at pp. 19–38; Stefan Oeter, 'Europäische Integration als Konstitutionalisierungsprozeß' (1999) 59 *Zeitschrift für ausländisches öffentliches Recht und Völkerrecht*, 901–17; Lucia Serena Rossi, '"Constitutionnalisation" de l'Union européenne et des droits fondamentaux' (2002) 38 *Revue trimestrielle de droit européen*, 27–52.

[10] Bruce Ackerman, 'The Rise of World Constitutionalism' (1997) 83 *Virginia Law Review*, 771–97; Norman Dorsen, *Comparative Constitutionalism* (St Paul: West Group, 2003).

example, are important topics. It is quite clear, however, that they do not (yet?) yield much common ground *within* Europe. Equal protection would have been a fertile topic, but ultimately the most important differences in this field would seem to lie in the realm of anti-discrimination policy. The most important issues in this context, however, such as the permissibility of affirmative action, are currently in flux both in Europe and in the United States.[11] Federalism is certainly an important topic insofar as it can be debated whether the US experience is significant for EU integration. This issue, however, has already been widely discussed.[12] Finally, the role of the constitution in its respective national, legal and political environment, its amendability and its entrenchment, are important background topics which should be kept in mind.

Do the five topics 'freedom of speech', 'human dignity', 'duty to protect', 'adjudication' and 'democracy and international influences' indeed yield characteristic differences between a European and a US constitutionalism? The purpose of this introduction is not to give conclusive answers, but to establish that the question is legitimate.

III. Freedom of speech

If average Europeans were asked which fundamental right is much more protected in the United States than in Europe, most people would probably give the answer: freedom of speech. Rightly so: hate speech, in particular Nazi propaganda, is not only tolerated but even to a large extent constitutionally protected in the United States. The same is not true in Europe. Most European states have enacted special legislation, in conformity with international human rights requirements, to ban incitement to racial hatred, and even to ban certain right-wing insignia and propaganda.[13] The European Court of Human Rights has accepted such legislation in principle, as have the

---

[11] *Gratz* v. *Bollinger*, 539 U.S. _ _ _ (2003).

[12] Von Bogdandy, *Europäisches Verfassungsrecht*, above, note 6, at pp. 60, 75, 99, 646, 932. Mauro Cappelletti, Monica Seccombe, Joseph H. H. Weiler, *Integration Through Law, Europe and the American Federal Experience* (Berlin, New York: Walter de Gruyter, 1986).

[13] UK, *Race Relations Act* 1976, see also the establishment of the 'Commission for Racial Equality'; France, Arts. 225–1 and 432–7 *Code pénal*; Germany, ss. 130, 185 *Strafgesetzbuch*; compare also European Commission against Racism and Intolerance, *Legal Measures to Combat Racism and Intolerance in the Member States of the Council of Europe*, CRI (95) 2 rev. (1996); for a general survey cf. Peter Rädler, *Verfahrensmodelle zum Schutz vor Rassendiskriminierung* (Berlin: Springer, 1999), pp. 198–203.

national Constitutional Courts in Europe. The two leading cases of
the European Court of Human Rights in this context are characteristic.
In *Jersild v. Denmark*[14] the Court declared that a journalist who
had conducted an interview with right-wing youths which was then
broadcast on television could not be punished for dissemination
of prohibited hate speech. A closer look at the judgment shows,
however, that the Court has very much restricted its holding to the
particular facts of the case. The Court found relevant the obvious
informational and non-associative nature of the programme and that
it was viewed by 'informed' recipients.[15] Therefore, the judgment is
rather a confirmation of the rule that the media can be restrained
when covering racist or extreme right-wing activities than an affirmation of media freedom.

The same is true for the case of *Lehideux v. France*.[16] In this case the
French authorities had applied a law which prescribed that French
history during the time of the German occupation may not be 'falsified'.
Two persons were convicted who had described General Pétain, the
leader of the Vichy puppet government, as a patriotic figure by empha-
sising certain of his deeds and leaving out others which most people
would regard as crucial, in particular the Vichy regime's policy of
persecution of Jews. These persons had not, however, denied this persecution or the holocaust as such. Again, the judgment of the European
Court is liberal only in a very limited sense: the Court took pains to
declare that holocaust denial and Nazi propaganda can be punished, and
are even outside the scope of protection of the freedom of expression,
and it only held that in the case at hand the issue was still within the
realm of legitimate historical debate.[17] Such a careful, some might even
say timid, case-by-case liberalism is not the style of the US Supreme
Court. The American Court has forcefully rejected any possibility of
'viewpoint-discrimination'.[18] It has thereby excluded special legislation
against certain ideological positions, even if they are expressed in the
form of otherwise unprotected hate speech. Such speech is defined as
speech which typically provokes immediate violent reactions and
thereby constitutes a clear and present danger.

[14] 298 Eur. Ct. H. R. (ser. A) 4 (1994).   [15] Ibid., pp. 24 et seqq., paras. 34 et seqq.
[16] 1998-VII Eur. Ct. H. R. 2864.   [17] Ibid., pp. 2886 et seq., paras. 54 et seq.
[18] *R. A. V.* v. *City of St. Paul*, 505 U.S. 377, 391 et seqq. (1992); see also *Hustler Magazine*
v. *Falwell*, 485 U.S. 46, 55 (1988).

This stark contrast in the free-speech jurisprudence between European and US courts is not necessarily predetermined by the respective instruments themselves. It is true that the American free-speech clause is phrased in absolute terms while the European provisions usually contain limitation clauses. At the same time, however, one must remember that until the First World War the judicial understanding of 'freedom of speech' in US law was rather limited.[19] It was not until 1968 and the case of *Brandenburg v. Ohio*[20] that the 'clear and present danger test' was firmly established. The European provisions with their limitation clauses could, on the other hand, permit the identification of 'hard cores' of free speech which would not be subject to much ad hoc balancing. It is indeed striking to read certain leading judgments of the European Court of Human Rights which resonate with ideas and concepts from the jurisprudence of the US Supreme Court. The oft-quoted formula of the European Court according to which freedom of expression also protects statements which 'offend, shock and disturb'[21] immediately reminds the reader of the US Supreme Court's formula in *New York Times v. Sullivan* according to which 'debate on public issues ... may well include vehement, caustic and sometimes unpleasantly sharp attacks'.[22] The same is true of some of the legal concepts which serve to circumscribe spheres of greater or lesser protection: while the US Supreme Court has afforded greater protection to attacks against public officials and public figures,[23] the European Court has found the same for speech which is directed against public officials and politicians.[24]

Already such a cursory glance at the different courts' jurisprudence raises profound questions which four authors address in their contributions. Roger Errera puts the European and the US jurisprudence into the general context of the development of judicial review and looks more closely at the areas of political speech, libel, personality rights and privacy. Frederick Schauer concentrates on the characteristic

---

[19] David M. Rabban, *Free Speech in its Forgotten Years* (Cambridge: Cambridge University Press, 1997), pp. 175–6.

[20] 395 U.S. 44 (1969).

[21] *Lingens* v. *Austria*, 103 Eur. Ct. H. R. (ser. A) 26 (1986), para. 41; *cf.* also *Lehideux* v. *France*, 1998-VII Eur. Ct. H. R. p. 2864, para. 55.

[22] 376 U.S. 254, 270 (1964).

[23] *Gertz* v. *Robert Welch, Inc.*, 418 U.S. 323, 343–5 (1974).

[24] *Lingens* v. *Austria*, 103 Eur. Ct. H. R. (ser. A) 26 (1986), para. 42; *Barfod case*, 149 Eur. Ct. H. R. (ser. A) 12 (1989), paras. 25 et seqq.

methodologies used by the courts and relates methodology and substance by adopting a broad historical perspective. In their comments,
Lorraine Weinrib and Wilfried Brugger pursue this broad inquiry from
their respective Canadian and German perspectives.

IV. Human dignity

Another reason why freedom of speech occupies such a different place in
European and US constitutionalism may be related to the second topic
of this book, human dignity. Human dignity is a comparatively modern
legal term.[25] It is therefore not surprising that the term is not mentioned
in the US Constitution, but is in a good number of post-war European
constitutions as well as in international human rights instruments. The
stimulus for the career of human dignity as a legal term is widely
perceived to come from the global sense of unprecedentedness which
the Nazi and other atrocities gave rise to, and the corresponding discovery of an even more fundamental legal right (or value) than the
classical 'life, liberty and property'.[26] In a sense, therefore, the reason
for recognising and proclaiming human dignity in post-war European
constitutional texts can be seen as being structurally similar to why a
need was felt to punish perpetrators for crimes against humanity and not
merely for murder or enslavement. This reading of the history of the
term human dignity as a constitutional concept easily explains why it
has been more prevalent in Europe than in the United States. In
America, the European experience which gave rise to the concept was
simply not felt to be relevant.

Such an explanation is, however, itself too narrow. The term human
dignity not only has an age-old philosophical tradition, but it is also
frequently used in discourses of all sorts, including in the judgments of
the highest courts on both sides of the Atlantic. The US Supreme Court
has indeed used and applied the term human dignity in a number of its
judgments. The most important of them concern the delimitation of
what is cruel and unusual punishment in the sense of the Eighth
Amendment,[27] the establishment of rights to a hearing under the Due

---

[25] *Cf.* David Kretzmer and Eckart Klein (eds.), *The Concept of Human Dignity in Human
Rights Discourse* (The Hague: Kluwer Law International, 2002).
[26] Horst Dreier, 'Art. 1 I', in H. Dreier (ed.), *Grundgesetz Kommentar* (1st edn, 3 vols.,
Tübingen: Mohr Siebeck, 1996), vol. I, paras. 20–1.
[27] *Atkins* v. *Virginia*, 536 U.S. ___ (2002); *Trop* v. *Dulles*, 356 U.S. 86, 100–1 (1958);
Rochin v. *California*, 342 U.S. 165, 174 (1952).

Process Clause,[28] the extent of the right to privacy (in the abortion context)[29] and, finally, the free speech area.[30] In all these cases, however, the concept of human dignity has remained in a rather limited role as a background concept. It has not been transformed into an operational legal term, as some dissenting opinions have suggested it should. This situation contrasts starkly with the role of human dignity in the German constitutional context in particular where voices have warned that the term not become 'small change' in constitutional interpretation.[31]

The German practice is, however, not fully representative of European constitutionalism. At the European level a picture emerges which, at first sight, resembles that in the United States. Like the US Constitution, the European Convention on Human Rights does not contain the term human dignity, and, like the US Supreme Court, the European Court of Human Rights has not used the term very frequently, and, when it does so, it uses it most often in connection with efforts to define what is degrading treatment in the sense of Article 3 of the European Convention.[32] In addition, the European Court has pronounced *dicta* which are similar to the one in the US Supreme Court judgment of *Gertz v. Robert Welch Inc.* in which the Court declares the fundamental importance of human dignity for the Convention system as a whole without, however, drawing many specific conclusions from it.[33]

Looking only at the use of the *term* 'human dignity', however, would not appropriately portray the situation. What is important is the substance of the concept. In this respect it is necessary to bear in mind that the European Court does not need to refer to the concept of human dignity when it can base its decisions on the right to privacy (Article 8 of the Convention). The right to privacy is the subject of a well-known

---

[28] *Goldberg v. Kelly*, 397 U.S. 254, 264 et seq. (1970); *State of LA. Ex Rel. Francis v. Resweber*, 329 U.S. 459, 468 (1947).

[29] *Thornburgh v. American College of Obstetricians*, 476 U.S. 747, 772 (1986); *Planned Parenthood of Southeastern Pennsylvania v. Casey*, 505 U.S. 833, 851 (1992).

[30] *Cohen v. California*, 403 U.S. 15, 24 (1971); *National Association for the Advancement of Colored People v. Claiborne Hardware Co.*, 458 U.S. 886, 918 (1982).

[31] Günter Dürig, 'Art. 1', in Theodor Maunz and Günter Dürig (eds.), *Grundgesetz* (1st edn, München: C. H. Beck, 1958), para. 16: "Art. 1 I ist keine 'kleine Münze'".

[32] *Tyrer v. The United Kingdom*, 26 Eur. Ct. H. R. 16 (1978), para. 33; *Ribitsch v. Austria*, 336 Eur. Ct. H. R. 26 (1995), para. 38; *Tekin v. Turkey*, 1998-IV Eur. Ct. H. R. 1518, para. 53.

[33] E.g. *Cossey judgment*, 184 Eur. Ct. H. R. (ser. A) 22, 24 (1990), para. 2.7 (dissenting opinion of Judge Martin); *Pretty v. The United Kingdom*, 2002-III Eur. Ct. H. R. 155, 194, para. 65.

debate in the United States, and the result of this debate, so far, seems to be that the invocation of the concept of human dignity in the famous *Roe v. Wade* decision[34] on the right to have an abortion is more the exception than the rule. The European Court of Human Rights, on the other hand, while not recognizing a right to have an abortion – not least because the concept of human dignity can be used against a right to have an abortion as well – has extensively interpreted this right of privacy in controversial areas. The European Court increasingly uses the term human dignity as a substantive and operative balancing factor, mainly in connection with privacy cases. This is true, for example, with respect to the obligations of the state towards transsexual[35] and disabled persons.[36] A classical contrast is the question of the permissibility of criminal prosecutions for homosexual acts where the US Supreme Court in *Bowers v. Hardwick*[37] came to a different conclusion than the European Court in the *Dudgeon* case.[38] Most recently, the US Supreme Court has made certain careful but important steps towards giving the concept of dignity more legal substance in US constitutional law. The Court used the concept of 'personal dignity' when it overruled the *Bowers* decision in its 2003 decision in *Lawrence v. Texas*.[39] In another recent decision, *Atkins v. Virginia*, the US Supreme Court even used the possibly more general concept of 'dignity of man' when it held that the execution of mentally retarded persons violated the Eigth Amendment's guarantee against 'cruel and unusual

---

[34] *Roe* v. *Wade*, 410 U.S. 113 (1973).

[35] *Goodwin* v. *The United Kingdom*, 2002-VI Eur. Ct. H. R. 1, 31, para. 90; *I.* v. *The United Kingdom*, Eur. Ct. H.R., judgment of 11 July 2002, para. 70, available at http://www.echr.coe.int.

[36] *Botta* v. *Italy*, 1998-I Eur. Ct. H. R. 412, 421, para. 27; *Pretty* v. *The United Kingdom*, 2002-III Eur. Ct. H. R. 155, 194, para. 65; *Keenan* v. *The United Kingdom*, 2001-III Eur. Ct. H. R. 93, 134, para. 113.

[37] *Bowers* v. *Hardwick*, 478 U.S. 186 (1986).

[38] *Dudgeon* v. *The United Kingdom*, 59 Eur. Ct. H. R. (ser. A) (1983).

[39] 539 U.S. _ _ _ (2003): in his Opinion for the Court, Justice Kennedy remarked: 'In explaining the respect the Constitution demands for the autonomy of the person in making these choices, we stated as follows: "These matters, involving the most intimate and personal choices a person may make in a lifetime, choices central to personal dignity and autonomy, are central to the liberty protected by the Fourteenth Amendment. At the heart of liberty is the right to define one's own concept of existence, of meaning, of the universe, and of the mystery of human life. Beliefs about these matters could not define the attributes of personhood were they formed under compulsion of the State.

Persons in a homosexual relationship may seek autonomy for these purposes, just as heterosexual persons do. The decision in *Bowers* would deny them this right."'

punishment'.[40] It is clear, however, that these steps by the US Supreme Court in the direction of opening its jurisprudence towards a vague concept like human dignity are rather timid if compared with the practice of the European Court of Human Rights.

Thus, although the *term* 'human dignity' is used restrictively by both the US Supreme Court and the European Court of Human Rights, the *concept* of human dignity seems to play a significantly larger role in Europe. This happens mostly under the guise of the right to privacy, but increasingly also as a factor in the reasoning of other cases. Put another way, interests of the human person *qua* person which are not explicitly protected by the constitution seem to have a greater chance of recognition in Europe than in the United States. The reasons for that are explored in more depth in four contributions. Giovanni Bognetti and James Whitman both adopt a broad historical approach, but from a different angle. While Bognetti looks at human dignity from the perspective of the state, its changing function, the history of ideas, and constitutional jurisprudence, James Whitman takes a sociological approach which leads to a surprising relativisation of the conventional wisdom. His theory that the relative lack of importance of the concept of dignity can at least partly be explained by the strictly non-aristocratic tradition in the United States is questioned by Eyal Benvenisti. Benvenisti insists on the importance of a distinction between the older concept of 'dignity' and the modern concept of 'human dignity' and makes a thought-provoking suggestion why this distinction has not gained much relevance in the United States. In addition, Benvenisti and Hugh Corder supplement and contrast the various European and the American uses of the concept of human dignity with the Israeli and the South African experiences respectively.

V. The protective function

The different emphasis which is put on human dignity in Europe and in the United States also seems to have significant consequences for the general question of whether fundamental rights only protect against state action or whether they also contain positive duties of the state to protect the rights-holders against infringements by private parties. Here, the US Supreme Court has preserved a purist position even in extreme

---

[40] *Atkins* v. *Virginia*, 536 U.S. _ _ _ (2002) (Slip Opinion at p. 13); *Lawrence* v. *Texas*, 539 U.S. _ _ _ (2003) (Slip Opinion at p. 12).

cases. The 1989 decision in *DeShaney v. Winnebago County*[41] is probably the best example: In this case the juvenile authorities had been alerted several times that a very young boy was regularly being severely beaten by his father. The US Supreme Court refused to recognise that the failure of the authorities to act in this case violated the boy's federal right to life or to bodily integrity. The simple reasoning of the Court was that the federal constitutional rights were designed to protect against state action and not to obligate the state to act and protect against private individuals.[42] Although this kind of reasoning has always been challenged, it now seems to be firmly entrenched in US constitutional law.[43]

The picture in Europe is very different. It is true that European constitutions vary considerably with respect to the extent that they guarantee positive rights. Constitutions of Northern and Western European countries tend to have no or very few explicit positive constitutional rights. Constitutions of Southern and Eastern European countries, on the other hand, tend to place more emphasis on rights which contain or imply a protective function of the state.[44] But here again, it is not the text which is decisive, but the recognition of protective dimensions of fundamental rights by the judiciary. And here, even those European courts whose constitutive documents contain no indication for an additional protective function of fundamental rights have recognised that such a function exists. This is true, in particular, for the German Constitutional Court which started its extensive jurisprudence on constitutional duties to protect in its well-known *Abortion Judgment*. In this decision the German Court declared that the right to life contained a duty of the state to protect life (the foetus) by means of criminal law.[45] Such a decision, at least in American eyes, completely turns around the function of fundamental rights. The European Court of Human Rights, however, has recognised the principle that fundamental

---

[41] *DeShaney v. Winnebago County Department of Social Services*, 489 U.S. 189 (1989).

[42] Ibid., 196.

[43] *Cf.* John E. Nowak and Ronald D. Rotunda, *Constitutional Law* (6th edn, St. Paul, Minn.: West Group, 2000), pp. 502 et seq.; Geoffrey R. Stone, Louis M. Seidman, Cass R. Sunstein and Mark V. Tushnet, *Constitutional Law* (2nd edn, Boston: Little, Brown and Company, 1991), pp. 1593 et seqq.

[44] *Cf.* Jörg Polakiewicz, 'Soziale Grundrechte und Staatszielbestimmungen in den Verfassungsordnungen Italiens, Portugals und Spaniens' (1994) 54 *Zeitschrift für ausländisches öffentliches Recht und Völkerrecht*, 340–91 (English summary).

[45] BVerfGE 39, 1 (1975), 37–40, translated in part in Donald P. Kommers, *The Constitutional Jurisprudence of the Federal Republic of Germany* (2nd edn, Durham: Duke University Press, 1997), pp. 337 et seq.

rights contain a protective function, albeit in less controversial settings. Thus, the European Court has insisted that the right to life and to bodily integrity gives rise to a duty of states to provide for the possibility of criminal prosecution against rape,[46] that the state must provide legislative protection against 'closed shop' agreements,[47] must protect against interferences against demonstrations by counter-demonstrators,[48] and must protect against excessive corporal punishment in private schools.[49] Article 8 of the European Convention, which enshrines the protection of privacy and family life, has been identified as a particularly rich source of positive duties of the states. In 2002, the European Court of Human Rights found in the case of *Yildiz v. Turkey* that the competent Turkish authorities had violated the rights to life and to property by not alerting the dwellers of a house which was haphazardly built in a slum area on land surrounding a waste dump that methane gas being given off by decomposing refuse in the dump might explode.[50]

This is not the place to give a full picture of the European jurisprudence on constitutional duties to protect. What does seem to be clear, however, is that courts in Europe today try to steer a middle course between a conception of the state which, as in the United States, provides basically only for the institutional machinery for citizens to obtain protection if they are able to bring together the necessary majorities for their cause on the one hand, and a conception of the state which, as was the case in the formerly socialist countries, is claiming the responsibility to guarantee the conditions for a 'real' and 'effective' freedom on the other. In short, in Europe, a minimum of welfare in the widest possible sense is constitutionally mandated, while this is not the case in the United States. This may itself well be a reflection of a different concept of political community, or better: the role of the individual within the political community. Frank Michelman and Dieter Grimm explore this issue in greater depth. While Grimm views the differences from a larger historical perspective and explains the concept of duty to protect as it has been developed by the German Constitutional Court, Frank

---

[46] *X and Y* v. *The Netherlands*, 91 Eur. Ct. H. R. (ser. A) 13 (1985), para. 27.
[47] *Young, James and Webster* v. *The United Kingdom*, 44 Eur. Ct. H. R. 22 et seq. (1980), para. 55.
[48] *Plattform 'Ärzte für das Leben'* v. *Austria*, 139 Eur. Ct. H. R. (ser. A) 12 (1988), para. 32.
[49] *Costello-Roberts* v. *The United Kingdom*, 247-C Eur. Ct. H. R. (ser. A) 57 et seq. (1993), paras. 26–8.
[50] *Yildiz* v. *Turkey*, Eur. Ct. H. R., judgment of 18 June 2002, paras. 62–6, available at http://hudoc.echr.coe.int.

Michelman explores a series of possible explanations for the perceived difference between European and US constitutionalism in this particular context. Heike Krieger's comments test his hypotheses on the basis of a thorough analysis of the jurisprudence of the European Court of Human Rights.

VI. Constitutional adjudication

The greater emphasis in Europe on human dignity and duties to protect, however, may not be due to Europeans attaching a greater intrinsic weight to such rights and concepts. It should not too readily be assumed that the political community in the United States values human dignity and mutual care and support less than Europeans do. The difference may simply be due to the fact that the role of the courts, in particular the function of constitutional adjudication, is conceived differently in the United States and in Europe.

The most conspicuous difference between Europe and the United States in terms of constitutional adjudication is obviously the existence of specialised constitutional courts in almost all European states. Even the United Kingdom, one of the few European countries which has not provided for a system of constitutional adjudication, has submitted important quasi-constitutional functions to a specialised tribunal: the European Court of Human Rights. This difference in the formal structure of constitutional adjudication is interesting in itself and Michel Rosenfeld, Lászlo Sólyom, and César Landa discuss the implications of each solution. Another important question is whether there exist significant differences in substance or style between European and US constitutional adjudication. Two issues arise in this context: the issue of what the Americans call the 'countermajoritarian difficulty' and, second, the issue of the tension between a 'rule-oriented' and 'case-oriented' jurisprudence.

As regards the countermajoritarian difficulty we are faced with a paradox. In the United States the power of judicial review of legislation has now been recognised for 200 years.[51] The US Supreme Court has exercised this power in a largely responsible and respected fashion which only twice gave rise to a crisis which called its role into question. European states, on the other hand, have long refused to adopt the idea of judicial review of legislation for themselves, the most respectable

---

[51] *Marbury v. Madison*, 1 Cranch (5 US) 137 (1803).

reason being the French understanding that such a function would put judges above the *volonté générale*.[52] Given this history, one is tempted to think that the problem of the countermajoritarian difficulty would still be more strongly felt in Europe. It appears, as Michel Rosenfeld describes in more detail, that the contrary is true today. It is not only due to the phase of judicial activism of the Warren Court era that decisions by the US Supreme Court are so frequently and passionately debated in terms of the bounds of legitimate judicial decision-making. Much of the retreat from the Warren Court era has been justified by the rather general consideration of the 'countermajoritarian difficulty'.[53] In Europe, on the other hand, the equivalent of the Warren Court era has never ended. The European Court of Human Rights is developing its jurisprudence, and there is no indication that it will reverse its expansive reading of the right to privacy, or reconsider its jurisprudence concerning duties to protect. There has been little opposition in principle against its basic approach. The same seems to be true for domestic constitutional courts. It is true that some decisions by national constitutional courts have from time to time provoked intense debates about their proper role, but these debates were sporadic and do not seem to have led to significant changes in the jurisprudence.

If the assumption is correct that the countermajoritarian difficulty plays a much greater role in the United States than in Europe, then why would that be so? One possibility is that the 'epochs' of jurisprudence are simply not synchronous. In that case, the European Warren Court era might end soon, perhaps spurred by a rebalancing of human rights and security interests in the face of global terrorism. Another possibility is that the parliamentary political system which prevails in most European states is more conducive to a more paternalistic form of judicial control.

Another possibility may be the tension between rule-oriented and case-oriented jurisprudence. A common cliché has it that legal systems from the common law tradition produce case law, while so-called continental legal systems strive for codification and a more systematic jurisprudence. The question, however, is whether the opposite is not true for today's constitutional adjudication. In its free speech

---

[52] Pasquale Pasquino, 'Constitutional Adjudication and Democracy. Comparative Perspectives: USA, France, Italy' (1998) 11 *Ratio Juris*, 38–50 at 45.

[53] Alexander Bickel, *The Least Dangerous Branch – the Supreme Court at the Bar of Politics* (Indianapolis: Bobbs-Merrill, 1962), pp. 16 et seqq.; see also Herbert Wechsler, 'Toward Neutral Principles of Constitutional Law' (1959) 73 *Harvard Law Review*, 1–35.

jurisprudence, for example, the US Supreme Court strives to develop 'tests' that are on a similar level of abstraction as legislation. One example is the 'reckless disregard for the truth' test for determining whether a defamation claim can be successful.[54] Such tests are meant to give lower courts as much guidance as possible. The European Court of Human Rights and the German *Bundesverfassungsgericht*, on the other hand, typically insist on a balancing of 'all the relevant factors' of the case in the light of certain criteria.[55] Thus, the permissibility of a particular expression can ultimately depend on the form of the publication, its presumed readership, whether it was an appropriate reaction to a previous expression, and similar issues which would not play a role in the United States. Such a 'balancing of all factors' approach has the disadvantage of making the law difficult to foresee, but it does have the advantage of being flexible, thus permitting the Courts to subtly change their approach without making this too clear – if one considers this to be an advantage. This less rigorous European approach to constitutional adjudication, at least to fundamental rights adjudication, with all the disadvantages it may entail, might contribute to the fact that constitutional adjudication is less confronted with the 'countermajoritarian difficulty'objection in Europe than in the United States.

But this is just a preliminary and narrow approach to an issue which also raises broader questions. Jeffrey Jowell's assessment of the British experience of 'constitutional adjudication', as being torn between its common law tradition which it shares with the United States and a continental-law-inspired European Court of Human Rights, demonstrates that developments in this area must not only be interpreted as emanating from within a particular legal system but may be connected with reflecting the spirit of the time and of opening to international currents of thought.

VII. Democracy and international influences

The problem of the countermajoritarian difficulty does not only arise between 'the people' and 'the Court'. In a sense it also arises between 'the

---

[54] *New York Times* v. *Sullivan*, above, note 22, at 279 et seq.
[55] *Ibrahim Aksoy* v. *Turkey*, 1996-VI Eur. Ct. H.R. 2260, 2280, para. 68; *Bundesverfassungsgericht, Lüth-Case*, in *Decisions of the Bundesverfassungsgericht* (published by the Members of the Court, 4 vols., Baden-Baden: Nomos, 1998), Vol. II/1: *Freedom of Speech*, p. 8; *cf.* also Kommers, *Constitutional Jurisprudence*, above, note 45, p. 361.

people' and 'the peoples'. This raises the issues of democracy and international influences. Today, constitution-making and legislation are no longer free from outside influence. Since the end of the Cold War there has been a wave of constitution-making around the world by states which are called 'states in transition' or 'new or restored democracies'.[56] Essentially, what has been happening is an emulation of western models of constitutionalism. This process was supported by three basic factors: the genuine desire by people(s) for freedom and the rule of law, economic motives and pressure by Western States. Thus, there was a dialectical and ambiguous relationship between an autonomous desire to establish the rule of law, democracy and freedom, and heteronomous pressure from the Western States to make that happen. International institutions and international law have played an important role in this dialectical process. More than other regions, Europe has tried to institutionalise the process of constitutionalisation of new and restored democracies. Europe, for the purpose of this process, is not only the EU, but also the Council of Europe. Institutions of the Council of Europe, in particular the Venice Commission, have contributed to making certain constitutional models acceptable to 'states in transition'. Judge Lech Garlicki writes on whether this has resulted in the adoption of more or less similar models which together could be classified as belonging to a European type of state organisation, as distinguished from the US model.

'Democracy and international influences', however, can also refer to another important constitutional question, the relationship of international law and domestic law. In this context we observe a multitude of different rules in different constitutional systems. On its face, the US Constitution is not unique or extraordinary in how it deals with international law. In its Article VI it declares that treaties are 'the supreme law of the land', leaving open the effect of customary international law in the domestic sphere. European constitutions, being mostly substantially younger, often contain clauses which enable the delegation of sovereign power to international organisations. It is quite understandable why the US Constitution does not contain such clauses and why such a clause has not been adopted in the meantime. The United States is in a different

---

[56] See Georg Nolte, Giorgio Malinverni, Jed Rubenfeld and Pál Sonnevend, 'The International Influences on National Constitutional Law in States in Transition', in (2002) 96 *Proceedings of the 96th Annual Meeting of the American Society of International Law*, 389–400.

position than the European states, it simply does not need international cooperation as much as European states do.

A characteristic difference, however, seems to lie in the constitutional practice with respect to the effect of international law in the domestic sphere. There is no state in Europe in which international norms are so hotly contested, restrictively applied and narrowly interpreted as in the United States. It is well known that the United States is comparatively reluctant to tie its hands by way of international treaty-making.[57] It is also well known that a number of treaties have deliberately not been given the self-executing effect that they could have had.[58] It is less well known that a serious academic debate is now taking place on whether it is indeed appropriate to give customary international law, in particular the modern customary law of human rights, the place of supreme law of the land.[59] This debate, and the US practice towards international law and international institutional cooperation, may well be a symptom of more fundamental differences of perspective between a European and a US view on the role and the concept of democracy in this era. Jed Rubenfeld suggests that such fundamental differences do indeed exist and even sees two conceptions of world order which arise from them, an international (European) and a democratic (US) concept of constitutionalism. His provocative contribution is criticised by Yasuaki Onuma from an internationalist perspective and by Armin von Bodgandy from a more constitutionalist perspective.

VIII. Final remark

This book is an attempt to test the legitimacy of a question which presents itself for at least two reasons. It is both the gradual intrinsic growth of the European entity and the challenges by recent political events from outside which seem to make the question of the emergence of a specific European constitutional identity pertinent, particularly vis-à-vis the United States of America. It is hoped that the multitude of perspectives which are assembled in this book will contribute to a clearer picture.

---

[57] See Pierre Klein, 'The Effects of US Predominance on the Elaboration of Treaty Regimes and on the Evolution of the Law of Treaties', in Michael Byers and Georg Nolte (eds.), *United States Hegemony and the Foundations of International Law* (Cambridge: Cambridge University Press, 2003), pp. 363–91 at pp. 365–71.

[58] *United States* v. *Alvarez-Machain*, 504 U.S. 655 (1992).

[59] Curtis A. Bradley and Jack L. Goldsmith, 'Customary International Law as Federal Common Law: A Critique of the Modern Position' (1997) 110 *Harvard Law Review*, 4.

PART II

Freedom of speech

2

Freedom of speech in Europe

ROGER ERRERA

Freedom of speech has a prominent place in both the European and the US constitutional order and the changes since the 1960s in the judicial interpretation of this freedom have been substantial. Half a century later it is time to assess the legal evolution on both sides of the Atlantic; to note differences and convergences and to link them to deeper historical, political and social trends.

This contribution is divided into two sections. The first section (I) examines the impact of two major developments in Europe since the 1950s on freedom of speech, the spread of judicial review and the creation of a system of European law, namely the European Convention on Human Rights with the case law of the Strasbourg court, and EC-EU law with the case law of the Luxembourg court. The second section (II) studies freedom of speech in Europe, in particular areas of political speech (1), libel of officials and of public figures (2), as well as personality rights and privacy (3). Comparisons with US-American constitutional law will be made as we go along.

I. The development of judicial review and its impact on freedom of speech

1. Judicial review

The creation and the development of judicial review represents one of the most important changes in the legal and political history of European countries since 1945.[1] Starting in Western Europe, in countries such

---

[1] On judicial review generally, see M. L. Volcancek (ed.), *Judicial Politics and Policy Making in Western Europe* (London: Cass, 2001); A. Stone Sweet, *Governing with Judges. Constitutional Politics in Europe* (Oxford: Oxford University Press, 2000); L. Favoreu and J. A. Jolowicz

as Germany,[2] France,[3] and Italy, it has spread since the 1990s to Central and Eastern European countries.[4] Outside Europe, it exists also in Canada,[5] Israel,[6] South Africa and India.[7] Judicial review has led to deep and definitive changes in the legal and political culture, bringing parliamentary supremacy to an end. Constitutional adjudication has transformed the legal and political realm with visible consequences on the attitude and behaviour of the executive, parliament and the judiciary as a whole. Constitutional courts are involved not only in law-making but, at times, also in policy-making.

In the field of civil liberties, the main tool of judicial review has been the interpretation of constitutional clauses or of Declarations of Rights.

(eds.), *Le Contrôle juridictionnel des lois* (Paris and Aix-en-Provence: Economica and Presses Universitaires d'Aix–Marseille, 1986); M. Cappelletti, *The Judicial Process in Comparative Perspective* (New York: Clarendon Press, 1989); A. R. Brewer-Carias, *Judicial Review in Comparative Law* (Cambridge: Cambridge University Press, 1989); M. Andenas and D. Fairgrieve (eds.), *Judicial Review in International Perspective. Liber Amicorum in Honour of Lord Slynn of Hadley* (The Hague: Kluwer, 2000).

[2] D. P. Kommers, *The Constitutional Jurisprudence of the Federal Republic of Germany* (2nd edn, Durham and London: Duke University Press, 1997); C. Landfried, 'Judicial Policy-Making in Germany. The Federal Constitutional Court' (1992) 15 *West European Politics*, 50–67; B. Schlink, 'German Constitutional Culture in Transition' (1993) 14 *Cardozo Law Review*, 711. See also C. Starck (ed.), *Main Principles of the German Basic Law* (Baden-Baden: Nomos, 1983).

[3] A. Stone, *The Birth of Judicial Politics in France. The Constitutional Council in Comparative Perspective* (Oxford and New York: Oxford University Press, 1992); J. Rivero, *Le Conseil constitutionnel et les libertés* (Aix-en-Provence and Paris: Economica and Presses Universitaires d'Aix–Marseille, 1984); T. Renoux and M. de Villiers, *Code constitutionnel* (2nd edn, Paris: Litec, 2001); B. Genevois, *La Jurisprudence du Conseil constitutionnel. Principes directeurs* (Paris: STH, 1984); L. Favoreu and L. Philip, *Les Grandes Décisions du Conseil constitutionnel* (11th edn, Paris: Dalloz, 2001); Conseil Constitutionnel (ed.), *Le Conseil constitutionnel à 40 ans* (Paris: LGDJ, 1999); J. Bell, *French Constitutional Law* (Oxford: Oxford University Press, 1992).

[4] H. Schwartz, *The Struggle for Constitutional Justice in Post-Communist Europe* (Chicago: Chicago University Press, 2000); A. E. Dick Howard, 'Constitutionalism and the Rule of Law in Central and Eastern Europe', in H. J. Cremer, T. Giegerich, D. Richter and A. Zimmermann (eds.), *Tradition und Weltoffenheit des Rechts. Festschrift für H. Steinberger* (Berlin: Springer, 2002), p. 755; see also A. Sajo (ed.), *Western Rights? Post Communist Applications* (The Hague: Kluwer, 1996).

[5] F. Iacobucci, 'Judicial Review in the Supreme Court of Canada under the Canadian Charter of Rights and Freedoms: The First Ten Years', in D. M. Beatty (ed.), *Human Rights and Judicial Review. A Comparative Perspective* (Dordrecht, Boston and London, 1994), p. 93; P. Macklem et al., *Canadian Constitutional Law* (2nd edn, Toronto: Emond Montgomery Publ., 1997).

[6] 'Israel Law. Forty Years. Proceedings of the Conference on 40 Years of Israeli Law' (1990) 3–4 *Israel Law Review*, 24; Cl. Klein, 'Les Droits de l'homme en Israël', in X. Robert (ed.), *Mélanges Jacques Robert* (Paris: Montchrestien, 1998), p. 519.

[7] V. N. Skukla, *Constitution of India* (9th edn, Lucknow: Mahendra P. Singh, 1997).

Two consequences deserve a special mention: a stronger guarantee of fundamental rights, including an attempt to define their proper scope and limitations under the Constitution, and a new impetus given to comparative constitutional law. This new comparative impetus has a two-fold dimension, as comparisons are drawn between European countries[8] and between European countries as a whole and the United States.[9]

The impact of judicial review on freedom of speech has been a spectacular one, as shown in particular by the German and French examples. Starting with the detailed regulation of freedom of expression in Article 5 of the Constitution[10] the German Federal Constitutional Court has built, over the years, a remarkable system. It has 'laid down . . . the doctrine of an objective order of values and clarified the relationship between fundamental rights and private law. More particularly, it has set forth the basic rationale for a regime of free expression, underscored the individual and social dimensions of speech, specified the purposes served by speech in the public forum, and identified the judicial standards to be applied in weighing the rights of speech against legally protected interests.'[11] It did so in a number of cases relating to libel, boycott, incitement to racial hatred, electoral campaigns, and public meetings. Of special interest is the sustained effort to give freedom of speech a prominent place in the constitutional order, the attention given to the delicate but necessary balancing between freedom of expression and other competing rights and values, e.g. personality rights and human dignity, and the high quality of the reasoning of the decisions.

The French example is somewhat different, the main cause being the differences of jurisdictional competence between the *Conseil Constitutionnel* and the Karlsruhe Court, in particular the exclusively 'abstract' character of the review performed by the former. In a number of cases relating both to the press and to broadcasting, the *Conseil Constitutionnel* had to interpret Article 11 of the 1789 Declaration. It affirmed the prominent importance of freedom of expression: in a

---

[8] Hence the creation of such international tools as the *Bulletin of Constitutional Justice* published by the European Commission for Democracy through Law (Venice Commission) in Strasbourg and of the *Annuaire international de jurisprudence constitutionnelle* (Aix-en-Provence: Presses Universitaires d'Aix–Marseille and Paris: Economica).

[9] E.g. P. Kirchhof and D. P. Kommers (eds.), *Germany and its Basic Law. Past, Present and Future. A German–American Symposium* (Baden-Baden: Nomos, 1993).

[10] Kommers, *Constitutional Jurisprudence*, above, note 2, chapter 8 on Freedom of Speech, pp. 360 et seqq.

[11] Ibid., p. 361.

1984 decision on the concentration of press ownership it mentioned 'the objective of financial transparency' which 'tends to reinforce an effective exercise of this freedom'.[12] It also held that

> the pluralism of daily newspapers dealing with political and general information ... is in itself an objective of constitutional value; ... in fact the free communication of ideas and opinions, guaranteed by Article 11 of the Declaration of the Rights of Man and the Citizen of 1789, would not be effective if the public to which these daily newspapers are addressed were not able to have access to a sufficient number of publications of different leanings and characters; ... in reality the objective to be realized is that the readers, who figure among the essential addressees of the freedom proclaimed by Article 11 of the Declaration of 1789, should be able to exercise their free choice without either private interests or public authorities substituting their own decision for it, and without it being possible to make them the subject-matter of a market.[13]

Such an emphasis on the right of the public to be informed is also to be found in Article 10 of the European Convention on Human Rights. In a 1986 decision on broadcasting the *Conseil Constitutionnel* held that 'the pluralism of currents of socio-cultural expression is in itself an objective of constitutional value; the respect for this pluralism is one of the conditions for democracy, the free communication of ideas and opinions would not be effective if the public to which the means of audio-visual communication address themselves were not able to have access, both within the framework of the public sector as well as in the private sector to programs that guarantee the expression of tendencies of different characters, respecting the necessity of honesty in information...'.[14] The same decision states that in broadcasting 'it is up to the legislature to reconcile, in the current state of technology and its control, the exercise of the freedom of communication resulting from Article 11 of the Declaration of the Rights of Man with, on the one hand, the technical constraints inherent in the means of audio-visual communication, and, on the other hand, with objectives of constitutional value such as the safeguarding of public order, respect for the freedom of others, and the preservation of the pluralistic character of socio-cultural

---

[12] *Conseil Constitutionnel*, Décision 84–181 DC, 11 October 1984, Recueil, p. 78, published in Journal officiel du 13 octobre 1984, p. 3200, also in J. Bell, *French Constitutional Law* (Oxford: Oxford University Press, 1992), p. 170.
[13] Bell, *French Constitutional Law*, note 12 above, p. 173.   [14] Ibid., p. 331.

currents of expression which these forms of communication, by reason of their considerable influence, are likely to infringe'.[15]

2. The creation of a system of European law

The creation of a system of European law since the 1950s has taken two forms: the European Convention on Human Rights (ECHR) and the treaties on the European Community/European Union (EC-EU).

a) The European Convention on Human Rights

The system of the ECHR is very remarkable for many reasons. It is the first general human rights treaty and a well-drafted one, creating a permanent Court and a right of application for individuals against states – an unprecedented move. The Strasbourg Court has developed, over the past half-century, a considerable body of law which has influenced domestic law.[16] However, the relationship between the Strasbourg case law and domestic law is not one-sided. The ECHR is not an atemporal

---

[15] On the ECHR, see P. Van Dijk and G. J. Van Hoof, *Theory and Practice of the European Convention on Human Rights* (3rd edn, The Hague: Kluwer, 1998); F. Sudre, *La Convention européenne des droits de l'homme* (6th edn, Paris: Presses Universitaires de France, 2004); M. de Salvia, *Compendium de la CEDH. Les principes directeurs de la jurisprudence relative à la Convention européenne des droits de l'homme* (2nd edn, Kehl: Engel, 2003) vol. 1: *Jurisprudence 1960 à 2002*; L. E. Pettitti, E. Decaux and P. H. Imbert (eds.), *La Convention européenne des droits de l'homme. Commentaire article par article*, preface by P. H. Teitgen (Paris: Economica, 1995); R. A. Lawson and H. G. Schermers (eds.), *Leading Cases of the European Court of Human Rights* (Nijmegen: Ars Aequi Libri, 1997); M. Janis, R. Kay and A. Bradley (eds.), *European Human Rights Law. Text and Materials* (2nd edn, Oxford: Clarendon Press, 2000); J. Abr. Frowein and W. Peukert, *Europäische Menschenrechtskonvention. EMRK-Kommentar* (2nd edn, Kehl: Engel, 1996); G. Cohen-Jonathan, *La Convention européenne des droits de l'homme* (Paris and Aix-en-Provence: Economica and Presses Universitaires d'Aix–Marseille, 1989); L. J. Clements, N. Mole and A. Simmons, *European Human Rights. Taking a Case under the Convention* (2nd edn, London: Sweet and Maxwell, 1999); J. L. Charrier (ed.), *Code de la Convention européenne des droits de l'homme* (3rd edn, Paris: Litec, 2005).

[16] P. Mahoney, 'The Comparative Method in Judgments of the European Court of Human Rights: Reference Back to National Law', in Schweizerisches Institut für Rechtsvergleichung (ed.), *The Role of Comparative Law in the Emergence of European Law* (Zürich: Schulthess, 2002); W.-J. Ganshof van der Meersch, 'Reliance on Comparative Law in the Case Law of the European Court of Human Rights' (1980) 1 *Human Rights Law Journal*, 13; R. Bernhardt, 'Comparative Law in the Interpretation and Application of the European Convention on Human Rights', in B. Salvino (ed.), *Mainly Human Rights. Studies in Honor of J. J. Cremona* (Valletta: Fondation Internationale de Malte, 1999), p. 33.

straitjacket to be applied mechanically irrespective of places and circumstances. It is a 'living instrument', as the Court repeatedly held, and it must
thus be interpreted according to the general legal evolution, especially of
constitutional law. The Court is a permanent and close observer of the
evolution of law in European countries. The overall result has been a two-
fold one: it has established relations between domestic courts and the
Strasbourg Court. Commentators have noted the use of the comparative
method and the significance of comparative law in the case law of the
Strasbourg Court.[17]

b) EC-EU law

The establishment of the EC law system, with the European Court of
Justice (ECJ) as its main author and actor, was the second major
European legal innovation in the second half of the twentieth century.
The system of preliminary rulings under Article 234 of the EC Treaty
and its success over the years has created an institutional framework for
a permanent judicial dialogue between domestic courts and the ECJ.
Such a dialogue may also have a domestic constitutional dimension: in
1987 the German Federal Constitutional Court held that the ECJ was,
when a referral was compulsory, the 'lawful judge' (*gesetzlicher Richter*)
in the sense of the German law from whose jurisdiction nobody may be
deprived under European law, under Article 101 (1) of the German
Constitution.[18]

Two articles of the European Treaties mention the domestic law of the
Member States. According to Article 6 (2) of the EU Treaty 'The Union
shall respect fundamental rights as guaranteed by the European
Convention for the protection of human rights and fundamental freedoms and as they result from the constitutional traditions common to
the Member States, as general principles of Community law'. Under
Article 288 (2), the EC Treaty provides: 'In the case of non-contractual
liability, the Community shall, in accordance with the general principles
common to the laws of the Member States, make good any damage
caused by its institutions or by its servants in the performance of their

---

[17] Cf. E. Guild and G. Lesieur, *The European Court of Justice on the European Convention on
Human Rights. Who Said What, When?* (The Hague: Kluwer, 1998).
[18] BVerfG (2001) 54 *Neue Juristische Wochenschrift*, 1267. The violation of the same article
had been invoked in an earlier case decided on 8 April 1987 (BVerfGE 75, 223). On the
first case, see M. Fromont's comments in (2001) XVII *Annuaire international de justice
constitutionnelle*, 429.

duties.'[19] As a result, comparative law is as used in Luxembourg as it is in Strasbourg.[20]

The overall result is a permanent triangular relationship between domestic courts, the European Court of Human Rights and the ECJ, leading to the slow growth of 'transnational constitutionalism'.[21] In today's Europe the protection of fundamental rights, freedom of speech being one of them, is achieved both at the domestic constitutional and at the European level. To borrow the subtitle of a study[22] there is both 'competition and complementarity' between domestic courts and the Strasbourg and Luxembourg Courts.

c) The European Court of Human Rights and Article 10 ECHR

There are very few absolute rights under the ECHR.[23] Freedom of expression is not one of them. The wording of most articles includes a description of the contents of the right guaranteed and then that of the permissible interferences in the exercise of this right by a public authority. In addition, both general[24] and specific[25] derogations and restrictions are allowed. Article 10 is no exception. A cursory reading of Article 10 could give the impression of an overly cautious if not restrictive approach to freedom of expression, reflecting probably the state of mind of the drafters and the legal situation in 1949–50. Licensing of broadcasting, television or cinema enterprises is mentioned;[26] the

---

[19] For two excellent comparative studies of this issue, see D. Fairgrieve, M. Andenas and J. Bell (eds.), *Tort Liability of Public Authorities in Comparative Perspective* (London: BIICL, 2002).

[20] See Y. Galmot, 'Réflexions sur le recours au droit comparé par la Cour de justice des Communautés européennes' (1990) 6 *Revue française de droit administratif*, 255.

[21] R. Dehousse, 'Naissance d'un constitutionalisme transnational' (2001) 96 *Pouvoirs: les cours européennes*, 19; E. Stein, 'Lawyers, Judges and the Making of a Transnational Constitution' (1981) 75 *American Journal of International Law*, 1. For an apt illustration, from the French legal scene, of such a dialogue, see D. Rousseau and F. Sudre (eds.), *Conseil constitutionnel et Cour européenne des droits de l'homme. Droits et libertés en Europe* (Paris: STH, 1990); *Les principes communs d'une justice des Etats de l'Union européenne* (Paris: La Documentation française, 2001) (on procedural rules derived from Article 6 (1) ECHR and the application of general principles of Community law); M. A. Eissen, 'Cours constitutionnelles et Cour européenne des droits de l'homme: leur influence mutuelle' (1991) *Revue trimestrielle des droits de l'homme*, 167.

[22] Conseil constitutionnel (ed.), *La protection constitutionnelle et la protection internationale des droits de l'homme: concurrence ou complémentarité?* (Paris, 1994).

[23] E.g. Articles 3, 4 (1) and 7.   [24] Article 15 (Emergencies).

[25] Article 16 (Restrictions on political activities of aliens).

[26] Article 10 (1), third sentence.

exercise of the freedoms mentioned in Article 10 (1) 'carries with it duties and responsibilities', an expression not to be found elsewhere in the Convention. Possible limitations are mentioned in broad generic terms: 'formalities, conditions, restrictions or penalties'. Finally, the grounds for possible limitations are many (ten) and they are worded in rather general terms.

Over the years, the case law of the European Court has been, on the whole, a very liberal one, influencing the law and practice in many countries. Its basis is the general conception of freedom of speech: 'Freedom of expression constitutes one of the essential foundations of a (democratic) ... society, one of the basic conditions for its progress and for the development of any man. Subject to paragraph 2 of Article 10, it is applicable not only to "information" or "ideas that are favourably received or regarded as inoffensive or as a matter of indifference", but also to those that offend, shock or disturb the State or any section of the population. Such are the demands of that pluralism, tolerance and broadmindedness without which there is no democratic society.'[27] Article 10 includes not only the right to express and disseminate information and ideas but also the right for the public to receive them, a 'right to know'.[28] This is of special relevance when the information relates to issues of general interest for the public.[29]

Such a conception of the foundations and of the scope of freedom of speech is not very different from that usually expressed in the decisions of the US Supreme Court or in American constitutional law treatises. Consequently limitations must meet two conditions: firstly, they must be 'prescribed by law', meaning that 'the law must be adequately accessible' ... 'a norm cannot be regarded as a "law" unless it is formulated with sufficient precision to enable the citizen to regulate

---

[27] *Handyside* v. *UK* 24 Eur. Ct. H.R. (ser. A) (1976), para. 49; *Otto-Preminger Institute* v. *Austria* 295-A Eur. Ct. H.R. (ser. A) (1994), para. 49; R. Errera, 'La Cour européenne des droits de l'homme et les limites de la liberté d'expression. Réflexions sur de singulières variations' (1995) *Gazette du Palais*, 21–2 June, 37; note F. Rigaux, 'La liberté d'expression et ses limites' (1995) *Revue trimestrielle des droits de l'homme*, 401; and G. Haarscher, 'Le blasphémateur et le raciste' (1995) *Revue trimestrielle des droits de l'homme*, 417.

[28] *Sunday Times* v. *UK* 30 Eur. Ct. H.R. (ser. A) (1978), para. 66; *Lingens* v. *Austria* 103 Eur. Ct. H.R. (ser. A) (1986), para. 41; *Oberschlick* v. *Austria* 204 Eur. Ct. H.R. (ser. A) (1991); note P. Lambert, 'La Liberté de la presse et la réputation de l'homme politique' (1992) *Revue trimestrielle des droits de l'homme*, 379; *Erdogdu and Ince* v. *Turkey* 1999-IV Eur. Ct. H.R., 185.

[29] *Bladet Tromso and Stensaas* v. *Norway* 1999-III Eur. Ct. H.R., 289.

his conduct'.[30] This concept is comparable to the twin notions of over-breadth and vagueness in US American law.[31] Secondly, the limitations must be proportionate to the legitimate aim pursued. The principle of proportionality is one of the key instruments of the Court's review of restrictions to freedom of speech. The Court usually requires a 'pressing social need'.[32]

The balancing exercise performed by the Court rests on the following notions: freedom of expression may have, in certain circumstances, to be balanced against other rights guaranteed by the Convention, such as freedom of thought, conscience and religion (Article 9)[33] or the right to a fair and public hearing by an independent and impartial tribunal (Article 6 (1)).[34] Maintaining the authority and the impartiality of the judiciary is also a legitimate ground for restriction.[35] Prior restraint is not excluded per se but invites a particularly close scrutiny by the Court in view of its inherent dangers.[36] The States have a certain margin of appreciation – a notion invented by the Court[37] – because of differences in the national context and also because domestic authorities may be, at times, in a better position to assess certain situations.[38] According to the Court such a margin 'varies according to circumstances, domains and

---

[30] *Sunday Times* v. *UK*, above, note 28, para. 49.

[31] *Grayne* v. *Rockford*, 408 U.S. 104 (19); *Connally* v. *General Construction Co.*, 269 U.S. 385, 391 (1926).

[32] *Wingrove* v. *UK* 1996-V Eur. Ct. H.R., 1937; note J. M. Larralde, 'La Liberté d'expression et le blasphème' (1997) *Revue trimestrielle de droits de l'homme*, 713; *Rekvenyi* v. *Hungary* 1999-III Eur. Ct. H.R., 423; note J. Callewaert, 'De la fausse vraie neutralité politique' (1999) 11 *Revue universelle des droits de l'homme*, 172; *Oztürk* v. *Germany* 73 Eur. Ct. H.R. (ser. A) (1983), para. 64; *Wille* v. *Liechtenstein* 1999-VII Eur. Ct. H.R., 279, para. 61. On the principle of proportionality see M. A. Eissen, 'Le Principe de proportionnalité dans la jurisprudence de la Cour européenne des droits de l'homme', in Pettitti, Decaux and Imbert, *Commentaire*, above, note 15, p. 65.

[33] *Otto-Preminger Institute* v. *Austria*, above, note 27 , para. 47.

[34] *Sunday Times* v. *UK*, above, note 28, para. 55; *News Verlags GmbH & Co.KG* v. *Austria* 2000-I Eur. Ct. H.R., 157, para. 56.

[35] *Oberschlick* v. *Austria*, above, note 28, para. 34; *De Haes and Gijsels* v. *Belgium* 1997-I Eur. Ct. H.R., 198, para. 37.

[36] *Observer and Guardian* v. *UK* 216 Eur. Ct. H.R. (ser. A) (1991), para. 60; *Sunday Times* v. *UK*, above, note 28, para. 51.

[37] S. C. Prebensen, 'The Margin of Appreciation and Articles 9, 10 and 11 of the Convention' (1998) 19 *Human Rights Law Journal*, 13; R. St. J. McDonald, 'The Margin of Appreciation', in R. St. J. McDonald (ed.), *The European System for the Protection of Human Rights* (Dordrecht: Nijhoff, 1993). For an example of abdication by the Court of the review of such a margin, see *Otto-Preminger Institute* v. *Austria*, above, note 27.

[38] *Tolstoy Miloslavsky* v. *UK* 316-B Eur. Ct. H.R. (ser. A) (1995), para. 48.

context'.[39] It is wider in such areas as morals[40] and narrower in others such as political speech[41] or criticism of the judiciary.[42] It is, however, always subjected to a review by the Court.

II. European and US attitudes towards freedom of speech

The topics of political speech, in particular libel of officials and 'public figures' (1), group libel and hate speech (2), and finally 'personality rights and privacy' (3) are particularly relevant for understanding the meaning of freedom of speech.

1. Political speech, libel of officials and 'public figures'

The European Court has emphasised the need to protect freedom of expression whenever speech relates to matters of public concern of which the public must be informed. This is certainly the case when political leaders are discussed.[43] There is no distinction here, the Court held, between political debate and the discussion of other issues of general interest.[44] Consequently the Court affirmed that in libel cases the limits of acceptable criticism are 'wider as regards a politician as such than as regards a private individual'.[45] The categorisation used by the Court seems to be a two-fold one, based on the kind of persons involved and on the nature of the issue discussed. As to the first element, the case law of the Court relates to politicians, elected or not.[46] The Strasbourg Court has not extended its case law to all public officials and to 'public figures' in the sense of the jurisprudence of the US Supreme Court.

---

[39] *Rasmussen* v. *Denmark* 87 Eur. Ct. H.R. (ser. A) (1984), para. 40.

[40] See *Handyside* v. *UK*, above, note 27, and *Müller and others* v. *Switzerland* 133 Eur. Ct. H.R. (ser. A) (1988).

[41] *Lingens* v. *Austria*, above, note 28; *Oberschlick* v. *Austria*, above, note 28; *Schwabe* v. *Austria* 242-B Eur. Ct. H.R. (ser. A) (1988); *Castells* v. *Spain* 236 Eur. Ct. H.R. (ser. A) (1992).

[42] *Prager and Oberschlick* v. *Austria* 313, Eur. Ct. H.R. (ser. A) (1995), § 34; *Weber* v. *Switzerland* 177 Eur. Ct. H.R. (ser. A) (1990); *Barfod* v. *Denmark* 149 Eur. Ct. H.R. (ser. A) (1989).

[43] *Lingens* v. *Austria*, above, note 28, para. 42; *Oberschlick* v. *Austria*, above, note 28.

[44] *Thorgeir Thorgeirson* v. *Iceland* 239 Eur. Ct. H.R. (ser. A) (1992).

[45] *Lingens* v. *Austria*, above, note 28, para. 42.

[46] Including candidates to an election: *Lopes Gomes Da Silva* v. *Portugal* 2000–X Eur. Ct. H.R., 85.

The case law relating to judges as individuals, as distinct from the judiciary as an institution,[47] deserves a special comment. In *Barfod v. Denmark* a person whose claim was rejected by a local court had written an article saying that the two lay judges, who were employees of the administration, 'had done their duty', thereby implying their bias and lack of impartiality. The person was fined for libel. The Court held the conviction did not violate Article 10, basing itself on two provisions of Article 10 (2): the protection of the reputation of others and the maintenance of the authority and impartiality of the judiciary.[48] Six years later, in *Prager and Oberschlick v. Austria* the European Court held that there had been no violation of Article 10 in a case where a journalist and a publisher had been found guilty of libelling a judge. The decision underlined the specific task of the judiciary in a democratic society. The judiciary needs the trust of the public. It could be necessary, in certain circumstances, to protect the judges against baseless and devastating attacks. The Court recalled that in view of their position judges are not well equipped to defend themselves in the public forum. As to the circumstances it held that the journalist's attack had not only damaged the judges' reputation 'but also undermined public confidence in the integrity of the judiciary as a whole'.[49] In *De Haes and Gijsels v. Belgium*[50] the European Court had to decide on a case in which an editor and several journalists had been sentenced for libelling four judges of the Antwerp Court of Appeal. The matter related to child custody. The journalists had criticised the decision of the court to give custody of the children to the father, against whom very grave accusations of mistreatment of the children had been brought forward. They highlighted his local political links as well as those of the judges, criticising violently the behaviour of the latter and their supposed partiality. The Court mentioned the public interest in the matter and the quality of the journalists' work and concluded that their conviction violated Article 10.

---

[47] See J. McBride, 'Judges, Politicians and the Limits to Critical Comment' (1998) 23 *European Law Review*, 76; Michael K. Addo, 'Are Judges Beyond Criticism under Article 10 of the European Convention on Human Rights?' (1998) 47 *International and Comparative Law Quarterly*, 425.

[48] *Prager and Oberschlick* v. *Austria*, above, note 42.   [49] Ibid., para. 20.

[50] *De Haes and Gijsels* v. *Belgium*, above, note 35; S. Peyrou-Pistouley, 'L'Extension regrettable de la liberté d'expression à l'insulte' (1998) *Revue trimestrielle des droits de l'homme*, 401.

Some comparison with the American case law following *New York Times v. Sullivan*[51] appears appropriate; in that case the US Supreme Court held that when a public official sues for libel in a case concerning a statement relating to his conduct *qua* official he has to prove, in addition to the falsity of the statement, that the statement was made with 'actual malice', i.e. that the author either knew that the statement was false or acted with 'reckless disregard of whether it was false or not'.[52] The decision relied both on general principle and on the position of officials. The Court cited 'a profound national commitment to the principle that debate on public issues should be uninhibited, robust and wide-open ... it may well include vehement, caustic, and sometimes unpleasantly sharp attacks on Government and public officials'. On the other hand public officials 'usually enjoy significantly greater access to the channels of effective communication and hence have a more realistic opportunity to counteract false statements than private individuals normally enjoy'. As to the scope of the new rule, the Court declined 'to determine how far down in the lower ranks of Government employees the "public official" designation would extend for purposes of this rule, or ... to specify categories of persons who would or would not be included' or 'the boundaries of the "official conduct" concept'.[53]

One of the justifications of *New York Times v. Sullivan* is that 'public officials' enjoy better access to the media than other people and thus are better equipped to defend themselves against accusations. This could in itself be a reflection of the status, legally and socially speaking, of officials in American society. For an English civil servant, a German *Beamter* or a French *fonctionnaire*, this is far from being evident.

The change contained in *New York Times v. Sullivan* is a very substantial one and subjects a category of plaintiffs to a special rule placing a very heavy burden on them. The initial indeterminacy of the new rule produced mixed results as to the very notion of 'public official'[54] and as to the meaning of 'official conduct' – 'anything that might touch on the fitness for office is relevant'.[55] An important issue was whether the privilege applied only to libel of public officials or 'whether it extended to libel of other persons as well'.[56] Following what for some was a

---

[51] 376 U.S. 254 (1964).   [52] Ibid., at 270.   [53] Ibid., at 283, n. 23.
[54] See *Rosenblatt* v. *Baer*, 387 U.S. 75 (1966).
[55] *Garrison* v. *Louisiana*, 379 U.S. 64 (1964).
[56] G. S. Stone, L. M. Seidman, C. R. Sunstein and M. V. Tushnet, *Constitutional Law* (3rd edn, Boston: Little, Brown, 1996), p. 1207.

slippery slope, and for others the logic of *New York Times v. Sullivan*, the Court applied the same standard to 'public figures involved in issues in which the public has a justified and important interest'[57] and then to all matters of 'public or general interest'.[58] After this, it was time to call for a retreat[59] – after years of legal uncertainty.

A probably unintended but nevertheless inevitable and logical fruit of *New York Times v. Sullivan* appeared in *Herbert v. Lando*.[60] A 'public figure' was trying to recover damages for defamation. The *Sullivan*-test applied. The Court had earlier held that there must be sufficient evidence to permit the conclusion that the defendant in fact entertained serious doubts as to the truth of his publication.[61] To prove 'actual malice' Herbert sought to interrogate the defendants and their colleagues about their beliefs and knowledge. The Court did not accept the defence according to which such an interrogation cast a heavy financial burden on the defendant and would have a 'chilling effect' on the willingness of the media to criticise public officials. Archibald Cox noted: 'The affront felt by editors and reporters when sharply questioned about their thoughts and emotions while preparing a story is readily understandable, but it too appears to be a consequence of the substantive law that attaches significance to an actor's state of mind'.[62] In 1984 the *Sharon*[63] and *Westmoreland*[64] cases struggled with the difficulties of determining actual malice.

---

[57] *Curtis Publishing Co.* v. *Butts* (for a University football coach) and *Associated Press* v. *Walker* (for a prominent retired Army general), 338 U.S. 130 (1967).

[58] *Rosenbloom* v. *Metromedia*, 463 U.S. 29 (1971): 'If the matter is a subject of public or general interest, it cannot suddenly become less so merely because a private individual is involved, or because in some sense the individual did not "voluntarily" choose to become involved.'

[59] *Gertz* v. *Robert Welch Inc.*, 418 U.S. 323 (1974); *Time Inc.* v. *Firestone*, 424 U.S. 448 (1976); *Wolston* v. *Reader's Digest Association Inc.*, 443 U.S. 157 (1979).

[60] 441 U.S. 153 (1979).   [61] *St. Amant* v. *Thomson*, 390 U.S. 727 (1968).

[62] A. Cox, *Freedom of Expression* (Cambridge and London: Harvard University Press, 1981), p. 66.

[63] *Sharon* v. *Time*, 599 F. Supp. 538 (S-D, NY, 1984). The jury decided that the *Time* article on Sharon was false but that there had been no reckless disregard for truth.

[64] *Westmoreland* v. *CBS*, 752 F. 2nd 16 (1984), cert. denied 472 U.S. 1017 (1985). Westmoreland withdrew his action during the trial. CBS published a declaration stating that the network did not mean to imply that the general had been unpatriotic or disloyal. On the Sharon and Westmoreland trials, see R. Adler, *Reckless Disregard: Westmoreland* v. *CBS and al. and Sharon* v. *Time* (New York: Knopf, 1986) and R. Dworkin's review of the book, '*The Press on Trial*', *New York Review of Books*,

There is no European progeny of *New York Times v. Sullivan* in the
sense of creating a distinct rule in libel law for certain categories of
plaintiffs. Indeed, in *Reynolds v. Times Newspapers Limited* the British
House of Lords in 1999 explicitly rejected *Sullivan*'s categorisation and
its characteristic reversal of the burden of proof, citing decisions by
many courts from other countries in support.[65] However, a few years
earlier, the House of Lords did take *New York Times v. Sullivan* into
account when it came to the right to sue; according to the highest British
Court a local authority does not have the right to bring an action for
libel and to claim for damages.[66] Such a possibility, it was held, could
inhibit free criticism of public authorities which could use other remedies, such as an action by its members or officers, a prosecution for
criminal libel, or an action for malicious falsehood. It seems that the
judgment ignores a fundamental issue: the right of a legal person, even a
public authority, to sue to protect its reputation. To completely deny
such a right to a local authority raises very serious issues concerning
equality before the law, equality before justice, and the very right of
access to the courts, as protected by Article 6 (1) ECHR.

2. Group libel and hate speech

The late nineteenth and the entire twentieth century saw the apparition
of new forms of political discourse: the rise of political anti-semitism,
the expression of anti-foreigner propaganda, xenophobic opinions,
campaigns, and writings directed against specific ethnic, national or
religious minorities. The aim was to denigrate certain persons belonging
or held to belong to certain groups, to make them responsible for all
kinds of social problems, evils or dangers such as unemployment, crime,
corruption of morality, erosion of national identity, treason, etc.

26 February 1987. The legal literature on *Sullivan* and its aftermath is immense. See e.g.
G. Gunther, *Constitutional Law. Cases and Materials* (9th edn, Foundation Press,
Mineola, NY, 1975), p. 1263; G. Gunther and K. M. Sullivan, *Constitutional Law* (13th
edn, Westbury, NY: Foundation Press, 1997), p. 1094. See also Elder, 'Freedom of
Expression and the Law of Defamation; the American Approach to Problems Raised
by the Lingens Case' (1986) 35 *International and Comparative Law Quarterly*, 891.

[65] *Reynolds* v. *Times Newspapers Limited* of 28 October 1999, available at http://
www. parliament.the-stationery-office.co.uk/pa/ld199899/ldjudgmt/jd991028/rey01.htm
(last visited 11 August 2004).

[66] *Derbyshire County Council* v. *Times Newspapers* [1993] AC 534; [1993] 1 All ER
1011, HL.

In the face of such a phenomenon two legislative attitudes are, broadly speaking, possible. The first would base the refusal to pass protective legislation mainly on a principled opposition to the idea of restricting speech on the sole basis of its content, however offensive and outrageous the opinion may be and whatever the offence, insult or social discomfort it creates. Such laws are interpreted as a new form of government censorship. Consequential arguments are added: group libel or hate speech expresses deep social and psychological currents that cannot be silenced by legislation. New laws will give its proponents the very publicity they seek or do damage to the very groups they aim to protect. The second attitude advocates such protective legislation, holding that it is needed not only in order to protect certain groups but for the well-being of society as a whole. The ultimate aim of such legislation would be to maintain a minimum of civility in the public discourse: the civility which forbids attacking an individual or a group on the grounds of their identity. Permitting vilification would harm the entire society. The use of legal instruments against what is, and is meant to be, an aggression would thus be legitimate. The legal basis for such protective legislation can be found in the central constitutional principles of equality, human dignity and non-discrimination. They are also enshrined by international human rights treaties, as shown by Article 10 ECHR and Article 4 a of the UN Convention for the Elimination of all Forms of Racial Discrimination.[67]

The First Amendment case law[68] is, broadly speaking, based on the principle of 'content neutrality', unless speech is a direct incitement to

---

[67] The Contracting States 'shall declare an offense punishable by law all dissemination of ideas based on racial superiority or hatred, incitement to racial discrimination, as well as all acts of violence or incitement to such acts against any race or group of persons of another colour or ethnic origin, and also the provision of any assistance to racist activities, including the financing thereof'. On the legislative history of Article 4 of the Convention, see W. McKean, *Equality and Discrimination under International Law* (Oxford: Clarendon Press, 1983), p. 160. On the international law dimension of hate speech and group-libel see D. McGoldrick and T. O'Donnell, 'Hate Speech Laws: Consistency with National and International Human Rights Law' (1998) 18 *Legal Studies*, 453; J. Cooper and A. M. Williams, 'Hate Speech, Holocaust Denial and International Law' (1999) 19 *European Human Rights Law Review*, 594; T. D. Jones, *Human Rights, Group Defamation, Freedom of Expression and the Law of Nations* (The Hague and Boston: Martinus Nijhoff, 1998). See also the decision of the UN Human Rights Committee of 8 November 1986 in the Faurisson case, Communication n°550/ 1993, (1997) 18 *Human Rights Law Journal*, 40.

[68] *RAV* v. *City of St Paul*, 505 U.S. 377 (1992); (1992) 13 *Human Rights Law Journal*, 327; *Collin* v. *Smith*, 578 F. 2nd 1197 (7th Circuit) 197; *Smith* v. *Collin*, 436 U.S. 953 (1978);

unlawful behavior likely to occur in the immediate future. This case law has led to a lively and meaningful debate.[69] Two features are of particular interest to a European observer. The first is the argument according to which 'group vilification poses ... [harms] both targeted groups and the political community as a whole'.[70] Gates[71] writes: 'A legal response to racist speech is a statement that victims of racism are valued members of our polity ... In a society that expresses its moral judgments through the law' the 'absence of laws against racial speech is telling'. The second feature is the use of central concepts such as those of individual autonomy and identity, human dignity, equality, civility, i.e. personality rights.[72]

The European answer is based on another attitude. European countries have adopted legislation against group libel, hate speech and racial incitement.[73] They did so because they felt that certain political and social trends needed a clear legal answer from government and parliament.

Smith v. *Collin*, 439 U.S. 916, 1978 (The *Skokie* case). As a result *Beauharnais* v. *Illinois*, 343 U.S. 250 (1952), sustaining an Illinois criminal group-libel law is no longer valid. See for a description R. G. Schneider, 'Hate Speech in the US: Recent Legal Developments', in S. Coliver (ed.), *Striking a Balance: Hate Speech, Freedom of Expression and NonDiscrimination*, Article XIX (London: University of Essex, 1992), p. 245.

[69] M. J. Matsuda, C. R. Lawrence III, R. Delgado and K. Williams Crenshaw, *Words that Wound: Critical Race Theory, Assaultive Speech and the First Amendment* (Boulder: Westview Press, 1993). On the aftermath of the *Skokie* case, see D. A. Downs, 'Skokie Revisited: Hate-Group Speech and the First Amendment' (1985) 60 *Notre Dame Law Review*, 629; L. C. Bollinger, 'The Skokie Legacy: Reflections on an "Easy Case" and Free Speech Theory' (1982) 80 *Michigan Law Review*, 617; L. C. Bollinger, *The Tolerant Society* (Oxford: Clarendon Press, 1986); see M. Rosenfeld's review 'Extremist Speech and the Paradox of Tolerance' (1987) 100 *Harvard Law Review*, 1457; D. Kretzmer, 'Freedom of Speech and Racism' (1987) 8 *Cardozo Law Review*, 445; Robert C. Post, 'Racist Speech, Democracy and the First Amendment' (1991) 32 *William and Mary Law Review*, 267; R. D. Bernstein, 'First Amendment Limits on Tort Liability for Words Intended to Inflict Severe Emotional Distress' (1985) 85 *Columbia Law Review*, 1749; Note D. Kahan, 'A Communitarian Defense of Group Libel Laws' (1988) 101 *Harvard Law Review*, 682; K. Greenawalt, *Speech Crime and the Uses of Language* (Oxford and New York: Oxford University Press, 1989), p. 292.

[70] Kahan, 'Group Libel Laws', above, note 69, 684.

[71] Henry Louis Gates Jr, 'Why Civil Liberties Pose no Threat to Civil Rights: Let Them Talk', *The New Republic*, 20–27 September 1993, 37 at 43.

[72] Greenawalt, *Speech*, above, note 69.

[73] See for a general survey: L. Greenspan and C. Levitt (eds.), *Under the Shadow of Weimar: Democracy, Law, and Racial Incitement in Six Countries* (Westport: Praeger, 1993); Coliver, *Striking a Balance*, above, note 68; D. Batselé, M. Hanotiau and O. Daurmont, 'La Lutte contre le racisme et la xénophobie, mythe ou réalité?' (1991) *Revue trimestrielle des droits de l'homme*, 319 and 435; F. Massias, 'La liberté d'expression et le discours raciste' (1993) *Revue trimestrielle des droits de l'homme*, 183.

A number of civil rights associations and political movements had repeatedly insisted that gaps needed to be filled in the existing law. The constitutional challenge, when it occurred, was met successfully,[74] as has been the
case in Canada[75] and in Switzerland, where legislation was adopted in 1994
by referendum.[76] Such pieces of legislation are not all identical. The main
issues to be answered are:

- Should criminal law or tort law be used?
- Under which criteria should the legislation define incitement (to
  hatred, violence or discrimination) or libel?
- Should legislation take into account public order or peace?

Truth is not a defence in every situation. Standing to sue is a key issue.
Exclusive reliance on the State prosecutor to bring every violation to
court is not sufficient to combat libel and incitement. Hence the interest
in allowing other bodies to initiate criminal proceedings. Under French
law any association which has been in existence for five years at the time
of the publication and the aim of which is to combat racism has standing
to bring proceedings. The victim's permission is needed if the cause of
action is an attack against an individual; in Canada the Human Rights
Commission is allowed to act under the 1977 Human Rights Act if
certain conditions are met, e. g. the use of telecommunications to spread
hate messages.

In a number of countries, in Europe as well as in the United States, the
negation or the gross minimisation of the Nazi genocide of Jews has been
the subject of books, essays and articles.[77] Should their authors be
protected by freedom of speech? The European answer has been in the

---

[74] Hungarian Constitutional Court, decision n° 30/1992 (V.18) AB, in (1995) 2 *East
European Case Reporter of Constitutional Law*, 9; see A. Sajo's comment, 'Hate Speech
for Hostile Hungarians' (1994) 3 *East European Constitutional Review*, 82. The Court
held unconstitutional Article 269 (2) of the Penal Code prohibiting the publication of
'offensive or denigrating expression' while holding constitutional Section 1 of the same
Article prohibiting incitement to hatred.

[75] As shown by *R. v. Keegstra*, (1990) CCC (3rd) I (SCC), see B. P. Elman, '*Her Majesty the
Queen* v. *James Keegstra*: the Control of Racism in Canada. A Case Study', in Greenspan
and Levitt, *Under the Shadow of Weimar*, above, note 73, p. 149.

[76] Penal Code, Article 261 bis, para. 4 and Military Penal Code, Article 171.

[77] See P. Vidal-Naquet, 'Un Eichmann de papier. Anatomie d'un mensonge', in *Les Juifs,
la mémoire et le présent* (Paris: La Découverte, 1981), p. 193; P. Vidal-Naquet, *Les
Assassins de la mémoire. Un Eichmann de papier et autres essais sur le révisionnisme*
(Paris: La Découverte, 1987); D. Lipstadt, *Denying the Holocaust. The Growing Assault
on Truth and Memory* (New York: Free Press, 1993); 'Négationnisme et révisionisme',
special issue, (1995) 65 *Relations internationales*.

negative: such writings are not only a perverse form of anti-semitism but also an aggression against the dead, their families, the survivors and society at large. They aim at the destruction of the only grave these dead have, that is, our memory and the very consciousness of the crime. A number of European countries have decided that such an aggression could not be tolerated. Criminal law has been used in Germany,[78] France[79] and Switzerland.[80] In Britain, David Irving lost a libel action against the author of a book.[81]

Group libel and hate speech is one of the areas where the differences in social attitudes and in the political and legal response between the United States and Europe is most visible. There is little doubt that the *Skokie* case[82] would have been decided differently in Europe. The limits of tolerance are obviously not the same. Recent historical experience is not the only explanation. After all, former neutral countries, such as Switzerland, or non-European ones, such as Canada, have adopted similar legislation against group libel and hate speech. Deeper cultural and social causes need further exploration in view of a necessary continuing transatlantic dialogue.

In a remarkable essay published after his death, Alexander Bickel, who was chief counsel for the New York Times Company in the *Pentagon Papers* case, left a warning. Quoting Justice Brandeis's dictum in *Whitney v. California* – 'discussion affords ordinarily adequate protection against the dissemination of noxious doctrine'[83] – he wrote: 'Disastrous, unacceptably noxious doctrine can prevail by the most innocent sort of advocacy. There is such a thing as verbal violence, a kind of cursing, assaultive speech that amounts to almost physical aggression, bullying that is no less punishing because it is simulated.' Some kinds of extreme speech, he added, 'may create a climate, an

---

[78] E. Stein, 'History Against Free Speech. The New German Law Against the "Auschwitz" and other "Lies"' (1996) 85 *Michigan Law Review*, 277. See the remarkable decision of the German Constitutional Court in the Holocaust Denial case, BVerfGE 90, 241, in Kommers, *Constitutional Jurisprudence*, above, note 2, p. 382.

[79] Article 24 bis of the 1881 Statute on the Press, as revised in 1990.

[80] Article 261 bis of the Penal Code, para. 4, last two lines.

[81] *Irving* v. *Penguin Books Ltd and Lipstadt*, High Court of Justice, 1996 I–1113, Queen's Bench Division, 11 April 2000; See D. Guttenplan, *The Holocaust on Trial. History, Justice and the David Irving Libel Case* (London: Granta Books, 2000); D. Guttenplan, 'The Holocaust on Trial', *The Atlantic Monthly*, February 2000, 45; D. Jacobson, 'The Downfall of David Irving. Holocaust Denial and Anti-Semitism have had their Day in Court', *The Times Literary Supplement*, 21 April 2000.

[82] *Smith* v. *Collin*, 439 U.S. 916 (1978) (The *Skokie* case).   [83] 274 U.S. 357, 375 (1927).

environment in which conduct and actions that were not possible before become possible'. His conclusion – 'Where nothing is unspeakable, nothing is undoable'[84] – deserves all our attention.

3. Personality rights and privacy

The progressive affirmation of personality rights, including the right to privacy and the necessity of balancing between freedom of speech and personality rights, has been one of the most important developments of the last decades in a number of European countries. Its origins are many: academic writings in Germany, France and elsewhere contributed to it. The famous article by Warren and Brandeis[85] mentions privacy 'as a part of a more general right to the immunity of the person, the right to one's personality'. Another influence has probably been the political and social trends and events of the twentieth century: the experience of communist and Nazi totalitarianism; new information technologies; bioethical issues, and others.

There is no closed list of personality rights, nor is there any need for one. They have, however, a central purpose, a conceptual unity resulting from their common purpose: the protection of the person as such, of his or her integrity, identity, autonomy and dignity. Such rights relate, by definition, to the individual, but their basis is not pure legal individualism. Such an affirmation and the legal protection that accompanies it are vital for the polity as a whole. An enumeration of personality rights would include personal honour, privacy, the right to one's name and image, protection against group libel and hate speech and respect for human dignity. German and French law are apt illustrations of the balancing exercise between the competing personality rights and freedom of expression.

The German example is notable for the strong affirmation, in the very beginning of the Constitution, of personality rights. Article 1 (1) of the German Constitution reads: 'Human dignity shall be inviolable. To respect and protect it shall be the duty of all State authorities.' This

---

[84] A. Bickel, *The Morality of Consent* (New Haven and London: Yale University Press, 1975), pp. 72–3; R. Errera, 'Group-Libel, Hate-Speech and Other Fighting Words', in B.S. Markesinis (ed.), *Law Making, Law Finding and Law Shaping: the Diverse Influences. The Clifford Chance Lectures* (Oxford: Oxford University Press, 1997), vol. II, p. 43.

[85] D. Warren and L. D. Brandeis, 'The Right to Privacy' (1890) 4 *Harvard Law Review*, 193.

article is covered by the eternity-clause contained in Article 79 (3), which reinforces its scope. Article 2 (1) is broader: 'Every person shall have the right to free development of his personality insofar as he does not violate the rights of others or offend against the constitutional order or the moral law.' Freedom of expression is guaranteed by Article 5 of the German Constitution. The judicial affirmation of the general right of personality came as early as 1954.[86] The right to privacy was duly recognised in 1973.[87] A detailed case law on privacy followed, using the principle of proportionality in the balancing exercise between the right to privacy and freedom of expression, particularly vis-à-vis the press.[88]

The affirmation of personality rights and of privacy is equally visible in French law, although the road to it has not been exactly the same. Academic writings have been influential.[89] The right to privacy was introduced into French law in several stages. Beginning in the mid-50s, the Paris civil court recognised privacy as a distinct right in tort actions against the press. The Court affirmed that everyone was entitled to respect for his privacy and it held that courts could use a number of remedies in addition to damages claims, especially in interlocutory proceedings (*référé*). At that time, there was neither a constitutional dimension to this question nor an international one, since France had not yet ratified the ECHR. Then, in 1970, a governmental and parliamentary initiative led to the introduction of Article 9 into the *Code Civil*: 'Everyone has the right to respect for his private life. – Courts are empowered, in addition to compensation for damage suffered, to order any measures, such as impounding, seizure or other to prevent or to put an end to an interference with the intimacy of private life. Such injunctions may, in case of urgency, be delivered through interlocutory proceedings.' This was a codification of the existing law and practice.

---

[86] BGHZ 13, 334 (*Schacht*). See also the Divorce Record Case, BVerfGE 27, 344, commented by Kommers, *Constitutional Jurisprudence*, above, note 2, p. 327.

[87] BVerfGE 34, 269, in Kommers, *Constitutional Jurisprudence*, above, note 2, p. 124.

[88] For a general study and discussion of the German case law on the protection of personality rights and privacy, see Kommers, *Constitutional Jurisprudence*, above, note 2, chapters 7 on 'Human Dignity and Personhood' and 8 on 'Freedom of Speech'; W. van Gerven, J. Lever, P. Larouche, Chr. von Bar and G. Viney (eds.), *Torts. Scope of Protection, Common Law of Europe Casebooks* (Oxford: Hart, 1998), p. 171.

[89] H. Nerson, 'La Protection des droits de la personne en droit privé français'(1963) 13 *Travaux de l'association H. Capitant*, 60; B. Beignier, *Le Droit de la personnalité* (Paris: Presses universitaires de France, 1992); Beignier, *L'Honneur et le droit* (Paris: LGDJ, 1995); P. Kayser, 'Les Droits de la personnalité. Aspects théoriques et pratiques' (1971) 69 *Revue trimestrielle de droit civil*, 445.

Article 9 of the *Code Civil* does not contain a definition of privacy and makes no provision for defences. Later, the *Conseil d'Etat* and lower administrative courts held that the rights to privacy and to intimacy were fundamental freedoms.[90] Finally, the *Conseil Constitutionnel* held that the right to privacy was a constitutional right.[91] In the absence of any mention of privacy in the 1789 Declaration or in the Constitution, it based its affirmation on the general right to liberty protected under the Constitution, a technique similar to that used earlier by the US Supreme Court in the cases of *Griswold v. Connecticut*[92] and *Roe v. Wade*.[93] The right to dignity has also been recognised[94] and has been used by the French courts vis-à-vis the press in a number of occasions.[95]

The example of English law may be taken as an illustration of the legal difficulties arising from the absence of recognition, by statute or by the courts, of a general right to privacy.[96] The development of the case law

---

[90] See e.g. Conseil d'Etat, 6 February 1980, Confédération syndicale des familles et al., Recueil p. 567.

[91] Conseil Constitutionnel, *Décision 94–352 DC*, 18 January 1995, Recueil, p. 170, published in: *Journal officiel du 21 janvier 1995*, p. 1154; *Décision 97–389 DC*, 22 April 1997, Recueil, p. 45, published in: *Journal officiel du 25 avril 1997*, p. 6271. *Décision 99–419 DC*, 9 November 1999, Recueil, p. 116, published in: *Journal officiel du 16 novembre 1999*, p. 16962; M. Fatin-Rouge Stefanini, 'France' (2000) 16 *Annuaire international de justice constitutionnelle*, 258.

[92] *Griswold* v. *Connecticut*, 381 U.S. 479 (1965).

[93] *Roe* v. *Wade*, 410 U.S. 113 (1973); on the scope and limits of this right and the nature of remedies, see Van Gerven et al., *Torts*, above, note 88, pp. 183; J. P. Gridel, 'Le Droit à la vie privée et la liberté d'expression: le fond du droit',(2003) *Bulletin d'information de la Cour de cassation*, March, 11; A. Lacabarats, 'Les Actions en justice pour atteintes à la vie privée', (2003) *Bulletin d'information de la Cour de cassation*, March, 18; C. Dupré, 'The Protection of Private Life Against Freedom of Expression in French Law' (2000) 20 *European Human Rights Law Review*, 627.

[94] B. Mathieu, *La Dignité de la personne humaine: quel droit? Quel titulaire?* (Paris: Dalloz, 1996), p. 282; B. Edelman, *La Dignité de la personne humaine, un concept nouveau* (Paris: Dalloz, 1997), p. 185; V. Saint-James, 'Réflexions sur la Dignité de l'être humain en tant que concept juridique du droit français' (1999) 115 *Revue du droit public et de la science politique*, 159; B. Jorion, 'La Dignité de la personne humaine, ou la difficile insertion d'une règle morale dans le droit positif' (1999) 115 *Revue du droit public et de la science politique*, 197. On the concept of human dignity, see D. Feldman, 'Human Dignity as a Legal Value' (1999) *Public Law*, 682; D. Kretzmer and E. Klein (eds.), *The Concept of Human Dignity in Human Rights Discourse* (The Hague: Kluwer, 2002).

[95] For a recent decision see Cass. civ. Ière, 12 December 2000, *Société C et H c. Erignac* (publication of the photograph of the corpse of Corsica's prefect lying on the ground just after his murder); P. Gridel, *Retour sur l'image du préfet assassiné; dignité de la personne humaine et liberté de l'information d'actualité* (Paris: Dalloz, 2001), p. 87.

[96] See Van Gerven et al., *Torts*, above, note 88, pp. 191; R. Singh and J. Strachan, 'The Right to Privacy in English Law' (2002) 22 *European Human Rights Law Review*, 129;

has been a twisted and interesting one.[97] Will the law of confidentiality forever be the only instrument available against the press in cases of invasion of privacy? Or will the combination of the *Human Rights Act* and of Article 8 ECHR, as interpreted by the recent decision of the Strasbourg court in *Peck v. UK*,[98] bring a substantial change in the case law and a recognition of the right to privacy?

In the United States we see a different legal landscape. The progeny of the Warren and Brandeis article has been a mixed one. Privacy has been recognised as a constitutionally protected right by the Supreme Court.[99] It is the subject of an abundant and lively literature.[100] To a European observer some personality rights are protected under four distinct torts recognised today (intrusion; public disclosure of embarrassing facts; false light; appropriation). But the protection of privacy and other personality rights vis-à-vis the press seems limited in view of the case law on the First Amendment.[101] What Bloustein wrote almost forty years ago in reply to Prosser is still valid: 'An intrusion on our privacy threatens our liberty as individuals to do as we will, just as an assault, a battery or imprisonment of our person does. Conceptual

---

Lord Bingham of Cornhill 'Opinion: Should there be a Law to Protect Rights of Personal Privacy?' (1996) 16 *European Human Rights Law Review*, 450; R. Singh, 'Privacy and the Media After the Human Rights Act' (1998) 18 *European Human Rights Law Review*, 712. For a comparison, see J. Craig and N. Nolte, 'Privacy and Free Speech in Germany and Canada: Lessons for an English Privacy Tort' (1998) 18 *European Human Rights Law Review*, 162; B. Markesinis, 'Privacy, Freedom of Expression and the Horizontal Effect of the Human Rights Bill' (1999) 115 *The Law Quarterly Review*, 47.

[97] See *Kayes v. Robertson*, (1991) FSR 62; *Douglas v. Hello!* I, Judgment of the Court of Appeal in the case of *Douglas and others v. Hello! Ltd.*, 21 December 2000, see http://www.courtservice.gov.uk/judgments/judg_home.htm; *Venables and Thomson*, Re Robert Thompson and Jon Venables, [2001] 1 *Criminal Appeal Reports* 401; *B and C v. A, [2002]* EWCA Civ 337 and, very recently *Douglas v. Hello!* II, *Douglas and others v Hello! Ltd.*, [2004] EWHC 63 (Ch).

[98] *Peck v. UK* 2003-I Eur. Ct. H. R., 123; *von Hannover v. Germany*, Eur. Ct. H. R., Application no. 59320/00, judgment of 24 June 2004.

[99] *Griswold v. Connecticut*, above, note 92; *Roe v. Wade*, above, note 93.

[100] W. L. Prosser, 'Privacy' (1960) 48 *California Law Review*, 383; E. J. Bloustein, 'Privacy as an Aspect of Human Dignity: an Answer to Dean Prosser' (1964) 39 *New York Law Review*, 96; J. R. Gavison, 'Privacy and the Limits of Law' (1980) 89 *Yale Law Journal*, 421; J. W. DeCew, 'The Scope of Privacy in Law and Ethics' (1986) 5 *Law and Philosophy*, 15; R. B. Hallborg Jr, 'Principles of Liberty and the Right to Privacy' (1986) 5 *Law and Philosophy*, 175; American Law Institute, *Restatement of Torts, Second, sec. 652a* (Washington D.C.: American Law Institute, 1997).

[101] *Time v. Hill*, 385 U.S. 374 (1967); *Cox Broadcasting v. Cohn*, 420 U.S. 469 (1975); *Florida Star v. BJF*, 491 U.S. 524 (1989); *Shulman v. Group W Productions Inc.*, 18 Cal. 4th 200, 955, P .2d 469 (1998).

unity is not only fulfilling in itself, it is also an instrument of legal development.'[102] Ten years later he added: 'In [public disclosure] cases the individual has been profaned by laying a private life open to public view. The intimacy and private space necessary to sustain individuality and human dignity has been impaired by turning a private life into a public spectacle. The innermost region of being has been bruised by exposure to the world.'[103]

4. The protection of journalists' sources

The central question concerning the protection of journalists' sources is: Should the press enjoy special protection? Several basic principles are at stake, guaranteed both at the constitutional and international level: freedom of expression; the right to a fair trial; equality before the law and before justice. May journalists who are called as witnesses before a court refuse to disclose their sources of information? The standard answer of the press is that the law of confidence or, in France, that the *'secret professionnel'* should be applied to journalists in such a situation. The European legal answer is on the whole more favourable to journalists than the American one. Under the US Supreme Court case law, the First Amendment may not be invoked by journalists who are called as witnesses or under a subpoena to refuse to disclose the source of their information.[104] In Britain, the courts have interpreted Section 10 of the Contempt of Court Act 1981 in a manner that did not bring much comfort to the press: 'No court may require a person to disclose, nor is any person guilty of contempt of court for refusing to disclose, the source of information contained in a publication for which he is responsible, unless it is established to the satisfaction of the court that it is necessary in the interests of justice or national security or for the

---

[102] E. J. Bloustein, 'Privacy as an Aspect of Human Dignity' (1964) 39 *New York University Law Review*, 962, at 1002 and 1004.

[103] E. J. Bloustein, 'The First Amendment and Privacy. The Supreme Court Justice and the Philosopher' (1974) 28 *Rutgers Law Review*, 41, at 54.

[104] *Branzburg* v. *Hayes*, 408 U.S. 665 (1972) (Grand jury investigation); *In re Farber*, 78 NJ 259, 394 A. 2nd 330, cert. denied 439 U.S. 997 (1978); on Farber, see R. Dworkin, 'The Farber Case: Reporters and Informers', in *A Matter of Principle* (Cambridge, Mass. and London, 1985), p. 373 and the exchange in *The New York Review of Books*: R. Dworkin, 'The Rights of Myron Farber', *NYR*, 26 October 1978, 34 and 'The Rights of Myron Farber: an Exchange', *NYR*, 7 December 1978; A. Lewis, 'A Preferred Position for Journalism?' (1979) 7 *Hofstra Law Review* 595, 610 et seqq.

prevention of disorder or crime.'[105] The courts have construed these two grounds rather broadly.[106] However the case law might be influenced in the future by the Human Rights Act of 1998[107] and by the *Goodwin* decision of the European Court of Human Rights.[108] In that case, the Court found a lack of reasonable relationship of proportionality between the legitimate aim pursued by the disclosure order and the means employed to achieve that aim. In France, a clause added in 1993 to the Code of Penal Procedure provides: 'Any journalist heard as a witness on information gathered in the exercise of his activity is free not to disclose his source.'

III. Conclusion

More than two hundred years after the adoption of Article 11 of the Declaration of the Rights of Man and the Citizen, forty years after *New York Times v. Sullivan* and almost twenty years after *Lingens v. Austria*, is it possible to try to evaluate elements of divergence and of convergence between European and US constitutionalism in the field of freedom of speech? The exercise requires some humility but is worth the attempt.[109]

On both sides of the Atlantic free speech enjoys high constitutional protection and is held to be one of the most fundamental pillars of democracy. On both sides the evolution of the past half-century has been a spectacular and a highly positive one for freedom of speech. As to

---

[105] In 1980, the House of Lords held that it was not in the public interest to recognise any immunity or testimonial privilege for the media: *British Steel Corp.* v. *Granada* (1981) AC, 1096. See Y. Cripps, 'Judicial Proceedings and Refusals to Disclose the Identity of Sources of Information' (1984) 43 *Cambridge Law Journal*, 266; C. J. Miller, *Contempt of Court* (2nd edn, Oxford: Clarendon Press, 1989), pp. 119 et seqq.

[106] See *Re an Inquiry under the Companies Securities (Insider Dealing) Act 1985* [1988] AC, 660; *Camelot Group plc* v. *Centaur Commission Ltd* [1998] 1 All ER, 251. For a comment on the situation at the beginning of the 90s, see S. Palmer, 'Protecting Journalists' Sources: Section 10, Contempt of Court Act 1981' (1992) *Public Law*, 61; J. Wadham and H. Mountfield, *Blackstone's Guide to the Human Rights Act, 1998* (London: Blackstone, 1999); G. Robertson and A. Nicol, *Media Law* (4th edn, London: Penguin, 2002), pp. 253 et seqq.

[107] See Wadham and Mountfield, *Human Rights Act*, above, note 106.

[108] *Goodwin* v. *UK*, 1996-II, Eur. Ct. H.R., 483; A. Sherlock, 'Protection of Journalists' Sources' (1996) 21 *European Law Review*, 496.

[109] For an earlier and partial attempt, see R. Errera, 'The Freedom of the Press: the US, France and other European Countries', in L. Henkin and A. J. Rosenthal (eds.), *Constitutionalism and Rights. The Influence of the US Constitution Abroad* (New York: Columbia University Press, 1990), p. 63.

differences, six of them can be readily assessed. They relate to the wording of constitutional instruments; the historical context; the respective role of parliaments; the tools of judicial review; the international context; and, finally, the substantive law.

There is a strong and objective difference between the wording of the First Amendment and, in Europe, the wording of Article 11 of the 1789 Declaration, Article 5 of the German Constitution or Article 10 ECHR. The latter articles state a fundamental but qualified right, thus directly inviting the courts to step into a balancing process. The European heritage of the nineteenth century is that of the rise of liberalism, that of the twentieth century is rather one of war and of authoritarian or totalitarian regimes. All these developments have left marks. As to US constitutionalism it seems that the case law of the Supreme Court in the 1960s and 1970s cannot be isolated from the social and political events of the times, the civil rights movement and the Vietnam War in particular.

Laws on the press exist throughout continental Europe. Parliaments have intervened in respect of group libel and hate speech. In the United States, such legislation is extremely rare.

The judicial attitude in Europe has been that of balancing between equally recognised rights, values and interests, as they are affirmed in the constitution itself or elsewhere. This is also true of the case law of the European Court of Human Rights. The categorisation used by the US Supreme Court is somewhat different. However, on both sides notions such as the public interest are commonly used.

Regarding the international context, two observations are in order: the international dimension of the law is visible everywhere in Europe, as illustrated by the case law of the Strasbourg Court and its influence on domestic law. This is in marked contrast to the American scene. The transatlantic trade in ideas on free speech needs to be increased. The dominant winds seem to be, for the moment, eastward ones.

Freedom of speech can be considered from two points of view: from the point of view of the state and from the perspective of individual rights. There is no doubt that, vis-à-vis the executive or parliament, in the United States freedom of speech is better protected than in most European countries. There is also little doubt that personality rights, such as privacy, human dignity, protection against racial incitement or group libel, are better recognised and protected in Europe. The outcome of the comparison shows a strong difference between the relevant European and US case law. The notion of a 'marketplace' of ideas is not enunciated or accepted in Europe as it is in the USA. Such a metaphor has already invited much discussion and criticism and the end of the discussion is not in sight. Whether or not it is 'rooted in *laissez-faire* economics'[110] it deserves a close examination.[111] But its very use and acceptance by the case law is significant.

[110] S. Ingber, 'The Market-Place of Ideas: a Legitimizing Myth' (1984) 34 *Duke Law Journal*, 1, at 4–5.
[111] See J. R. Pole, 'A Bad Case of Agoraphobia. Is there a Marketplace of Ideas?', *Times Literary Supplement*, 4 February 1994.

3

Freedom of expression adjudication in Europe and the United States: a case study in comparative constitutional architecture

FREDERICK SCHAUER

Constitutional and human rights doctrines and rights differ across cultures not only in their substance, but also in their architecture. Some rights are worded broadly and vaguely while others are written in narrow and precise terms; for some rights the determination of the scope of the right is merged with the determination of its strength, while for others questions of scope and strength are sharply delineated; some rights are seemingly absolute, yet others allow for overrides; some rights are universally applicable within their jurisdictional scope, while others apply only to some people, or at some times, or in some places; and some rights are non-derogable, while others are subject to suspension in cases of catastrophe, or in circumstances of emergency or crisis.

Although such differences in the architecture of rights pervade the topic of constitutional and human rights,[1] the architectural issues have been especially visible and especially contested with respect to the rights variously described as freedom of speech, freedom of communication and freedom of expression, and including the freedom of the press, the right of assembly, the freedom of association and various other rights (academic freedom and artistic freedom, for example) commonly associated with or part of the cluster of communicative rights. In part because the concepts of speech, communication and expression are themselves so capacious, and in part because the countervailing interests often both appear and are especially weighty, there has been an explicit

---

[1] For my own thoughts on the structure of rights generally, see Frederick Schauer, 'A Comment on the Structure of Rights' (1993) 27 *Georgia Law Review*, 415–34; Frederick Schauer, 'Exceptions' (1991) 58 *University of Chicago Law Review*, 871–99; Frederick Schauer, 'Can Rights Be Abused?' (1981) 31 *Philosophical Quarterly*, 225–30.

concern with the design of freedom of communication rights in virtually all countries with sophisticated constitutional or human rights cultures and legal protection. This concern with the structure and design of rights of communication has emerged out of a seeming need to delimit the scope of rights that if taken literally would have unlimited breadth, and there has thus been careful attention to the need to design the rights so as simultaneously to ensure their effective protection and also to provide appropriate breathing room for a multiplicity of important countervailing interests.

Yet although issues relating to the architecture of rights have arisen with particular frequency in the context of freedom of communication, there exists an important divide in terms of just what that architecture should be. More particularly, there is a view, widespread in Canada, in Europe and in South Africa, and sometimes seen in other countries as well, that American free-speech adjudication is obsessed with categorisation and definition.[2] Under this view, American free speech

[2] A sampling of the comparative literature on this point includes Nadia Ahmad, 'The Canadian Charter of Rights and Freedoms: an Example of Canadian Dependence on the United States or Commitment to International Law' (1998) 7 *Detroit College of Law Journal of International Law and Practice*, 89; Donald L. Beschle, 'Clearly Canadian? *Hill v. Colorado* and Free Speech Balancing in the United States and Canada' (2001) 28 *Hastings Constitutional Law Quarterly*, 187; Paul Horwitz, 'Law's Expression: the Promise and Perils of Judicial Opinion Writing in Canadian Constitutional Law' (2000) 38 *Osgoode Hall Law Journal*, 101; Vicki C. Jackson, 'Ambivalent Resistance and Comparative Constitutionalism: Opening Up the Conversation on "Proportionality", Rights and Federalism' (1999) 1 *University of Pennsylvania Journal of Constitutional Law*, 583; Vicki C. Jackson, 'Comparative Constitutional Federalism and Transnational Judicial Discourse' (2004) 1 *International Journal of Constitutional Law*, 91; Simon Mount, '*R v. Shaheed*: the Prima Facie Exclusion Rule Reexamined' (2003) 1 *New Zealand Law Review*, 45; Aaron J. Polak, 'Free Legal Trade: American First Amendment Theory Fails to Persuade Canadian Courts' (1994) 8 *Emory International Law Review*, 579; Cedric Merlin Powell, 'The Mythological Marketplace of Ideas: R. A. V., Mitchell, and Beyond' (1995) 12 *Harvard Blackletter Law Journal*, 1; Adrienne Stone, 'The Limits of Constitutional Text and Structure: Standards of Review and Freedom of Political Communication' (1999) 23 *Melbourne University Law Review*, 668; Nadine Strossen, 'Recent U.S. and International Judicial Protection of Individual Rights: a Comparative Legal Process Analysis and Proposed Synthesis' (1990) 41 *Hastings Law Journal*, 805; Clive Walker and Russell L. Weaver, 'The United Kingdom Bill of Rights 1998: the Modernisation of Rights in the Old World' (2000) 33 *University of Michigan Journal of Law Reform*, 497; Lorraine C. Weinrib, 'The Supreme Court of Canada and Section One of the Charter' (1988) 10 *Supreme Court Law Review*, 469; Lorraine C. Weinrib, 'Hate Promotion in a Free and Democratic Society: R. v. Keegstra' (1991) 36 *McGill Law Journal*, 1416. See also Eric Barendt, *Freedom of Speech* (Oxford: Oxford University Press, 1985); Kent Greenawalt, *Fighting Words: Individuals,*

adjudication disingenuously decides that certain forms of communication are beyond the scope of the First Amendment's protection of freedom of speech and freedom of the press, and in the process of such categorial exclusion masks the difficult weighing process that the Canadian, European and South African structure both facilitates and makes more transparent. The American approach, say its critics abroad, produces results that are both substantively undesirable and procedurally inappropriate, both being the consequence of a preoccupation with categories and an unwillingness to recognise the importance of numerous values that often conflict with the values of freedom of communication.

My goal in this paper is to address this contrast and this controversy, relating some of the controversy to more abstract questions about the theory of rights, some to larger questions of constitutional method, and some to genuine disagreements about the substance and strength of the right rather than about its structure. It is not my aim here to take an especially strong position on the desirability of one approach or structure rather than another, although I will suggest that the critics of the American approach, scarcely less than the Americans, ignore the extent to which they rely on categorisation and the extent to which they disguise or neglect the choices that such categorisation reflects. My goal is thus primarily descriptive and explanatory, although I suspect that both the description and the explanation will have some of the flavour of a defence of the American approach against the charges of its critics. Insofar as this is true, however, the defence should not be understood as a prescription that other jurisdictions follow the American lead, but is best taken as an explanation of why the American approach follows more naturally than is often understood from deeper choices in the American constitutional culture.

I. The difference described

The basic difference between the American and non-American approaches can best be described in the formal and literal structure of the relevant guarantees, although differences in formal structure are the beginning and not the end of the analysis. Still, the formal differences provide a good entry into the issue. In terms of those differences, the

Communities, and Liberties of Speech (Princeton: Princeton University Press, 1995), especially chapter 2.

most notable part of the guarantee of freedom of speech (and freedom of the press) in the First Amendment to the Constitution of the United States is that it appears on its face to speak in absolute terms: 'Congress shall make no law ... abridging the freedom of speech or of the Press.'[3] Although the text of the First Amendment refers to 'Congress,' it is now accepted that, by virtue of the 'incorporation' of the First Amendment by the Fourteenth Amendment, the First Amendment delimits the powers of the states as well as those of the federal government.[4] As written, this guarantee makes no reference to the strength of potentially competing interests, no reference to the possibility of the right being outweighed or overridden, and no reference to any circumstances in which an exercise of the right might nevertheless be restricted. According to its literal terms, the First Amendment is absolute.

By contrast to the seeming absoluteness of the First Amendment, the typical modern non-American protection of roughly the same right differs from its American counterpart in two important respects. First, most obvious in Article 10 of the European Convention on Human Rights, is the presence of an explicit listing of various qualifications or exceptions to the right. So although Article 10 (1) of the Convention protects the freedom of expression in seemingly absolute terms (except for the explicit authorisation in that section of broadcast and motion picture licensing), Article 10 (2) proceeds to allow restrictions in the name of 'national security, territorial integrity or public safety, for the prevention of disorder or crime, for the protection of health or morals, for the protection of the reputation or rights of others, for preventing the disclosure of information received in confidence, or for maintaining the authority and impartiality of the judiciary'. Just as Paragraph 1 grants the right, therefore, Paragraph 2 appears significantly to circumscribe it.

Second, and more significantly, the typical non-American protection of freedom of communication[5] explicitly authorises a process of

---

[3] The full text is as follows: 'Congress shall make no law respecting an establishment of religion, or prohibiting the free exercise thereof; or abridging the freedom of speech, or of the press; or the right of the people peaceably to assemble, and to petition the Government for a redress of grievances.'

[4] *Stromberg* v. *California*, 283 U.S. 359 (1931); *Gitlow* v. *New York*, 268 U.S. 652 (1925).

[5] For purposes of this analysis, I will draw no distinction between freedom of speech, freedom of expression and freedom of communication. The different forms may at times make a genuine difference, but for my purposes here, little depends on variations in the way in which the right is formally articulated.

balancing the interest in freedom of communication against other countervailing interests. In the European Convention on Human Rights, the balancing methodology is contained directly in Article 10 (2), which precedes the foregoing list of approved countervailing interests with the statement that the freedom of expression, 'since it carries with it duties and responsibilities, may be subject to such formalities, conditions, restrictions or penalties as are prescribed by law and are necessary in a democratic society'. More commonly, such qualifications are contained in a limitations clause applicable to all rights, as for example in the Canadian Charter of Rights and Freedoms, which protects freedom of expression (as well as the related freedoms of thought, belief, opinion, press, assembly and association) in Section 2, but in which Section 1, the limitations clause, allows the rights in section 2, as well as all other rights, to be 'subject ... to such reasonable limits prescribed by law as can be demonstrably justified in a free and democratic society'. Similarly, South Africa designates some rights as nonderogable, but for all the others, including the right to freedom of expression, the rights may be 'limited only in terms of law of general application to the extent that the limitation is reasonable and justifiable in an open and democratic society based on human dignity, equality and freedom, taking into account all relevant factors, including (a.) the nature of the right; (b.) the importance of the purpose of the limitation; (c.) the nature and extent of the limitation; (d.) the relation between the limitation and its purpose; and (e.) less restrictive means to achieve the purpose'.[6]

The Canadian model of a general limitations clause, embellished by the South African proportionality inquiry, has become the dominant model among advanced constitutional democracies. Israel's quasi-constitutional Basic Laws allow rights to be limited when the limitation is one 'fitting the values of the State of Israel, designed for a proper purpose, and to an extent no greater than required.'[7] The Federal Republic of Germany's Basic Law explicitly allows restrictions of basic rights as long as done explicitly, by a

---

[6] Constitution of the Republic of South Africa, Section 36. The right to freedom of expression is contained in Section 16, and associated rights to assembly, demonstration, picketing, petition and association are contained in Sections 17 and 18. And although Section 16 is subject to the general limitations clause, Section 16 itself makes clear that its protections do not extend to 'propaganda for war', 'incitement of imminent violence', or 'advocacy of hatred that is based on race, ethnicity, gender or religion, and that constitutes incitement to cause harm'.
[7] State of Israel, Basic Law – Human Dignity and Liberty, § 8.

law of general application, and in a way that preserves the 'essence' of the right affected.[8] New Zealand's Bill of Rights Act 1990 expressly authorises limitations in language virtually identical to that in the Canadian Charter of Rights and Freedoms,[9] and the limitations provisions of the European Convention on Human Rights are now the law, whether directly or by incorporation,[10] throughout Europe.

As the contrast has been developed, the issue is not just the one of whether the limitations should be omitted, as in the United States, or attached to specific rights, as in the European Convention, or applied to all or almost all rights, as in Canada, Germany, South Africa and New Zealand.[11] Rather, the importance of the issue stems from the way in which, textually, the different formulations might be thought to produce different processes of adjudication. Under the American approach, it appears as if the sole task is to delineate the contours of a right which is then to be treated as having infinite stringency, such that all of the 'action', as it were, is at the stage of definition. By contrast, the non-American approach appears explicitly to authorise a two-step process, in which the first step is to delineate the scope of the right, and then, if some activity or some governmental restriction falls within that scope, thereafter to determine whether the limitations are justified according to the designated burden of justification and the designated proportionality inquiry.

II. The current debate

The current debate between these two approaches in fact involves two different debates. One is a debate about the formal structure of rights, and flows from the description provided above. On one side of the debate is the view that rights should be designed and delineated so that they are absolute, with the best structure of rights being a list of specifically and (probably) narrowly defined but infinitely stringent rights.[12] Under this approach, crisp articulations of specific rights are

---

[8] Basic Law for the Federal Republic of Germany, Article 19.

[9] New Zealand Bill of Rights Act 1990, § 5.

[10] See, for example, the United Kingdom Human Rights Act 1998.

[11] On this distinction, see David Kretzmer, 'Basic Laws as a Surrogate Bill of Rights: the Case of Israel' in Philip Alston (ed.), *Promoting Human Rights Through Bills of Rights: Comparative Perspectives* (Oxford: Oxford University Press, 1999), pp. 75–92.

[12] Such an approach is developed in Charles Fried, *Right and Wrong* (Cambridge: Harvard University Press, 1978).

set forth with the understanding that the rights so described will be absolute. No weighing, balancing or proportionality testing is involved or permitted, and the rights, as a matter of structure, are designed so that they may not be overridden or declared inapplicable with respect to any conduct falling within their linguistic scope.

According to its proponents, the advantages of this form of rights architecture reside largely in the domain of worries about slippage in application.[13] If overrides are permitted, so the argument goes, then overrides will be found, especially because the right-holders of certain rights – especially rights to freedom of speech and fair procedure in criminal law – will disproportionately be unpopular (or guilty) individuals espousing unpopular ideas or engaging in antisocial behaviour.[14] Given this phenomenon, so the argument goes, allowing for rights overrides is effectively to encourage such overrides, and to encourage them in a milieu in which it is highly likely that the exercise of the right will seem unfortunate and the reasons for override compelling. With such a psychological, sociological and political environment, so the argument goes, rights will be overridden, outweighed or outbalanced with great frequency. The only remedy, it is said, is to devote considerable effort early on to defining the rights carefully, but having done so then to set up a system such that the non-overridability of the rights makes them as durable in the cauldron of practical application as was imagined when the right was first designed.[15]

On the other side of this argument is the argument from unpredictability. Carefully designed but non-overridable rights resemble the precisely written, publicly accessible and non-interpretable codes so celebrated by Jeremy Bentham,[16] and they suffer from similar flaws. Just as no code of laws can anticipate all eventualities in advance, so too

---

[13] See John Hart Ely, 'Flag Desecration: a Case Study in the Roles of Categorization and Balancing in First Amendment Analysis' (1975) 88 *Harvard Law Review*, 1482; Mark Tushnet, '"Of Church and State and the Supreme Court": Kurland Revisited' (1989) *The Supreme Court Review*, 373 at 382, 400.

[14] See Frederick Schauer, 'Slippery Slopes' (1985) 99 *Harvard Law Review*, 361; Frederick Schauer, 'Codifying the First Amendment: *New York* v. *Ferber*' (1982) *The Supreme Court Review*, 285; Frederick Schauer, 'Categories and the First Amendment: a Play in Three Acts' (1981) 34 *Vanderbilt Law Review*, 265.

[15] See Kathleen M. Sullivan, 'Foreword: the Justices of Rules and Standards' (1992) 106 *Harvard Law Review*, 22; Kathleen M. Sullivan, 'Post-Liberal Judging: the Roles of Categorization and Balancing' (1992) 63 *University of Colorado Law Review*, 293.

[16] See Gerald M. Postema, *Bentham and the Common Law Tradition* (Oxford: Clarendon Press, 1986).

can no listing of rights anticipate *ex ante* all possible reasons for overriding such rights, or even anticipate all of the possible types of exercises of those rights. And just as no code, whether in Bentham's writings or in actual civil law codified legal systems, has been able to survive without incorporating mechanisms for continuous internal modification, so too with rights. Unless rights contain the flexibility to allow for their own modification, and unless they allow for the possibility that unpredicted and unpredictable events will necessitate their override, it is argued, the rights will be widely ignored, destined to be replaced by something far more flexible or, even worse, doomed to ineffectiveness in guaranteeing the very rights whose protection is their rationale.

This debate about rigidity, flexibility, slippage and the structure of rights, however, is, as noted above, only one of two related debates. The other debate, also a debate based on structure but with a different focus, is largely a debate about honesty. The American approach is flawed, say large numbers of Canadians, Europeans and South Africans, among others, not (or not only) because it represents a mistaken resolution of the debate about rigidity, flexibility and slippage. It is also flawed because Americans have wound up doing surreptitiously and disingenuously what the rest of the advanced constitutional world does honestly and transparently. Sometimes, so the charge goes, this is merely a matter of appending exceptions and qualifications and elaborate tests to seemingly absolute rights. So when American courts allow free-speech rights to be overridden by compelling interests,[17] or in the service of intricate three- and four-part tests,[18] they are engaging in a similar proportionality or balancing inquiry, but less honestly, and in a far less disciplined manner. Even worse, say the critics, is what happens in the first stage of the inquiry. Recognising that free-speech rights will be extraordinarily strong, Americans, say the critics, do their balancing and proportionality testing when they define the rights,[19] disingenuously claiming that certain activities are beyond the scope of the right when it would be wiser, more transparent and more

---

[17] See *New York* v. *Ferber*, 458 U.S. 747 (1982).

[18] See *Miller* v. *California*, 413 U.S. 15 (1973) (obscenity); *Central Hudson Gas & Electric Corporation* v. *Public Service Commission of New York*, 447 U.S. 557 (1980) (commercial advertising).

[19] In the American literature, such a process has occasionally been referred to as 'definitional balancing'. See Melville Nimmer, 'The Right to Speak from Times to Time: First Amendment Theory Applied to Libel and Misapplied to Privacy' (1968) 56 *California Law Review*, 935; Melville Nimmer, 'The Meaning of Symbolic Speech Under the First Amendment' (1973) 21 *University of California Los Angeles Law Review*, 29.

honest to do this balancing more openly. By insisting that outweighed rights were not really rights in the first place, say the critics, Americans do under the table what most others do far more openly.

III. In search of explanation

Like far too many other debates, there is a risk that this debate about free expression architecture will degenerate into a simple normative debate between advocates trumpeting the virtues of their own country's position. And although there may be value in such normative debates, there is also value in trying to search simply for explanation, and that is what I propose to do in this section. As a result, I will offer here some explanations for why American and other approaches might differ so markedly, yet without arguing that one is better or worse than the other. Indeed, my point is largely that it is not a matter of better or worse, but rather a function of the way in which different architectures emerge from different substantive commitments, different experiences, and different views about the locus of decision-making authority.

1. The question of age

The American approach to freedom of speech is not only characterised by the use of complex tests, as noted above, and not only by determinations of what is inside or outside of the coverage of the First Amendment,[20] but also by a wide range of qualifications, exceptions, principles, rules and presumptions. At first glance the temptation is to see this as baroque, formal and faintly ridiculous. Yet however tempting this characterisation is, the temptation should be resisted. After all, three- and four-part (or more) analyses are a common part of numerous statutes and regulations throughout the world, and principles, rules, presumptions, qualifications and exceptions pervade virtually all mature legal topics. Once we see this, and once we see freedom of communication as an area of law and not just an abstract and contentless manifesto to be trumpeted on national holidays, the question shifts, and we confront the possibility that the law of freedom of speech, no less than the law of contract, tort, real property, unfair competition or securities regulation, is simply a mature legal topic – a well-developed

---

[20] On the issue of 'coverage,' the American equivalent of the first stage inquiry in Canadian, European and South African adjudication, see Frederick Schauer, 'The Boundaries of the First Amendment' (2004) 117 *Harvard Law Review*, 1765.

area of legal doctrine – with all of the characteristics that such maturity can be expected to bring.

To put the same issue in a different way, one possibility is that the American approach, as compared to that which prevails elsewhere, is largely a function of experience, and of the increasing array of cases and challenges that come from time. At this writing, the First Amendment is 214 years old. And although serious First Amendment application has hardly occurred for that entire period, it does date back to no later than 1919,[21] thus producing in the United States no less than eighty-six years of intensive judicial (as well as public and political) engagement with free-speech adjudication. By contrast, the experience under the European Convention on Human Rights is, with respect to freedom of expression issues, closer to twenty-five years, under the Canadian Charter of Rights and Freedoms slightly over twenty, and in most of the other countries mentioned above somewhat closer to ten.

There is no reason to believe that this experience has made the United States any better or wiser at free-speech adjudication than are its architectural competitors. The claim here is not that older is necessarily sounder. Yet the enormous differential in the simple quantity of free-speech experience has made the United States more experienced, in the non-evaluative sense of that term, and it has thus allowed American courts to confront a much larger quantity and diversity of free-speech issues. And as large numbers of different free-speech issues have arisen, these issues and cases have, not surprisingly, arranged themselves into patterns, patterns that may be less apparent and more fluid than in countries with a substantially smaller experiential base. Just as the common law has become substantially less fluid as dispute patterns have repeated themselves over hundreds of years, and just as codes in civil law countries have become more refined with more experience in the transactions that those codes must govern, so too does freedom of expression decision-making codify itself over time and with experience. What appears to Canadians and Europeans as an American obsession with categories, boundaries, definitions, tests and rules may well be an

---

[21] On earlier discussions and applications of the First Amendment, primarily in the lower courts, see David M. Rabban, *Free Speech in Its Forgotten Years* (Cambridge: Cambridge University Press, 1997). The modern era of free-speech adjudication in the Supreme Court is commonly taken to begin with a series of important 1919 cases, including *Schenck* v. *United States*, 249 U.S. 47 (1919); *Frohwerk* v. *United States*, 249 U.S. 204 (1919); *Debs* v. *United States*, 249 U.S. 211 (1919); and *Abrams* v. *United States*, 250 U.S. 616 (1919).

obsession, but it is likely an obsession borne of experience, and little different from the obsession with all of the impedimenta of legal doctrine that characterises a vast number of other equally old and equally dense legal topics. When the European Court of Human Rights first dealt in the *Sunday Times (Thalidomide)* case[22] with the issue of pre-trial publicity, it dealt with an issue entirely new to that court, albeit against a background of considerable national experience with the issue in the various member countries. Still, the issue was novel for the European Court of Human Rights itself, and it should come as no surprise that the matter was decided in a substantially open-ended fashion, albeit with due regard for the margin of appreciation that the Convention and the Court allows for national practices, national histories and national variation. But it would come as a great surprise to discover that in the year, say, 2029, half a century after the *Thalidomide* case, the same court were to be treating every contempt case as if it were a case of first impression. It is far more likely that the Court in 2029 would itself have had increasingly more experience with the issue, that national courts would have had increasingly more experience in working out various details within the interstices of the law under Article 10 of the Convention and that this experience would have produced not only precedents, but also rules, principles, canons, maxims, presumptions and all of the other devices of the increased complexification of legal doctrine. In theory, it remains possible that freedom of expression adjudication in Canada, in Europe and in other countries other than the United States will remain, in Q'adi-like fashion, continuously open-ended and continuously case- and context-specific. But this possibility is highly remote, and were it to occur it would constitute a challenge not only to American free-speech development, but to all we know about the growth and rigidification of the common law generally.[23] Far more likely is that as more and more cases are presented, there will be as many rules outside of the United States as there are within, and that seeming differences in 2005 are far more a function of differential experience than of anything deeper or more permanent.

---

[22] *The Sunday Times Case*, 30 Eur. Ct. H.R. (ser. A) (1978).
[23] On American constitutional adjudication as largely a common law process, see David A. Strauss, 'Common Law Constitutional Interpretation' (1996) 63 *University of Chicago Law Review*, 877. For application to freedom of speech, see David A. Strauss, 'Freedom of Speech and the Common-Law Constitution', in Lee C. Bollinger and Geoffrey R. Stone (eds.), *Eternally Vigilant: Free Speech in the Modern Era* (Chicago: University of Chicago Press, 2002), pp. 33–59.

This issue is especially apparent at the edges rather than at the centre of free-speech doctrine. In Canada, in Europe and in South Africa, free-speech cases have looked quite traditional, at least in the sense of presenting issues that free-speech adjudicators and free-speech theorists have been dealing with for generations, such as defamation, pornography, commercial advertising in the mass media, hate speech and speech alleged to be threatening to national security. And although such cases still dominate the free-speech docket of American courts, American courts have also been involved (perhaps 'plagued' is the better word) with a large number of cases raising free speech claims that are somewhere between attenuated and preposterous. Claims that the First Amendment limits the securities laws, the antitrust laws, the fraud laws and many, many others, are a staple of the current American free speech environment,[24] and it is thus a matter of vital importance in the United States to distinguish the legitimate from the frivolous claims of abridgment of freedom of speech, even though the frivolous and the legitimate claims alike are ones involving the word 'speech' in the ordinary language sense of that term.

This feature of American free speech adjudication takes place against a background in which most non-American free expression adjudication has rarely been presented with such problems. Although the Supreme Court of Canada, for example, has tended to find that almost all claims presented to it are encompassed by Section 2 of the Canadian Charter of Rights and Freedoms,[25] it has yet to have occasion to decide whether 'freedom of expression' includes the expression by which corporate officers fix prices, whether 'freedom of the press' includes published offerings of securities and other investment instruments, and whether 'freedom of association' includes non-political criminal conspiracies.[26] And if and when it does, as American courts have had to decide just these issues, two possibilities emerge. One is that all or most of such activities will be held to be encompassed by the right, in which case it will become apparent that the scope (or ambit, or coverage) of the right has no limits, and that what is textually designed as a two-stage process is in fact a one-stage process. More plausibly, the court will look at the purposes of the constitutional

---

[24] On this phenomenon, see Schauer, 'Boundaries of the First Amendment', above, note 20.

[25] See Richard Moon, *The Constitutional Protection of Freedom of Expression* (Toronto: University of Toronto Press, 2000); W. J. Waluchow (ed.), *Free Expression: Essays in Law and Philosophy* (Oxford: Clarendon Press, 1994).

[26] See Roger A. Shiner, *Freedom of Commercial Expression* (Oxford: Oxford University Press, 2003).

guarantee, and determine that whatever the single purpose is or the multiple purposes are, activities like securities trading and price-fixing are so far
beyond any plausible purpose that the right is not triggered in the first
place, the presence of what is literally 'expression', 'association' or 'press'
notwithstanding. And if this is the case, the court will find itself doing
exactly what American courts have done (controversially) with obscenity,
and far less controversially with numerous other topics. It is too soon to tell
exactly what Canada, South Africa, New Zealand, European national courts
and the European Court of Human Rights will do with such claims, but
until these courts confront such a wide range of cases involving what is
literally expression but is implausibly about freedom of expression it may
be too soon to brand the American approach as mistaken. What now looks
to non-Americans like a mistaken approach may simply be a function of
greater experience and a much greater array of free expression challenges,
and what at first sight looks to most non-Americans like a different or
unique or exceptional American approach may be little more than the
natural progression from simplicity to complexity that we have witnessed
in almost all forms of common law development.

2. On the relationship between structure and substance

As noted above, many of the arguments for a precisely delineated set of
non-overridable rules are premised on the importance of preserving a
strong free speech culture and protecting strong free speech rights. Yet
it is obvious that this is not a goal shared by most non-American
constitutional cultures, at least not in the form in which, and to the
extent in which, it is held in the United States. As is well known,
American First Amendment doctrine protects incitement to racial
hatred,[27] Holocaust denial[28] and other forms of hate speech widely
criminalised in the rest of the world, and explicitly excluded from free
expression principles in numerous human rights documents. American

---

[27] See *Brandenburg v. Ohio*, 395 U.S. 444 (1969). See also the so-called 'Skokie' cases,
protecting the communicative actions of the American Nazi Party, *Collin v. Smith*, 578
F 2d 1197 (7th Cir. 1978), stay denied, 436 U.S. 953 (1978), cert. denied, 439 U.S. 916
(1978); *National Socialist Party of America v. Village of Skokie*, 432 U.S. 43 (1977), as
well as, on cross-burning, *R. A. V. v. St. Paul*, 505 U.S. 377 (1992).

[28] That there is no American counterpart to the Canadian case of *R. v. Keegstra*, 3 S. C. R.
697 (1990), is solely a function of the fact that it is entirely implausible under current
American free-speech doctrine that Holocaust denial could be subject to either criminal
or civil sanctions.

First Amendment doctrine also constrains the law of libel to a degree
virtually unthinkable even to those numerous countries that have explicitly considered (and rejected) the American approach,[29] treats freedom
of the press as far more important than the rights of defendants and
victims in criminal trials,[30] applies the First Amendment almost as
vigorously to illegally obtained information as to information obtained
legitimately[31] and treats claims of national security with a dose of
scepticism far larger than that seen in much of the developed world.[32]
In all of these dimensions, and many more, the United States, as a matter
of substance and not a matter of structure, is a free speech outlier,
insisting that its 'exceptional' approach to freedom of speech and freedom of the press is both wiser and more faithful to American political
and legal traditions than would be the American analogue to Canadian
and European views on these and related issues.[33]

   This is not the occasion for me to address the possible explanations
for American substantive exceptionalism on free speech and free press
issues, and certainly not the occasion to offer an opinion on whether
the American approach is better or worse than that seen in most
of the balance of the open, liberal, democratic, constitutional world.
This is, however, the occasion on which to address the issue whether
there is a relationship between the American approach on matters
of substance and the American approach on matters of free speech
architecture. And on this issue, it does appear that there is a significant
relationship. This relationship is illustrated by an American debate on
the Supreme Court that took place in the 1950s and 1960s, and in the
academic literature of the same time, and extending somewhat beyond.
As this debate was framed, it had on one side those who contended,
more metaphorically than literally, that the First Amendment was an

---

[29] See Leonard Leigh, 'Of Free Speech and Individual Reputation: *New York Times Co.* v.
Sullivan in Canada and Australia' in Ian Loveland (ed.), *Importing the First Amendment:
Freedom of Speech and Expression in Britain, Europe and the USA* (Oxford: Hart
Publishing, 2000), pp. 51–68.

[30] *Richmond Newspapers, Inc.* v. *Virginia*, 448 U.S. 555 (1980); *Florida Star* v. *B.J.F.*, 491
U.S. 524 (1989); *Cox Broadcasting Corp.* v. *Cohn*, 420 U.S. 469 (1975).

[31] *Bartnicki* v. *Vopper*, 121 S.Ct. 1753 (2001); *Landmark Communications, Inc.* v. *Virginia*,
435 U.S. 829 (1978).

[32] *New York Times* v. *United States* (Pentagon Papers Case), 403 U.S. 713 (1971).

[33] On the differences between the United States and the rest of the modern developed
liberal world on freedom of speech and freedom of press issues, see the various essays in
Ian Loveland (ed.), *Importing the First Amendment: Freedom of Speech and Expression in
Britain, Europe and the USA* (Oxford: Hart Publishing, 2000).

absolute. Prominent contestants on this side of the debate included Justices Hugo Black[34] and to a lesser extent William O. Douglas[35] on the Supreme Court, and Alexander Meiklejohn[36] and Laurent Frantz[37] among a large number of academic commentators. And on the other side were Supreme Court Justices such as Felix Frankfurter[38] and John Marshall Harlan,[39] and commentators like Wallace Mendelsohn,[40] all of whom advocated a 'balancing' approach in which free speech values were weighed against potentially countervailing values on more or less a case-by-case basis.

As with most such debates, there was no clear winner. Yet even with the absence of a winner, it was widely understood then, and to a considerable extent is widely understood now, that those on the 'absolute' side of the debate tended to be the more enthusiastic free speech proponents, and those who advocated 'balancing' were more likely to believe that free speech, whatever its importance, was hardly the only important interest, and hardly an interest that did or should be granted presumptive priority in cases in which free speech and other interests were in conflict.[41] Moreover, the debate, not surprising against the background of a Supreme Court that was largely passive in the face of McCarthyism, and not surprising during a time when it was just beginning to be recognised that a Communist revolution in the United States was far less likely than many had previously thought, was significantly about a distrust of discretion and significantly about a fear of the official ability to assess accurately the

---

[34] See *Konigsberg* v. *State Bar of California*, 366 U.S. 36 (1961) (Black, J., dissenting); Hugo Black, 'The Bill of Rights' (1960) 35 *New York University Law Review*, 865. See also Harry Kalven Jr., 'Upon Rereading Mr Justice Black on the First Amendment' (1967) 14 *University of California Los Angeles Law Review*, 428.

[35] *Brandenburg* v. *Ohio*, 395 U.S. 444 (1969) (Douglas, J., concurring); *Roth* v. *United States*, 354 U.S. 476 (1957) (Douglas, J., dissenting).

[36] Alexander Meiklejohn, 'The First Amendment is an Absolute' (1961) *The Supreme Court Review*, 245.

[37] Laurent Frantz, 'Is the First Amendment Law: a Reply to Professor Mendelsohn' (1963) 51 *California Law Review*, 729; Laurent Frantz, 'The First Amendment in the Balance' (1962) 71 *Yale Law Journal*, 1424.

[38] *Dennis* v. *United States*, 341 U.S. 494 (1951) (Frankfurter, J., concurring in the judgment).

[39] *Konigsberg* v. *State Bar of California*, 366 U.S. 36 (1961).

[40] Wallace Mendelsohn, 'The First Amendment and the Judicial Process: a Reply to Mr. Frantz' (1964) 17 *Vanderbilt Law Review*, 479.

[41] For the view that a balancing process could in theory be strongly speech protective, see Gerald Gunther, 'In Search of Judicial Quality on a Changing Court: the Case of Justice Powell' (1972) 24 *Stanford Law Review*, 1001.

dangers that might come from speaking, writing and printing. For the absolutists in this debate, what was wrong about balancing was not anything structurally problematic about the idea of balancing, but rather the worry that in the actual balance, free speech interests would be balanced too lightly and countervailing interests would be balanced too heavily.

This attitude of distrust of the balancing process still pervades American free speech culture, a culture of extreme distrust existing within what is itself a culture of distrust. And in such a culture, strong protection of free speech goes hand in hand with distrust of structures that allow, encourage or even require a weighing of interests. If one takes as a given – for these purposes – the American commitment to an exceptionally strong protection of freedom of speech and freedom of the press, then the American preference for categorisation at the first stage and limited balancing at the second is not an example of disingenuousness or dishonesty or ignorance of the extent to which some balancing takes place even at the first stage, but rather a deliberate commitment to the view that balancing categorially and not in individual cases is far less likely to result in erosion of strong free speech principles. As a result, it is plausible to argue that the debate ought to be joined at the level of substance, but that if we acknowledge non-evaluatively the differences between the cultures on questions of substance, then we should not be surprised that the American approach has grown out of a peculiarly American approach to the strength and breadth of free speech and free press protection, and that the Canadian and European approach has grown out of a non-American commitment to free speech being important but not necessarily more important than, say, equality, or the rights of those accused of crimes, or national security, or any of the other values listed as qualifications to freedom of expression in Article 10 (2) of the European Convention on Human Rights.

3. The role of the courts

Once we appreciate the importance about the debate between absolutes and balancing, better understood as a debate between categorisation and case-specific balancing,[42] it turns out that much of the debate is a debate about judicial review, judicial authority, and the nature of constitutional adjudication. And here there are important differences that may explain

---

[42] See Schauer, 'Slippery Slopes', above, note 14; Ely, 'Flag Desecration', above, note 13; Sullivan, 'Post-Liberal Judging', above, note 15.

part of the difference in approach between the United States, on the one hand, and Europe, Canada and South Africa, among others, on the other hand.

Among the more important of those differences is the fact that judicial review in the United States remains a source of active debate, in part because of the absence of any explicit authorisation in the constitutional text for the power itself. Although it is now more than 200 years since the Supreme Court first exercised the power in *Marbury v. Madison*,[43] and although there are no longer serious calls for the elimination of the power of judicial review in the United States, the very fact that it is implied rather than explicit has produced more of a continuing debate in the United States than elsewhere about the very legitimacy of the power, and about the implications for the breadth and strength of the power in light of its textually and historically fragile provenance.[44] Thus, although judicial review itself may be so well entrenched in the United States as to occasion few wholesale challenges, there is more of a concern in the United States than there is in most other countries with strong judicial review about a court that might be closely and continuously monitoring the details of government action, and about a court that might be intimately involved with the empirical and policy issues that such monitoring and evaluation necessarily entails.

Given this ongoing scepticism about the wisdom of allowing courts in general or the Supreme Court in particular to get too far down into the weeds of governmental policy decisions, it is not surprising that there is more preference for categorisation and wholesale decision-making in the United States than there is in many of its counterparts in the developed liberal world. To make decisions about proportionality, and thus about what is 'necessary' in a democratic society, is of course something that American courts do with great frequency, sometimes explicitly and even more implicitly. Yet this task is undertaken in the United States with reluctance more than enthusiasm, and it is done under the shadow of continuing criticism of its very exercise.[45] In light of this, it should come as little surprise that, at least at the margins, at

---

[43] 1 Cranch (5 US) 137 (1803).

[44] For a flavour of the issues and the debates, even today, see the various essays in John H. Garvey and T. Alexander Aleinikoff, *Modern Constitutional Theory: a Reader* (St Paul: West Group, 1999).

[45] On the current Supreme Court, the most prominent critic of anything resembling 'balancing' has been Justice Scalia. See Antonin Scalia, 'The Rule of Law as a Law of Rules' (1989) 56 *University of Chicago Law Review*, 1175. And although Justice Scalia

least where there is some choice about the matter, American courts are far more reluctant explicitly to see themselves as weighing the full panoply of interests, facts and factors that would support a careful proportionality analysis.

The phenomenon of some aversion to case-by-case proportionality or balancing analysis is exacerbated by the nature of the Supreme Court's workload in the United States. In the 2002–3 term of the Court, the Court was asked to decide somewhat in excess of 8,000 cases, but in fact decided only seventy-four on the merits and with full opinion. In almost all of the remainder of the cases, the Court let stand the result below on the basis of no briefs except those urging review in the first instance, on the basis of no oral arguments, with no written opinions being issued, and with no precedential effect for the Court's decision to let the ruling below stand. But for a court that these days decides seventy to eighty cases a year, and which during even its most active period rarely decided more than 150, the guidance function looms larger, and the disadvantages of a case-by-case approach seem more apparent. When the Supreme Court decides a case, it is not only deciding that case, but is also giving instructions to literally thousands of lower courts, and literally hundreds of inferior appellate courts. In addition, it is giving instructions to Congress, to the President, to vast numbers of federal administrative agencies and to the legislatures, governors, and executive and administrative apparatus of fifty states, the District of Columbia and to various territories and protectorates. Although the Court may be less self-conscious about and attentive to this guidance function than some of us would prefer,[46] it still looms large in judicial self-understanding, and still exercises substantial force in making the Court reluctant to do too much in a case-specific manner.

Given the Court's role and resources, therefore, it is not implausible to see the Supreme Court as engaged in what is essentially a rule-making process as much as if not more than an adjudicatory one. And given that freedom of expression claims are disproportionately likely to be championed and litigated by what Justice Frankfurter, in a different context,

may make the argument in a stronger and bolder form, and although in many respects his remains a minority voice on this issue, the prominence of his voice is useful evidence of the way in which American judges and commentators remain leery of too much explicit balancing and weighing in the process of constitutional adjudication.

[46] See Frank H. Easterbrook, 'Ways of Criticizing the Court' (1982) 95 *Harvard Law Review*, 802; Frederick Schauer, 'Opinions as Rules' (1995) 62 *University of Chicago Law Review*, 1455.

referred to as 'not very nice people',[47] a rule-based approach to freedom of speech is hardly surprising. And although rule-based approaches will necessarily ignore particular features of particular cases that may in fact be important, that is simply what rules do and how rules operate.[48] There may be a difference between freedom of expression adjudication and a routine highway speed limit, but the difference between American and non-American approaches to freedom of expression adjudication are not totally unrelated to the differences between 'Speed Limit 100 Kilometers Per Hour' and 'Drive Reasonably'. There are good arguments for both approaches at different times, different places and under different circumstances, but the difference between the two may help us understand the differences between various national approaches to free expression decision-making.

IV. A one- or two-stage process?

As a conceptual matter, the rationale behind a rule or a principle is distinct from the reasons that may exist for overriding it or for refusing to apply it. To take the classic jurisprudential chestnut,[49] a rule prohibiting vehicles in the park may reflect an underlying rationale of safety or noise prevention, but these rationales are analytically distinct from the reason we may decide to override the rule when the Queen seeks to visit the park in the royal limousine. That there is a good reason to allow the Queen to do so, and that that good reason may be deemed more important than following the rule in this instance, does not change the fact that the rule itself reflects safety and noise-reduction rationales. More importantly, if we decide that the rule does not prohibit erecting a statue of a vehicle as a war memorial because such an enterprise fails to implicate the rationales behind the rule,[50] we have not decided that those rationales are overridden. To override an applicable rationale, as in the case of the Queen's limousine, is different from concluding that

---

[47] *United States* v. *Rabinowitz*, 339 U.S. 56, 69 (1950) (Frankfurter, J., dissenting). See Frederick Schauer, 'The Heroes of the First Amendment' (2003) 101 *Michigan Law Review*, 2118–33.

[48] See Frederick Schauer, *Playing By the Rules: a Philosophical Examination of Rule-Based Decision-Making in Law and in Life* (Oxford: Clarendon Press, 1991).

[49] H. L. A. Hart, 'Positivism and the Separation of Law and Morals' (1958) 71 *Harvard Law Review*, 593–629.

[50] Lon L. Fuller, 'Positivism and Fidelity to Law – a Reply to Professor Hart' (1958) 71 *Harvard Law Review*, 630–72.

the rationale is inapplicable, as in the case of the vehicle-based war memorial.

Once we understand this commonplace distinction between overriding a rule and holding it inapplicable, we can see that American free-speech adjudication, at its first stage, is far more often a matter of a rule's inapplicability than of an applicable rule's less than infinite stringency. So when the Supreme Court of the United States in *Roth v. United States*[51] and subsequent cases held that obscenity was not encompassed by the freedom of speech that it is the function of the First Amendment to protect, it was doing little more than saying, prior to any process of evaluating the reasons for restriction, that, like the statute of a vehicle case, obscenity was not part of what the First Amendment encompassed and not part of the rationale lying behind it. Now it is quite possible that the Supreme Court was wrong in so concluding, as many commentators have urged,[52] but there is nothing analytically flawed or necessarily disingenuous about the approach, and a process in which the scope of the right is decided at the first stage, without reference to the reasons for overriding it, and in which the arguments for override are considered at the second stage, simply reflects the deep structure of all rules and all principles.

Interestingly, therefore, the American approach to freedom of speech appears, in practice, to be more faithful to the non-American textual structure than is much of the non-American approach. As is well known, Canadian adjudication at the first stage is virtually all encompassing, holding that 'freedom of expression' applies to any human act of communicating a message.[53] And because the first stage determination in Canada is so encompassing, in fact all of the difficult work is dealt with at the second stage, including, often more implicitly than explicitly, the determination of whether the values behind the right are even implicated at all. Under such an approach, what is textually designated as a two-stage approach turns out to collapse into a one-stage approach, and thus, ironically, turns out to be less faithful to the textual demarcation of two stages under the Charter of Rights and Freedoms than is an American approach that reflects a two-stage process even though the text, literally, makes no such rigid demarcation.

---

[51] 354 U.S. 476 (1957).
[52] See Harry Kalven Jr., 'The Metaphysics of the Law of Obscenity' (1960) *The Supreme Court Review*, 1.
[53] See Reference re §§ 193 and 195.1(1)(c) of the Criminal Code (Man.) (1990) 56 CCC (3d) 65.

Because all rights *necessarily* involve just such a two-stage process – no right has infinite coverage, and few have infinite stringency – it is far from fanciful to suggest that any process that actually divides the two steps is not only more faithful to what Canada, South Africa, New Zealand and the European Convention on Human Rights have expressly incorporated into the relevant texts, but more accurately embodies something important about the deep structure of rights. At times the American approach has erred in incorporating a weighing process at the first stage, and at times other jurisdictions appear to have erred as well by largely ignoring the first stage of the process. But once we recognise that the process has two stages, and that the first stage, at its best, is not and should not be a process of weighing interests as much as engaging in the non-weighing process of determining the delineation of a right in light of the language of its formulation and the rationale behind *its* existence, we will find it easier to understand and evaluate different approaches, and perhaps be more reluctant as well to criticise as disingenuous a process that seeks to keep separate two inquiries whose separation lies at the heart of the structure of all rules, all principles and therefore of all rights.

Comment

LORRAINE WEINRIB

The proposition that there are different approaches to constitutionalism in Europe and the United States would precipitate little controversy in Canada. In fact, one might say that the adoption of the Canadian Charter of Rights and Freedoms, 1982 (by amendment to the Canadian Constitution) offered Canadians the opportunity to choose between an American and a European approach to rights protection. The Charter text demonstrates a preference for the European model. The interpretation and application of the relevant Charter provisions in a number of cases carries on that preference, as is evident in cases involving the guarantee of freedom of expression.

The Canadian Charter of Rights and Freedoms, although entrenched as part of the Canadian Constitution in 1982, almost forty years after the end of the Second World War, is best understood as a post-WWII constitution. In fact, the political work that paved the way for the Charter's adoption began immediately after the war as part of Canada's road to full independence from the colonial arrangements of the British Empire. The long gestation period of the Charter gave the country the opportunity to consider various models of rights protection that emerged just after the war. It also gave time for the lessons learned in the war to be developed into modes of legal entitlement and analysis at both the national and international levels elsewhere. The text of the Charter reflects these legal structures.

The post-war period was a particularly important period in the development of Canada's sense of nationhood. Immediately after the war, the Supreme Court of Canada became the highest court of appeal for Canada (replacing the Judicial Committee of the Privy Council) and Canadian citizenship replaced British subject status as the form of membership in Canadian society. While Canada had no constitutional bill of rights at the time, its federal structure had established a strong judicial review function in the judiciary.

70

One of the earliest developments of the Supreme Court's new role as highest appellate court was to begin to use rights analysis. In a number of cases in the shadow of the war, the Court invoked age-old legal precepts to negate abusive laws and executive action. The Court also began to invoke the idea of basic rights and liberties in its analysis of questions raised in the exercise of federal-provincial powers. Various members of the Court introduced the idea that the Canadian Constitution's text or, more broadly, the fact that Canada was a liberal, parliamentary democracy meant that its legal system included certain inherent or implied liberties, including a variety of freedoms – of the press, expression, assembly, religion, etc. – as well as equality rights. Some of the judges used these implied or inherent liberties as guides in their allocation of legislative or executive power to the federal or provincial levels. The result was that a number of restrictive provincial statutes were invalidated. Two of the judges expressed a more expansive inclination. They said that they would strike down laws restricting fundamental rights at the federal level of government as well. This approach ultimately failed to garner the support of a majority of the Supreme Court of Canada and fell by the wayside as did later efforts to create higher law protections of basic rights and liberties through ordinary statute.

It is important to note that this short flowering of judicial protection of rights in the 1950s had its parallel in other countries. The extra-judicial writing by the judges who used this approach reveals the strong influence of the Warren Court in dismantling racial segregation and rationalising some of the strictures of the criminal law process and procedure. One might also refer to the great judgments rendered by Justice Oliver Schreiner in South Africa in this period, opposing some of the early legal steps that eventually led to the rule of apartheid.

The ultimate rejection of this approach to rights protection by the Supreme Court of Canada demonstrated the need for an entrenched bill of rights. Interest group participation in parliamentary hearings made it clear that Canadians wanted the post-WWII commitment to basic human dignity and equal citizenship to permeate the work of all three branches of government. Refugees from Europe in the aftermath of the war were not satisfied with Canada's inheritance from Great Britain of legislative sovereignty combined with conventions of restraint. An increasingly diverse and secularising population wanted strong protections for democratic government, the rule of law and, also, basic rights and freedoms.

The value structure of the Charter is most clearly encapsulated in its opening provision:

> The Canadian Charter of Rights and Freedoms guarantees the rights and freedoms set out in it subject only to such reasonable limits prescribed by law as can be demonstrably justified in a free and democratic society.

This clause alone might be enough to indicate the extent to which the Charter adopts a European mode of rights protection, rather than an American one. The formulation is not merely a negation of state power, as one finds in the US Bill of Rights, but a guarantee of stipulated rights and freedoms in the mode of post-war national constitutions in Europe as well as the European Convention. Detailed debate as to the effect of entrenching the Charter elicited strong public support for strong and effective rights protection and that desire resulted in this preference. The value structure, as well as the institutional framework to enforce its norms, were express imports from Europe and the Commonwealth, not the United States, which had by that time rejected the Warren Court's modernisation of the Bill of Rights.

The Charter's guarantees are not expressed in absolute terms, but qualified by a statement of the exclusive grounds upon which rights may be limited. The first stipulation is prescription by law, a term that invokes the values that the rule of law instantiates, such as general laws, formulated by formal law-making processes. The requirement of 'demonstrable justification' makes clear that the permissibility of limitations retains the primacy of the rights except where evidence and argumentation suffice to displace that primacy. It also requires the two-stage sequence of argumentation now common in post-war national and supra-national rights-protecting systems. The first focuses on the scope of the right or liberty and the fact of its infringement, engaging purposive or teleological analysis; the second focuses on the state's submissions as to the justification of the limitation upon the guaranteed interest, which take the form of the now familiar sequenced stages of proportionality analysis. Finally, the clause 'free and democratic society' invokes the idea that legislative supremacy is henceforth to be disciplined to the modern values of liberal democracy – pluralism, respect for human dignity and equality, tolerance and multiculturalism.

No cases demonstrate the working of this model of rights protection in Canada more clearly than those adjudicated to enforce the state's obligation to respect freedom of expression. One of the most important cases challenged the national Criminal Code's prohibition of the public, wilful promotion of hatred. The accused was a high school teacher, prosecuted for teaching classical anti-Semitic material as well as Holocaust denial in his public high school classes as indisputable historical truth. He was successful in establishing that the criminal charges infringed his Charter right to freedom of expression. The federal Attorney General bore the onus of establishing the justification of this infringement. To that end, he invoked the implementation of similar suppression of freedom of expression in other countries and in international human rights instruments in order to protect the rights to full human dignity and equal citizenship of all members of Canadian society, especially historically vilified identity groups.

The Supreme Court of Canada's majority ruling demonstrates the powerful logic of the post-WWII approach to rights protection as applied to speech rights. The Court rejected the idea of the marketplace of ideas, pointing out that truth was not necessarily the same thing as what the majority might at any point in time accept as truth. Moreover, it noted, with reference to European history, that even if truth eventually prevailed, the cost to vilified minorities in the interim period was unacceptable.

The Court's analysis fully integrates the two-stage model of rights adjudication. In so doing, it rejects the American preoccupation with the definition of the right. Moreover, the Court concerned itself not with the American idea that speech rights must be absolute but with the idea that speech rights must be analysed to ensure that there is no abuse of rights. Accordingly, the analysis tested whether the foundational values, in furtherance of which the Charter guarantees freedom of expression, were better fulfilled by honouring the right as exercised or by vindicating the legislative infringement. It concluded that the legislative infringement promoted 'a free and democratic society' more than honouring the right in this particular instance. What was at stake was the human dignity and equal citizenship of the target group as an historically vilified and vulnerable minority.

This example demonstrates not merely a preference for the mode of analysis in the post-WWII European constitutions and international human rights instruments; it also invokes the very values that emerged in Europe in the wake of the war. Other cases have followed this pattern. So, for example, the Supreme Court has restricted the expression rights of other teachers who have been active outside the classroom in anti-Semitic activities and Holocaust denial.

In other contexts the Court has restricted speech rights to forward equality values as well. In a case emanating from Quebec, the Court invalidated legislation that mandated the exclusive use of French in all commercial signs. The Court made clear that protecting the French-speaking community overwhelmed by English-speaking North America was a proper purpose under the Charter, but stipulated that this promotion could not extend to the prohibition of the use of all other languages. The Court's analysis emphasised that the state must respect a variety of language communities because language is both the carrier of culture and the mode of expression of individual personality.

The Supreme Court has also departed from the US approach to restriction of explicit sexual material. The Court ruled that such material may be the subject of criminalisation if it involves children and if it degrades women. As in the hate promotion case, the Court was concerned that the equal human dignity of women as well as their equal citizenship were undermined by exploitative material. In a later case involving child pornography, the Court read down the statutory prohibition to permit the production of sexually explicit material involving children if it was created for private consumption only, as a product of the imagination.

These examples demonstrate a stark contrast to the US case law in analysis and result. They demonstrate a contrast in the most basic values of the societies under discussion. For the Americans, freedom of speech invokes the glory of the American Revolution and its establishment of a democratic society endorsing individual freedom as its highest aspiration. The testing ground for truth is the marketplace of ideas. Accordingly, this right must be as wide as possible despite the costs that market failure might impose upon some sectors of society.

For Canadians, freedom of expression is one of a group of rights that together create the fabric of freedom and democracy for a multicultural, pluralistic and tolerant society. What is paramount is not the speech right but the values that it forwards. In the adjudication of each claim of a breach of the right, the state has the opportunity to establish that its underlying purpose is fulfilled by the encroachment that the state has imposed. Here we have not merely rights, but the idea that rights are the building blocks of a liberal democratic order committed to equality. Rights, therefore, are not merely subjective, individual entitlements. They are best understood as the crystallisation of an abstract, normative, objective order, the preservation of which falls to a vigilant judiciary mindful of the failings of the majoritarian mechanisms in the twentieth century.

Comment

WINFRIED BRUGGER

Professors Roger Errera and Frederick Schauer emphasise the special importance of freedom of speech for liberal democracies while pointing out the differences between the United States and Europe, especially France and Germany. This raises the question of the *importance of free speech*. I think that the United States and Europe agree on a two-level rationale for determining the value of communicative freedoms:

Free speech is important because it allows the individual to express his personality and his authenticity. While actions are also important, the opinion-forming content of freedom of speech is even more important since by communicating we form our self which only then expresses itself in actions. Thus, to put it briefly, the formation of a personality in communication comes before this personality engages in physical acts. For this reason communicative acts should receive a special place in the values of our constitutions; they typically are better protected than rights to the free development of one's personality or general liberty rights.

While this first rationale for freedom of speech is based on autonomy and refers to expressive individualism irrespective of good or bad consequences of opining, the second rationale is based on an assessment of the consequences of speech. Do certain forms of speech further or hinder the finding of truth, do they further or damage an open process of political decision-making, do they establish a safety valve for high emotions in the form of letting off steam, or do they exacerbate intensive feelings by turning them into actions? This level is consequentialist. It relies on prognoses and it leads to various complications and to disputes between the United States and Europe, especially with regard to the consequences of hate speech.

The constitutional importance of certain categories of speech can to a considerable degree be explained by this two-level-analysis.[1] The

---

[1] See Winfried Brugger, *Einführung in das öffentliche Recht der USA* (2nd edn, Munich: Beck, 2001), ch. 14 II.

following three situations can be distinguished: if the autonomy argument and the argument based on prognosticated consequences strengthen each other, as is the case with most political speech, liberal constitutions and courts strongly, maybe even absolutely, protect such speech. In the United States, for example, such speech is called high-value speech and has the status of a preferred right. In Germany, the Federal Constitutional Court speaks of a strong presumption in favour of freedom of political speech, which, in election times, even transforms itself into an especially strong presumption in favour of political speech.

If the two functional levels of speech do not interact with one another, the tendency of constitutional law is toward a 'regular' or strong, but not absolute, protection of the respective speech.

If the two levels collide with each other, one can think of two ways of dealing with such low-value speech. One can either disqualify it as speech in the constitutional sense – in this case it is not covered by the free speech provision, but at most by a weaker general right to liberty – or one can qualify it as speech in the constitutional sense, but allow it to be regulated or prohibited because of the conflict with other constitutionally acknowledged values; thus it would constitute low-value speech or 'speech minus'. The first approach was used, for example, when the United States Supreme Court in *Chaplinsky v. New Hampshire* said that 'certain well-defined and narrowly limited classes of speech', 'including the lewd and obscene, the profane, the libelous, and the insulting or "fighting" words', do not count as protected speech. The Court's language in that decision, though, can be understood to stand for the other method, too: if such speech should be protected by the First Amendment, at least it can be regulated or prohibited because 'such utterances are no essential part of any exposition of ideas, and are of such slight social value as a step to truth that any benefit that may be derived from them is clearly outweighed by the social interest in order and morality'.[2] Another example is Holocaust denial which is criminalised in Germany.[3] The German Federal Constitutional

---

[2] *Chaplinsky* v. *New Hampshire*, 315 U.S. 568, 571 (1942), explained in Brugger, *Einführung*, above, note 11, pp. 164–5. Since *Chaplinsky*, the categories of such non-speech or 'speech minus' have been reduced by the US Supreme Court. In recent decisions, the Supreme Court also tends to avoid declaring categories of speech to be 'non-speech'; the tendency is towards solving difficult cases through reference to implicit or explicit limitation clauses in the form of salient judicial tests. See *R.A.V.* v. *St. Paul*, 505 U.S. 377 (1992), section I of Justice Scalia's opinion of the Court.

[3] See s. 130 (3) of the Federal Criminal Code, and Winfried Brugger, 'Constitutional Treatment of Hate Speech', in Eibe Riedel (ed.), *Stocktaking in German Public Law*

Court had no difficulties legitimising this prohibition because although the speaker might believe that there was no Holocaust, this assertion is clearly wrong and thus cannot further truth. In this conflict between the autonomy function and the truth function of speech, the German Court sided with the truth function. It denied from the outset that such obviously false allegations are covered by the free speech clause.[4]

Turning to some differences between US and European notions of free speech, both Schauer and Errera point out that the wording of the free speech clauses is different. In the American Bill of Rights, freedom of speech is the first and foremost right, whereas in Art. 10 of the European Convention of Human Rights and in Art. 5 of the German Basic Law it is one of many rights. The First Amendment does not specify textual limitations, whereas the European Convention and the Basic Law establish several such limitation clauses. One should not overstate the textual difference, because, in reality, the US Supreme Court as well as European Courts use a balancing approach. This can clearly be seen by consulting any American casebook on constitutional rights. There, in the respective First Amendment chapter, we find sub-chapters characterising clusters of cases which in essence formulate court-established categories of low-value speech that can be curtailed within court-established limitation clauses: 'expression that induces unlawful conduct', 'criticism of the judicial process and speech that threatens', 'expression that provokes a hostile audience reaction', 'expression that discloses confidential information', 'false statements of facts', 'non-newsworthy disclosure of private information', 'commercial advertising', 'obscenity'[5] and protection of young people.[6] In the interpretation of the salient limitation clauses, the US Supreme Court sometimes differs from European Courts, as Professors Schauer and Errera point out, but there is no categorical difference between the methodologies the Courts use on this side and the other side of the Atlantic. Sometimes the categories that are used may differ, but in substance the methodologies are similar. For example, the strict scrutiny test used by the Supreme Court when government encroaches on free

---

(Baden-Baden: Nomos, 2002), pp. 117, 142 et seqq., also available at www.germanlaw journal.com, vols. 3–12 and 4–1; Brugger, 'Ban or Protection of Hate Speech? Some Observations Based on German and American Law' (2002) 17 *Tulane European and Civil Law Forum*, 1, 15 et seqq.

[4] BVerfGE 90, 241, 247.

[5] This (incomplete) list is taken from Cass R. Sunstein, Geoffrey R. Stone, Louis M. Seidman and Mark Tushnet, *Constitutional Law* (4th edn, New York: Aspen, 2001), ch. 7.

[6] See Brugger, *Einführung*, above, note 1, pp. 169–70.

speech parallels the strict proportionality test used by the European
Court of Human Rights and the German Federal Constitutional Court
in comparable cases.

As far as substantive differences are concerned, both contributors
mention and analyse the most striking examples: hate speech, group
libel, defamation and the role of the media. Especially with regard to the
first two of these categories, a striking difference between Europe and
the United States indeed exists. Schauer speaks of 'American exceptionalism' which, although he repudiates this view, suggests to me that a
feeling of American superiority remains. After all, 'exceptionalism' in
the United States, I think, means more than 'exception to some general
rule' – it also includes notions of being superior or having a good
mission to carry out. The reason for my supposition is also based
on the observation that American authors who are critical of the prevailing libertarian free speech doctrines use words such as 'isolationism'
or 'being out-of-step' instead of the expression 'exceptionalism'.[7]
For comparativists having to explain such different assessments
between states which all call themselves democratic and liberal, this is
fascinating. The textual difference obviously does not take the analysis
very far; for the most part it can be explained by the fact that
the United States Constitution is old and short and European constitutions tend to be younger and more comprehensive. Both Schauer and
Errera present an array of reasons for the differences and I agree with
most of them.

There is indeed a major difference with regard to the role of the state.[8]
Despite having endured two major catastrophes in the twentieth century, Europe in general and Germany in particular put more trust in the
healing and beneficial power of government than in societal forces and
individual citizens. If one compares the role of the state in the twentieth
century in the United States and in Europe, one should expect
Europeans to mistrust their governments much more than Americans,
and one should expect Americans to trust their governments much
more than Europeans, but the opposite is true. Why is that? The answer
must be linked to the founding of the American republic, which grew
out of major repressions of the colonists by their European kings.
Although one could argue that this historical background has long ago

---

[7] References in Brugger, 'Hate Speech', above, note 3, at p. 117.
[8] See Winfried Brugger, *Demokratie, Freiheit, Gleichheit. Studien zum Verfassungsrecht der
USA* (Berlin, 2002), pp. 83–4, 189.

vanished into irrelevance, the collective instinct of the American public, law and lawyers is still based on that 'defining moment' of American history.[9] In addition, one might point out that the influx of millions of immigrants from repressive countries over the last two centuries has contributed its share to keeping this tradition alive.

Another difference centres around the notion of dignity.[10] Since the end of the Second World War, dignity has been a major and often the foremost value and right of the polity. Germany's Article 1 Section 1 of the Basic Law is a fitting example of this world-wide tendency which can be observed in many new constitutions and human rights treaties. 'Dignity' refers to inalienable rights, and tends to include liberty, equality and reciprocal respect, as equally important sub-categories as can be seen from the foremost philosopher of dignity, Immanuel Kant. Such an architecture of dignity makes it possible to argue in cases of conflict between liberty, on the one hand, and equality and reciprocal respect, on the other hand, as they usually occur in hate speech, for a balancing of these values. This is the dominant approach in Europe. In the United States, the philosophical background is different. There, John Locke with his rights to life, liberty and property is the main source of legitimation, as can be seen from their inclusion into the due process clauses of the US Constitution, not Kant's version of dignity. Thus, liberty claims a higher place in the hierarchy of moral and constitutional values. Liberty in the United States, one could say, is the major component of dignity, or possibly replaces dignity. It is no surprise, then, that some authors call the US Constitution a constitution of liberty, whereas the German Constitution is called a constitution of dignity.[11] Liberty in the United States trumps equality and reciprocal respect as far as speech is concerned, whereas in Europe and Germany the legal orders and constitutional courts try to balance these values in such a way that a 'practical concordance' can be achieved. One should mention that the minority view in US jurisprudence with regard to hate speech espouses

---

[9] See Richard S. Kay, 'American Constitutionalism', in Larry Alexander (ed.), *Constitutionalism* (Cambridge: Cambridge University Press, 1998), p. 19: 'The [American] constitutionalist instinct is that the use of collective power of society is a special source of danger.'

[10] See Brugger, *Demokratie*, above, note 8, pp. 37 et seqq.

[11] See Donald Kommers, 'Kann das deutsche Verfassungsrechtsdenken Vorbild für die Vereinigten Staaten sein?' (1998) 37 *Der Staat*, 335, 338–9, and Edward Eberle, *Dignity and Liberty. Constitutional Visions in Germany and the United States* (Westport, Conn.: Praeger, 2002), pp. 254 et seqq.

the European view.[12] It points to such constitutional values as racial equality to make the case against racist hate speech, and the need for reciprocal respect among individuals and groups in order to have a healthy and inclusive community life, but the dominant free speech jurisprudence so far has not been convinced.[13]

Related to these dignity arguments are differences with regard to the *legal protection of honour and reputation*. In Germany, a three-level approach of legal protection exists.[14] On the first level, the constitutional value of dignity protects against attacks on one's status as a human person with equal status among all human beings. On the second level, one's social honour or reputation is protected against crude insults; in Germany, one has to abide by certain basic rules of civility. On the third level, the German legal order protects against false assertions of fact that damage one's reputation; in such cases there is often a connection to the capacity of the attacked person to present himself or herself as a reputable citizen and to earn money.

In the United States, the first two levels are for the most part not protected by law.[15] There is no protection against verbal attacks against one's status as a human being with equal normative footing, as the *Skokie* controversy and the *R.A.V.* case make clear.[16] Americans are free to propagate the superiority of their race and the inferiority of other races. In the United States, there is also no protection against mere normative criticism, bad language or epithets that attack 'honour'. The American legal order does not level up the quality of discourse among its citizens; it allows them to level down the quality of their

---

[12] See, e.g., Mari Matsuda et al. (eds.), *Words that Wound. Critical Race Theory, Assaultive Speech, and the First Amendment* (Boulder, Col., 1993), and the comparative analysis by Winfried Brugger, 'Schutz oder Verbot aggressiver Rede? Argumente aus liberaler und kommunitaristischer Sicht' (2003) 42 *Der Staat*, 77, 90 et seqq.

[13] Dignity, although not incorporated in the text of the United States Constitution, has been incorporated into the jurisprudence of the Supreme Court. The major groups of cases in which dignity arguments are being voiced refer to (1) the death penalty (on the side of its critics), (2) free speech (mainly on the speaker's side), (3) due process rights (the right to be heard), and (4) abortion (the dignity of the pregnant woman to decide for or against an abortion). See the references in Brugger, *Einführung*, above, note 1, pp. 123, 172–3, 226, 230.

[14] See Brugger, 'Constitutional Treatment', above, note 3, pp. 134–5; Brugger, 'Ban or Protection', above, note 3, pp. 9–10.

[15] See the comprehensive comparative analysis by James Q. Whitman, 'Enforcing Civility and Respect: Three Societies' (2000) 109 *Yale Law Journal*, 1279 et seqq.

[16] See Brugger, *Einführung*, above, note 1, pp. 172 et seqq. and *R.A.V.* v. *St. Paul*, above, note 2.

conversations. But it does so in the hope that in 'society', among the citizens and communities, other mechanisms will step into the shoes of the legal order in order to ensure some degree of civility among conversationalists. And indeed, the sensitivity among Americans, at least in educated circles, for offensive language is much higher than in Germany. One could also say that political correctness in the United States plays a much more prominent role than in Germany. Finally, false assertions of a damaging character are prohibited in Germany as well as in the United States, although the hurdles for suits by politicians and public figures against critics in the United States tend to be higher than in Germany, as both Schauer and Errera point out.

The reason for this difference seems again to be founded in historical experience. The early colonists and later Americans tended to be (or simply had to be) strong individuals, physically and psychologically. Small wonder that later on, free speech jurisprudence concentrated on the values of 'robust' discussions, 'free men [and women]', not afraid to speak their minds.[17] Europe, in contrast, pays more attention to minorities, weak and poor groups, and fragile personalities that, in its opinion, need protection through the strong arm of the state against rhetorical aggression. A second explanation for the difference between the United States and Europe in its treatment of hate speech is that hate speech, in Europe, is mainly or even exclusively seen from the perspective of the worst possible outcome – pogroms, ethnic cleansing and mass murder. In the United States, in contrast, the consequences of hate speech or aggressive speech are seen in a more complex light. Of course these dangers exist, Americans admit, although, they hasten to add, they probably would not materialise in their country of the free. It should be remembered that aggressive speech can also lead to positive results. In the 1960s and 1970s, for example, civil rights activists and critics of the Vietnam war often used excessive speech to fight for their points of views. And their communicative attacks were successful. Thus, a typical

---

[17] The famous dictum by Justice Brandeis, concurring in *Whitney* v. *California*, 274 U.S. 357, 375 et seq. (1927): 'Those who won our independence by revolution were no cowards. They did not fear political change. They did not exalt order at the cost of liberty. To courageous, self-reliant men, with confidence in their power of free and fearless reasoning applied through the processes of popular government, no danger flowing from speech can be deemed clear and present, unless the incidence of the evil apprehended is so imminent that it may befall even before there is opportunity for full discussion. If there be time to expose through discussion the falsehood or fallacies, to avert the evil by the processes of education, the remedy to be applied is more speech, not enforced silence.' See Brugger, 'Schutz oder Verbot', above, note 12, pp. 77 et seqq.

American citizen, when asked about the good or bad consequences of aggressive speech, would probably say: 'Sometimes they are beneficial to society, sometimes they are harmful, but most of the time you don't know in advance.' And then the liberal mantra would consist of the motto: In cases of doubt, prefer more speech to less speech.

PART III

Human dignity

4

The concept of human dignity in European and US constitutionalism

GIOVANNI BOGNETTI

I. Models of constitutionalism

In order to assess the role played by the concept of human dignity in European and US constitutionalism, it is expedient to briefly recall the two phases that western constitutionalism went through during the last two centuries.[1]

In the nineteenth century, the state model prevailing on both sides of the Atlantic was the *classical liberal model*. The legal system was composed of relatively few stable norms, some of which were modified from time to time by special legislation. The special norms were meant to be interpreted narrowly. The system would define and protect the autonomy of the individual in all areas of social life, in particular the economy, culture and politics. Where formal, written constitutions existed, they usually contained solemn guarantees for individual autonomy, the fundamental institutes of which were already defined and protected by sub-constitutional, ordinary law. In addition, these constitutions usually proclaimed a general principle of formal equality of all citizens before the law. The constitutional guarantees were judicially enforceable against executive state action. In the United States they were, in principle, also enforceable against unconstitutional legislation.

The twentieth century witnessed the advent and the expansion of the model of the *interventionist state*. The progress of the new model was

---

[1] A detailed outline of the two phases of western constitutionalism, from the point of view embraced in this paper, is contained in G. Bognetti, *Lo spirito del costituzionalismo americano* (vol. I), *La costituzione liberale* (vol. II), *La costituzione democratica* (Milan: Giuffré, 1999–2000). Also G. Bognetti, *La divisione dei poteri. Saggio di diritto comparato* (Milan: Giuffré, 2001), and G. Bognetti, *Federalismo* (Turin: Utet, 2001).

primarily connected with the industrialisation of society. Industrialisation carried with it:

- a weakening of autonomy rights in the area of economic relationships in order to protect important interests which were not sufficiently provided for by the mechanisms of the free market;
- a reinforcement of civil rights and freedoms in the areas of culture, politics and the strictly personal life of the individual, perhaps as a sort of compensation for the diminished force of economic freedoms;
- a variety of state-supported services that were offered to the less fortunate individuals in order to provide them with at least a modicum of social security.

Such huge changes, present in all legal systems, have been brought about by way of ordinary legislation. Old, written constitutions, as in the United States, were conveniently re-read and adapted to the new needs of the interventionist model. All new written constitutions dating from the period following the Second World War phrased the guarantees of fundamental rights in ways that reflected the new interventionist model. It is important to notice that the new interventionist model has been adopted in two different versions: a version which is more responsive to the old idea of individual freedom (the neo-liberal version), and a version which is more open to the values of social solidarity (a version that may be called 'democratic-social').

The United States' twentieth-century legal system is the typical embodiment of the neo-liberal version. Federal legislation created systems of social security, health care and labour law which, however, provided only a minimum level of protection for 'social' values. The Constitution, as interpreted by the Supreme Court, still protects only encroachments on individual rights by public authorities. It does not restrict the powers of private persons in the exercise of their respective autonomy. The Supreme Court refused to read the due process clause, the equal protection clause or the Ninth Amendment in a way that would oblige the state to provide even a minimum of public services.[2] The state is free to provide social services; if it chooses to provide them, it is free to choose to what extent. The state is only required to refrain from contravening

---

[2] *Dandridge v. Williams*, 397 U.S. 471 (1970); also *De Shaney v. Winnebago County Department of Social Services*, 489 U.S. 189 (1989).

the principle of formal equality,[3] and impairing fundamental freedoms.[4] In contrast, the US Supreme Court has frequently interpreted political and strictly personal rights rather broadly. Such interpretations would have been unthinkable during the classical liberal period and they usually have no counterpart in the present legal systems of the European countries (for example, with respect to the freedom of expression,[5] and to the right of privacy[6]). In these areas the US Constitution has been interpreted in ways which severely limit the freedom of the legislature to enact rules of its choice.

European legal systems, on the other hand, are generally more prone to embody 'social' values and less ready to advance the boundaries in favour of freedom of expression and neighbouring areas. Ordinary legislation has everywhere provided for social services of conspicuous dimensions. European labour law supplies protection to the worker far beyond that afforded by American law. Employment is less governed by the rules of the market and, in some systems, workers' participation in the management of enterprises is guaranteed. Constitutions either contain provisions which require the state to furnish specific forms of social services (France, Italy) or a general clause affirming the 'social' character of the state which works practically to the same effect (Germany). Traditional constitutional guarantees of civil and political rights are no longer conceived as binding only the sovereign powers of the state. They now also restrict, at least to a certain point, the exercise of such private rights as property and contract, either directly (Italy) or indirectly through 'general clauses' in the Civil Code (Germany: *Drittwirkung der Grundrechte*).

In European systems there is more reluctance to read freedom of speech in ways that would sacrifice other constitutional values, such as the security of the state or important interests of the person, such as reputation, honour or privacy. At times the necessity of preserving the values of liberal democracy has been felt so intensely as to lead to the prohibition of political parties and to deny legitimacy to speech that has been seen to undermine these values. As far as such outcomes are

---

[3] However, the equal protection clause does not require taking into account possible conditions of poverty: *San Antonio* v. *Rodriguez*, 411 U.S. 1 (1973).

[4] Such as the freedom to travel: *Shapiro* v. *Thomson*, 335 U.S. 1 (1948); *Saenz* v. *Roe*, 526 U.S. 489 (1999).

[5] *Brandenburg* v. *Ohio*, 395 U.S. 444 (1969); *New York Times* v. *Sullivan*, 376 U.S. 254 (1964); *Miami Herald* v. *Tornillo*, 418 U.S. 241 (1974).

[6] *Roe* v. *Wade*, 410 U.S. 113 (1973).

mandated by the constitution the ordinary legislator is left with little room to choose among alternative policies dealing with unorthodox forces. Finally, in Europe the right of the woman to have an abortion was never defined in such broad terms as in *Roe v. Wade*.[7] German constitutional law, in particular, was initially extremely negative on the point. In the long run, however, ordinary legislation in all parts of Europe has been able to reach solutions which are rather liberal in practice.

II. The philosophical justifications of fundamental rights

The ideological and political movements of the eighteenth and the nineteenth centuries which caused legal systems to adopt the classical liberal rights of the individual held a firm belief in the philosophy of natural rights and in the contractual origin of the state as an association intended to protect such rights (Locke). During the nineteenth century, this belief gradually faded away and its place was taken by two other philosophical justifications for the moral and practical desirability of these rights. On the one hand, notable success was enjoyed by utilitarianism according to which fundamental individual liberties were the necessary condition and the best institutional means to promote the greatest happiness of the greatest number (Bentham; Mill). On the other hand, a certain success was also enjoyed by the theory of civilisation as being the progressive unfolding of reason which recognised that civilisation in the highest phase of its progress required strong institutions for the safeguarding of individual autonomy (Hegel; Spencer). With the twentieth century the scenario changed again. Absolute relativism became the dominant theory in the philosophy of values, and many tried to base the institutions of liberal democracy solely on the relativity of all values. Only the acceptance of the democratic method, they said, would prevent unreasonable attempts to impose a simple personal preference as a truth by force (Kelsen). As of late, resulting from a combination of relativism, the value of self-interestedness, and a concern for a viable coexistence of different life-styles, a liberal-democratic theory of justice has had a remarkable impact on public opinion (Rawls).

After the dramatic events of the Second World War there was a latent but diffuse feeling that none of the theories in circulation regarding the foundation of fundamental rights was really satisfactory. All these theories either had a weak philosophical basis or they did not sufficiently defend the rights so as to avert the possibility of the return of some of the

---

[7] Ibid.

worst experiences of the recent past. The idea began to emerge that the only valid, ultimate justification for the existence of inviolable individual rights was to be found in the inherent quality of the human being as a distinct subject existing in the midst of a complex universe: in the special dignity of man.

The formula 'human dignity' first appeared in solemn international documents, in particular the United Nations Charter and the UN Declaration of the Rights of Man of 1948. It was made the cornerstone of the new German Constitution (1949), appearing in the opening provision of its first article. Human dignity was also utilised, though marginally, by other constitutions of the period (Italy 1948, Art. 41). The jurisprudence of many European courts has subsequently derived the principle of human dignity out of diverse constitutional provisions, using it for many different purposes. Human dignity presently occupies a central place in recent European constitutions (Hungary, Switzerland) and in the Nice Charter of Rights of the European Union. It is also beginning to appear in US State Constitutions (Montana). Many legal writers now believe that human dignity offers the best guide for measuring the validity of laws in most areas of the legal system, and for suggesting reforms or warnings against dangerous temptations.

Despite its present large popularity, the concept of human dignity is far from having a clear, undisputed meaning. The reasons for this are relatively simple. The origins of the concept can probably be traced back to the core of the Jewish–Christian tradition, which held man to be made in the image of God.[8] Aquinas defined rights and duties of man in a similar key. However, such a lofty concept of man did not prevent philosophers and jurists, in the Middle Ages and after, from accepting as just the division of society into pre-established classes endowed with different rights: a division that is repugnant to present-day liberal-democratic society.

Most appropriately, the father of the modern concept of human dignity is considered to be Kant, with his theory that man is a morally autonomous being, who as such deserves respect and must never be treated, in general and especially by the law, as only a means to contingent ends but always (also) as an end unto himself. Almost nobody, however, today dares to recall that Kant propagated a strictly retributive concept of the purpose of criminal law as a necessary consequence of his

---

[8] See D. Kretzmer and E. Klein (eds.), *The Concept of Human Dignity in Human Rights Discourse* (The Hague, London, New York: Kluwer Law International, 2002).

theory of man's autonomy. From this theory he deduced the obligatory infliction of the death penalty for the most serious crimes, and a theory of the state of the classical liberal mould, with property at its centre. Both the death penalty and the sanctity of property are often characterised by the present champions of human dignity as stumbling blocks to the full realisation in law of that dignity.

The truth is that, so far, there has been no systematic re-elaboration of the concept of human dignity which has been able to command if not universal, then at least widespread, acceptance. Human dignity has been used to express underlying philosophical beliefs of quite different kinds for the purpose of reinforcing them with its powerful appeal. In the writings of jurists and in the decisions of courts the principle of human dignity does not usually give rise to a distinct fundamental right in the same sense as other traditional rights. It is rather a conceptual instrument that helps to give a particular turn to the interpretation of certain principles concerning the liberty of the individual and to the interpretation of the principle of equality. For most jurists using it, the concept of human dignity lies at the very basis of all fundamental rights and is the true reason for them; therefore, human dignity determines and influences the purport, extension and limits of all other rights (e.g. Dürig).[9]

There is almost total agreement that the dignity principle should be used for the purpose of condemning certain institutions or practices that either destroy or seriously impair the physical or mental freedom of the individual. The areas in which this strand of the principle is mostly applied are criminal law and criminal procedure. The death penalty is widely considered to be intrinsically incompatible with the respect due to the dignity of the person. Also the penalty of life imprisonment, unless substantially mitigated with some prospect of future release, is seen as violating the principle. Among the means used to gather evidence in a criminal cause, not only torture and physical pressure, but also other less oppressive methods, such as the lie detector or the use of

---

[9] G. Dürig, 'Der Grundrechtssatz von der Menschenwürde' (1954) 81 *Archiv des öffentlichen Rechts* 117–57; G. Dürig, 'Art. 1', in T. Maunz and G. Dürig (eds.), *Grundgesetz* (1st edn, Munich: C. H. Beck, 1958). Some authors, however, consider human dignity a fundamental right distinct from the others though at the same time the very basis for all of them: H. C. Nipperdey, 'Die Würde des Menschen', in F. L. Neuman, H. C. Nipperdey and U. Scheuner (eds.), *Die Grundrechte* (2 vols., Berlin: Duncker and Humblot, 1954), vol. I, p. 1. So also, recently, P. Häberle, 'La dignità umana come fondamento della comunità statale', in *Cultura dei diritti e diritti della cultura nello spazio costituzionale europeo* (Saggi, Milan: Giuffré, 2003), p. 1.

statements contained in a strictly personal diary, are held to be below the level of the respect that is due. In this area, the dignity of the individual generally operates in favour of the culprit and of a more lenient and humane treatment of prisoners.

In contrast, in private law the appeal to the dignity of the individual is frequently made in order to justify restrictions of the private rights of others. The autonomous person must have control of the data concerning his private life, not only vis-à-vis unjustified desires of the state to know, but also with respect to possible intrusions of fellow citizens who gather and spread information. The law, in order to ensure human dignity, must therefore not only adopt rules against defamation and, at the level of groups, against hate speech, it must also regulate the activities of all persons who collect data for the sake of business or for the idle curiosity of the people at large. It is also appropriate to enact prohibitions against the exercise of economic activities which put the basic respect which is due to a person at risk, even if the persons involved are voluntarily agreeing to accept their own degradation, as for instance in public presentations in which human beings are used as mere valueless objects.

In the examples just provided the principle of human dignity was applied to all persons without distinctions. But the champions of the principle believe that there is also a dignity relative to special social conditions which requires no less attention. In contemporary western societies, the dignity of the less fortunate citizens must be taken care of through robust, adequate and free social services. If such services are not expressly provided for in the constitution, they must be read into its general clauses. The state ought to assure a minimum standard of living to all citizens. Decent housing ought to be provided to them through public funds as a distinct, officially recognised 'social' right, or otherwise human dignity would be offended.[10]

Thus far, mention has been made of cases of convergence among the supporters of the principle. They are, however, fiercely divided in other, important areas. For some the very dignity of the woman requires a substantial freedom for her to decide whether to continue or to terminate her pregnancy. Likewise, the dignity of a person who is terminally ill ought to be respected by giving him the right to choose to be assisted in committing suicide. Others, who claim to be equally faithful to the principle, think that none of these rights ought to be granted.

[10] So, for instance, Häberle, 'La dignità umana', above, note 9, p. 62.

A person would betray the respect owed to all members of the human species should he voluntarily sacrifice the life of a foetus or even his own life. Life, all human life, must be regarded as sacred, or the duty of unconditional respect for it would make no sense, and the law should give force to this conclusion.

Divergences also exist with regard to the enormous moral and political problems created by the recent developments in the fields of genetics and bioengineering. Some maintain that individuals ought to be able to organise transmission of life to their descendants by having recourse to artificial insemination or by manipulating genes, the latter not only to remedy possible grave defects but also to improve well-being at will, perhaps even by cloning. Others reject these practices with horror, holding them to be an intolerable offence to the very idea of mankind, whose nature would hereby be deeply violated. The great majority of the medical profession worldwide is opposed to at least the extreme forms of such practices. For the moment, public opinion and the political classes seem to firmly share its negative position.[11]

Once the main outlines of the legal theory and practice of human dignity have been elucidated, it is possible to assess how the present democratic systems reflect its requirements.[12] The responses of the systems in various countries are indeed quite different. Some appear to have accepted most of its implications, others are much less receptive; in some systems, the courts have made expansive, conscious use of the concept to shape their jurisprudence, in others, they have not.

III. European constitutionalism and human dignity

1. Germany

The German legal system is a 'democratic social' version of the model of the interventionist state. The system has been largely shaped by ordinary legislation at the *Bund* and the *Länder* levels. However, the contribution made by the *Grundgesetz*, as interpreted and enforced by the

---

[11] On the moral and legal problems raised by the discoveries in the field of bioengineering and on the problems of bioethics in general see, among the many recent contributions, G. P. Smith II, *Human Rights and Biomedicine* (The Hague, London, Boston: Kluwer Law International, 2000); G. Marini (ed.), *Bioetica e diritto penale* (Turin: Giappichelli, 2002).

[12] E. J. Eberle, *Dignity and Liberty. Constitutional Visions in Germany and the United States* (Westport, Conn., London: Praeger, 2002).

Constitutional Court, in directing, correcting, and streamlining this legislation, has been considerable and it is a contribution which has been greatly influenced by the concept of human dignity. The concept is stated in the first sentence of Art. 1 of the *Grundgesetz* and is held to posit a *Grundwert*, a basic value, supreme within the system (Dürig).[13] The *Grundrechte* from Art. 2 to Art. 19 were perhaps conceived by the framers as mere *Abwehrrechte*,[14] but the jurisprudence of the Constitutional Court transformed them into something different: into values requiring the legal system to assume institutional shapes that enable the effective, equal enjoyment of those rights for everyone. In so shaping this system the Court went to great lengths to ensure that the supreme *Grundwert*, human dignity, was always duly considered and never compromised. This is particularly visible in the judicial development of the general right to self-determination (Art. 2 (1)), the right to life (Art. 2 (2)), freedom of expression (Art. 5) and equality before the law (Art. 3).

The German law regarding freedom of expression must be explained in this context. This fundamental right has been appropriately recognised since the 1958 *Lüth* decision.[15] Apart from the strong special limitations for the protection of the democratic order, other limits are directly related to the idea that the reputation, the privacy and the intimate feelings of other persons must be vigorously defended. The defence originates from the inviolable value of the human dignity. Decisions such as *Soraya* (1973),[16] *Mephisto* (1971),[17] *Peep-show* (1981)[18] and *Holocaust Denial* (1994)[19] set boundaries as to the rights of the press and the media.

The *Grundgesetz* outlaws the death penalty altogether (Art. 102). The Constitutional Court, in the name of human dignity, has reduced the impact of life imprisonment sentences on the freedom of the offenders by making it obligatory to leave them the hope for a future release in the case of good conduct (*Life Imprisonment* case – 1977).[20] On the same grounds, it was decided that a terminally ill accused has the right not to be arrested even in the case of most serious crimes and when the danger of flight exists (*Honecker* case – 1993).[21] In a similar vein, the Court has judged that human dignity, together with the general right of

---

[13] Dürig, 'Menschenwürde', above, note 9.

[14] E. Forsthoff, *Rechtsstaat im Wandel* (Stuttgart: Kohlhammer, 1964), pp. 27, 147.

[15] BVerfGE 7, 198.   [16] BVerfGE 34, 115.   [17] BVerfGE 30, 173.

[18] BVerfGE 64, 274.   [19] BVerfGE 90, 241.   [20] BVerfGE 45, 187.

[21] This decision was actually made not by the federal, but by the Berlin Constitutional Court, arguing on the basis of federal law and precedents: BerlVerfGH NJW 1993, 515.

self-determination, requires that entries in a strictly personal diary cannot, at least in principle, be used as evidence in a criminal process (*Personal Diary* case – 1989).[22] Confidential personal information given to certain professionals is generally protected, ultimately because the right of the human personality would otherwise be violated (*Medical Records* case – 1972;[23] *Social Worker Privilege* case – 1972;[24] *Medical-Psychological Reports* case – 1993[25]). The power of the state to obtain information about the personal data of citizens by way of the census has also been restricted by the Court (*National Census* case – 1983).[26] Finally, the Constitutional Court has extended the protection of the human dignity principle to the case of the life of the unborn and this has contributed to the judgments on abortion (*First Abortion* case – 1975;[27] *Second Abortion* case – 1993[28]).

The German Constitution has adopted the 'democratic-social' model, but it has decided to express this choice by way of one simple formula (the *Bund* and the *Länder* must be 'social states': Art. 20, Art. 28), without specifying which social services in particular must be offered to the citizens. This does not mean, however, that it is entirely up to the legislator to determine how extensive the social services should be, the Court remaining totally extraneous to the matter. Rather, the Court thought that at the bottom of the matter lay a question of human dignity, a value which it was its duty to preserve. Therefore, the Court stated that Art. 1 (1) of the *Grundgesetz*, in conjunction with Art. 20 and Art. 28, imposes an obligation on the state to provide at least minimal subsistence to every individual.[29] The Court went further, requiring the legislature to distribute benefits according to a rigorous principle of equality whenever services are provided. This rule not only excludes different treatment based on 'suspect categories' (race, gender, religion, etc.), but also compels the legislature to treat groups alike which possess the same characteristics since unjustified differentiation might affect the dignity that is equally due to all persons.[30]

The Constitutional Court has played a significant role in shaping the German legal system towards defending and advancing the respect for the value of human dignity. Of course the Constitutional Court has not been the only factor that gave the legal system a shape that so

---

[22] BVerfGE 80, 367.   [23] BVerfGE 33, 367.   [24] BVerfGE 33, 367.   [25] BVerfGE 89, 69.
[26] BVerfGE 65, 1.   [27] BVerfGE 39, 1.   [28] BVerfGE 88, 203.
[29] BVerfGE 84, 133, 158 (1991).
[30] BVerfGE 55, 72, 88 (1980); BVerfGE 82, 126, 148–52 (1990).

distinctively bears the mark of this value. The legislators, both on the federal and on the *Länder* level, have also made very significant contributions. When one considers the extent to which human dignity has been embedded in the administration of criminal justice, in the protection of privacy and of personal data, and, finally, with the organisation of large and efficient welfare services, one must acknowledge that German legislation in these areas has reached quite remarkable results, and has even gone beyond the directions of the Court.

The performance of the German legal system as a whole can be summed up, from the point of view of the concept of human dignity, in the following way: it is inclined to leniency in the persecution of crimes, affords substantial protection – in a strong conservative tone – to the rights of man's personality when exposed to the dangers of possible aggressions on the part of private action (of all kinds), and it is extremely generous in providing the people with adequate social services.

2. Italy

The Italian Constitution twice expressly mentions 'dignity' as a fundamental value. These occasions are 'social dignity', which all citizens enjoy on the same footing (Art. 3) and 'human dignity', that 'private economic initiative' must not 'damage' (Art. 41). In addition, Art. 27 states that criminal penalties must not contravene the 'sense of humanity' and must tend to 're-educate' the prisoner, while Art. 32 prohibits compulsory medical treatments that are incompatible with the 'respect for the human person'. Furthermore, given that there are many provisions regarding social services, a concern for people in danger of being injured in their basic human expectations can be inferred as part of the constitutional model which the Italian Charter has adopted. However, jurists and courts have only recently tried to elaborate a general theory of human dignity as a legal value, and these tentative explorations are still rather scant. Besides making use of the textual basis just cited, they have relied heavily on the general principles contained in Art. 2, which makes the human person as such the holder of 'inviolable rights', and in Art. 3, where the citizens are proclaimed equal before the law in all respects and where the state is called on to promote the cause of their 'factual liberty and equality'.

In practice, the Italian legal system has presently attained a position which is comparable to that of the German system, both at the constitutional level and at the legislative level. In the area of criminal justice the Constitutional Court, though in theory retaining the penalty of life imprisonment, has granted the prisoner a right to a reduction of the sentence for good conduct in prison.[31] It has also protected the situation of prisoners in other ways, in the name of humanitarian considerations.[32] As the Italian Constitution does not permit the death penalty in peacetime, the Court has prohibited the extradition of suspected criminals to countries which permit capital punishment for their crimes.[33] Through legislation, Italian criminal law has been progressively revised in a generally lenient sense, in some cases out of a desire to enact more humane sanctions and to favour the rehabilitation of the culprits as 'worthy' human beings.

In the areas of defamation and exposure by the media, Italian law is perhaps less protective of the rights of individuals than German law. The Italian legislation on the collection and use by private individuals of data concerning other persons is, however, very strict. The existence of a distinct informational 'right to privacy' is now undisputed.[34] Many jurists believe that this right not only has constitutional roots, but that it even enjoys a strong constitutional guarantee. They argue that Art. 2 of the Constitution concerning the 'inviolable rights' of the person is open ended and that 'informational privacy' is an 'unnamed' right. Alternatively, they maintain that it is a part of the right of the person to self-determination which is acknowledged by Art. 2 and Art. 3 in view of the 'dignity' that belongs to all persons. Obviously the right 'to be let alone' is also recognised, and there are traditional constitutional protections against unjustified state intrusions.[35]

The concept of 'human dignity' also occasionally surfaces in the Court's decisions in the areas of family law, labour law, and criminal and civil procedure. However, the most significant and creative interpretations of the concept are perhaps to be found in the field of social rights. Unlike the German Constitution, the Italian Constitution is rich in provisions that describe specific services for people whose needs would not be adequately met by the free market. In the eyes of some, these provisions leave gaps and ought to be read in an evolving way. The Constitutional Court has often embraced such doctrines, and has, for

[31] Giur. Cost., 1983, I, 1757 (n. 274).
[32] Giur. Cost., 1989, I, 1740 (n. 386); Giur. Cost., 1999, I, 176 (n. 26).
[33] Giur. Cost., 1979, I, 413 (n. 54).   [34] Law n. 675 of 1996.
[35] On the question of the constitutional standing of the right of 'information privacy' in Italy see G. M. Salerno, 'La protezione della riservatezza e la inviolabilità della corrispondenza', in R. Nania and P. Ridola (eds.), Il diritti costituzionali (Turin: Giappichelli, 2001), vol. I, p. 417.

instance, 'discovered' that human dignity requires that decent housing be secured for all citizens as a constitutional 'social right'.[36] Even more than its German counterpart, the Court has applied the equality principle to extend benefits which the legislator has generously granted to groups of its choice on to groups which have been left out by the law. The Court did this in order to redress the unequal respect paid to the dignity of equal citizens. To achieve this aim, the Court occasionally did not even hesitate to sacrifice the integrity of the budget.[37]

As in Germany, the Italian constitutional jurisprudence has recognised 'human dignity' and the 'right to life' of the foetus. However, in balancing the latter right with the freedom of the woman, it has adopted solutions in which penalisation plays a lesser role, placing emphasis, in accordance with the legislator, on the right of the woman to choose.[38]

3. France

The jurisprudential 'discovery' of a fundamental principle of human dignity occurred much later in the French legal system. Its official recognition by the *Conseil Constitutionnel* took place in 1994 and was formally based on the Preamble to the Constitution of 1946 which condemns the regimes which in the Second World War had tried to 'enslave and degrade the human person'.

On the other hand, France has been the first major country in which the thorny problems of bioethics have been faced at the level of constitutional adjudication and have received significant (though inevitably partial) answers. The *Conseil Constitutionnel* decided in 1994 that the '*bloc de constitutionnalité*' of the French system includes the principle of human dignity but that it does not require that the respect due to the life of all human beings be extended to the foetus;[39] nor that it is a constitutional principle that the genetic heritage of mankind be preserved intact and that it is the right of a child to know the identity of its parents. Consequently, the legislator was free to enact a law that allowed, in a medically assisted form, both homogamous and heterogamous insemination. At the same time the law prohibited

---

[36] Giur. Cost., 1988, I, 1789, n. 404.
[37] G. Bognetti, 'Social Rights, a Necessary Component of the Constitution? The Italian Case', in R. Bieber and P. Widmer (eds.), *Der Europäische Verfassungsraum* (Zurich: Schülter Verlag, 1995), p. 85.
[38] Giur. Cost., 1975, I, 117 note 27; Giur. Cost., 1981, I, 140; 951, note 26 e and note 109.
[39] 343–344 DC – 1994.

investigating the identity of the donor of the gametes and the commercial trading of embryos, but permitted, under certain conditions, the transfer of embryos from one couple to another. By establishing a number of principles the *Conseil Constitutionnel* meant to protect important values concerning the transmission of human life and at the same time to ensure the respect of the freedom of the woman. Therefore, the law as a whole was not considered to be in conflict with the general principle of 'human dignity'.[40]

Prior to the decision of 1994, the *Conseil Constitutionnel* had already established that the right to life, belonging to all human beings, also applied to the foetus.[41] After the 1994 decision, the principle of human dignity easily entered into other areas than that of procreation. The *Conseil Constitutionnel* has found in particular that the possibility for all persons to obtain decent housing is an objective of constitutional value.[42] It is up to the state to fulfill that objective. Human dignity has also helped to contain certain improper initiatives of private economic interest. The *Conseil d'Etat*, for instance, has validated the prohibition, issued by the authorities, of public amusements called '*lancer de nains*' (dwarf-throwing).[43]

4. Other European systems

Other European legal systems, besides Germany, Italy and France, have recently made use of the concept of human dignity, both at the constitutional level and at the level of the ordinary law. In general, the applications have fitted into the patterns of the prevalent version of the interventionist state adopted by European legal systems: the 'democratic-social' version. Human dignity has at times been invoked, as it is done in German jurisprudence, to provide a new philosophical justification for fundamental rights of an old, well-established standing. As far as the production of new legal results is concerned, the concept has been useful in developing

---

[40] See L. Favoureu and L. Philip (eds.), *Les Grandes Décisions du Conseil constitutionnel* (9th edn, Paris: Dalloz, 1997), p. 861, with a long editorial note. The law, among other things, prohibited the creation of embryos *in vitro* for commercial and industrial purposes and, at least in general, also for purposes of research and scientific experiments.

[41] *Abortion* Decision, 54 DC, 1975; Favoureu and Philip, *Les Grandes Décisions*, above, note 40, p. 305.

[42] Favoureu and Philip, *Les Grandes Décisions*, above, note 40, p. 876 (359 DC/1994).

[43] M. Long, P. Weil and G. Raibant, *Les Grands Arrêts de la jurisprudence administrative* (11th edn, Paris: Dalloz, 1996), no. 119.

limitations on the free exercise of private rights in accordance with a general tendency in the 'democratic-social' version of the interventionist state. It has also been useful in developing the duty of the state to furnish significant social services along the lines of the 'generous' idea of the welfare state which is typical of the European continent.

The concept of human dignity has not been able to reinforce the claim that the 'right to life' also belongs to the foetus to the extent of substantially restricting the right of the woman to terminate a pregnancy.[44] The battle about the implications of human dignity on the laws on bioethics has probably only just begun, and it has so far yielded different results.[45] The Netherlands have just passed the first European law recognising the 'right to die' of the terminally ill. No European constitutional court has as yet upheld such a right nor has the Strasbourg Court.[46]

IV. The United States and human dignity

Considering that the United States presently represents a neo-liberal version of the interventionist state, it is logical that the role of human dignity should be rather limited in the writings of jurists and in the developments of law, especially constitutional law.

As for the theory of the rights of the individual, American jurists did not have the same reasons for turning to the doctrines of Aquinas or Kant, cast in a modernised form, in order to revise their interpretations of the Bill of Rights. It was enough for them to read the ideology of Locke, Mill and the Founding Fathers 'with new glasses' and to rely on a more intransigent conception of democracy as a government by equals, as the best tradition of the country suggested. Support could also come from the tenets of an intelligent utilitarianism and, if

---

[44] The constitutional decisions in Austria, France and Italy have recognised the right of the foetus, but have on the other hand also recognised, in more or less generous terms, the right of the woman to decide to interrupt the pregnancy. For a direct comparison of the several abortion decisions of the seventies – including the less liberal German one – see *L'aborto nelle sentenze delle Corti Costituzionali – USA, Austria, Francia, RFT* (Milan: Giuffré, 1976).

[45] The German Embryo Protection Act of 1990 categorically forbids any genetic interference with human reproductive cells. The Italian law – approved in 2004 – is equally severe and does not permit, among other things, heterogamous inseminations. Clearly more liberal is the British Human Fertilization and Embryology Act of 1990.

[46] See the decision of the Court in the case *Pretty* v. *The United Kingdom*, 2002-III Eur. Ct. H.R.

necessary, from a reborn ideal of the social contract. Besides, Americans, unlike Europeans, did not have to react against the history of a state that, through a totalitarian regime, had treated some of its citizens as beasts, and therefore did not have to vindicate the figure of man as such.

However, the true cause of the minimal (if any) role played by the concept of human dignity in US law probably lies elsewhere. It has to do with the way in which the classical liberal model of the state was superseded in the 1930s and in which the new 'social' model was developed in its place. At the time of the New Deal, under the pressure of public opinion and of other factors, the Supreme Court abandoned its traditional doctrines of economic due process and of interstate commerce, two fundamental pillars of the old model. From that moment onwards, the Court decided to exercise judicial review in the broad area of economic-social relations with only a minimal degree of scrutiny. In practical terms this meant the abolition of judicial review in that area, and the delivery of it to the free, democratic choices of the federal and state legislators. Regulation of the economy and the setting up of social services were left to the sovereign decisions of the political powers, trusting that the democratic political mechanism would, all in all, produce the best results without judicial interference. The Court, on the basis of this fundamental choice, did not develop the technical means that would have allowed a judicial defence of the dignity of man against possible encroachments by private economic activities and against a lack of sufficient provision of social services by the state. Theoretically, the Court could have undertaken a revolutionary reading of certain clauses of the Fifth, Ninth and Fourteenth Amendments. Instead, among other things, the Court rejected any new theory of *substantive due process* in the economic area, and stuck firmly to the classical theory of *state action*.

It is true that later, with the Warren Court and for some time after, the judicial deference towards the political powers and democracy gave way to a new season of judicial activism and of suspicious 'distrust' of majorities.[47] This movement, however, was a distrust that was directed chiefly against the legal obstacles that made it difficult for overlooked and isolated minorities to participate fully in the democratic processes, or in favour of rights whose unfettered strength was held to be a precondition for the

---

[47] J. H. Ely, *Democracy and Distrust. A Theory of Judicial Review* (Cambridge: Harvard University Press, 1980).

good functioning of democracy, such as free speech and free press. Even in the new reading of the equal protection clause since *Brown v. Board of Education*[48] the emphasis was not on the offended human dignity as such but on the right of the citizen not to be discriminated against by the law on unjustifiable grounds, such as race, religion, gender, etc. The new activism of the Court also touched areas in which the rhetoric of human dignity could have easily played some part: criminal law, criminal procedure and 'privacy'. However, the judicial protection of interests of the individual in these areas has also been based simply on the classical concept of individual liberty in the sense that the state cannot limit and repress beyond a certain point. Besides, although the activism of the Court was almost aggressive in the beginning,[49] in the long run it has moderated its course.

This all means that the US Constitution, as interpreted by the Supreme Court, seems to offer less protection to values and rights associated with the idea of human dignity than the average European Constitution. Even at the level of ordinary legislation these rights and values appear to enjoy a lesser standing in America.

The death penalty, which the Court has refused to declare unconstitutional, is still inflicted in a number of states. It is up to the legislators to decide whether social services are to be offered to the citizens and of what kind. Good social services do exist in the United States, but the system is incomplete and the quality and quantity of American welfare is not comparable with that of the average European state. The right to privacy as a shield against gossip and unwanted diffusion of personal news was 'invented' in America,[50] but today laws forbidding private individuals from making computerised use of personal data are much stricter in Europe.

The American legal system, through its Constitution, leaves legislators much more room than in Europe for their choices in economic and social matters, out of respect for their democratic stature. Legislators, in turn, out of respect for the prominent importance of the market and its values, are less ready than in Europe to impose strict regulations on economic initiatives and to pay large sums for extended social

---

[48] 347 U.S. 483 (1954).
[49] See for instance *Mapp* v. *Ohio*, 367 U.S. 643 (1961); *Miranda* v. *Arizona*, 384 U.S. 436 (1966); *Roe* v. *Wade*, 410 U.S. 113 (1973).
[50] S. Warren and L. D. Brandeis, 'The Right to Privacy' (1890) 4 *Harvard Law Review*, 193–220.

services, even if that would be justified by the requirements of human dignity. Against this background, the American jurists and judges who speak the language of human dignity are obviously 'progressive' champions of reforms that would bring the American legal system closer to the European version of the 'social' state.

In a beautiful essay Professor Louis Henkin of Columbia University has rewritten the entire history of the rights in the American Constitution, from the time of the Framers to our times, in the light of the concept of the dignity of man: he has in some ways successfully applied Dürig's conceptual approach to the *Grundgesetz* to US constitutionalism.[51] In the name of human dignity he has asked that the death penalty be adjudicated unconstitutional and has stated that the Constitution should proclaim the right to work and to leisure, the right to food, housing, health care and education, and the right to an adequate standard of living: all rights not less 'essential to human dignity' than the traditional liberties.

Human dignity has occasionally been mentioned or alluded to in American judicial decisions[52] or it was perhaps implicitly relevant in other well-known cases.[53] More often the feeling for it has made its

---

[51] L. Henkin, 'Human Dignity and Constitutional Rights', in M. J. Meyer and W. A. Parent (eds.), *The Constitution of Rights. Human Dignity and American Values* (Ithaca, NY, London: Cornell University Press, 1992), p. 210. The book of Meyer and Parent contains other valuable essays dealing with the concept of human dignity, in general and in relation to the United States legal system. Among them, one by Professor R. Berger convincingly demonstrates that, from a strictly *historical* point of view, the Amendments to the Constitution were not intended to include the protection of human values that their present champions read into them.

[52] *Goldberg* v. *Kelly*, 397 U.S. 254 (1970); *Price* v. *Johnston* concerning prisoners, 334 U.S. 266 (1948); *Hutto* v. *Finney*, 437 U.S. 678 (1978); *Hudson* v. *Palmer*, 468 U.S. 517 (1984); *Turner* v. *Safley*, 428 U.S. 78 (1987); in part *Gertz* v. *Welch Inc.* in the area of defamation, 418 U.S. 323 (1974). In *Gertz* the value of the individual reputation – as an important component of the dignity of the person – was used by the Court to justify refusing the application of the extremely liberal *Sullivan* rule to the case of private figures. *Gertz* was only concerned with the amount of protection that the Constitution grants to free speech – which was decided to be relatively limited in cases not involving public figures. But the Court – unlike what the German Court has done in *Mephisto* and other cases – did not say that the reputation of the person *must*, according to the Constitution, be effectively protected by the law: that remains up to the legislature (state or federal) to freely decide. See also, in the same sense, *Paul* v. *Davis*, 424 U.S. 693 (1976).

[53] E.g. *Skinner* v. *Oklahoma*, 316 U.S. 535 (1942) which however failed to formally overrule the notorious *Buck* v. *Bell*, 274 U.S. 200 (1927), where a compulsory sterilisation statute applicable to mental defectives in state institutions was sustained (opinion by Holmes).

appearance in dissenting opinions. And the figures who stand as the best American representatives of the concept of human dignity in judicial dissent are Justices Brennan and Marshall. The fight they have conducted in vain to have the death penalty completely ostracised from the American legal system under an adapted reading of the provision of the Eighth Amendment remains prominent in their record.

V. Concluding remarks

I am a follower of a philosophical theory that comes down from Vico's and Hegel's historicism and believes that the ultimate meaning of the adventure of the human species, thrown in the midst of a mysterious universe, lies in the effort to unfold all the potentials of reason, to make civilisation progress, and to increase indefinitely the power of man over himself and over nature. Such a conception does not allow for the existence of principles of socio-political organisation that are equally valid for all times and all places, and therefore does not allow for the existence of legal rights – be they called 'natural' or 'inalienable' or 'inviolable' or otherwise – of universal application. Nor does it accept the idea that there is a 'human dignity' that requires a fixed set of equal and minimum legal treatments for a member of the species under all possible circumstances. Instead, the theory of historicism knows that, in the course of the evolution of the species and of its culture, the invention at a certain point, and on the part of some nations, of the institutions of individual liberty was a great but difficult step which contributed to the growth of civilisation. Further advances, by way of experiments through trial and error, in the direction of higher stages of civilised life are always possible, but problematic. While it would be a naive illusion to believe that there is an infallible method to determine what are, at a certain stage of the process, the precise institutional solutions that best fit the situation, the historicist approach permits the formulation of some necessarily brief but important remarks about the merits of human dignity as a conceptual tool used in the processes of political evaluation, legal reasoning and judicial decision in the western systems of our time.

In the experiences of the legal systems we have examined, the concept of human dignity has functioned essentially as a means to reinforce the weight of one or another of the individual rights that each system respectively recognises: extending the scope of one right, limiting the extension of another, at times giving more specific content to the meaning of a constitutional provision. In the European systems, the concept of human dignity has helped to make criminal law and criminal procedure more humane; it has contributed to set limits on private economic initiatives and forays of the press, to the advantage of social customs and practices which are more respectful of the individual human person; human dignity has supported as just and necessary a broad system of social services useful to the needy. Its practical impact on the American system has been far less, if any at all: the neo-liberal version of the interventionist state has proved – at least for now – adamant towards most of the suggestions of the concept that have been accepted in Europe.

It would be easy, taking the side of human dignity, to draw the rash inference that the European systems are more advanced on the scale of civilisation than the American one; and that they better meet the true needs of our contemporary societies. Things are not so simple, however. Obviously, the basic individual rights that are indispensable for a western society of our time are present in the United States today. Once that level is attained, the humane features of a system are not the only value that counts. Their absence, or their limited extent, could be compensated for by the presence of other features.[54]

A certain ruggedness of the American system may be the unavoidable reflection of its strong, general reliance on individual initiative, which wants to move in open spaces. The extreme freedom granted to speech and the press may be the necessary fuel for a vigorous democracy to function appropriately. Fewer social services run by the state may mean less bureaucracy and fewer inefficiencies in the system. All this may turn out to be a sign of greater youth, and may prove to be of advantage in the harsh competition which will characterise the future world of nations. Therefore, it is at least prudent to suspend the comparative judgment concerning the respective positions of Europe and the United States on

---

[54] One example: it is often said that the human dignity of the worker is better protected in Europe than in the United States, owing to the legal rules that in European systems strictly limit the power of the employer to fire or to lay off. On the other hand, experts maintain that these very rules are one of the factors that, by making the labour relation less flexible, contribute to the higher rates of unemployment existing for decades in Europe (roughly averaging twice as high as in America). The dignity of those having an employment seems here to be assured at the indirect expense of the dignity of those who would like to work (a fundamental way to express one's personality and to participate meaningfully in community life) and are not able to get a job. The larger number of persons employed in the United States might in a sense abundantly compensate for the lesser protection of the worker within the labour relation (not to speak of the resulting more dynamic character of the economic system as a whole).

the scale of civilisation, and to refuse a conclusion based only on the simple yardstick of human dignity.

Another observation has to do with a more subtle technical aspect of the uses that jurists and courts can make of the concept of human dignity. Once the formula of 'human dignity' is inserted in the text of a constitution – or has become a recognised part of constitutional law by virtue of successful doctrinal and judicial elaboration – it can be noticed, as a matter of fact, that legal reasoning tends to deduce as many consequences or 'implications' or 'derived sub-principles' from the new established principle as possible. This process of deduction from general principles is a natural and useful element of the methods by which the law normally develops. In the case of 'human dignity', however, there is a risk that the legal system may acquire too much rigidity at the constitutional level too soon.

Perhaps the special strictures that the German jurisprudence has put on freedom of expression in the name of human dignity are justified in the particular context of German society and history: Germany is in many respects not the United States. However, one wonders whether it would not have been more suitable if such structures had been adopted in Germany by ordinary legislation rather than derived by application of the constitutional principle of human dignity. Other examples of this kind can easily be supplied. They all suggest that without self-restraint in the application of the principle of human dignity too much political space would be taken away from the legislature by creative constitutional interpretation.

From this point of view, again, US jurisprudence does not necessarily appear inferior to that of the European systems. American judicial review has established precise constitutional principles in the areas of political and civil rights and with respect to the application of the equal protection clause against suspect discriminations, while its scrutiny is minimal in economic and social matters. It is perhaps not harmful that the idea of applying the principle of human dignity to economic and social matters has not yet come to the US Supreme Court. Judicial review in Germany, Italy and France does not know sectors where the principle of human dignity does not apply, or where it operates only perfunctorily. Some maintain that the political life in those countries has been subjected to an inflexible, suffocating, universal juridical armature. As their constitutional systems have already incorporated an operative general principle of human dignity, a cautious use of the principle is advisable for them so as to avoid aggravating an already difficult situation. A very cautious use of the principle of human dignity seems particularly recommendable to the doctrinal and judicial treatment of the new problems posed by the new sciences of bioethics and bioengineering.

Finally, a warning against an activist use of the human dignity principle seems to be especially justified with respect to the jurisprudence of the two European Courts of Strasbourg and Luxembourg. The principle of human dignity has been given a prominent place in the Nice Charter of Human Rights (Art. 1), now incorporated in the Constitutional Treaty of the Union. It will probably also play a role in the future decisions of the European Court of Human Rights. European nations have very good reasons for accepting to be bound by charters of rights that reflect a compromise between their different traditions on the subject and that are authoritatively interpreted by international or supra-national courts. However, Europeans are not, in general, naive 'universalists', who believe that there are supreme values which are valid under all circumstances for all the members of mankind and capable of being best identified by international courts. There are probably many more ethico-political sceptics and absolute relativists in Europe than there are in the United States. Sceptics and relativists also know the advantages of pragmatism. And pragmatism might be the true driving force that presently induces European nations, unlike the United States, to sign international covenants that are not likely to be always and immediately respected by the signing parties promptly and willingly: they are tools to be used in the complicated game of world politics. With respect to the European charters of rights, however, the game is entirely different. Here, the decisive element is the fundamental interest of forming a Union: a Union comparable, in dimensions and power, to the giants of the world. In the interests of forming a strong Union, many factors can make a useful contribution. As the history of US constitutionalism teaches, a Bill of Rights, as interpreted by a federal Court and overriding the different laws of the component states, can in the long run generate a firm sense of belonging and of common destiny. This is why it is perfectly reasonable for Europeans today to hand over to European Courts the task of defining their common heritage in the field of rights, even if that may sacrifice some of their different points of view and perhaps a part of their national pride.

If this is a realistic picture of the situation it becomes immediately evident, however, why the European Courts should be very cautious in handling the principle of human dignity. The principle extends its possible influence to highly delicate areas in which there are sharp differences of opinion among the peoples of the several states of Europe. It might prove counter-productive to judicially read into the principle of human dignity implications that contradict national opinions, laws and judicial doctrines held just and dear by relevant sections of the Continent. Interpreters should be careful when going beyond what is strictly required by specific provisions and refrain from further extrapolating a system of guarantees which is already, in my opinion, overly extensive and complex. An activist European jurisprudence of rights, instead of helping the formation of a common conscience and of bringing together the peoples of the several states, may, at least at the present moment, run the risk of operating in the opposite direction.

5

'Human dignity' in Europe and the United States: the social foundations

JAMES Q. WHITMAN

The United States of America makes a woeful impression on many Europeans. Of course this is partly because of the overwhelming, and more or less unbridled, way in which Americans exercise military and economic power on the international stage. It is inevitable that a dominant power like the United States should face resentment. But there is more to the distrust and dislike of the United States than that. Europeans are also frequently troubled by the internal structure of American society. America is a harsh place. This has to do in part with economics. American governments have largely abandoned the project of redistributing wealth, showing little commitment to social welfare states of the European type.[1] Even inheritance taxes, which lie at the core of modern state socialism, are under heavy and largely successful attack in the United States.[2]

Economics are only part of what can make American society seem harsh, though. 'Human dignity', as Europeans conceive it, is remarkably weak in the United States as well. The most striking evidence for this is the American record of rejecting international conventions on human rights, or accepting them with crippling reservations. To take only one

---

[1] For discussion, see e.g. Alberto Alesina and George-Marios Angeletos, 'Fairness and Redistribution: US versus Europe', *National Bureau of Economics Working Paper* (October 2002), available at http://post.economics.harvard.edu/faculty/alesina/pdf-papers/ Alesina-Angeletos1nov2002.pdf; Alberto Alesina, Edward Glaeser and Bruce Sacerdote, 'Why Doesn't the United States have a European-Style Welfare State?' (2001) 2 *Brookings Papers on Economic Activity*, available at http://post.economics.harvard.edu/faculty/ alesina/pdf-papers/0332-Alesina2.pdf. For the classic treatment, see also Werner Sombart, *Warum gibt es in den Vereinigten Staaten keinen Sozialismus?* (Tübingen: Mohr, 1906).

[2] E.g. Carl Hulse, 'Ads Push Estate Tax as Issue in Campaigns', in *New York Times*, 14 July 2002, p. A22.

dramatic example, until recently the United States continued to inflict the death penalty for crimes committed when the offender was a minor, in the face of the International Covenant on the Rights of the Child.[3] Criminal justice offers many other examples of American practices that Europeans reject as not only harsh, but no less than barbarous.[4] In other realms of the law, too, we see parallel phenomena. Europeans bring a sense of the imperatives of 'dignity' to their legislation that is simply lacking in America. The difference made itself felt most recently with regard to the protection of private information, and especially of consumer information. Europeans have a long tradition of protecting privacy as an aspect of 'personality', or of the 'control of one's image'. Following that tradition, they introduced legislation preventing merchants from sharing most consumer data. No such protections were possible, or perhaps even conceivable, for most American legislators and lawyers. The result was a draining conflict in international commerce, only problematically resolved by a 2000 'safe harbour' agreement.[5] Europeans still issue constant complaints that Americans do not accept the importance of protecting consumer data.[6] Many more examples can be offered as well. Indeed, when it comes to 'dignity', there is not just a contrast, but a kind of conflict of cultures that divides the states on either side of the Atlantic.

Why do these differences exist? One would not expect to see such far-reaching contrasts between societies that are, by many socio-economic measures, quite similar, and that grow out of a common western cultural soil.

In this paper, which summarises a great deal of research that I present in detail elsewhere, I will focus on our conflicts over 'dignity' and 'human dignity'. And I will try to account for the differences between continental Europe and the United States using historical sociology. In my view, we cannot understand the comparative *law* of dignity unless we understand the comparative *sociology* of dignity: there is no point in talking about the high theory of 'human dignity' if we do not understand the everyday social forms of dignity. Nor can we understand the law of

---

[3] But see now the important Supreme Court decision, with significant attention to foreign law, in *Roper v. Simmons*, No. 03-633 (March 1, 2005).

[4] Presented at length in James Q. Whitman, *Harsh Justice: Criminal Punishment and the Widening Divide between America and Europe* (New York: Oxford University Press, 2003).

[5] See e.g. the materials collected in Daniel J. Solove and Marc Rotenberg, *Information Privacy Law* (New York: Aspen, 2003), pp. 713–63.

[6] E.g. Adam Clymer, 'Privacy Concerns: Canadian and Dutch Officials Warn of Security's Side Effects', *New York Times*, 28 February 2003, p. A14.

dignity if we do not understand the *history* of dignity. The contemporary social forms of dignity are the products of a long history – a history that reaches back at least to the eighteenth century.

The historical claim that I will offer focuses on Germany and France, the dominant legal cultures of continental Europe. In simplified form, the claim is this: We cannot understand the pattern of 'dignity' in continental Europe today unless we begin with the forms of 'dignity' that existed in the aristocratic-monarchical orders of the *ancien régime*. Of course, the 'dignity' of the *ancien régime* was not *human* dignity. Two hundred and fifty years or so ago, continental law included elaborate and obnoxious rules, intended to guarantee that high-status persons would be treated better than low-status persons: whether the issue was punishment, privacy, or any other aspect of daily life, only high-status persons received respect and dignified treatment. Well into the twentieth century, only high-status Europeans could expect their dignity to be protected by the law. This world was utterly objectionable from the point of view of anyone committed to human rights as we conceive of them today.

In fact, it may seem a clumsy scholarly error to suppose that the old high-status forms of 'dignity' bear any real relationship to the new 'human' forms. Yet in my view the old and the new forms are intimately related. 'Human dignity' as contemporary Europeans embrace it has been shaped by a rich and complex collective memory of the obnoxious past of the old regime. The core idea of 'human dignity' in continental Europe is the idea that old forms of low-status treatment are no longer acceptable. Every European – or at least, every citizen of a European country – is now supposed to be possessed of a 'dignity' protected by law. 'Human dignity', as we find it on the Continent today, has been formed by a pattern of *levelling up*, by an extension of formerly high-status treatment to all sectors of the population.

The proof of this proposition, I will try to show, lies in the doctrinal history of some of the main institutions of 'dignity' in continental law today. To a remarkable extent, those institutions began as institutions of privilege – of specially reserved rights for high-status persons. Whether the issue is punishment, privacy, or any other aspect of daily life, all members of continental society can now expect to receive treatment that was historically reserved to their 'betters'. Strange as it may sound, there is in fact a genetic relation between the old, obnoxious forms of 'dignity' and the contemporary human forms. Continental Europe is a world in which former status privileges have been generalised. Indeed, we can say that continental Europe is in many ways less a world of rights than a world of generalised privileges. Nothing comparable has happened in the United States, and this helps us to understand how the two heartlands of the occidental world have come to differ so dramatically.

Now, this may sound like an overly simple account of the differences that separate Americans from French and Germans. Nevertheless, I will try to show that, presented with the appropriate caveats and the appropriate care, it is correct. The history of continental law, in this regard, is not different from the history of continental society more broadly. Many continental commentators, from Rudolf von Jhering to Norbert Elias, have made the same observation: continental societies have been formed by a drive to guarantee that everyone should enjoy high status, by the effort to create a world in which, as Philippe d'Iribarne puts it, 'You shall all be masters!'[7] The same drive has shaped the continental law of 'human dignity' as well. This is a sociological truth, and it is a truth that challenges some familiar European ideas about the origins of 'dignity' and 'human dignity' in their law. Many Europeans, especially many Germans, credit their law of dignity to the influence of Immanuel Kant.[8] In my view, the magnificent abstractions of Kant, with their talk of the categorical imperative, of treating persons as 'ends in themselves' and so on – these magnificent abstractions have little to do with the socio-historical reality of dignity in Europe. Nor is it only the importance of Kant that we should doubt. Many Europeans, of all nationalities, regard their law of 'human dignity' as the product of a reaction against Fascism and Nazism. I believe the place of the fascist era in the making of European dignity is much more complex and ambiguous than that – though that is a topic about which I will say nothing further in this paper.[9]

[7] Norbert Elias, *Über den Prozess der Zivilisation. Soziogenetische und psychogenetische Untersuchungen* (2nd edn, Bern: Francke, 1969); Rudolf von Jhering, *Der Zweck im Recht* (4th edn, Leipzig: Breitkopf and Härtel, 1904), vol. II, p. 524; Philippe d'Iribarne, *Vous serez tous des maîtres: la grande illusion des temps modernes* (Paris: Éditions du Seuil, 1996).

[8] See e.g. *Bonner Kommentar zum Grundgesetz* (4th edn, München: Vahlen, 1999–2001), Art. 1, paras. 7–10; and for a French example: e.g. Philippe Pedrot, 'La Dignité de la personne humaine: principe consensuel ou valeur incantatoire', in P. Pedrot (ed.), *Éthique, Droit et Dignité de la Personne: Mélanges Christian Bolze* (Paris: Economica, 1999), p. 16.

[9] See my fuller argument in James Q. Whitman, 'On Nazi "Honour" and the New European "Dignity"', in Christian Joerges and Navraj Ghaleigh (eds.), *The Darker Legacy of European Law: Perceptions of Europe and Perspectives on a European Order in*

Leaving much aside, I will take the following approach. The bulk of the paper will summarise the history of one area of law: the law of criminal punishment. Afterwards I will touch briefly on the law of hate speech and the law of dignity in the workplace; and finally I will turn to the law of privacy. Inevitably I will do no more than sketch each of these areas of law. At the close of the paper, I will turn to the sociological assessment of the material I have presented.

I. The law of criminal punishment

Let me begin with criminal punishment. American society *is* harsh, and nowhere more so than in its criminal punishment. As I have tried to show in a recent book, the differences are profound, and indeed often shocking. The contrast only begins with the death penalty, reintroduced in the United States during exactly the period that it was definitively abolished in Europe. Prison sentences are far longer in the United States – probably something like five to ten times as long as sentences for comparable offences in Germany and France. Indeed, in Germany and France, prison is no longer the ordinary sanction at all. The widely reported result is that American rates of imprisonment, which are the highest in the world, run as high as *ten times* the per capita rate in Europe. A much wider range of offences is criminalised in the United States than in Europe. Offences are graded higher. And it goes on.[10]

Why is American justice so much harsher? There are some explanations that deserve more space than I can give them – that American society is more violent, for example (which is true), or that American society is more racist (which is probably false). Here I simply want to concentrate on one facet of the difference between the United States, on the one hand, and France and Germany on the other. American criminal punishment is more *degrading*. Indeed, American criminal punishment is degrading in ways that the continental traditions have vigorously rejected. This is most obviously true in the case of certain notorious American practices, such as the use of chain gangs. But there are many other related phenomena that are far less well known. Prisons make the most striking example. Continental systems have generally moved to

Legal Scholarship during the Era of Fascism and National Socialism (Cambridge: Hart, 2003), pp. 243–66.

[10] Detailed comparison of doctrine, practice and some statistics are offered in my *Harsh Justice*, above, note 4. Readers seeking a more carefully substantiated account of the arguments in this section of the paper are referred to that book.

abolish such aspects of imprisonment as degrading uniforms, and barred doors that leave inmates exposed to constant view. They also have rules – very remarkable from the American point of view – requiring that inmates be treated with respect, in such things as forms of address: inmates are ordinarily to be addressed as 'Herr so-and-so' or 'Monsieur so-and-so'. Most broadly, punishment professionals in both France and Germany are committed to some version of what German law calls the *Angleichungsgrundsatz*, the 'principle of approximation'. This principle holds that life in prison should resemble life in the outside world as closely as possible, and in Germany it includes such remarkable practices as the application of ordinary labour law within prisons. All of this conveys an important symbolic message: the message that offenders are to be treated like ordinary members of society, and not like status inferiors. To be sure, these ideals are not fully realised in practice. Ideals are never fully realised, and life in prison is certainly not pleasant in Europe – especially not in France. But whatever its failings, continental law *is* intended to dramatise symbolically the proposition that inmates are not persons of a different and lower status – that they are not degraded by comparison with ordinary civilians.

This effort to guarantee that punishment is not degrading permeates both French and German systems, and in my view it is of outsize importance for understanding the comparative differences that separate the continent from the United States. Degradation matters immensely, because the urge to degrade is of critical importance to the dynamic of punishment. When we view the person we are punishing as an inferior, as a person of lower status, we punish more harshly in every way. Conversely, when we regard the offender with respect, we punish more mildly. This helps us to understand why the prevalence of degradation in American punishment sustains the broad culture of American harshness.

But *why* is American punishment more degrading? It is here that we must turn to the historical understanding of the formation of American and continental cultures. In particular, we must understand the comparative history of status relations over the last two centuries. The continental commitment to the elimination of degradation in punishment is very old, and indeed is founded in resentments that date to the eighteenth century. Let us remember the social world that pre-dated the French Revolution. As of roughly 1750, everywhere in western Europe – as indeed, in all complex human societies – there were two classes of punishments: high-status punishments and low-status punishments.

These differences in the forms of punishment served everywhere as vivid markers of status differentiation. In the occident, the most familiar form of status differentiation came in the practices of execution. Following a tradition that reached back into antiquity in the western world, high-status persons were beheaded, while low-status persons were ordinarily hanged. The forms of execution made for a peculiarly resonant symbol, as they always do, but they were only one aspect of a wider system of status differentiation. Tradition held that imprisonment never served as a punishment as such for low-status prisoners. Nevertheless, in the eighteenth century, they were imprisoned in various settings, all of which subjected them to forced labour, ordinarily in chains, ordinarily whipped. In fact, this was not so much imprisonment as penal slavery, typically ending with an early death. Other more traditional forms of low-status punishment also continued: especially various forms of mutilation, branding and (once again) whipping. All of these low-status forms of punishment involved a good measure of humiliating public exposure.

But what happened to high-status persons who were not executed? For them, imprisonment *was* the ordinary punishment – but it was not the form of enslavement to which low-status persons were subjected. Quite the contrary: high-status persons – aristocrats, political agitators and the like – were subjected to what in France would later be called 'the special regime' and in Germany would later be called *Festungshaft*, fortress confinement. Typically held in fortresses or cloisters – the institutions that had held high-status prisoners since the Middle Ages – detainees like Voltaire or Mirabeau were confined to relatively pleasant apartments. They were permitted to wear their own clothing, to have servants, to enjoy visits from friends and doctors, to dine well and so on. And of course they engaged in intellectual activities. There was indeed a long tradition of prison writing, dating at least to Voltaire, and perhaps to Boethius and Ovid. And of course, high-status prisoners were shielded from public exposure.

The subsequent social history of punishment in continental Europe can be captured in a surprisingly simple formula. Over the last two and a half centuries, the high-status punishments have gradually driven the low-status punishments out. The commitment to ending the social practices of the *ancien régime* has expressed itself as a commitment to ending degradation in punishment. This has been a complex process of which I can only summarise broad outlines. Once again, the forms of execution offer the most symbolically resonant examples. After the

French Revolution, as we all know, beheading, the old high-status form of execution, was generalised to all citizens in both France and (eventually) Germany. This was a potent symbol indeed of a kind of high-status egalitarianism, ghoulish though it may seem. In fact, it mattered a great deal for the shape of revolutionary equality on the continent that, by the latter part of the nineteenth century, the section on punishment in all continental penal codes began with a version of the phrase *every person condemned to death shall be beheaded*. For those who believe that the only question of 'dignity' raised by the death penalty is whether we kill offenders or not, be advised: for a very long time, the principal question of dignity was *how* we killed them.

At any rate, the change in the form of the death penalty is only one aspect of a much broader pattern of change. As every European commentator of the nineteenth century knew, the history of punishment in their time was the history of the piecemeal abolition of the old forms of low-status, degrading, treatment. One by one, mutilation, branding, whipping, public exposure, degrading forced labour, humiliating uniforms – one by one, they were all abolished. This was a very slow process – indeed, hardly completed before the end of the twentieth century. But it happened. And what took the place of the old low-status punishments? This too is a complex story, and one that had hardly ended by the end of the twentieth century. Nevertheless, the fundamental answer is that, within the limits of the possible, the old terms of high-status 'fortress confinement' became normal for all offenders who were imprisoned – though even they became a minority. 'Fortress confinement', the 'special regime': these old high-status forms were slowly generalised, first to political prisoners and (in Germany) the 'morally upright'. By the 1970s and 1980s, the old rules for aristocrats and clerics applied, in principle, to every offender. This extension of high-status forms of punishment happened only within the limits of the possible: There is no way that every prisoner can be treated in the way that Voltaire was once treated. Nevertheless, within the limits of the possible, it happened.

Not so in the United States. The United States is a study in profound contrast – as is Britain. In the Anglo-American world, the old high-status punishments were not generalised. Instead, they were abolished. The decline in the old high-status punishments can probably be traced back as far as the early seventeenth century in England. But certainly by the 1750s, the Anglo-American tradition had taken a very different route. Hanging was generalised as the normal form of execution, where beheading was generalised on the continent. Once again, this is simply typical of a much broader pattern. The period after 1800 was of course one of the most famous in the history of American punishment: this was the period of the rise of the American penitentiary, which had a worldwide influence. Let me just emphasise the most important point for my purposes here: within the penitentiaries, the old low-status forms of punishment remained the norm. Prisoners were whipped, subjected to senseless forced labour, branded, and so on. Americans showed almost no sense that there was anything inappropriate about such degrading treatment. European observers, on the other hand, were shocked. This includes Beaumont and Tocqueville, the most famous of the European visitors to American penitentiaries. Beaumont and Tocqueville noted something that Americans themselves often noted: that American prisoners were treated as *penal slaves* – degraded, whipped – just as low-status persons had been before the Revolutions of 1789 and 1830. This worried the French observers, who were afraid that their countrymen would not accept a system that involved forms of degradation that had been abolished at home. Nevertheless, they expressed confidence that Americans would soon abandon such barbarities. They were wrong. Not only did whipping and the like continue – indeed, whipping has *never* been formally abolished in American prisons – but the American Constitution itself, in its Thirteenth Amendment, expressly permitted prisoners to be reduced to slaves. Indeed, until the mid-1970s, the technical status of American prisoners was 'slaves of the state', a phrase that American law borrowed from the ancient Romans and Greeks. In Britain too, the mid-nineteenth century saw the passage of so-called 'penal servitude' acts, and whipping was only abolished in 1948.

The main point is this: after 1750 or so, northern continental Europe levelled up, abolishing historically low-status punishment and extending relatively respectful high-status treatment to all offenders. After the same date, the United States and Britain levelled down, abolishing high-status treatment outright. Over the long run, this established a fateful toleration for degradation in punishment which survives into the present in my country.

II. The law of hate speech and of dignity in the workplace

The practices of punishment are always of special symbolic importance, and the rise of contemporary continental punishment makes for a peculiarly dramatic example of how modern 'human' dignity can grow out of a long history of status differentiation and status conflict. Punishment is only part of the law, though; and to get a full feel for the power of the social forces at work, we have to look further afield. When we do so, we discover that the symbolic pattern of punishment is only typical of a much wider pattern. French and German law display the same deep-seated commitment throughout the law: a commitment to guaranteeing norms of respect for historically low-status persons.

This is something we see, for example, in a wide range of legal topics all connected with the law of 'insult' – the law of 'injuries' or '*Beleidigung*'.[11] This body of law, which is entirely lacking in the United States, is the doctrinal descendant of the ancient Roman law of *injuria*. It is the classic body of law that protects the interest in 'personal honour'. And indeed, 'personal honour' is a protectable legal interest in continental systems – something that is simply not the case in my own country. This is a fact of critical comparative importance. It matters for the continental law of defamation, which vindicates two interests, the interest in reputation *and* the interest in honour. It also matters for the narrower law of insult itself. In the continental tradition, insults are actionable. This is especially true of Germany, where there is a lively popular culture of the law of *Beleidigung*. But it is also true to a lesser degree of France. The personal honour of a German or of a Frenchman is protected, and theoretically it is protected in all settings.

So where does the continental concern with personal honour come from? It should be no surprise to observe that, historically, the protection of 'personal honour' did not extend to all members of continental society. To be sure, in eighteenth-century Germany, the personal honour of persons on many levels of society was protected by the law. But that was not true of eighteenth-century France, and it was not true in either country in the nineteenth century. Well into the twentieth century, indeed, continental courts everywhere restricted the protection of 'personal honour' to *respectable* people. The law of insult in particular was a law that applied to people who were '*satisfaktionsfähig*', in the German term – who were of social status high enough that they might duel. Only since the First World War, and especially since the 1930s, have things changed. But since then they have changed extraordinarily. It is indeed little short of amazing to acknowledge how the protection of

---

[11] The following three paragraphs summarise work presented more fully in my 'Enforcing Civility and Respect: Three Societies' (2000) 109 *Yale Law Journal*, 1279–398.

personal honour has extended its social reach on the Continent. As we have just seen, it has extended into the prisons: even prison inmates, the persons of the lowest conceivable status, are protected by the law of insult in continental Europe. Even *they* must be addressed as 'Herr so-and-so' or 'Monsieur so-and-so'. This represents, it hardly needs to be said, an astounding expansion beyond the historic social limits of the law of insult. Other low-status persons have also come to benefit from similar protections.

This is most noticeably the case in an area of special importance for the comparison of American and European human rights regimes: the continental law of hate speech. At least in principle, it is forbidden, in continental Europe, to direct humiliating or disrespectful words at Jews or Turks or Gypsies. In practice, the law of hate speech in continental Europe has many obnoxious defects. Nevertheless, the fact remains that the personal honour of racial minorities enjoys protection in continental European law. Here again, the law of insult has breached its historic social limits. Most broadly, the same thing has happened in continental constitutional law. Some continental constitutions expressly guarantee the protection of personal honour for all. In the constitutional law of other countries, we see concepts of personal honour entering jurisprudence in various ways. Perhaps the most important expansion of the protection of personal honour is the protection of 'dignity' and 'personal dignity' as we find it in German constitutional law.

Today, probably the liveliest area in which these European traditions are expressing themselves is in the law of the workplace. All modern legal systems have to answer the same fundamental question: Do workers have the right to be treated respectfully? The answer in contemporary continental Europe, unsurprisingly, is *Yes*.[12] Indeed, the answer in continental Europe is not only *Yes*, but *Yes and increasingly so*: historically, it hardly needs to be said, continental law did not protect the right of low-status workers to respect in the workplace. On the contrary: the workplace law of insult was geared entirely towards guaranteeing the workers behaved deferentially towards their superiors. All that has changed dramatically over the last seventy years or so, and especially over the

---

[12] The following paragraphs summarise work presented more fully in James Whitman and Gabrielle Friedman, 'The European Transformation of Harassment Law: Discrimination Versus Dignity' (2003) 9 *Columbia Journal of European Law*, 241; and (for the historical background), Whitman, 'Nazi "Honour" and the New European "Dignity"', above, note 9, pp. 243–66.

last five or ten years. Particularly important and interesting is the rise of the law of something the Germans call 'Mobbing' and the French call 'moral harassment', '*harcèlement moral*'. The law of mobbing or moral harassment, completely unknown in the United States, is found everywhere in continental Europe, sometimes in statutory form (as in France), sometimes through juristic interpretation (as in Germany), sometimes in a burgeoning popular culture of the law. It is a relatively new area of the law – though one with some very old roots. In part it is founded on studies in industrial psychology. But of course it has an older pre-history as well, and a pre-history that has to do once again with the continental predilection for 'personal honour'.

The law of 'moral harassment' or 'mobbing' concerns itself with a long list of workplace sins. But in point of fact many of those sins, inevitably, represent slights to individual *dignity*, of the type that were once regulated by the law of insult. 'Moral harassment', in the continental mind, includes insults. It also includes assigning workers tasks that are beneath their dignity, such as photocopying. Most generally, it includes conduct that makes workers feel singled out, shamed – conduct that makes workers feel anything less than members of the community of equal worth. Perhaps most strikingly, from the American point of view, the movement against *moral* harassment has begun to change the continental attitude towards *sexual* harassment. The law of sexual harassment was theoretically imported into continental Europe from the United States. But it is a body of law that has never meant the same thing in France or Germany that it has meant in its country of birth. The American law of sexual harassment, at its core, is a law that protects a *financial* interest, an interest in *career advancement*. It has in effect never protected an interest in dignity as such. It hardly could, in a country in which there is no tradition of protecting personal honour. Inevitably, things are different in Europe. From the beginning, the continental law of sexual harassment has been a law that protects an interest in the victim's *dignity*. This is true by statute in Germany, where the legislator chose specifically to protect '*Würde*'. It has been true in the decisional law of France as well, where courts have taken it for granted that '*dignité*' must somehow be at stake, even though the French statute has never used the term. It is true on the European level too. Europeans may think that they have adopted the American law of sexual harassment. In fact, they have *adapted* it, making it a law of interpersonal respect and dignity of the continental type.

The world of continental workers is thus akin to the world of continental prison inmates, or to the world of continental racial minorities.

These are worlds in which the law reflects a felt social need, a felt social imperative. It is the imperative to extend norms of respectful treatment to everybody in the population, and especially to persons of historically low status. It is a world transformed since 1770 or 1870, or indeed since 1920, and what has transformed it is not just a redistribution of wealth. There has also been a redistribution of honour. Everyone – such at least is the ambition of the law – is supposed to count as a high-status person.

All this is utterly alien to anything we find in the contemporary United States. Paradoxically, Europeans typically imagine that the law against 'mobbing' is an American invention. Nothing could be further from the truth. In fact, the term, and the concept, are essentially unknown in the United States. In a way entirely typical of American law, workers in fact enjoy essentially no protections of the European kind for their dignity in the workplace. As for hate speech: American constitutional law is legendary for its resistance to any such doctrine. Protection of personal honour is simply not a matter of concern for American law.

III. The law of privacy

I will observe only in the briefest way that similar things can be said of the law of privacy. Europeans sometimes assert that privacy is not protected in the United States at all. This is something that was said with particular vehemence and relish after the notorious Monica Lewinsky scandals;[13] but the Lewinsky matter is by no means the only example of an American law that can seem disturbingly oblivious to privacy interests.[14] Yet of course there is something strange about saying that Americans do not care about privacy: anybody who has spent time in the United States knows that we are as obsessed with the topic as our continental cousins. There is a large volume of American law on privacy, dating back in particular to the famous 1890 article of Warren and Brandeis, 'The Right to Privacy'.[15] Today we can point to common-law, statutory and constitutional protections for 'privacy' in the United States, and some of the most controversial social issues, such as

---

[13] E.g. 'Le Recours à l'intimité est de règle aux Etats-Unis', *Le Monde*, 22 April 2002.

[14] This section summarises research presented more fully in James Q. Whitman, 'The Two Western Cultures of Privacy: Dignity versus Liberty' (2004) *Yale Law Journal*, 1151–1221.

[15] Samuel Warren and Louis D. Brandeis, 'The Right to Privacy' (1890) 4 *Harvard Law Review*, 193–220.

abortion, have been framed as 'privacy' questions.[16] It is manifestly false to say that Americans do not care about privacy. What then is the difference?

The fundamental answer is that while 'privacy' matters everywhere in the west, in practice the core conception of 'privacy' differs on either side of the Atlantic. To put it in an overly simplified formula: American privacy protections are, at their conceptual core, protections against the *state*; while European privacy protections are, at their conceptual core, protections against *the media* and *the general public*.

Thus the European right of privacy is, at its base, a right to the control over one's image, and especially to keep one's name and photograph out of the newspapers. This is a concept of privacy whose history dates well back into the early nineteenth century. It bears a close and evident connection to concepts of personal honour.[17] It hardly needs to be added that it is a concept of privacy whose link to high-status patterns of behaviour is written on its face. One is tempted indeed to call it a 'Princess Caroline of Monaco' concept of privacy:[18] What sort of person, after all, is worried about keeping his name or image out of the newspapers? And indeed, as we trace its history into the nineteenth century, we discover, unsurprisingly, that the protection of continental 'privacy' was at first a protection afforded overwhelmingly to members of high society.[19] But to say that it is a high-status concept of privacy is not to deny the moral force of the continental urge to extend these protections to everybody. On the contrary: the progress of 'privacy' in continental law has been the product of the same noble, and morally serious, urge I have been tracing throughout: the urge to guarantee that everyone should benefit from high-status treatment. It is an urge that is absent in the United States.

---

[16] For a survey, see Richard Turkington and Anita Allen, *Privacy Law: Cases and Materials*, (2nd edn, Saint Paul: West, 2002).

[17] Indeed, its doctrinal roots lie once again in the law of insult, for early examples in France: Amable Guillaume Prosper Brugière, baron de Barante, *La Vie politique de monsieur Royer-Collard, ses discourses et ses écrits* (Paris: Didier, 1863), vol. I, pp. 474–5; Loi Relative à la Presse, 11 Mai 1868, Art. 11; for the German history: Dieter Leuze, *Die Entwicklung des Persönlichkeitsrechts im 19. Jahrhundert* (Bielefeld: Gieseking, 1962); Wolfgang Pleister, *Persönlichkeit, Wille und Freiheit im Werke Jherings* (Ebelsbach: Gremer, 1982), pp. 203–5.

[18] Cf. *Caroline von Monaco II*, BVerfGE 101, 361.

[19] E.g. *Moitessier c. Féral*, in (1878) 23 *Annales de la Propriété Industrielle, Artistique et Littéraire*, 93–5.

Of course, the protection of one's image is not entirely alien to American law. Nevertheless it is a commonplace that such protection is in practice weak, and indeed shockingly weak from the European point of view.[20] As the Lewinsky scandals suggest, there is little by way of protections against such invasions of privacy in American practice. What is it, then, that American law protects? The fundamental answer is that American concerns about privacy are concerns that reflect primarily anxieties about invasions on the part of the state. It is for this reason, most obviously, that the abortion question can be conceived as presenting the key privacy problem in the United States – alongside many other problems whose origins lie in the Fourth Amendment's regulation of criminal procedure. Americans care primarily about keeping the government out of their affairs. To repeat, this does not mean that the continental concept of privacy is wholly absent: the differences I describe are relative, and not absolute. Those differences are unmistakably present, though: by and large, Americans simply do not share the continental obsession with the control over one's image as an aspect of the maintenance of personal honour. So it is that Americans experience comparatively little anxiety over whether they can control the dissemination of their consumer information, just as they experience comparatively little anxiety over the intrusive use of discovery in civil procedure.[21] Underlying sensibilities about the control of one's image simply differ in these two worlds.

They differ similarly when it comes to the state. Indeed, when we focus on state intrusions, we discover that it is continental law that seems, to the American eye, to lack protections for privacy. Continental law includes many protections against state violations of privacy, of course: the differences, to say it again, are relative and not absolute. Nevertheless, there are many recesses of the continental world in which we can detect the absence of an American sensibility. One thinks, for example, of the continental practice of allowing the state to maintain a list of permissible baby names.[22] This is a practice that would be simply inconceivable in the United States, and that would seem to Americans to constitute a flagrant violation of privacy rights. Or again, one thinks of

---

[20] For a vigorous, readable and indignant study, see Jeffrey Rosen, *The Unwanted Gaze: the Destruction of Privacy in America* (New York: Random House, 2000).

[21] Cf. Oscar G. Chase, 'American "Exceptionalism" and Comparative Procedure' (2002) 50 *American Journal of Comparative Law*, 277–301.

[22] Compare the decision Eur. Ct. H. R., *Guillot* v. *France*, Reports 1996–V, S. 1593.

the German *Meldepflicht*, the obligation to be registered with the authorities at all times.[23] The *Meldepflicht* seems like an irksome duty to ordinary Germans, but it does not seem a fundamental violation of privacy rights. That is exactly how it would surely seem to ordinary Americans.

IV. Conclusion

In all of these things, we see the consequences of the same continental sensibility – a sensibility one might call, both mockingly and admiringly, a Princess-Caroline-of-Monaco sensibility. Everyone in continental Europe is supposed to be entitled to respect. This pattern does not, of course, capture every aspect of European law about 'human dignity', nor every nuance of European mentalities. There remain many other corners of European law, some of them very dark and mysterious to Americans. One thinks, for example, of European anxieties over genetically modified food – anxieties that seem passing strange to an American, and that have no obvious connection to the history of status I have focused on here. Questions of historic status do not make themselves felt everywhere.

Nevertheless, those questions do make themselves felt over the most remarkable range of legal topics. 'Dignity' of the kind I have described matters *throughout* French and German law, and it is more or less absent *throughout* American law. Indeed, the differences that I have discussed show how much profit there is in regarding grand questions of constitutional law against the background of everyday social beliefs and sensibilities. The law, even in its most intellectually ambitious and grandiose moments, is the product of quotidian prejudices and assumptions. This is as true of 'human dignity', magnificent as it sounds, as it is of any other legal construct. Human dignity, as continental lawyers advocate it, is the product of continental traditions and continental resentments. That hardly means that there is anything wrong, dishonourable, or unattractive about continental ideas. It means only that we must try to look beneath what lawyers are saying if we are to explain why what they say seems appealing to the people to whom they address themselves. Legal ideas never seem legitimate on the strength of their own coherence or beauty. They seem legitimate only if they speak to the beliefs and anxieties of a given culture. The right way to characterise this phenomenon is to invoke, without embarrassment, Montesquieu, saying that the

---

[23] Melderechtsrahmengesetz (MRRG) of 24 June 1994.

spirit of the law differs on either side of the Atlantic. And it differs because social traditions differ.

Comparative law will thus always grope blindly if it does not allow itself to be guided by historical sociology. For that matter, historical sociology has a great deal to gain from comparative law. Indeed, the research I offer here sheds some useful light on our sociology. The idea that continental culture is the product of a generalisation of high-status norms is not new: As I have already noted, Norbert Elias and Pierre Bourdieu have famously made that argument, and Rudolf von Jhering made it long before them. Most recently, the same claim has been offered by Philippe d'Iribarne. All of these authors speak of the pattern of the generalisation of high-status norms as though it were universal, however. It is not. It is a continental pattern, distinctly not shared by the United States, just as it is probably not shared by contemporary China. Something similar can be said of the sociology of Tocqueville, who believed that 'democracy' meant the end of aristocratic values. This is true of the United States, but distinctly false of Tocqueville's own continental Europe. There is in short no single model of modernity, but at least two.

Finally, let me not be misunderstood: my claim is not that either of these western patterns lacks equality. Both American society and the societies of northern continental Europe are *egalitarian* societies. What we must understand, though, is that human societies display more than one form of equality. There is equality at the high end of the historic status ladder, and equality at the low end. We may prefer one of these forms of equality over the other, but nothing in the abstract concept of equality itself dictates any choice between the two. The choice we make is the product of political preference, conditioned by generations of historical experience – or to state it a shade more forcefully, by generations of *ressentiment*.

Comment

EYAL BENVENISTI

Bognetti's paper analyses the work done by the concept of human dignity in European and US constitutional law. Whitman explores the underlying social forces that led to the adoption of the human dignity concept in Europe and its more limited role in the United States. Despite the different approaches both papers expose one fundamental difference between the US and continental Europe with respect to the role of law in society, in particular constitutional law. Whereas the US attitude reflects a strong belief in the markets: economic, political, social, marketplaces of ideas, to protect reputation for example, Europe demonstrates misgivings about the strengths of these markets and favours governmental involvement, including judicial involvement to protect personal honour. Bognetti's observation about a shift in the US Supreme Court's approach during the 1930s, with respect to its role, from protecting the economic market during the Lockner era to protecting the political market is pertinent. This shift is very clear in the decision of Carolene Products in 1938. The concept of human dignity was not necessary for that task. In contrast, Bognetti shows how the human dignity concept is used in continental Europe as a judicial tool to explain the increasingly active role of the courts in protecting the economic market: to protect against market failures and promote welfare policies. It is important, I think, to note that the human dignity concept in and of itself is neither a necessary nor a sufficient concept to explain a more active role for legal regulation. It is not a necessary tool, because courts can explain intervention in the market and welfare policies by using the concept of equality. Welfare policies can be described as providing equal opportunities or correcting past wrongs. Human dignity is not a sufficient tool, because courts that see their role as limited can restrict its meaning to its most basic message: namely, that all human beings should be treated as human beings, regardless of their gender, race or religions. This message says nothing about welfare or market regulations. And, in fact, the human dignity concept can even be used to explain why State efforts to promote disadvantaged groups are unconstitutional.

To give one example: human dignity was used by the US Supreme Court to subject race-based preferences to the strict scrutiny test which led to their rejection. Justice Kennedy explains in *Rice v. Cayetano* (2000) that classifications based on race, even if designed to promote historically disadvantaged minorities, are forbidden under the US Constitution, because 'it demeans the dignity and worth of a person to be judged by ancestry instead of by his or her own merit and essential qualities'. If human dignity is neither necessary nor sufficient to explain state intervention in the markets, why was it chosen? The answer lies in my view in what Bognetti and Nolte refer to as the universalist message that permeates the international law of human rights and post-WWII state constitutions. This universalist message is one that Whitman does not address. He views dignity as an *intra*-societal matter whereas its deeper universalist message is an *inter*-societal one. What Whitman does not sufficiently address, I think, is the tension between dignity and *human* dignity. These two terms carry remarkably different meanings. The concept of human dignity does not necessarily imply protection of reputation or honour, not even respect as such. It implies respect to each individual *qua* individual. Its message is universalistic, positing that each human being is subject to the same basic rights and freedoms regardless of race, gender, nationality, etc., but, not necessarily, and certainly not only, the right to protection of honour. And so this discussion identifies, I think, a second difference between the United States and Europe. This is a different attitude towards the human person who is subject to constitutional protection. Post-WWII Europe embraced a universalist sentiment moving away from nationalism and the concomitant distinction between citizens and non-citizens. As Nolte puts it, Europe has embraced a concept that would reflect the worthiness of a human person *qua* person. The US remains suspicious about aliens and continues to celebrate citizenship as one of the strongest ties, if not the only tie, that binds Americans together. Whereas equality leaves open the question 'equality between whom', human dignity provides a clear and universalistic answer. Human dignity aims at blurring and limiting the distinction between citizens and others in the context of constitutional protection. It stipulates that the government may have duties towards non-citizens at home and even abroad. Even in wartime. It implies commitment to international law in general, and human rights law in particular. It challenges the distinction between 'we, the people' and 'aliens'. It questions why civil rights merit protection, while human rights do not.

It is beyond the scope of this comment to offer alternative suggestions as to why American anxieties project themselves in the context of distinguishing between US citizens or non-US citizens, whereas continental Europe is more comfortable with reducing barriers between different citizens. Perhaps this is a European reaction to the nineteenth-century nationalism and twentieth-century devastating wars. Perhaps it reflects the American preoccupation with limiting access to the new world. Germany, France or Italy may rely on social or other paralegal systems to define their demos or nation, and do not need the law for that. In contrast, the American society may be comfortable with leaving issues of personal honour beyond legal regulation, but needs the law to sharpen distinction between members and non-members, perhaps to regulate entry to the unregulated markets.

Or perhaps the weakness of human dignity in American law derives from its international pedigree. Rubenfeld analyses the US difficulty with the legitimacy of international law. Human rights in general, and human dignity in particular, suffer from democratic deficiencies in American eyes. But human dignity is not intimately linked to international law. One can be dismissive about international law but embrace the universalist vision of human dignity.

Let me end by invoking the Israeli jurisprudence. Israel shares the US concern with international law. Israelis, even more than Americans, view international law with much concern and even hostility. Thus, the Israeli Court has difficulty invoking international law as an authority in its decisions. But the Israeli court can and does invoke the *Israeli* law on human dignity. And, in fact, in the last ten years it has developed the concept of human dignity following the European model. But in Israel, human dignity as such is an Israeli concept, namely based on the Israeli Basic Law. It serves as a powerful justification to extend constitutional protection to non-Israelis also beyond the Israeli borders.

Comment

HUGH CORDER

In this comment I will try to do two things. First, I will refer to some aspects in the papers of Whitman and Bognetti which resonate with the South African experience. Secondly, I will briefly set out the extent to which the right to human dignity has become very rapidly a central feature of South African constitutional law over the past decade since political liberation and the advent of a written constitution.

In Nolte's discussion of human dignity,[1] the sentence which summed it up for me, and which Benvenisti also relies on, was that 'the interests of a human person *qua* person, which are not explicitly protected by the constitution, seem to have a greater chance of recognition in Europe than in the United States'. That certainly was the theme which resonates most with our experience in South Africa. Whitman's paper characterises the United States, and particularly its criminal justice system, as a harsh place, a place where conflicts of cultures take place, and vividly describes the degrading criminal punishment system and the notion of higher-status treatment being gradually extended to lower-status persons. All this too resonates hugely with anybody who has had any experience with South Africa, where we have in our prison regime followed Britain and the United States, with status until recently being determined by race.[2] There is no question that anybody would be addressed as Mr or Ms or Mrs in the South African criminal justice system.

On the other hand, when one moves to Whitman's discussion of privacy, that is something alien to our experience, because in that area our whole law of delict and particularly defamation is based on the

---

[1] Georg Nolte, above, 'European and U.S. constitutionalism: comparing essential elements' in this volume at pp. 10–13.

[2] See the leading authority on prison law in South Africa, Dirk van Zyl Smit, *South African Prison Law and Practice* (Durban: Butterworths, 1992).

Roman concept of *injuria* and that is the value system which infuses our legal system.[3]

In the context of Bognetti's description of the phases of constitutionalism, again South Africa clearly falls, with the development of its current constitution,[4] into the category of 'democratic-social'. The sentence which strikes me as relevant is: 'Europe is more prone to embody social values and less ready to defend extreme boundaries of liberty in the field of expression.'[5] Once more, the discussion of horizontality sounds very familiar to South African ears.[6]

So where is dignity in the South African constitutional system of today? In general, without indicating a preference, it will be quite clear that South Africa, by inclination, by historical context, by the drafting influences in its constitution[7] and by judicial approach has developed a strongly 'European' style. There are two obvious comments in the context of the discussion of human dignity.

Firstly, above all the evil things that were done in the name of Apartheid, perhaps the most striking was that the system was fundamentally an affront to the human dignity of every single South African: mostly black, but also white South Africans were demeaned. Human dignity was overwhelmingly undermined by policies of segregation and Apartheid over several centuries.

Secondly, South Africa as a legal system has come only lately to embrace the values of constitutionalism and constitutional democracy. Our current constitution is less than ten years old.[8] We were therefore able to draw in the drafting process substantially on the lessons learned

---

[3] See the discussion in Jonathan Burchell, *Principles of Delict* (Cape Town: Juta, 1993). The best general overview of the origins and development of this system is to be found in Herman R. Hahlo and Ellison Kahn, *The South African Legal System and its Background* (Cape Town: Juta, 1968).

[4] Constitution of the Republic of South Africa, Act 108 of 1996, the 'final Constitution' which came into force on 4 February 1997.

[5] Giovanni Bognetti, 'The concept of human dignity in European and American constitutionalism', in this volume p. 85.

[6] The Bill of Rights in the Constitution provides for a degree of direct horizontality (Section 8) as well as indirect horizontality through the 'realignment' of the common law with the values of the Constitution (Section 39(2)).

[7] For details of which see Richard Spitz and Matthew Chaskalson, *The Politics of Transition* (Johannesburg: Witwatersrand University Press, 2000) and Lourens du Plessis and Hugh Corder, *Understanding South Africa's Transitional Bill of Rights* (Cape Town: Juta, 1994).

[8] The final Constitution was preceded by the transitional or interim Constitution, Act 200 of 1993, which acted as the 'bridge' between the apartheid regime and the first democratically elected Parliament, of April 1994.

by centuries of constitutional democracy in Europe and the United States and to be influenced by some of the more recent developments in the second half of the twentieth century. So the experiences of Canada as a member of the British Commonwealth, with its Charter of Fundamental Rights and Freedoms in 1982, and Germany, particularly with its constitutional expression of the move away from Nazism, resonated with the drafters of the South African constitution.[9] Naturally, we could also rely on the language of the United Nations Charter, the Universal Declaration of Human Rights and various other international documents in regard to the protection of human rights. Within Africa we have the Preamble to the Charter of the Organisation of African Unity of 1963 and the African Charter, also known as the Banjul Charter, of 1981. In order to emphasise the importance of the doctrines and values of international law, the Constitution of South Africa provides expressly for the circumstances in which it plays a role in the determination of legal disputes (see Sections 231 to 233).

The provisions in the South African Constitution related to dignity are sixfold.

Firstly, the founding values of the Constitution are to be seen in Section 1 as follows: 'South Africa is one sovereign democratic State founded on the following values: ... Human dignity, the achievement of equality and the advancement of human rights and freedoms. ...'[10]

Secondly, Section 7(1), the Preamble to the Bill of Rights, provides that: 'The Bill of Rights is a corner-stone of democracy in South Africa. It enshrines the rights of all people in our country and affirms the democratic values of human dignity, equality and freedom.'

Thirdly, the right to human dignity in Section 10 reads: 'Everyone has inherent dignity and the right to have that dignity respected and protected.'

Fourthly, the general limitations clause in Section 36(1) stipulates that: 'The rights in the Bill of Rights may be limited only in terms of law of general application to the extent that the limitation is reasonable and justifiable in an open and democratic society based on human dignity, equality and freedom ...'

---

[9] See the works cited above, note 7.

[10] This section is the most protected provision in the Constitution, requiring a 75 per cent majority in the National Assembly to amend it as opposed to the more usual two-thirds majority support needed for a constitutional amendment – see the Constitution, Section 74.

Fifthly, Section 37(5) provides that in a state of emergency one of the non-derogable rights is the right to human dignity.

And finally, Section 39(1) requires that, 'when interpreting the Bill of Rights, a court, tribunal or forum must promote the values that underlie an open and democratic society based on human dignity, equality and freedom'.

It is clear, therefore, as was the case in the interim constitution, that dignity features large. Its influence in practice has been considerable.[11] I note seven areas in which it has been expressed.[12]

Firstly, in regard to dignity *as an underlying value*, the South African Constitutional Court has frequently expressed itself on this point. Effectively it comes down to this: dignity is relevant in three ways: to determine whether there has been discrimination; to determine whether that discrimination is unfair; and, if unfair, to determine whether the discrimination is unjustifiable.[13] This approach is particularly relevant in relation to disputes which turn on equality. Moving on to the intimate relationship between *dignity* and *equality* the court has said in its earliest judgments: 'In our view unfair discrimination principally means treating people differently in a way which impairs their fundamental dignity as human beings who are inherently equal in dignity.'[14] In regard to *dignity* and *personal freedom*, again one of the earlier judgments of the court in 1995 provides a good illustration: 'Human dignity has little value without freedom: for without freedom ... human dignity is little more than an abstraction. Freedom and dignity are inseparably linked. To deny people freedom is to deny them their dignity.'[15]

The second point concerns *dignity* and *punishment*. In the first and seminal judgment of the Constitutional Court in which the death penalty was outlawed, the *State v. Makwanyane* decision,[16] each of the eleven judges gave a separate concurring opinion and each concurred in the opinion of the President of the Court. The judgments proceeded from the following starting point: the rights to life and dignity above all

---

[11] A good discussion of this influence can be found in Susie Cowen, 'Can "Dignity" Guide South Africa's Equality Jurisprudence?' (2001) 17 *South African Journal on Human Rights*, 34–58 and Arthur Chaskalson, 'Human Dignity as a Foundational Value of our Constitutional Order' (2000) 16 *South African Journal on Human Rights*, 193–205; I have found these particularly useful in preparing what follows.

[12] To some extent I have been guided by the approach of Johan de Waal, Iain Currie and Gerhard Erasmus, *The Bill of Rights Handbook* (4th edn, Cape Town: Juta, 2001), chapter 10.

[13] See Cowen, 'Dignity', above, note 11, 36–7.

[14] *Prinsloo* v. *Van der Linde* 1997 (3) SA 1012 (CC).

[15] *Ferreira* v. *Levin NO* 1996 (1) SA 984 (CC) at para. 49.   [16] 1995 (3) SA 391 (CC).

others give content to the right against cruel, inhuman and degrading punishment which is the fundamental basis the Court used for outlawing the death penalty. That same year, respect for human dignity was deemed to include an acceptance by society that even 'the vilest criminal remains a human being possessed of common human dignity'.[17] This resonates with the European approach to the treatment of prisoners, at least in theory in South Africa, although much remains to be done to translate it into practice. In regard to dignity and life imprisonment, on which the Court has yet to rule, again the approach likely to be followed is that in Germany, that it would violate human dignity simply to banish a prisoner to a cell without hope of release.[18]

Thirdly, in regard to *dignity* and *the law of delict*, it must be noted that the South African Constitution is now spreading the tentacles of its value system generally into private law and particularly into the field of defamation. It does this through the provision for the horizontal operation of the Bill of Rights (Section 8), as well as the obligation (Section 39) of the courts to develop the common law in accordance with the values of the Bill of Rights. In this regard, human dignity is the key value in determining the existence and extent of *injuria*, thus strengthening the traditional approach of the common law.[19]

Fourthly, in regard to *marriage and family life*, the South African Constitutional Court has recently used the dignity argument to hold that same-sex couples should be accorded the legal capacity to jointly adopt a child.[20] In the words of another judgment: 'A central aspect of marriage is cohabitation, the right (and duty) to live together, and legislation that significantly impairs the ability of spouses to honour that obligation would also constitute a limitation of the right to human dignity'.[21]

Fifthly, most critically, human dignity helps as a transformative value to give *expression to socio-economic* rights, of which we have several in our Constitution.[22] Our Chief Justice has said in an extra-curial piece: 'As an abstract value common to the core values of our Constitution, dignity informs the content of all the concrete rights and plays a role in the balancing process necessary to bring different rights and values into

---

[17] In *S. v. Williams* 1995 (3) SA 632 (CC) at para. 58.
[18] See De Waal et al., *The Bill of Rights Handbook*, above, note 12, p. 35.
[19] On this issue, see Burchell, *Principles of Delict*, above, note 3.
[20] *Du Toit* v. *Minister for Welfare and Population Development* 2002 (10) BCLR 1006.
[21] *Dawood* v. *Minister of Home Affairs* 2000 (3) SA 936 (CC), at para. 37.
[22] Notably in Sections 26 and 27, in respect of housing, health care, food, water and social security.

harmony. It too, however, must find its place in the constitutional order. Nowhere is this more apparent than in the application of the social and economic rights entrenched in the Constitution … These rights are rooted in respect for human dignity, for how can there be dignity in a life lived without access to [basic services]?'[23]

Sixthly, *dignity as a collective right* has begun to assume importance.[24] This is an aspect which has not come out in other presentations, but in the South African context reliance is placed not on the work of Immanuel Kant but on the concept of something called *Ubuntu*. This is a distinctly African notion, and it effectively means that 'a person is a person because of other people' or 'a person achieves personhood through the quality of their association with other people'. The courts gave prominence to this idea in the first judgment, the death penalty decision, and have built upon that subsequently.[25] Thus the idea of the collective nature of dignity has become a prominent element in our law.

Finally, dignity is regarded as a *forward-looking concept*. It is especially helpful in the sphere of the implementation of socioeconomic rights that dignity is seen as a constantly developing expression of human advancement.[26] In the oft-quoted words[27] of retired Justice Brennan of the Supreme Court of the United States: 'I do not mean to suggest that we have in the last quarter of the century achieved a comprehensive definition of the constitutional ideal of human dignity … For if the interaction of this Justice and the constitutional text over the years confirms any single proposition, it is that the demands of human dignity will never cease to evolve.'

To conclude: it is clear that dignity is the single most significant value, but its meaning remains deliberately vague in the South African constitutional jurisprudence. The courts have used it almost as a vehicle, as a means to other ends, as a social value. Perhaps we can rest content with that at present for, in the words[28] of a famous American, Bob Dylan, although not often quoted in legal circles:

> 'Trying to read a note that someone wrote about dignity …
> Someone showed me a picture and I just laughed
> Dignity [has] never been photographed …
> Sometimes I wonder what it's gonna take to find dignity …'

---

[23] See Chaskalson, 'Human Dignity', above, note 11, 204.
[24] See Cowen, 'Dignity', above, note 11, 50–4.
[25] Such as *S. v. Makwanyane* 1995 (3) SA 391 (CC) at paras. 224, 263 and 308.
[26] See Cowen, 'Dignity', above, note 11, 54–8.
[27] See Chaskalson, 'Human Dignity', above, note 11, 205.
[28] In the song 'Dignity', originally released in May 1995.

PART IV

The protective function

6

The protective function of the state

DIETER GRIMM

I. The different approaches in German and US constitutional law

The question whether the state must only *respect* or also actively *protect* fundamental rights still divides US and German constitutional doctrine and practice. In its *First Abortion Decision* of 1975, the German Constitutional Court explicitly recognised that the *Grundgesetz* imposes a duty on the state to protect fundamental rights against intrusions by third parties. The court argued: 'The obligation of the state to furnish protection is comprehensive. It forbids not only – self-evidently – direct state attacks on developing life, but also requires the state to take a position protecting and promoting this life, that is to say, it must, above all, preserve it against illegal attacks by others.'[1] In sharp contrast, Chief Justice Rehnquist wrote for the US Supreme Court in *DeShaney v. Winnebago County*: 'Nothing in the language of the due process clause requires the state to protect the life, liberty, and property of its citizens against invasion by private actors. ... Its purpose was to protect the people from the state, not to insure that the state protected them from each other. The framers were content to leave the extent of governmental obligation in the latter area to the democratic political processes.'[2]

The German Court left no doubt as to whose task it was to fulfil the duty to protect. The decision concerned an amendment to the Penal Code permitting abortions during the first three months of pregnancy. The Court declared this amendment to be unconstitutional because the

---

[1] BVerfGE 39, 1 at 42; English translation in Donald P. Kommers, *The Constitutional Jurisprudence of the Federal Republic of Germany* (2nd edn, Durham: Duke University Press, 1997), pp. 336 et seqq.; Vicki C. Jackson and Mark Tushnet, *Comparative Constitutional Law* (New York: Foundation Press, 1999), pp. 115 et seqq.; Norman Dorsen, Michel Rosenfeld, Andras Sajo and Susanne Baer, *Comparative Constitutionalism* (St Paul: Thomson/West, 2003), pp. 542 et seqq.
[2] *DeShaney* v. *Winnebago County Department of Social Services*, 489 U.S. 189 (1989).

legislature had thereby failed to sufficiently protect unborn life. Consequently, the legislature was obliged to repair the law. The US Supreme Court, on the contrary, has never gone so far as to impose an obligation to legislate on Congress. Two judgments concerning freedom of broadcasting show the difference quite clearly. Both Courts started from the assumption that this freedom is not guaranteed in the interest of the broadcaster or the journalists but in the interest of the general public and of democratic government. Yet, the German Court concluded from this that parliament *must* regulate broadcasting, whereas the American Supreme Court came to the conclusion that Congress *may* regulate broadcasting.[3] Hence, the difference is not only one of fundamental rights theory. It extends to the institutional relationship between the legislature and the judiciary as well. In Germany, the Constitutional Court cannot only declare a law null and void when the legislature went too far in limiting a fundamental right, but also when it did too little in order to protect a fundamental right against injury by private actors. The US Supreme Court refuses to recognise such a power. How can this difference be explained?

II. Historical roots

One may be inclined to attribute the striking difference to text and time. The American Bill of Rights dates back to the eighteenth century. The German *Grundgesetz* was enacted only after the Second World War. And, of course, the texts differ. But both documents are framed in the traditional liberal manner, and no clear intention to add a positive function to the negative one can be found in the *Grundgesetz*. Regarding time, it is quite common to call the negative function of fundamental rights the classical function, meaning also that it is their original function. As a matter of fact, this was the argument of the Austrian Constitutional Court when it reviewed an abortion law that looked more or less like the German one. The Court argued that the Austrian Bill of Rights dates from 1867 when liberalism was at its peak and fundamental rights were exclusively understood as limits to state action. Since the state neither undertook abortions itself nor required

---

[3] BVerfGE 12, 205 at 263 (1961); and even more clearly BVerfGE 57, 295 at 319 et seqq. (1981); English translation in: *Decisions of the Bundesverfassungsgericht*, vol. 2 part I, (Baden-Baden: Nomos, 1998), pp. 31 et seqq. and pp. 199 et seqq.; *Red Lion Broadcasting Co., Inc., et al. v. Federal Communications Commission et al.*, 395 U.S. 367 (1969).

private persons to perform abortions, the Court was unable to identify a constitutional issue regarding the abortion law.[4]

Yet, a closer look at the historical origins shows that the difference in time does not fully explain the difference in function. The classical theory correctly describes the American but not the European situation.[5] The difference has its roots in the eighteenth century, when the idea of innate rights that the state had to recognise and respect was turned into binding law, first in the American Revolution in 1776, then in the French Revolution in 1789. The different circumstances under which these two revolutions occurred and, caused by these circumstances, their different purposes can supply an explanation: the American Revolution aimed at independence from the British motherland and at self-government. The French Revolution aimed primarily at a different social and legal order, and only when it became clear that the desired reform could not be reached within the framework of the existing political order did the French revolutionaries move to overthrow the monarchical government. In Europe the political revolution was a means to achieve social reform, in North America political reform was an end in itself.[6]

This difference had consequences for the function of fundamental rights. The American colonists lived under the English legal order, yet without the remnants of the feudal and the canon law still alive in their motherland. They enjoyed the rights of Englishmen and they invoked these rights when they felt unlawfully treated by the British motherland. They were forced to realise, however, that in the English legal system these rights were fundamental, but not supreme.[7] Supremacy, on the contrary, was attributed to Parliament. Parliament was not subject to fundamental rights, but placed above them. From this the Americans

---

[4] VfSlg 7400/1974.

[5] Dieter Grimm, 'Grundrechte und Privatrecht in der bürgerlichen Sozialordnung', in Günter Birtsch (ed.), *Grund- und Freiheitsrechte im Wandel von Gesellschaft und Geschichte* (Göttingen: Vandenhoeck and Ruprecht, 1981), pp. 359 et seqq.; also in Dieter Grimm, *Recht und Staat der bürgerlichen Gesellschaft* (Frankfurt: Suhrkamp, 1987), pp. 192 et seqq.; Dieter Grimm, 'Die Grundrechte im Entstehungszusammenhang der bürgerlichen Gesellschaft', in Jürgen Kocka (ed.), *Bürgertum im 19. Jahrhundert* (3 vols., Munich: dtv, 1988), vol. I, pp. 340 et seqq.; also in Dieter Grimm, *Die Zukunft der Verfassung* (3rd edn, Frankfurt: Suhrkamp, 2002), pp. 67 et seqq.

[6] Jürgen Habermas, 'Naturrecht und Revolution', in Jürgen Habermas, *Theorie und Praxis* (Neuwied: Luchterhand, 1963), pp. 52 et seqq.

[7] For this difference see Gerald Stourzh, *Wege zur Grundrechtsdemokratie* (Vienna: Böhlau, 1989), no. 1–8; Gerald Stourzh, *Alexander Hamilton and the Idea of Republican Government* (Stanford: Stanford University Press, 1970).

concluded that the rights of Englishmen, as good as they might have been in substance, were inferior in rank and therefore unsafe. Consequently, the colonists referred to natural law as the true source of fundamental rights in order to justify the break with the motherland. In establishing their own political system, they placed these rights above government, the legislature included. Hence, the function of fundamental rights was to make the pre-existing liberty more secure by preventing government, including its legislative branch, from interfering in individual rights. To fulfil this function negative rights were sufficient.

The pre-revolutionary French legal system was the opposite of a liberal order. It was characterised by the feudal structure of society, a thoroughly regulated economy and the claimed right of the absolutist monarch to control all spheres of life according to his superior insight into the common good. The French Revolution aimed at modernising society by abolishing feudalism and paternalism and replacing them by a legal order based on the principles of individual freedom and equality. But instead of immediately taking up this task the National Assembly decided to start with a declaration of the rights of men and citizens. This decision was not uncontested in the Assembly. A number of deputies found it necessary to liberalise the legal system first and only when this task was achieved to guarantee the new order by a bill of rights. The majority's counter-argument was that the complete change of a social and legal system was such a long-drawn-out, complex and difficult task that the legislature needed guidelines and principles on its way towards a totally renewed society.

The Declaration of Rights was meant to furnish such guidelines. In their capacity as guidelines the fundamental rights were, in the first place, directed towards the legislature. Enacted at a time when the old legal system was still in existence, they could not exclusively function as negative rights from the very beginning. This becomes quite obvious with regard to property. In the Declaration, property is called a sacred and inviolable right (Article XVII). At that time, however, the feudal property law, the legal basis of the *ancien régime*, still existed. Its transformation into a liberal system based on the principles of individual freedom and equality with the effect of modernising the economy was one of the most important goals of the revolution. Yet, this was not a matter of a single stroke of the pen, but of years of legal reform. Had the sacred right to property been understood as a negative right from the outset it would have prevented the legislature from reforming the system, and instead would have functioned as a safeguard of the pre-revolutionary order. Consequently the first function of the

Declaration of Rights was to guide the legislature in adapting the legal system to the new principles. Only when the legal system had been liberalised could these principles operate as negative rights and protect the individual against the state.

Germany differed from the United States and France in the absence of a liberal revolution in the late eighteenth or early nineteenth centuries.[8] Although liberal ideas were quite popular with the middle classes at the time, neither self-government as in America nor national sovereignty as in France were achieved. Attempts to modernise Germany in order to strengthen it after the defeat by Napoleon stagnated after the collapse of the Napoleonic Empire. The Revolution of 1848, which set out to create a unified and liberal Germany, failed. The monarchical state remained in place throughout the nineteenth century and never gave up its responsibility for the structure and development of society. Nevertheless, most of the German monarchs of the early nineteenth century granted constitutions. This does not mean that they were convinced of the project of constitutionalism. Their motive rather was dynastic self-preservation in an age of growing delegitimisation of the old order. But since the monarchs continued to be the legitimate rulers, the constitutions did not produce a fundamental change of the political system. They were granted as a voluntary self-limitation of the monarchs, not – like the American and French prototypes – as the constitutive basis of the political system.

Still, most of the German constitutions of the nineteenth century contained bills of rights. But, being granted by the monarchs instead of being imposed on them by the citizens, they had no basis in natural law, were not considered as rights of men but only of citizens, and did not acquire the power to override the existing ordinary laws. Thus lacking supremacy, they remained more or less promises of future changes. However, this did not prevent most liberal scholars of constitutional law from interpreting fundamental rights as obligations of the legislature to adapt the legal system according to the constitutional principles.[9] Likewise, the newly established parliaments used them as a constitutional basis for their constant effort to bring the existing laws

[8] For the following see Dieter Grimm, *Deutsche Verfassungsgeschichte* (3rd edn, Frankfurt: Suhrkamp, 1995), pp. 71 et seqq., pp. 110 et seqq.

[9] Dieter Grimm, 'Die Entwicklung der Grundrechtstheorie in der deutschen Staatsrechtslehre des 19. Jahrhunderts' in Günter Birtsch (ed.), *Grund- und Freiheitsrechte von der ständischen zur spätbürgerlichen Gesellschaft* (Göttingen: Vandenhoeck and Ruprecht, 1987), pp. 234 et seqq.; also in Dieter Grimm, *Recht und Staat der bürgerlichen Gesellschaft* (Frankfurt: Suhrkamp, 1987), pp. 308 et seqq.

into accordance with the respective bills of rights. It is true that most attempts failed since legislation required the consent of the non-elected upper houses of parliament and the monarchs, who were both unwilling to transform the system radically. But it was this failure that kept the idea of fundamental rights as positive obligations of the state alive in Germany in the first half of the nineteenth century.

This brief historical survey of the origins of bills of rights shows that the recognition of a positive dimension of fundamental rights, which has become characteristic of German constitutional law and was later on adopted by many other legal systems, has a basis in history that did not exist in the United States. The historical roots made it easier to extend the scope of fundamental rights. The addition of a positive dimension was not a breach with tradition, but a revival of a tradition. However, before this happened, a long period intervened in Germany in which the importance of fundamental rights decreased not only in practice, where their impact had been small anyway, but in theory and doctrine as well.[10] After the failed revolution of 1848, the German middle classes lost interest in fundamental rights for fear that they might lead to disorder and that the working class might base their social claims on these rights. Legal theory reflected this general attitude when it denied any impact of fundamental rights on legislation. Fundamental rights were deemed binding for the executive only, but as they could be limited by law their remaining effect was that infringements without a basis in the laws were illegal. The laws themselves were not subjected to the bills of rights.

When the monarchy finally collapsed in 1918 the parties that had been in opposition during the Empire (especially the Social Democratic Party and the Catholic *Zentrum* Party) gained a vast majority in the constituent assembly of the Weimar Republic. This made possible a fresh attempt to give greater importance to fundamental rights. The National Assembly added a considerable number of economic and social rights to the classical liberal rights, thereby showing again that fundamental rights were regarded as more than purely negative rights. Most of these rights, however, could not take effect without intervention of the legislature that had to provide the necessary means and to determine the conditions and the extent of the promised benefits. Yet, the practical effect of this reform remained small. The legal community was not prepared to understand fundamental rights as binding directives for

---

[10] Dieter Grimm, 'Die Entwicklung der Grundrechtstheorie', above, note 9.

the legislature.[11] Continuing on the old train of thought that fundamental rights did not bind the legislature, they were interpreted as a mere expression of political intent instead of binding law. A constitutional court with the power to enforce fundamental rights was not established by the Weimar Constitution.

Only the experience of the total neglect of human rights during Nazi rule in Germany brought this minimalist concept of fundamental rights to an end. The *Grundgesetz* begins with a guarantee of human dignity which the state has not only to *respect* but also to *protect* (Article 1 Section 1). In addition, it declares all guarantees in the Bill of Rights to be enforceable law, binding all branches of government, the legislature included (Article 1 Section 3). Moreover, a constitutional court was established with the power to review any governmental act as to its conformity with the Constitution. This was an important step. But it left many questions open. No doubt the main function of fundamental rights was to erect boundaries for state action in favour of individual liberty and to give the individual the legal means to defend himself or herself against intrusions by the state. But it remained quite unclear whether the fundamental rights were intended to function as negative rights only, or, in addition, as positive rights; whether they were limited to vertical application or extended also to horizontal application; and whether the duty to protect, as pronounced in Article 1, applied only to human dignity or to the other fundamental rights as well.

III. Foundations of *Schutzpflicht*

These questions were subsequently resolved by the Constitutional Court. The landmark case for almost everything that follows is *Lüth*, decided in 1958.[12] The case originated in the ordinary courts which had to deal with a question under the Civil Code. Veit Harlan, a prominent movie director of the Nazi period and known for his anti-Semitic films, reappeared on the post-war movie scene with a film called '*Unsterbliche Geliebte*'. Erich Lüth, head of the Hamburg press club and active in

---

[11] Christoph Gusy, 'Die Grundrechte in der Weimarer Republik' (1993) 15 *Zeitschrift für Neuere Rechtsgeschichte*, 163 et seqq.; Michael Stolleis, *Geschichte des öffentlichen Rechts in Deutschland* (3 vols., Munich: C. H. Beck, 1999), vol. 3, pp. 109 et seqq.

[12] BVerfGE 7, 198. English translation in *Decisions*, above, note 3, pp. 1 et seqq.; Kommers, above note 1, pp. 361 et seqq.; Jackson and Tushnet, *Comparative Constitutional Law*, above, note 1, pp. 1403 et seqq., pp. 1424–6; Dorsen et al., *Comparative Constitutionalism*, above, note 1, pp. 824 et seqq.

Jewish-German reconciliation, urged the owners of movie theatres not to show Harlan's film. He called upon Germans not to watch the movie, should it be shown in the cinemas. The film companies sought an injunction against Lüth not to repeat his call for a boycott. The injunction was granted by the civil courts based on a provision of the Civil Code that provides liability for damages caused by acts offending good morals. Fully in line with civil law doctrine and jurisprudence of the time, the civil courts found that a call for boycott fell under the prohibition of Section 826 of the Civil Code. Lüth, in turn, filed a constitutional complaint with the Constitutional Court and invoked his right to free speech guaranteed in Article 5 of the *Grundgesetz*, while the movie companies argued that fundamental rights were only applicable in relationships between state and the individual, but not in private law relationships.

The question presented to the Constitutional Court by this case was the question of horizontal application of fundamental rights. To answer this question, the Court started by asserting that fundamental rights are not only subjective rights of the individual against the state but also expressions of objective values. In this latter capacity their influence is not limited to the sphere of public law but extends to all fields of law, civil law included. This approach barred the alternative of a solely vertical application of fundamental rights. But it still left the question open as to how these rights were to operate in private law relationships. The Court reaffirmed that all private law provisions had to be compatible with the Bill of Rights. But it added that the influence of fundamental rights did not stop there. Whenever the application of private law affected the exercise of a fundamental right, this fundamental right had to be taken into account in the interpretation of the pertinent provision of private law. The Constitutional Court called this a 'radiating effect'. It thereby chose a middle way. On the one hand, the only addressee of fundamental rights remained the state. On the other hand, the state had to give effect to fundamental rights in private law relationships as well.

Lüth was not the end but the beginning of an extremely productive line of jurisprudence. In *Lüth* the German Constitutional Court needed the notion of objective values in order to demonstrate that fundamental rights were not confined to vertical application. In the following years, the objective-value approach served as the basis for a number of effects attributed to fundamental rights of which *Schutzpflicht* (duty to protect) soon became the most important one. When the Court coined this notion in the *First Abortion Case* of 1975, it had already rendered a number of decisions that hinted in that direction. Freedom of the press, for instance, was interpreted not only as individual freedom of the editor or the journalist from state intrusion, but also as freedom of the press as a social institution (so-called institutional interpretation). This implied that freedom of the press as a whole could justify limitations of the individual freedom of an editor or journalist when, by exercising their individual liberty, they endangered the larger institutional freedom.[13] Likewise, the Court had obliged the state to ensure academic freedom as well as freedom of broadcasting by requiring a legal framework capable of fulfilling the objectives of the constitutional guarantees (protection by organisation).[14] In the *numerus clausus* case it was recognised in principle that fundamental rights may oblige the state to grant citizens certain means necessary to make use of constitutional guarantees (fundamental rights as claims to benefits).[15]

Because of these precedents, commentators at first regarded the duty to protect as yet one more function that was derived from the objective element of fundamental rights. Only later did it become clear that *Schutzpflicht* was a more comprehensive notion, the long forgotten 'other side' of fundamental rights. While fundamental rights as negative rights protect individual freedom against the state, the duty to protect derived from fundamental rights is designed to protect fundamental rights against threats and risks stemming not from the state but from private actors or societal forces or even social developments that are controllable by state action. Today in Germany, duties to protect are considered to be the counterpart to the negative function of fundamental rights.[16] This is why the duty to protect cannot be seen as another word for economic and social rights. Economic and social rights as so-called second-generation civil rights allocate material benefits to needy individuals. The duty to protect is a function of

---

[13] BVerfGE 20, 162 (1966) – Spiegel Case. English translation in *Decisions*, above, note 3, pp. 21 et seqq.; Kommers, *Constitutional Jurisprudence*, above, note 1, pp. 397 et seqq.

[14] BVerfGE 12, 205 (1961) – First Television Case, above, note 3; BVerfGE 35, 79 (1973) – University Case; English translation in Kommers, *Constitutional Jurisprudence*, above, note 1, pp. 437 et seqq.

[15] BVerfGE 33, 303 (1972); English translation in Kommers, *Constitutional Jurisprudence*, above, note 1, pp. 282 et seqq.; Dorsen et al., *Comparative Constitutionalism*, above, note 1, pp. 1244 et seqq.

[16] E.g. Josef Isensee, 'Das Grundrecht als Abwehrrecht und als staatliche Schutzpflicht', in Josef Isensee and Paul Kirchhof (eds.), *Handbuch des Staatsrechts* (Heidelberg: C. F. Müller, 1992), vol. V, pp. 143 et seqq. The amount of literature on *Schutzpflicht* has become immense. A very detailed survey is given by Peter Szczekalla, *Die sogenannten grundrechtlichen Schutzpflichten im deutschen und europäischen Recht* (Berlin: Duncker and Humblot, 2002).

first-generation civil rights, traditional liberties. It is concerned about individual freedom instead of welfare, yet not in the vertical, but in the horizontal dimension.

Of course, the fact that the goods protected by fundamental rights are threatened not only by the state but also by private persons is by no means new. The state owes its very existence to this fact. It has always drawn its legitimacy from the degree to which it safeguards its citizens against attacks by foreign forces or fellow citizens. Safety is the basic task of the state. A great deal of its laws are designed to fulfil this function. In that sense, there is no difference between the United States and Germany. Some of the early state constitutions in America recognised security or safety of the people as a task of the state. Others, such as the New Hampshire Bill of Rights of 1784, even contain a right of the citizen to be protected by the state in the enjoyment of his life, liberty and property (Article I No. XII). Yet, safety in this context means the general safety that humans earn, according to natural rights theory by which the American Revolution was guided, when they leave the state of nature and enter into civil society. It should not be confused with the specific obligation that is derived from basic liberties and which obliges the legislature to protect individual freedom against intrusions by fellow citizens.[17]

As long as the protection rendered by ordinary legislation seemed sufficient the question of a constitutional obligation to make such laws was not raised. It is therefore not by chance that the idea of a specific *Schutzpflicht* first appeared when the legislature abolished a long-existing protection in criminal law, that of unborn human life. However, the fact that abortion (where even the US Supreme Court came close to recognising such a duty[18]) did not remain the only application of the *Schutzpflicht* idea has deeper reasons. The general safety-guaranteeing function of the state was turned into a specific constitutional obligation when it became apparent that the conditions for maintaining individual liberty were changing.[19] Most of the cases following the *Abortion Decision* concerned risks to constitutionally guaranteed goods or

---

[17] Josef Isensee, *Das Grundrecht auf Sicherheit: Zu den Schutzpflichten des freiheitlichen Verfassungsstaates* (Berlin: de Gruyter, 1983); Gerhard Robbers, *Sicherheit als Menschenrecht: Aspekte der Geschichte, Begründung und Wirkung einer Grundrechtsfunktion* (Baden-Baden: Nomos, 1987).

[18] Frank Michelman, 'The protective function of the state in the United States and Europe: the constitutional question', in this volume, pp. 156 et seqq.

[19] Dieter Grimm, 'Rückkehr zum liberalen Grundrechtsverständnis?', in Grimm, *Die Zukunft der Verfassung*, above, note 5, pp. 221 et seqq.

interests produced by modern technologies and their commercial use.[20] Atomic energy, genetic manipulation of food, airplane noise and their impact on life and health; electronic data processing and its threats to free personal development; biogenetics and their manipulative potential for the human nature are among the modern developments that mobilised the constitutional instrument of a duty to protect. In all these cases the question was not whether the legislature, by regulating private activities, had overstepped the limits drawn by fundamental rights, but whether it had furnished sufficient protection against newly appearing risks.

Another strong motivating factor for the extension of the duties to protect is the present wave of privatisation of services formerly rendered by the state, such as railways, postal services, telecommunication, or energy supply. While operated by the state these institutions were directly bound to observe fundamental rights and the principle of the social state. Privatisation of such services means not only a change of ownership. It also means that those who render the services change sides with regard to fundamental rights. They are no longer bound by the Bill of Rights but, on the contrary, enjoy the liberty that fundamental rights grant to private persons. The expectation that these services are to be rendered in accordance with basic principles of fairness, equality and social acceptability which were formerly safeguarded by the direct applicability of fundamental rights are now provided by the legislature via the duty to protect. This example shows that not only the right to life and physical integrity, but any fundamental right can serve as a basis of the *Schutzpflicht*.

However, in a growing number of cases the legislature loses the ability to furnish sufficient protection of fundamental rights against private actors by way of substantive law. More and more laws regulating the commercial use of new technologies are unable to clearly determine safety standards. This is particularly true vis-à-vis highly complex or rapidly changing technologies. The legislature finds itself limited to formulate very broad guidelines whose specific meaning very often is determined in *ad hoc* negotiations between administrative agencies and private actors. Under these circumstances, one cannot rely on a legal review of the final result in order to guarantee sufficient protection.

---

[20] Dietrich Murswiek, *Die staatliche Verantwortung für die Risiken der Technik* (Berlin: Duncker and Humblot, 1985); Georg Hermes, *Das Grundrecht auf Schutz von Leben und Gesundheit. Schutzpflicht und Schutzanspruch aus Art. 2 Abs. 2 Satz 1 GG* (Heidelberg: C. F. Müller, 1987).

Rather, the constitutional safeguards must intervene earlier and allow those whose fundamental rights may be affected by the decision to participate in administrative procedures authorising the establishment and operation of plants which use the technology. According to the German Constitutional Court this procedural avenue is not only an option that the legislature may choose but a constitutional requirement: fundamental rights protection by way of a procedure that allows the potentially affected persons to defend their constitutionally guaranteed interest.[21]

The *First Abortion Decision* was a 5:3 decision, with two justices filing a vigorous dissenting opinion. The decision was also harshly criticised within the legal community. Yet, most of the criticism was not directed against the idea of a *Schutzpflicht* inherent in fundamental rights, but against the opinion of the Court's majority that in this case the duty had to be fulfilled by criminalising abortion since equally effective means to protect unborn life were not conceivable. Some critics complained that the Court had failed to demonstrate on what grounds it reached the conclusion that fundamental rights contain a *Schutzpflicht*. This seemed necessary since the textual basis is unclear. With few exceptions (like Article 6 *Grundgesetz*, which guarantees special protection for marriage and family by the state), the rights contained in the *Grundgesetz* are formulated in the classical liberal manner of negative rights. The 'duty to respect and protect' in Article 1, which the court quotes, refers to dignity, and it cannot be taken for granted that it equally applies to all other rights.

Authors have offered a number of possible grounds from which the same result could have been reached.[22] The most convincing among them takes up the ruling of *Lüth* according to which fundamental rights are not only subjective rights of the individual vis-à-vis the state, but also objective principles or values. If one describes these values as expressions of the general idea of freedom and autonomy of the various sub-systems of society, it is possible to conclude that the defence against state action is not an end in itself, but a means to secure individual freedom and autonomy. Since this defence works only vis-à-vis the state it is unable to reach its end completely. Insofar as freedom and autonomy are threatened by private actors an additional means is necessary. In this

---

[21] BVerfG 53, 30 (1979); even more clearly the dissenting opinion of Justices Simon and Heussner, BVerfG 53, 30 (1979), pp. 69 et seqq.

[22] Johannes Dietlein, *Die Lehre von den grundrechtlichen Schutzpflichten* (Berlin: Duncker and Humblot, 1992), pp. 34 et seqq.

understanding, *Schutzpflicht* is the other means to protect freedom and autonomy, and only together can they reach the ultimate goal of the Bill of Rights. Today, in spite of some remaining doubts as to its normative basis, in Germany the *Schutzpflicht* is generally accepted as the second basic function of fundamental rights. Fundamental criticism was and is rare.[23]

IV. Practice of *Schutzpflicht*

The most important question then is how the concept of a duty to protect operates in practice. First of all, it seems necessary to mention that the judicial development of the *Schutzpflicht* did not change the addressee of fundamental rights. Fundamental rights continue to oblige the state and nobody else. This means that *Schutzpflicht* is not identical with horizontal application of fundamental rights. What has been enlarged is merely the mode of obligation. The state is not only obliged to abstain from certain actions that would violate fundamental rights. It is also obliged to act when the goods protected by fundamental rights are threatened by private actors. This means that the state finds itself in a double position vis-à-vis fundamental rights. On the one hand, the state, possessing the monopoly on legitimate force, is regarded as a potential foe of fundamental rights. Fundamental rights set limits to its actions. On the other hand, the state, owing its existence to the fact that life, liberty and property are constantly threatened and must be secured by a powerful public authority, is the friend of fundamental rights.

Like the duty to respect fundamental rights, the duty to protect them binds all branches of government. However, the primary way to fulfil the protective function is through legislation. The other organs are but in a subsidiary function. The main reason for this is that the dangers and risks against which the state is obliged to protect citizens emerge from private actors who themselves enjoy the protection of fundamental rights. Hence, fulfilment of a duty to protect often requires a limitation of certain liberties (e.g. freedom of property, economic liberties, Articles 12 and 14 *Grundgesetz*) in the interest of other liberties (e.g. right to life and physical integrity, personality

---

[23] Bernhard Schlink, 'Freiheit durch Eingriffsabwehr – Rekonstruktion der klassischen Grundrechtsfunktion' (1984) 11 *Europäische Grundrechtezeitschrift*, 457 et seqq.; Ernst-Wolfgang Böckenförde, 'Grundrechtstheorie und Grundrechtsinterpretation' in Böckenförde, *Staat – Gesellschaft – Freiheit. Studien zur Staatstheorie und zum Verfassungsrecht* (Frankfurt am Main: Suhrkamp, 1976), pp. 221 et seqq.

rights, Article 2 *Grundgesetz*).[24] Limitations of fundamental rights, however, can be effectuated only by a general law or pursuant to such a law. This means that the idea of a duty to protect that is to be fulfilled by legislative limitations of individual rights may entail an increase in restrictions. Yet, the purpose is to enhance overall freedom in society and make it a reality for all bearers of fundamental rights. Viewed from this angle, what appears as a curtailment for one group of persons may be an enablement for another group.

The legislature, in a constitutional system that recognises the protective duty of the state, is no longer free to decide whether it enacts certain laws or not. However, in contrast to fundamental rights in their capacity as negative rights, the German Constitution does not tell us how duties to protect are to be fulfilled. There is, however, a significant difference between the negative and positive aspects of fundamental rights.[25] The duty to respect fundamental rights requires the state to abstain from certain actions. Consequently, there is only one way to comply with this duty, namely to omit acts violating fundamental rights. If, in spite of the prohibition, such an act has occurred, the only way to heal the fault is the reverse act: annulment. The duty to protect fundamental rights, on the contrary, requires the state to act in the interest of endangered liberties. This duty can be fulfilled in various ways, which are all in accordance with the Constitution. It follows that the legislature is free to choose the means to fulfil its duties to protect. The *First Abortion Decision*, which had acknowledged this in theory but denied it in practice, obliging the legislature to protect unborn life via criminal law, has been modified by subsequent decisions and was overruled by the *Second Abortion case* of 1993.[26]

The Constitutional Court requires, however, that the legislature choose a means that is suitable to reach the purpose of the law. In addition, in the *Second Abortion Decision*, the Constitutional Court developed a prohibition of doing too little in protecting a fundamental right against violations by private actors (the so-called *Untermaßverbot*

---

[24] Rainer Wahl and Johannes Masing, 'Schutz durch Eingriff' (1990) 45 *Juristenzeitung*, 557 et seqq; as to the danger this entails see Peter Preu, 'Freiheitsgefährdung durch die Lehre von den grundrechtlichen Schutzpflichten' (1991) 46 *Juristenzeitung*, 265 et seqq.

[25] Robert Alexy, *Theorie der Grundrechte* (Baden-Baden: Nomos, 1985), pp. 395 et seqq.; Gertrude Lübbe-Wolff, *Die Grundrechte als Eingriffsabwehrrechte* (Baden-Baden: Nomos, 1988), pp. 37 et seqq.

[26] BVerfGE 88, 203 (1993); English translation in Kommers, *Constitutional Jurisprudence*, above, note 1, pp. 349 et seqq.; earlier cases modifying the First Abortion Decision are BVerfGE 46, 160 (1977) – Schleyer, and BVerfGE 77, 170 (1987) – Chemical Weapons.

being complementary to the *Übermaßverbot* which is applicable when fundamental rights function as negative rights).[27] Relevant criteria are the importance of the right at stake and the likelihood and intensity of harm. These criteria can be understood as an adaptation of the principle of proportionality to the positive function of fundamental rights. As a matter of fact, there is not much difference between the duty to respect and the duty to protect fundamental rights when it comes to deciding whether a law is constitutional or not. Since almost every law contains some limitation of a fundamental right and since the justification is almost always the protection of another fundamental right or a constitutionally recognised value, the task of the legislature is to bring competing values into harmony, preserving as much as possible of each of them (the so-called *praktische Konkordanz*).[28]

There is much controversy surrounding the concept of proportionality in the United States.[29] In Germany this concept has become a generally accepted tool to decide fundamental rights cases. With the exception of human dignity (Art. 1 *Grundgesetz*), which is regarded as the source of all following guarantees in the Bill of Rights, the German Constitutional Court does not recognise a hierarchy of fundamental rights. In the absence of such a hierarchy there is hardly another way to solve conflicts among different rights than proportionality and balancing. If this is true, the prohibition to go too far (*Übermaßverbot*) and the prohibition to do too little (*Untermaßverbot*) are the same device, viewed from different angles. When a fundamental right is invoked in its capacity as a negative right the question is whether the legislature went too far. When it is invoked in its capacity as a positive right or a duty to protect, the question is whether it did too little in order to protect the endangered right. This does not mean, however, that the limits for legislative activities are the same. Since the legislature enjoys wide discretion in the fulfilment of a duty to protect and since the *Untermaßverbot* is but a guarantee of the minimum standard, a decision to grant more protection is not necessarily a violation of the proportionality principle.[30]

---

[27] BVerfGE 88, 203 (1993) at 254.

[28] Konrad Hesse, *Grundzüge des Verfassungsrechts der Bundesrepublik Deutschland* (Reprint of the 20th edn, Heidelberg: C. F. Müller, 1999), paras. 317 et seqq.

[29] For a recent example see *Ewing* v. *California* 538 U.S. 11 (2003).

[30] Karl-Eberhard Hain, 'Der Gesetzgeber in der Klemme zwischen Übermaß- und Untermaßverbot', (1993) 108 *Deutsches Verwaltungsblatt*, 982 et seqq.

Duties to protect, being primarily fulfilled by legislation, do not leave much room for the other branches of government. If a law that is required by the *Schutzpflicht* is missing completely, the executive and the judiciary can act on their own only if the obligation has a sufficiently clear basis in the Constitution itself and if no limiting effect on fundamental rights of third parties ensues. Such cases will be fairly rare. They may occur when the laws, under exceptional circumstances, do not provide the bare necessities of a dignified life. The Constitutional Court has had no occasion to decide a case like this, but the lower courts have rendered judgments in this vein.[31] When laws exist, the administrative agencies and the judiciary can but apply these laws. In doing so, they have to take the fundamental rights affected by their decision into account as guiding principles for their decision-making. But this function does not differ from the so-called radiating effect already stated in *Lüth* and cannot go beyond the limits of the text.

In some decisions of the 1990s the German Constitutional Court extended the *Schutzpflicht* to contractual relations of private parties. In cases where the balance of power among the contracting parties was distorted to such an extent that freedom of contract did not lead to a fair balance of interests but severely hampered the right to free development of one's personality (Art. 2 Section 1 *Grundgesetz*) the civil courts were obliged to take this right into account when granting remedies on the basis of the Civil Code.[32] Such cases remained small in number, but they met more criticism than the *Schutzpflicht* decisions which were addressed to the legislature. Some authors condemned them as an attack on the autonomy of private law and as a paternalistic protection of a person against himself or herself, whereas others praised them as a necessary limitation of freedom of contract, the precondition of this freedom being a more or less balanced relationship between the contracting parties.[33]

Since the duties to protect are derived from fundamental rights in their capacity as objective principles, the question is whether and to what extent the objective law is transformed into individual rights. As a general rule, the

---

[31] For a list of cases see Rüdiger Breuer, 'Grundrechte als Anspruchsnormen', in Otto Bachof (ed.), *Verwaltungsrecht zwischen Freiheit, Teilhabe und Bindung. Festgabe aus Anlass des 25jährigen Bestehens des Bundesverwaltungsgerichts* (Munich: C. H. Beck, 1978), pp. 89 et seqq.

[32] BVerfGE 81, 242 (1990) – Salesman; BVerfGE 89, 214 (1993) – Declaration of Surety.

[33] Wolfram Höfling, *Vertragsfreiheit* (Heidelberg: C. F. Müller, 1991); Christian Hillgruber, *Der Schutz der Menschen vor sich selbst* (Munich: Vahlen, 1992).

Constitutional Court does not recognise a (subjective) right to have a law passed by the legislature, unless such a claim has an explicit basis in the Constitution and the applicant belongs to the beneficiaries of the said constitutional provision. Again, these are very rare cases. This is different, however, with regard to the duty to protect. One can observe a general tendency to 'subjectivise' the objective elements of fundamental rights, and so does the Constitutional Court with regard to the *Schutzpflicht*. This means that the individual whose constitutionally protected interest may be infringed upon by third parties has a claim against the state if the existing laws do not protect him or her sufficiently. The legislature that remains inactive, or refuses to act, not only violates objective constitutional law but an individual right of the citizen as well.

Consequently, the Constitutional Court is prepared to accept individual complaints based on the allegation that the legislature violated a *Schutzpflicht* that exists in the complainant's interest. However, since constitutional complaints are admissible only after the complainant has exhausted all other means, the question reaches the Constitutional Court mostly in incidental form. The complaint is directed against decisions of lower courts. The actual object of constitutional review is an administrative act, say a permission granted to a private corporation to build a nuclear plant, and the complaint is based on the alleged failure of the underlying law to efficiently protect the neighbours of the planned location. In such cases, the Constitutional Court does not content itself with declaring the administrative act void because the underlying law is unconstitutional. Rather, it obliges the legislature to amend the law within a certain period of time in a way that is compatible with the duty to protect.

There can be no doubt that, in consequence of this development, the legislature loses power. To be precise, the legislature loses the power to remain inactive vis-à-vis a manifest danger for a fundamental right or the power to grossly disadvantage one constitutionally protected interest in favour of another one. The power lost by the legislature is gained by the Constitutional Court. Thus, the duties to protect present a problem of separation of powers. Yet, separation of powers cannot be an argument for not giving effect to the requirements of the Constitution. The Constitution does not offer a different measure for behaviour of the legislature and for control of the legislature. If the Constitution contains a certain obligation, it is difficult to argue that the legislature is nevertheless free to choose whether to comply with it. The crucial question, therefore, is whether a duty to protect can reasonably be derived from the Bill of Rights. For Germany, this question must be answered in the affirmative. Duties to protect are sufficiently rooted in the idea of and purpose behind fundamental rights. They are an answer to modern conditions of effectively realising the idea of constitutional freedom, and it cannot be seen as an interpretation contrary to the clear wording of the text.[34] The rest is a matter of degree.

V. The contrast in context

There remains a striking contrast to the American approach which cannot only be explained by differences in text or time. Moreover, it seems doubtful whether the contrast is merely due to a difference in enforcement and not in substance as Frank Michelman suggests referring to Lawrence Sager's notion of under-enforced constitutional rights in the US.[35] But even if he were right, the difference in judicial behaviour remains to be explained, and again the constitution itself does not give the answer. Rather, the contrast seems to be deeply rooted in different historical experiences; different perceptions of dangers; different trust in the state on the one hand, the market on the other; different ideas about the role of political and of legal institutions; a different balance between individual freedom and communal interests. Constitutional law, constitutional theory and constitutional interpretation rest on such a cultural context, and if this is so, it seems difficult to argue that one approach is right and the other one wrong.

It should be of interest, however, that the idea of a duty to protect as derived from fundamental rights was adopted by a great number of countries that had freed themselves of all sorts of authoritarian regimes or dictatorships inside and outside Europe in the last quarter of the twentieth century. Either the duty to protect was explicitly incorporated into the text of the constitution or the newly established constitutional courts derived it from their bills of rights. A closer look shows that most of these countries share some characteristics with post-war Germany that are not present in the United States: the experience of a society not accustomed to self-government; a legal order that, to a large extent, dates from a pre-constitutional era with the consequence that it has to be adapted to the new principles by way of legislation or adjudication; a less

[34] Grimm, 'Rückkehr zum liberalen Grundrechtsverständnis,' above, note 19.
[35] Frank Michelman in this volume, pp. 156–180; Lawrence Sager, *Justice in Plainclothes: a Theory of American Constitutional Practice* (New Haven: Yale University Press, 2004).

individualistic background than the United States. In these circumstances, the German system may have offered a better solution than
the American one. Still, one should not forget that the recognition of a
duty to protect has a price, as has the refusal to recognise such a duty.
There is not one universally valid best solution for every country and
every situation. But when a country makes its choice, it should be aware
of the alternatives and their risks and benefits.

7

The protective function of the state in the United States and Europe: the constitutional question

FRANK I. MICHELMAN

I. The comparison drawn: a difference in legal doctrines

A seminar is in progress. The general theme is relationships and comparisons between US and European constitutionalism. The programme includes, as one topic for discussion about which you, as an American constitutional lawyer, are especially invited to comment, 'the protective function of the state'. What question, exactly, is being put to you?

Is the issue supposed to be 'ESR', economic and social rights? In relation to constitutional law, the question of the state's 'protective' function easily could be taken to mean – or to include – the question of obligating the state, by constitutional-legal mandate, to ensure provision to all citizens of the means of satisfying certain material interests such as subsistence, housing, health care and education. I take the meaning, though, to be a different one. By its reference to the state's 'protective function', I understand the seminar programme to mean the state's function of safeguarding inhabitants effectively against various forms of violation and intrusion at the hands of fellow inhabitants. Thus, I envision the comparative seminar's agenda listing, as two separate topics for discussion, 'ESR' and 'the protective function of the state'.

Thus understanding the 'protective function' question, it seems the response to it might be both short and sweet. Alike in US and European law, everyone enjoys a range of civil rights against abusive treatment by other members of society. The applicable definitions of abusive treatment are found mainly in the jurisdictions' respective legal doctrines of tort (delict) and crime, and they are reasonably similar on both sides of the Pond – close enough, anyway, to keep eyebrows from rising too sharply on either side.

At least, that will be the assumption here. In order to keep a sharp focus on the protective-function question, precisely defined, we concentrate on civil rights regarding bodily integrity and security. If *D* physically assaults *P* causing *P* bodily harm, *P* has legal recourse against *D* (aside from which *D*'s act is prosecutable as a crime) in all the jurisdictions that concern us. To that extent, all of them routinely – one might loosely say constitutionally – recognise and carry out a protective function of the state. Who, after all, is providing *P* with a cause of action, if not the state? Who, if not the state, establishes and funds the court system required to process claims, issue and execute remedial orders, and so on? Of course, there is no commitment anywhere to absolutely guaranteed recompense for bodily harm inflicted by one person on another, regardless of intention, fault, justification or excuse. Still, all the states in view readily accept and perform, in the manner described, a substantial protective function.

In all of these jurisdictions, moreover, it is the case that state law establishes, and state coercive authority in the form of tax collection supports, protective agencies – police forces, child welfare departments, and the like – that have among their state-assigned functions that of anticipating and preventing, or detecting and stopping, physically abusive treatment of some inhabitants by others. Of course, there is no commitment anywhere to perfect protection, or to prevention regardless of the costs to other values, such as, for example, the costs to liberty that some preventative policies might carry.[1] Still, all the states in view readily accept and perform, in the manner described, a substantial protective function.

---

[1] In South Africa, where constitutional jurisprudence develops the state's protective function exceptionally clearly and strongly, see e.g. *Carmichele* v. *Minister of Safety and Security* (2001) 10 BCLR 995 (CC), 2001 SACLR LEXIS 64, the Constitutional Court has made clear its view that the Constitution also requires due allowance for the liberty rights of accused or suspected assailants. See *S.* v. *Baloyi* (2000) 2 SA 425 (CC). The question was whether a certain statutory text should be construed to place the onus of proving non-violation on a man charged with violating a judicial order to refrain from assaulting his wife. The Constitution, Section 39 (2), requires courts to construe statutes with a view to 'promot[ing] the spirit, purport, and objects of the Bill of Rights'. Relying partly on this requirement, the Court concluded that the statute should *not* be given the contested, reverse-onus interpretation, writing as follows:

> the Constitution ... require[s] effective measures to deal with the gross denial of human rights resulting from pervasive domestic violence. At the same time the Constitution insists that no one should be arbitrarily deprived of freedom or convicted without a fair trial. The problem, then, is to find the interpretation of the [statutory] text which best fits the Constitution and

I have now been able to write that sentence twice over. Are we finished with the topic, then? Is the discussion complete?

No, the seminar leader says; it is only just getting started, because the topic is the protective function of the state in *constitutional* law, not in private or common law or under the civil code. We did not mean thus to ask only whether state performance of protective functions is *authorised* by constitutional law, or is *expected* by constitutional law, we meant to ask how constitutional law responds – if at all – to a state's failure to perform these functions. Just because protection of both of the two kinds mentioned above is a well-understood, even pre-supposed, commitment of state policy, that does not mean the commitment always will be kept. What consequences – what *legal* consequences – ensue if it is not?

The 'constitutional' question, then, is this: Are the state and its functionaries held answerable to some paramount law for their culpable failures to carry out one or both of the two protective functions I have just said are everywhere accepted as a matter of general public expectation and state policy? By 'culpable failures', we mean failures defined as culpable by the paramount law – they might be malicious, or reckless, or grossly negligent failures. By 'paramount law', we mean a law that binds state officials regardless of anything declared to the contrary by national parliaments, congresses or judiciaries interpreting the civil code, or judiciaries construing the common law. We mean something like the Constitution of the United States or the European Convention for the Protection of Human Rights and Fundamental Freedoms (the 'Convention on Human Rights' or 'European Convention'). Our comparative question concerns those two bodies of paramount law specifically. As interpreted and applied by their respective courts of last resort, are those two bodies of law the same, or are they different, regarding the question of the legal consequences of the state's failure to carry out protective functions as defined above?[2]

> balances the duty of the state to deal effectively with domestic violence with its
> duty to guarantee accused persons the protection involved in a fair trial.
>
> (At para. 26.)

[2] As I have indicated already, one must take care to keep the protective-function comparison, strictly understood, distinct from comparisons of substantive value orderings in the systems under consideration. Take, for example, the recent decision of the European Court of Human Rights in the case of *von Hannover* v. *Germany* (Application no. 59320/00, decided 24 June 2004, available on the internet at http://hudoc.echr.coe.int). The Court found that the government of Germany would have to pay substantial damages to the plaintiff, Princess Caroline of Monaco, because of the failure of the German civil courts to prevent publication by private companies in Germany (magazine publishers) of photographs of the plaintiff, where publication was found to violate the plaintiff's

If that is the question, the answer still can be short, although this time it may not be quite so sweet. The answer is: The two bodies of paramount law are different. All one need do by way of support is to point to two, leading judicial decisions, that of the Supreme Court of the United States in *DeShaney v. Winnebago County*[3] and that of the European Court of Human Rights in the *Case of Z and Others v. The United Kingdom.*[4]

The two cases are closely comparable. In both, a young child (or children) had suffered hideous abuse by a parent (or parents). In both, the responsible state protection agencies were charged with culpable failures to rescue the children from risks and threats of grave and imminent harm of which they knew. In both, the surrounding legal debates recognised the difficulty, as a matter of policy, of saying just how broadly agencies and their personnel ought to be exposed to legal liability for non-intervention. At stake in such decisions – it was recognised in both cases – are not only the familial-privacy interests of parents, including their interests in freedom from state domination in the realm of child-rearing, but also the interests of the children and society in long-term successful outcomes, inasmuch as these might, in many cases, depend on holding families together rather than tearing them apart.[5]

---

right to respect for her private life guaranteed by Article 8 of the European Convention. In so concluding, the Court obviously enforced a 'protective function' of state parties to the Convention. The Court also (and this is a distinct point) relied on a certain, controversial, ordering and balancing of the Convention's commitments to personal privacy and to freedom of publication – an ordering and balancing that probably would be rejected by constitutional adjudicators in some liberal democracies. Jurists in such countries might nevertheless accept without question that the state is under constitutional obligation to protect citizens actively against *some* privacy-infringing publications by commercial publishers. They might disagree with the case result only with regard to its substantive (value-ordering) claim that the publications *in this case* deserved to be subjected in any way to legal suppression or sanction.

[3] *DeShaney* v. *Winnebago County Department of Social Services*, 489 U.S. 189 (1989).

[4] (2001) 10 Butterworths Human Rights Cases 384.

[5] See *DeShaney* v. *Winnebago County Department of Social Services*, 489 U.S. 189 (1989), at 203 ('In defense of [the responsible state officials] it must . . . be said that had they moved too soon to take custody of the son away from the father, they would likely have been met with charges of improperly intruding into the parent–child relationship, charges based on the same Due Process Clause that forms the basis for the present charge of failure to provide adequate protection'); *Case of Z* (2001) 10 Butterworths Human Rights Cases 384, at para. 74 ('The Court acknowledges the difficult and sensitive decisions facing social services and the important countervailing principle of respecting and preserving family life. The present case, however, leaves no doubt as to the failure of the system to protect these applicant children from serious, long-term neglect and abuse').

For all their similarities, the two cases resulted in what look like radically clashing constitutional-legal decisions. In *DeShaney*, the Supreme Court of the United States decisively and flatly construed our Fourteenth Amendment's guarantee against arbitrary deprivation of life and liberty by the state[6] as *not* making states, their officials, or their protective agencies legally answerable for failures, of whatever degree of culpability, to prevent one person in civil society from committing mayhem on another.[7] In the *Case of Z*, the Strasbourg Court decisively construed to an exact opposite effect Articles 3[8] and 13[9] of the European Convention, even as applied in the admittedly treacherous business of intra-familial relations. So the answer is clear. In Europe, paramount or 'constitutional' law imposes a protective function on the state and holds the state legally accountable for culpable failure to perform; in the US, it does not.

Is that all? Are we finished? If not, where shall we go from here? Perhaps in search of explanation for the contrasting postures of the Supreme Court and the Strasbourg Court?

II. Explanations for the divergence

1. Not federalism

Scanning for possible explanations, an American constitutional lawyer's mind might move quickly to 'federalism'. American constitutional law and culture maintain a pronounced commitment to a balance of authority between the national and state levels of government. What is more, they treat 'police' work – the work of protecting inhabitants against each

---

[6] See U.S. Const. Amend. XIV, § 1 ('. . . No State shall . . . deprive any person of life, liberty, or property, without due process of law').

[7] 489 U.S. 189, 197 (1989) ('A State's failure to protect an individual against private violence simply does not constitute a violation of the Fourteenth Amendment'). If the maiming was intentional on the part of some official exercising state authority – if the official, in effect, conspired with the non-state actor to permit the latter to inflict the harm – an action would lie against that official for *actively* depriving the victim of a right secured by the Constitution, namely, the right not to be deprived of life or liberty *by the state* without due process of law. Cf. *Adickes* v. *S. H. Kress & Co.*, 398 U.S. 144 (1970); *United States* v. *Price*, 383 U.S. 787 (1966).

[8] 'No one shall be subjected to torture or to inhuman or degrading punishment or treatment.'

[9] 'Everyone whose rights and freedoms as set forth in [the] Convention are violated shall have an effective remedy before a national authority notwithstanding that the violation has been committed by persons acting in an official capacity.'

other's depredations – as belonging primarily and mainly to the province of the state governments. In combination, these impulses doubtless tend to steer American judges away from finding in our national constitutional law a doctrine that would give national officials (including federal judges) a corrective authority over the arrangements by which the states carry out their police responsibilities.

Historically, it is clear that a judicial concern for maintaining a balance of authority between the national and state governments has provided major support for the so-called 'state action' doctrine in the United States. The doctrine is that the Fourteenth Amendment's ban against depriving persons of life, liberty, or property applies only to state governments and their officials ('state action'), imposing no legal duties or restraints on private citizens. Suppose the doctrine were otherwise, to the effect that citizens at large are placed under direct obligation of national constitutional law to refrain from committing against their fellows whatever sorts of harm the national legal authorities may find to be covered by the Fourteenth Amendment's ban against 'deprivations' of 'life' or 'liberty' or 'property'. Then – the worry has been – organs of the national government would have become, in effect, the close supervisors and controllers of virtually the full run of private law in the states. The said national organs would include both the national judiciary hearing cases under the Fourteenth Amendment's anti-deprivation guarantee and the Congress, which is empowered by the Amendment to 'enforce' that guarantee by legislation.[10]

A similar set of concerns probably is stirred by suggestions that the Fourteenth Amendment might impose a protective duty on the governments of the states, even though the protective-duty question does not

---

[10] See U.S. Const. Amend. XIV, § 5; *Civil Rights Cases*, 109 U.S. 3, 11, 23 (1883) ('[The Fourteenth Amendment] does not invest Congress with power to legislate upon subjects which are within the domain of State legislation ... It does not authorize Congress to create a code of municipal law for the regulation of private rights; but to provide modes of redress against the operation of State laws, and the action of State officers executive or judicial, when these are subversive of the fundamental rights specified in the amendment. [Congressional] legislation cannot properly cover the whole domain of rights appertaining to life, liberty and property, defining them and providing for their vindication. That would be to establish a code of municipal law regulative of all private rights between man and man in society. It would be to make Congress take the place of the State legislatures and to supersede them'); *Slaughter-House Cases*, 83 U.S. 36, 77–8 (1872) (restrictively construing, for like reasons, the Fourteenth Amendment's guarantee against state deprivations of 'privileges or immunities of citizens of the United States').

pose so stark a threat to the balance of state and national powers as the 'private action' question does.[11] Nevertheless, it seems plain that an American constitutional policy of solicitous regard for the 'area' powers (i.e. the states) in a federalised system of governance cannot explain the opposing decisions in *Z's Case* and *DeShaney's Case*. Commitments to subsidiarity and margin-of-appreciation can hardly have been thought less strong in European human rights law, where full-fledged Westphalian nation-states are the area units and the existence of a European 'nation' remains deeply contested (despite the recent onset of a Constitution), as in American constitutional law, where the area units are the admittedly *sui generis*, but certainly non-Westphalian, 'states' in relation to the American national republic.

2. Text?

It seems the first place to look for a possible source of the doctrinal disparity between *Z's Case* and *DeShaney's Case* must be the texts of the two paramount bodies of law involved, and in fact these do appear to differ in ways that match the clash of decisions. Article 3 of the European Convention speaks impersonally, in the passive voice ('No one shall be subjected to . . . inhuman or degrading treatment') and Article 13 builds from there ('Everyone whose rights . . . are violated shall have . . . remedy'). The primary right thus framed by Article 3 appears to be a right against maltreatment by anyone, not just by the state, while the secondary right framed by Article 13 – to a national-venue remedy for violations of the primary right – is one that only a state can fulfil. Putting the two together, one moves smoothly to the conclusion that the Convention has imposed upon states a legally enforceable, active or positive duty to provide effective legal remedies for one person's inhuman or degrading treatment of another, regardless of whether the perpetrator of the treatment has or has not acted as a state agent. Add the

---

[11] By holding that private conduct can violate the guarantees of the Fourteenth Amendment, it has been feared, we would open the *content* of state private law to national judicial or congressional revision, through the device of demanding that the said content conform in substance to the requirements of the Fourteenth Amendment, construed however Congress and the national courts might construe them. (See e.g. for an exceptional and well-known instance in which exactly that has occurred, *New York Times Co.* v. *Sullivan*, 376 U.S. 254 (1964).) The protective-duty question, by contrast, is narrower. It is a question only of holding the states to a duty to provide effective prevention of and requital for violations, by non-state actors, of interests of persons that the states' respective bodies of private law routinely recognise as legally protected.

words of Article 1 of the Convention – 'The High Contracting Parties shall secure to everyone within their jurisdiction the rights and freedoms defined in ... this Convention' – and the conclusion easily follows that states have been placed under some degree of legally enforceable, active duty to prevent such harmings, as well as to requite them.[12]

The Fourteenth Amendment speaks ostensibly in a quite different way: 'No state shall deprive', not 'no one shall suffer deprivation'.[13] To say that S 'deprives' P of life, liberty or freedom from assault, when the plain fact is that the assailant in the case is D and not S (although S may have failed inexcusably to intervene) is undoubtedly to stretch the application of 'deprive' beyond what most would find to be the word's plainest meaning – not unsustainably, perhaps, but still palpably.[14] So we can say at least this much: the texts of the Convention and the Constitution respectively point in the divergent directions respectively followed by the Strasbourg Court and the Supreme Court in *Z's Case* and *DeShaney's Case*.

[12] See *Case of Z* (2001) 10 Butterworths Human Rights Cases 384, para. 73 ('The obligation on High Contracting Parties under Article 1 ... to secure to everyone ... the rights and freedoms defined in the Convention, taken in conjunction with Article 3, requires States to take measures designed to ensure that individuals ... are not subjected to torture or inhuman or degrading treatment, including such ill-treatment administered by private individuals').

[13] See *DeShaney v. Winnebago County Department of Social Services*, 489 U.S. 189 (1989) at 195 ('The [Fourteenth Amendment's Due Process] Clause is phrased as a limitation on the State's power to act, not as a guarantee of certain minimal levels of safety and security').

[14] The difficulty under discussion here, to be clear, is the one inherent in the words 'no State shall ... deprive any person'. An inquiry also could be launched into how readily, in various settings, American judges would construe the words 'of life, liberty or property' to cover non-lethal but substantial violations of the personal interest in bodily integrity and security, in cases where the state or its agents have committed the violation actively and directly. For present purposes, it is enough to say that the door certainly is open to reading those words to cover such cases. See *Cruzan* v. *Director, Missouri Department of Health*, 497 U.S. 261, 279 (1990) ('Petitioners insist that under the general holdings of our cases, the forced administration of life-sustaining medical treatment, and even of artificially delivered food and water essential to life, would implicate a competent person's liberty interest. ... [W]e think the logic of the cases discussed above would embrace such a liberty interest [and we so assume] ... for purposes of this case ...'); cf. *Ingraham* v. *Wright*, 430 U.S. 651, 673–4 (1977) (holding that infliction of corporal punishment by public school officials affects an interest in 'liberty', as that term occurs in the Fourteenth Amendment, sufficiently to support a constitutional claim to procedural niceties such as notice and fair hearing) ('While the contours of [the] historic liberty interest in the context of our federal system of government have not been defined precisely, they always have been thought to encompass freedom from bodily restraint and punishment').

But a textual explanation here may well strike us as incomplete, even superficial. For why, then, should the texts differ as they do? Do social conditions in the two places, or culturally embedded value orderings, differ in some way or ways that might have led constitutional law makers in two such different directions? Or is the difference simply mindless, accidental, arbitrary?

The latter conclusion may strike us as unlikely or unsatisfying, for the following reason. The texts do differ in ways that comport with the differing constitutional-legal doctrines of *Z's Case* and *DeShaney's Case*, but to many lawyers – perhaps most – the texts will not seem fully decisive in themselves.[15] If the relevant, salient, social and cultural conditions were in both places the same, and in both places were strongly influencing judicial interpreters, the texts need not have prevented convergent results in the two cases. It would not be linguistically preposterous for a court to say that the state deprives someone of liberty when it (a) by its general laws and practices creates a police force charged with preventing assaults (within certain bounds of practicability), but then (b) condones – refuses remedy for – an admittedly inexcusable failure by that very police force to stop an assault when they easily might have done so. Nor, if deep-set social understandings and expectations happened to be so aligned, would it be linguistically grotesque to interpolate 'by the state' into a constitutional guarantee that 'no one shall be subjected to ... inhuman or degrading treatment'.[16]

3. History and original understanding?

If text is not decisive, what about history? Might differences in constitutional culture at the respective, framing moments of the two texts

---

[15] As one indication that the American text is not fully decisive, consider that the anti-deprivation guarantee made applicable to the national government (as distinct from the state governments) by the US Constitution's Fifth Amendment is cast, like Article 3 of the European Convention, in the passive voice. See US Const. Amend. V ('No person shall ... be deprived of life, liberty, or property, without due process of law'). I have never heard of a suggestion that this phrasing, by contrast with the 'no state shall deprive' phrasing of the parallel clause of the Fourteenth Amendment (directed to the state governments), should be read to cast an active duty of protection on the national government.

[16] Were the right defined by Article 3 of the Convention to be thus confined, so likewise would the duty imposed on states by Article 1 to 'secure' that right. That is, states would be obliged by Article 1 to take any measures that might be required to secure their inhabitants against cruel, inhuman or degrading treatment by state functionaries.

explain the differences either in the ways in which the texts are phrased or in the meanings detected in them by their respective judicial masters, regarding the state's active, legal duties of protection?[17] Suppose we could assume that both sets of judicial masters were strict interpretative 'originalists', who take for granted that the proper application of a legal text is fixed forever by the probable expectation of its original promulgators, at least when and insofar as that is discoverable. Bearing in mind the drastically discrepant birth dates of our two constitutional instruments – 1868 for the Fourteenth Amendment, 1950 for the European Convention – it seems that differing judicial perceptions of the respective original understandings could help to explain the divergent doctrines of *DeShaney's Case* and *Z's Case*.

I make that suggestion having in mind some well-known remarks by a leading American judge, Richard Posner. Ruling against a Fourteenth-Amendment-based protective-duty claim in the pre-*DeShaney* case of *Jackson v. Joliet*,[18] Judge Posner reminded his readers that the American constitutional framers' own study and experience of history taught them that the holders of government powers, with popular majorities goading them on, face dangerously weak incentives to refrain from turning those powers against citizens they find troublesome or irksome – to muzzle, prosecute, humiliate, isolate, expropriate or otherwise harass them. The framers plainly meant for constitutional law to make up some of that motivational deficit.

By contrast, there is no evidence, and no reason to believe, that the framers perceived any comparable motivational deficit when it came to government's daily common task of protecting citizens against *each other's* assaultive, larcenous and trespassory tendencies. Ordinary majoritarian politics, the framers would have believed, would suffice to punish governments that failed them on that score, and the prospect of such punishment would suffice to keep governments up to the mark. Thus, it would have made perfect sense for the framers to write constitutions containing special guarantees against *active* abuse of citizens *by the state* – guarantees that they would see no need to extend either to

---

[17] I follow Robert Post's definition of 'constitutional culture' as 'the beliefs and values of nonjudicial actors' regarding 'the substance of the Constitution'. Post posits a continuous exchange between constitutional culture and the constitutional law pronounced by judges. See Robert Post, 'Foreword: Fashioning the Legal Constitution: Culture, Courts, and Law' (2003) 117 *Harvard Law Review*, 4, 8, 9.

[18] *Jackson v. City of Joliet*, 715 F.2d 1200 (7th Cir., 1983) (Posner, J.), cert. denied, 465 U.S. 1049 (1984).

mere neglect of inhabitants by the state or to common-law abuse (as we may call it) of some inhabitants by others. So runs Judge Posner's plausible account of the probable original understanding of the anti-deprivation clause of the Fourteenth Amendment.[19]

The European Convention, we might speculate, is the product of a generation far removed from 'the height of laissez-faire thinking'[20] – a generation for whom a prime lesson of the intervening history had been that a liberal, industrial society (ideological commitments to the contrary notwithstanding) sustains differentials of power that make possible the replication by non-governmental actors of forms of abuse that traditional liberalism had connected specifically to governments. This was, to be sure, a lesson loudly taught by American Legal Realism,[21] but the Realists did not teach until three generations had passed after the adoption of the Fourteenth Amendment. Thus, however nicely Judge Posner's account may capture the probable expectations of those who wrote the Bill of Rights and the Fourteenth Amendment at the times when they wrote them, that account can tell us nothing about the probable understandings of the authors of the European Convention at their post-War, post-Universal Declaration, founding moment.

---

[19] Judge Posner states it more succinctly:

> The men who wrote the Bill of Rights were not concerned that government might do too little for the people but that it might do too much to them. The Fourteenth Amendment, adopted in 1868 at the height of laissez-faire thinking, sought to protect Americans from oppression by state government, not to secure them basic governmental services. Of course, even in the laissez-faire era only anarchists thought the state should not provide the type of protective services at issue in this case. But no one thought federal constitutional guarantees or federal tort remedies necessary to prod the states to provide the services that everyone wanted provided. The concern was that some states might provide those services to all but blacks, and the equal protection clause prevents that kind of discrimination.

(Ibid. at 1203.)

The Supreme Court's opinion in *DeShaney* is still more succinct. See 489 U.S. 189 (1989) at 196 ('The Fourteenth Amendment's purpose was to protect the people from the State, not to ensure that the State protected them from each other. The Framers were content to leave the extent of governmental obligation in the latter area to the democratic political processes').

[20] See above, note 19.

[21] See e.g. Morris R. Cohen, 'Property and Sovereignty' (1927) 13 *Cornell Law Quarterly*, 8; Walter W. Cook, 'Privileges of Labor Unions in the Struggle For Life' (1918) 27 *Yale Law Journal*, 779.

An originalist approach to constitutional interpretation thus might help to justify or to explain the divergent results in our two leading cases.

4. Contemporary constitutional (professional) culture?

But, of course, originalism will not justify the divergent results to those who reject originalism as a normatively proper, sovereign guide to constitutional interpretation. Nor can originalism explain these results to those who do not envision our two judiciaries as driven strongly by originalist interpretative premises. Therefore, we cannot think our work is done when we have suggested an originalist explanation or justification for the discrepancy in American and European doctrines regarding the state's protective obligation in constitutional law. Earlier, we surmised that if socially prevalent understandings had pushed for similar results in Europe and America in cases like those of *DeShaney* and *Z*, differences in the governing legal texts need not have stood in the way. For most legally trained observers, I would guess, a like proposition holds for perceived historical differences in original understandings. For this fraction of the audience, the question will persist whether some *contemporaneous* discrepancy of political philosophy or constitutional culture must not lie behind the doctrinal discrepancy.

We deal first with constitutional culture – defined, please recall, as 'the beliefs and values of nonjudicial actors' regarding 'the substance of the Constitution'.[22] Our question is whether there may be some current divergence between European and American constitutional cultures that jibes with the discrepant results in our two cases. As a possible example, we might consider the wide circulation among European (but not American) constitutionalists of the idea – it appears to be of mainly German origin[23] – that the rights-affirming clauses in a constitutional bill of rights are to be read not merely as conferrals of 'subjective rights' on individuals, but as expressions of 'objective principles' of the constitutional order.

As used here, the term 'subjective rights' refers to constitutional-legal guarantees in their guise as statements of fixed, legal entitlements of individuals – entitlements 'to be respected by the state in [one's]

---

[22] Post, 'Foreword', note 17 above.
[23] See e.g. Bernhard Schlink, 'German Constitutional Culture in Transition', in Michel Rosenfeld (ed.), *Constitutionalism, Identity, Difference, and Legitimacy* (Durham: Duke University Press, 1994), p. 197.

individual freedoms, to participate as an individual in the practice of state power, or to be considered in the distribution of positions, means, and opportunities'.[24] The term 'objective principles', by contrast, refers to 'maxims according to which social relationships, as well as the relationship between state and society, are to be ordered'.[25] Subjective rights reflect norms governing the state's immediate treatment of persons, while objective principles point to more comprehensive states of social affairs that the constitution commits the state to pursue and uphold.

To illustrate, consider a constitutional guarantee of freedom of expression. Construed *qua* subjective right, 'freedom of expression' signifies the immunities of individuals from legal regulation of what they, as individuals, or severally, choose to say or to publish. Construed *qua* objective principle, 'freedom of expression' signifies the state's positive obligation to enact and enforce such measures as may be required to induce a state of social affairs in which expression is free – in which, in other words, everyone who so chooses is able to contribute effectively to communicative exchange. The two aims are not identical, and indeed the two often have been thought non-congruent in practice. For example, legal restrictions on the flow of money in electoral politics, which an objective principle of freedom of expression may be thought to require, seem to many incompatible with subjective rights of freedom of expression.[26]

Now, suppose a constitution contains a textual guarantee of the safety of persons against physical violence. Subjective right? Objective principle? Both? How we see it can make a difference. Guarantees of constitutional law are meant especially to bind the state. (This must be so because, if a guarantee were to bind only non-state actors, there would be no need to write it into *constitutional* law; statute law or common law would serve as well.) Suppose a constitutional guarantee respecting freedom from inhuman or degrading treatment is perceived to register solely in the modality of subjective right. Then the corresponding obligation of the state is to refrain from perpetrating such treatment. But now suppose the same textual guarantee registers in the *two*

---

[24] Ibid. at p. 199.   [25] Ibid.
[26] For a classic illustration from US constitutional law, see *Buckley* v. *Valeo*, 424 U.S. 1, 48–9 (1976) ('The concept that the government may restrict the speech of some in order to enhance the relative voice of others is wholly foreign to the First Amendment . . .').

modalities of subjective right and objective principle. Then the resulting obligation on the state is two-fold: to refrain from infringing the guarantees and to exert itself, within reason, towards the achievement of a social state of affairs in which infringements do not occur. As a lesser, included form of the latter obligation, the state would be duty bound to prevent infringements when it can do so at a proportionally small cost, including cost measured in terms of compromise of other constitutional values; in other words, the state is constitutionally at fault for negligent – or reckless, or disproportionate – failure to protect.

It seems, then, that if the US constitutional culture today were as generous as the European with objective-principle ideas and their implications for constitutional law, US courts might be more open than they have been to reading our Fourteenth Amendment's anti-deprivation clause to impose a protective duty on the state. It would be easy, I think, to document that objective-principle ideas have not, in fact, spread nearly as widely and deeply in American as in European constitutional culture. Does the *Z's Case* / *DeShaney's Case* discrepancy thus stand explained by this discrepancy of professional-cultural discourses?

Again, it seems that such an explanation would be less than complete. The cultural contrast I have presented is merely one between professional cultures that have and have not taken on board a certain technical notion, that of constitutional guarantees as expressions of 'objective principles' of the constitution. To be sure, it is plausible that a professional culture having this notion in wide circulation is likelier than one from which it is mainly missing to be receptive to a legal result like that in *Z's Case* as opposed to that in *DeShaney's Case*. The question that remains is whether the degree of a legal culture's receptivity to the objective-principle approach is likely to be independent of that culture's more general ideological leanings. Perhaps we can no more assuredly speculate that objective-principle thinking in a professional legal culture explains that culture's support of a judicial finding of a state's protective duty in constitutional law, than we might speculate, oppositely, that the ideological biases of jurists who favour finding a protective duty explain the emergence in their professional culture of the notion of 'objective principle'. Perhaps all we have done so far, with our suggested constitutional-cultural divide, is to restate our question in a somewhat arcane form: Why is it that European constitutionalists circulate and nurture the objective-principle idea, while Americans, by and large, remain non-conversant with it?

5. Prevailing political 'philosophy'?

An obvious suggestion would be that the answer lies in general, political cultures (as distinct from professional, 'constitutional' cultures), in the form of some difference in what I shall call prevailing political 'philosophy', a term I use loosely to refer to what others may prefer to call ideology. Here would be a crude version, which I use only to convey the general idea. An ideological spectrum or axis runs from red to blue, from left to right. To the left lies 'social' democracy, to the right lies 'liberal' democracy. To the left lies the community, to the right, the individual. Comparatively speaking, European society heaves more to the left, American society heaves more to the right. Those, then, would be the vectors decisively explaining the discrepant doctrines of *Z's Case* and *DeShaney's Case*. The other vectors we have surveyed – federalism, the texts and their probable original understandings, professional-cultural differences – may all be implicated in the sense that they adapt easily to the doctrinal choices respectively represented by our two decisions. But the *driving*, the *decisive* vector is the one we all probably suspected in the first place, left–right philosophical difference. Case closed.

III. Against ideological closure

If we do close the case on those terms, we shall have before us a simple instance of what we may call a 'mirror' use of comparative analysis in the field of constitutional law, meaning that we treat legal-doctrinal differences as disclosing or confirming the existence of differing ideological or cultural factors in the respective sponsoring societies.[27] From there, we could launch the debate over whether such seemingly explanatory cultural differences represent a healthy diversity, therefore to be affirmed and cherished, or rather a meretricious retreat from true and universal values of liberal constitutionalism, therefore to be resisted and debunked. My aim here does not require entry into that full debate. I want simply to raise a doubt about how far the particular doctrinal disparity before us can warrant any finding at all of an ideological divide between the United States and Europe.

Basically, my doubt is one about how reliably and confidently we can 'read back' from legal-doctrinal evidence to deep, socio-cultural difference. I suspect the answers vary from instance to instance. In this

---

[27] See Frank I. Michelman, 'Reflection' (2004) 82 *Texas Law Review*, 1737.

particular instance, my sense is that a strong reaching-back is not securely warranted, and for two reasons: first, the legal-doctrinal difference we study here occurs only at the level of constitutional law, not that of general law. Second, even focusing on constitutional law, the difference may be less than meets the eye. I will take up the latter reason first.

1. How thoroughly does American constitutional law exclude the state's protective duty from constitutional analysis?

Consider the South African case of *Christian Education South Africa v. Minister of Education*.[28] A statute prohibited any use of corporal punishment in a school, public or private. A group of religiously dedicated private schools complained of violation of their constitutionally protected rights of freedom of religion.[29] The Constitutional Court assumed that the statute did infringe on this constitutionally protected right,[30] but it found the infringement to be lawful under the Constitution's so-called limitation clause, which permits limitation of constitutionally guaranteed rights by 'law of general application' that is 'reasonable and justifiable in an open and democratic society based on human dignity, equality and freedom'.[31]

A chief factor cited by the Constitutional Court in support of its conclusion was the fact that 'the state is ... under a constitutional duty to take steps to ... protect all people and especially children from maltreatment, abuse or degradation'.[32] The Court observed approvingly that the state, in reaching its judgment to prohibit corporal punishment even in Christian private schools, evidently was 'directly influenced by its constitutional obligations'.[33]

The *Christian Education* case illustrates a point that we shall need to bear in mind: judicial recognition that a given principle or value is

---

[28] 2000 (10) Butterworths Constitutional Law Reports 1951 (CC).

[29] See SA Const. § 15.

[30] See 2000 (10) Butterworths Constitutional Law Reports (CC), at 27.

[31] SA Const. § 36 (1).

[32] 2000 (10) Butterworths Constitutional Law Reports (CC), at paras. 40, 47. The Constitution declares the state's relevant duty explicitly. It contains a guarantee to everyone of 'freedom and security of the person', which includes the rights 'to be free from all forms of violence whether from public or private sources' and 'not to be treated or punished in a cruel, inhuman or degrading way' (SA Const. § 12(1) (c), (e)) and it furthermore expressly obligates the state not only to 'respect', but also to 'protect, promote and fulfil the rights in the Bill of Rights' (SA Const. § 7(2)).

[33] Ibid. at para. 50.

constitutionally embedded can register in constitutional adjudication in more than one way, of which direct judicial enforcement of the principle or value, against a passive or recalcitrant government, is only one. Another, which *Christian Education* typifies, is to allow the government's evident purpose of complying with the principle, or pursuing the value, to serve as justification for infringement by the government of some *other*, and circumstantially competing, principle or value enjoined by the constitution. In *Christian Education*, the Constitutional Court allowed the principle of the state's duty to protect all inhabitants against private physical abuse to justify a fairly obvious infringement on freedom of religious practice. In so doing, the Court ranked the protective-duty principle as a recognised and weighty one in South African constitutional law.

In like manner, when an American court accepts a government's argument that the state has, in the case at hand, a sufficiently 'compelling' justification for infringing on a constitutionally protected interest (such as, for example, freedom of expression), that court is accepting that the principle or maxim of the government's justification is one that carries distinct constitutional weight.[34] On several occasions, our Supreme Court has acted thus on behalf of what appears to be the principle of the state's protective function, as we have been defining it in this discussion. I will mention a few notable examples here.

In *Cruzan v. Director, Missouri Department of Health*,[35] the Supreme Court dealt with a claim pressed in the name of a comatose young woman by her parents, as legal representatives. The young woman, who had suffered accidental injury, had no chance of regaining consciousness. Demanding that she be disconnected from life-sustaining hydration and nutrition, her parents asserted on her behalf a traditionally recognised, constitutionally protected right to refuse physically invasive treatment of any kind, even if necessary to preserve one's life. Hospital personnel refused to comply without a supporting court order,

---

[34] For leading American scholarship on this point, see Stephen E. Gottlieb, 'Compelling Governmental Interests and Constitutional Discourse' (1992) 55 *Albany Law Review*, 549; Stephen E. Gottlieb, 'Compelling Governmental Interests: an Essential but Unanalyzed Term in Constitutional Discourse' (1988) 65 *Boston University Law Review*, 917. See also Richard H. Fallon Jr., 'Individual Rights and the Powers of Government' (1993) 27 *Georgia Law Review*, 343, 389 (' . . . judicial identification of rights represents only one medium through which constitutional interests are . . . protected. This point emerges clearly in considering the interests that underlie government powers').

[35] 497 U.S. 261 (1990).

and the Supreme Court of Missouri eventually concluded that state law prohibits termination of life-preserving treatment of a person currently unable to express her wishes, in the absence of a prior written declaration by her or other clear and convincing evidence that she had formed the wish not to be kept alive in circumstances such as those obtaining.

The US Supreme Court accepted the premise that the Fourteenth Amendment grants a substantial degree of protection for the interest in refusing treatment, even at the risk of death, but found the Missouri law's infringement of that interest to be justified by important interests of the state, including not only a diffuse interest in upholding the general value of human life and its preservation[36] but also a more concretely focused, police-like interest in protecting particular vulnerable persons against possible abusive treatment at the hands of legal surrogates.[37]

In *Hill v. Colorado*,[38] the Supreme Court refused to invalidate a state statute prohibiting any person, within one hundred feet of a health care facility's entrance, to approach within eight feet of another person to make an oral presentation, or hand a leaflet, to the person approached. Would-be protesters at abortion clinic entrances challenged the statute as an infringement of their constitutionally guaranteed rights of free speech. The Supreme Court agreed, as it had to, that some degree of infringement was occurring, but it nevertheless upheld the statute, citing the state's legitimate, 'traditional', and 'special' concerns both to maintain freedom of access to health care facilities and to protect patients and others seeking entry from the potential 'trauma' associated with confrontational protests.[39] Similarly, in *Madsen v. Women's Health Center, Inc.*,[40] the Court sustained a judicial injunctive order directed against participants in a particular ongoing protest at an abortion clinic. The order excluded demonstrators from a 36-foot buffer zone around the clinic entrances and driveway, restricted loud noise-making within earshot of patients inside the clinic, and prohibited protesters within a 300-foot zone around the clinic from approaching patients and potential patients without their consent. The Court mainly upheld the injunction,[41] citing the state's 'significant' and 'strong' interest in 'protecting a

---

[36] See ibid. at 281.   [37] See ibid.   [38] 530 U.S. 703 (2000).
[39] Ibid. at 715 ('It is a traditional exercise of the State's police powers to protect the health and safety of their citizens. That interest may justify a special focus on unimpeded access to health care facilities and the avoidance of potential trauma to patients associated with confrontational protests').
[40] 512 U.S. 753 (1994).
[41] The Court required modification of the 300-foot buffer zone as unnecessarily large.

pregnant woman's freedom to seek lawful medical or counseling services'.[42]

You may be tempted to object that the *Hill* and *Madsen* decisions are no particular sign of the Court's according constitutional weight to a state's general protective function or duty – they rather being, in your view, instances of the Court's vindicating a specially defined, 'fundamental' right to obtain an abortion. However, the cases cannot be read in the latter way. The Supreme Court repeatedly has made clear its view that the constitutional so-called right to an abortion is not what that name says. The right is only a right to 'choose' an abortion; it is not a right to *have* one when one lacks the means of getting it. It is, in other words, only a right not to have the government cast serious obstacles (such as criminal liability for abortion providers or consumers) in the way of a woman seeking an abortion and otherwise able to obtain one.[43] There being thus no special constitutional right to the government's assistance, of any kind, in obtaining an abortion, the *Hill* and *Madsen* decisions have nothing left to rest on, apart from the Court's recognition that the state's general protective function weighs significantly in the Constitution's scales of value.

Now, there happens to be a more dramatic indication of such recognition by the Court, and it lies, ironically, in the famous case establishing the libertarian right to choose an abortion, *Roe v. Wade*.[44] In that case, the Court established the doctrine, from which it has never wavered, that, once a pregnancy is past some relatively advanced stage of foetal development, the state's interest in 'protecting' the potential life of the foetus overtakes the pregnant woman's constitutionally protected interest in free choice of physical destiny, and abortion can be restricted or prohibited.[45]

The Court there spoke in terms of protection of the foetus's 'potential' life. Why? Because it believed the Constitution bars a state from 'adopt[ing] one theory of life', which it would do by decreeing that a human life begins at some point in time prior to birth or that a foetus has the moral and legal status of a 'person' from the instant of conception.[46] In the Court's view, this ruling by it – that a state cannot decide, for purposes of constitutional analysis, that life begins prior to birth – was crucial to the success of Roe's libertarian claim. Were the conclusion

---

[42] *Madsen* v. *Women's Health Center, Inc.*, 512 U.S. 753 at 764, 767.
[43] See *Harris* v. *McRae*, 448 U.S. 297 (1980); *Maher* v. *Roe*, 432 U.S. 464 (1977).
[44] 410 U.S. 113 (1973).   [45] See ibid. at 154.   [46] See ibid. at 156–62.

otherwise, the Court reasoned – were the state free to classify the foetus as a 'person' from the moment of conception – 'the appellant's case [would] ... collapse[ ],' because 'the fetus's right to life' would then be 'guaranteed specifically by the [Fourteenth] Amendment'.[47]

Guaranteed against whom, or what? Guaranteed against harm by a non-state actor such as a pregnant woman or her doctor? Guaranteed against the state's possible failure to protect against such privately inflicted harm? The Court did not explain.

Nor did the Court refer to its reasoning in *Roe* when it decided *DeShaney* sixteen years later, but how can the *Roe* reasoning survive? *DeShaney* insists that the Fourteenth Amendment's anti-deprivation guarantee imposes no duty of protection on the state. Yet according to *Roe v. Wade*, the state's responsibilities under that same constitutional guarantee would give it clear justification to override a constitutionally elevated liberty interest of a pregnant woman to control her own physical destiny, in order to protect a foetus, assuming a foetus were a 'person'. How can both propositions hold simultaneously?

Protection as an under-enforced constitutional right in American constitutional law?

An answer is available, in two parts. First, what we perceive in the decisions reviewed above is affirmation of the state's general duty of protection, but it is affirmation entering constitutional law by the back door, so to speak, at the justification stage as opposed to the claiming stage of a lawsuit. Second, this back-door-open, front-door-closed judicial posture is symptomatic of the existence in American constitutional law of what has been called an 'under-enforced' constitutional right – specifically, here, an under-enforced constitutional right to the state's protection against physically abusive treatment by others in society.

The notion of under-enforced constitutional rights has been persuasively developed by Lawrence Sager.[48] Sager maintains that the refusal of courts to give direct remedial effect to one or another claimed principle of constitutional right does not necessarily signal the absence of that principle from American constitutional law. There may, he argues, exist sound institutional reasons for *judicial* abstinence from direct

---

[47] See ibid. at 156–7.
[48] See, e.g., Lawrence Sager, *Justice in Plainclothes: a Theory of American Constitutional Practice* (New Haven: Yale University Press, 2004); Lawrence Sager, 'The Domain of Constitutional Justice', in Larry Alexander (ed.), *Constitutionalism: Philosophical Foundations* (Cambridge: Cambridge University Press, 1998), p. 235, at pp. 240–1.

enforcement, observance of which does not deny or refute the principle's subsistence as one having the force of constitutional law for *other* actors in the legal system to whose conduct it may apply – and even for judges when the principle is invoked in some way other than as a ground for direct judicial enforcement. Other ways might include, for example, invocation of the principle as a ground of justification for otherwise constitutionally questionable government action.

The kinds of institutional considerations that may inhibit direct judicial enforcement of certain constitutional rights are well known to constitutional lawyers around the world. There may be lacking a crisp, justiciable standard for deciding questions of compliance and violation. Enforcement may require forms of judicial intervention in public affairs that strain the relations between the judiciary and the executive and legislative branches of government; or it may involve the judiciary in making too many subsidiary, administrative decisions that belong properly to the popularly accountable 'political' branches.[49]

All of these problematic features – uncertain standards, strain on inter-branch relations, excessive judicial 'engineering' – are likely to be salient when the claims of right that judges are called on to enforce directly are claims to the government's active assistance of some kind. That is why ESR rights stand high on Sager's candidate list of existent American constitutional rights that are, appropriately, judicially under-enforced.[50] A right to protection is a right to the government's active assistance, and it fits Sager's model neatly. But note that the problematic features either vanish or grow much more manageable when the right to protection – more precisely, the corresponding protective duty of the state – is invoked as justification for action the government spontaneously chooses to take. By endorsing the justification, the court neither ignites inter-branch controversy nor takes on the role of social engineer; and although the exact constitutional standard of protective obligation may remain cloudy, a court upholding justification shares with the political branches the judgment that the protective obligation is fairly implicated by the case at hand.[51]

I propose, therefore, that, for purposes of comparison of American with European constitutional law, the apt conclusion is not that American

[49] See, e.g., Sager, 'Domain of Constitutional Justice', above, note 48.   [50] See ibid.
[51] See Fallon, 'Individual Rights', above, note 34, p. 389 ('For reasons [of] ... comparative competence ... courts may rightly hesitate to translate every interest of constitutional magnitude into a constitutional right and may even defer to the judgments of non-judicial officers concerning what the Constitution requires').

constitutional law denies or excludes the state's protective function or duty. It is rather, and somewhat to the contrary, that American law confirms the duty principle's force in our system of legal norms by visibly under-enforcing it. What this would mean, in effect, is that the distinction between US and European constitutional law on this point may be not that America stands indifferent to a principle of human right that Europe proclaims, but rather that the two professional constitutional cultures entertain somewhat different ideas regarding limits on the appropriate role of the judiciary, and of adjudication, in the implementation of a political principle that both cultures nurture.

This, then, is the second time we have sought explanation for the *Z's Case / DeShaney's Case* discrepancy in differences of professional cultures. There is, however, an important distinction to be drawn between this second professional-cultural difference and the one we previously considered. That one – the difference between professional cultures that do and do not speak routinely of constitutional guarantees as objective principles – may be thought to collapse into a supposed left–right ideological divergence in the general, political cultures. This one resists any explanation of that kind. There is nothing particularly 'left' or 'right' about a more or less constricted conception of the judicial role in a constitutional system of government. If you doubt that, consider that an American tilt towards a relatively constricted role for the judiciary is an undoubted legacy of revulsion from 'Lochner',[52] and rejection of 'Lochner' historically was a leftward, not a rightward, impulse. Consider, further, that relatively populist conceptions of constitutional democracy are generally considered to be 'left', while relatively Madisonian conceptions are generally considered to be 'right'. The apparent American tilt towards a more constricted judicial role is a tilt away from Madisonianism, towards populism – a tilt toward the red, not the blue.

2. Is the doctrinal difference in constitutional law a 'real' social difference?

One could compare the actual, ground-level, political and social practices of two societies respecting the state's protective function. Social scientists could devise ways to measure whether state protection against private violence is more committed or effective in Europe than in America. Legal experts could inquire whether the laws in the countries of Europe – I mean the ordinary laws, not the constitutional laws – set

---

[52] See, e.g., Sujit Choudhry, 'The Lochner Era and Comparative Constitutionalism' (2004) 2 no. 1 *International Journal of Constitutional Law*, 4–15.

higher effective standards of state protection than do the counterpart laws in the United States. Public finance specialists could report on whether Europeans tax themselves harder to fund state protection than Americans do. The social scientists, again, could look to see whether Europe has been more resistant than America to displacement of public police forces by private guards in gated communities (and the like), or otherwise has been less prone to political abdication from public protection. They could inquire whether one is less likely in Europe than in America to find severely under-served districts in which visible public law enforcement shrinks out of sight.

It might be the case – I have no idea whether it is – that Europe would be found, or has been found, to score higher on such social measures of state-protective functioning than America does. If so, one might accept that as a true basis for inferring the relatively social-democratic or communitarian leanings of Europeans as compared with the relatively libertarian, individualist leanings of Americans.

But suppose it is not so. Suppose that – for all we really know just now – Europe and the United States score just about the same on the sorts of empirical social measures I have mentioned. In that case, would the bare fact that European *constitutional* law provides a legal remedy against egregious defaults in state protection, while US *constitutional* law does not, give us any real ground for inferring some deep ideological divide between the two populations? Why should it? Constitutions and constitutional law comprise one set of devices among others – some of them of a legal nature, some not – for constraining public actors to desired levels of performance of certain key public functions and of respect for preferred political values. Why should the fact that the *constitutional* devices are somewhat differently arranged in the two places make us think the ideologies must be divergent, as long as the actual governmental performances (so far as we know) are roughly comparable? Why should we fetishise constitutional law in that way?

Because, you might answer, constitutions and constitutional law are *not* simply devices for constraining public actors to desired levels of performance and respect. Constitutions, you might say, serve expressive as well as instrumental uses. They earn their keep by performing an 'integrative' as well as a 'legitimating' function.[53] They serve to 'embody

[53] Ulrich K. Preuss, 'Patterns of Constitutional Evolution and Change in Eastern Europe', in Joachim J. Hesse and Nevil Jonson (eds.), *Constitutional Policy and Change in Europe* (Oxford, 1995) p. 95, at pp. 101–3.

common goals, ... values, and beliefs that bind together the members of the polity', and not just to 'justify political authority'.[54] A country's constitution is an expression of its national ethos, a focal point for national identity. A constitution, indeed, is a 'mirror reflecting the national soul'.[55] Therefore, you say, it is quite in order to treat attention-grabbing discrepancies between the constitutional-legal doctrines of two societies as indicators of underlying ideological differences.

I see two hazards in this line of thought, as applied to the particular discrepancy before us. The first and relatively minor hazard is presented by my discussion in the preceding section. Supposing that American constitutional law does mirror the American national soul, our soul may then appear to be one that gravitates to a form of political life in which public protection against private violence is a basic premise and commitment, reflected visibly in our constitutional law as an under-enforced constitutional principle.

The second and larger hazard lies in the argument's dependence on rejection of a strictly instrumental view of constitutions, as being simply one device among others for constraining governmental conduct in certain ways. Mainstream American jurists may possibly differ from mainstream European jurists over just that view. Americans who engage professionally in the practice of constitutional law, a group in which I include judges, typically do so, I believe, with a hard-nosed, instrumentalist approach to the work. They think of the constitution as a law to be used and deployed more or less as other laws.[56]

---

[54] Ibid.

[55] *S v. Acheson* 1991 (2) SA 805 (Nm) at 813A–B (1991 NR 1 at 10A–B) (Mahomed AJ).

[56] Two clarifications are in order. First, the instrumentalist aims for which lawyers try to make constitutions serve may be highly 'idealist' in nature; for example, achievement of a non-racial, non-sexist society. Second, lawyers and judges may very well take account of the inevitable, expressive consequences of legal-doctrinal choices in their instrumentalist calculations, in the manner suggested, for example, by Richard Pildes and Richard Niemi, 'Expressive Harms, "Bizarre Districts", and Voting Rights: Evaluating Election-District Appearances After *Shaw v. Reno*' (1993) 92 *Michigan Law Review*, 483, 485, 502, 506–7. Pildes and Niemi use the term 'expressive harm' to designate a class of effects that '[result] from the ideas or attitudes expressed through a governmental action, rather than from the more tangible or material consequences the action brings about'. They suggest that, in the Supreme Court's view, legislative districting that appears to 'reduce' the problem of due or fair representation to one of racial representation 'demonstrates inappropriate respect for relevant public values' or 'express[es] a value structure that offends constitutional principles'. Such mere expressions of disrespect for values, Pildes and Niemi suggest, can have practical consequences. They can 'undermine collective understandings' or jeopardise political legitimacy. Thinking in this practical-minded way about the expressive effects of doctrinal choices is not at all the same thing as treating constitutional law as a national *cri de coeur* that reveals the soul within.

Might it be that American legal professionals are less romantically disposed toward their Constitution than their European counterparts are? I raise this possibility for consideration because, if there is anything to it, it could point towards an explanation for the *Z's Case* v. *DeShaney's* case discrepancy to compete with the hypothesis of a left–right ideological gulf between our two societies.

Comment

HEIKE KRIEGER

The classical liberal interpretation views human rights as areas of liberty for the individual which the State may not infringe upon. However, private persons can also endanger human rights. Landlords may terminate rent contracts on the basis of race. Children may suffer abuse at the hands of their parents. A woman's decision to have an abortion interferes with the foetus' possible right to life. Although such actions are private actions they take place within the legal system provided by the state. Thus, the state is always somehow involved in private actions.[1] Does the state therefore have a positive obligation to protect the individual against other individuals? And does the individual have a corresponding right to the state's protection?

A comparison of the jurisprudence of the US Supreme Court with the jurisprudence of the European Court of Human Rights seems to demonstrate that the American constitutional system, as opposed to the European one, rejects any protective duty of the state or any corresponding constitutional right of protection for the individual. In the case of *DeShaney v. Winnebago County*,[2] concerning a failure of public authorities to prevent child abuse, the Supreme Court held that the US Constitution

> forbids the State itself to deprive individuals of life, liberty, or property without 'due process of law', but its language cannot fairly be extended to impose an affirmative obligation on the state to ensure that those interests do not come to harm through other means. Nor does history support such an expansive reading of the constitutional text. The clause's purpose was to protect the people from the state, not to ensure that the state protected them from each other. The Framers were content to leave the

---

[1] M. Tushnet, 'The Issue of State Action/Horizontal Effect in Comparative Constitutional Law' (2003) 1 *International Journal of Constitutional Law*, 79.

[2] *DeShaney* v. *Winnebago County Department of Social Services*, 489 U.S. 189 (1989).

extent of governmental obligation in the latter area to the democratic political processes.[3]

In two comparable European cases, *Z v. United Kingdom*[4] and *E v. United Kingdom*,[5] the competent authorities had been aware of the occurrence of child abuse but they did not act to stop the abuse. In these cases, the European Court of Human Rights found this to be a breach of Art. 3 of the European Convention. Indeed, the Court has not limited its jurisprudence to particularly vulnerable persons or to certain fundamental human rights provisions, but has recognised a much broader range of positive obligations.

I. The jurisprudence of the European Court of Human Rights

The European Court of Human Rights has developed an abundant jurisprudence on the individual's rights to be protected by the state. Different dimensions of these positive obligations can be distinguished. As Frank Michelman explains,[6] there is a basic distinction between positive obligations to protect the individual against harmful actions by private persons and the obligation to grant financial support or take specific social measures. The European Court of Human Rights fully accepts a duty to protect the individual from harmful actions of other private persons,[7] but it has so far essentially rejected any right that would imply larger financial obligations.

1. Protection of social and economic rights?

The European Court is reluctant to accept positive obligations if they imply financial support or specific social measures. The Court has repeatedly found that there is no right to be provided with a home,

---

[3] *DeShaney* v. *Winnebago County Department of Social Services*, 489 U.S. 189, 195 et seq. (1989).

[4] *Z* v. *The United Kingdom*, 2001-V Eur. Ct. H.R.

[5] *E* v. *The United Kingdom*, Eur. Ct. H.R., judgment of 26 November 2002, available at http://www.echr.coe.int.

[6] F. Michelman, 'The protective function of the state in the United States and Europe: the constitutional question', in this volume p. 156.

[7] *Young, James and Webster* v. *The United Kingdom*, 44 Eur. Ct. H.R. (ser. A) (1980), para. 49; *X and Y* v. *The Netherlands*, 91 Eur. Ct. H.R. (ser. A) (1985), para. 23; *Plattform 'Ärzte für das Leben'* v. *Austria*, 139 Eur. Ct. H.R. (ser. A) (1988), para. 32.

work or education.[8] When gypsy families complained that the United Kingdom violated their right to private life by not allowing them (as members of an internationally protected minority) to temporarily occupy land where they wished the Court rejected a duty of the state to provide them with an adequate number of suitably equipped sites. The Court refused 'such a far-reaching positive obligation of general social policy'.[9] With regard to poverty, the Court has not as yet accepted a right to minimum welfare[10] whereas the German Constitutional Court acknowledges the state's duty to guarantee a minimum level of subsistence.[11] This difference may be due to the lack of an explicit provision on human dignity in the European Convention. The European Court is aware of the resistance of the States to being subject to financial obligations that might be imposed by an international court. The rejection of specific social rights is consistent with the general approach of European constitutions and the European Charter of Fundamental Rights.[12] Although constitutions of southern European states, such as

---

[8] *Chapman* v. *The United Kingdom*, 2001-I Eur. Ct. H.R. 41, para. 99; *Beard* v. *The United Kingdom*, Eur. Ct. H.R., judgment of 18 January 2001, para. 110, available at http://www.echr.coe.int; *Coster* v. *The United Kingdom*, Eur. Ct. H.R., judgment of 18 January 2001, para. 113, available at http://www.echr.coe.int; *Lee* v. *The United Kingdom*, Eur. Ct. H.R., judgment of 18 January 2001, para. 111, available at http://www.echr.coe.int; *Jane Smith* v. *The United Kingdom*, Eur. Ct. H.R., judgment of 18 January 2001, para. 106, available at http://www.echr.coe.int; *Petrovic* v. *Austria*, 1998-II Eur. Ct. H.R. 579, para. 25; see also M. Villiger, *Handbuch der EMRK* (Zurich: Schulthess, 1993), note 100, 572, 634, 646.

[9] *Chapman* v. *The United Kingdom*, 2001-I Eur. Ct. H.R. 41, para. 98; see *Beard* v. *The United Kingdom*, Eur. Ct. H.R., judgment of 18 January 2001, paras. 109–10, available at http://www.echr.coe.int; *Coster* v. *The United Kingdom*, Eur. Ct. H.R., judgment of 18 January 2001, para. 112, available at http://www.echr.coe.int; *Lee* v. *The United Kingdom*, Eur. Ct. H.R., judgment of 18 January 2001, para. 110, available at http://www.echr.coe.int; *Jane Smith* v. *The United Kingdom*, Eur. Ct. H.R., judgment of 18 January 2001, para. 105, available at http://www.echr.coe.int.

[10] *Pancenko* v. *Latvia*, Eur. Ct. H.R., decision of 28 October 1999, para. 2, available at http://www.echr.coe.int; see C. Dröge and T. Marauhn, 'Soziale Grundrechte in der Europäischen Grundrechtecharta – aus der Perspektive der EMRK', in Bundesministerium der Arbeit et al. (eds.), *Soziale Rechte in der Europäischen Union* (2001), pp. 77–94 at pp. 90–1; J. Frowein, 'Wirtschaftliche und soziale Rechte in der Rechtsprechung der Straßburger Organe', in S. Vassilouni (ed.), *Aspects of the Protection of Individual and Social Rights* (Athens: Hestin, 1995), pp. 203–17 at p. 215.

[11] BVerfGE 82, 60 (85 et seqq.); 87, 153 (169 et seqq.).

[12] See for the German debate on the European Charter of Fundamental Rights, C. Calliess, 'Die Charta der Grundrechte der Europäischen Union' (2001) *Europäische Zeitschrift für Wirtschaftsrecht*, 261, 265; I. Pernice, 'Eine Grundrechtecharta für die Europäische

Spain and Italy, contain social rights these are not read as judicially enforceable rights[13] because of their imprecise nature and the potential conflict with the budgetary competences of the legislature.[14]

The jurisprudence of the European Court does demonstrate, however, that the distinction between the protective function and social rights may eventually collapse. In the case of *Botta v. Italy* a physically disabled person could not gain access to the beach of a private bathing establishment during his holidays. While the European Commission for Human Rights found that the rights which the applicant asserted were social in character and that what he claimed went beyond the concept of the legal obligations inherent in the right to private life, the European Court analysed the case in terms of the duty to protect.[15] Ultimately, the distinction seems to depend on whether the involvement of private persons or of the state is emphasised. Are third parties responsible for a violation of Art. 8 ECHR because private bathing establishments were not equipped with special facilities? Or does Mr Botta have a right to receive state support to make the life of a handicapped person easier?

2. The duty to protect against infringements by third parties

It can be argued that protective duties are contained in all human rights guaranteed under the Convention. The Court and the European Commission on Human Rights have accepted positive obligations in relation to the right to private and family life,[16] freedom of assembly,[17]

Union' (2000) *Deutsches Verwaltungsblatt*, 847, 853; P. Tettinger, 'Die Charta der Grundrechte der Europäischen Union' (2001) 14 *Neue Juristische Wochenschrift*, 1010, 1014; A. Weber, 'Die Europäische Grundrechtecharta' (2000) 8 *Neue Juristische Wochenschrift*, 537, 540–1.

[13] C. Dröge, *Positive Verpflichtungen der Staaten in der Europäischen Menschenrechtskonvention* (Berlin: Springer, 2003), 264–5.

[14] D. Currie, 'Positive and Negative Constitutional Rights' (1986) 53 *The University of Chicago Law Review*, 864, 889; see on the German debate C. Starck, 'Art. 1 Sect. 3', in H. v. Mangoldt, F. Klein, C. Starck (eds.), *Das Bonner Grundgesetz: Kommentar* (4th edn, 3 vols., Munich: Vahlen, 1999), vol. I, note 154.

[15] *Botta v. Italy*, 1998-I Eur. Ct. H.R. 412, para. 35.

[16] *X and Y v. The Netherlands*, 91 Eur. Ct. H.R. (ser. A) (1985), para. 23; *Powell and Rayner v. The United Kingdom*, 172 Eur. Ct. H.R. (ser. A) (1990), paras. 41 and 45; *López Ostra v. Spain*, 303-C Eur. Ct. H.R. (ser. A) (1994), para. 51; *Velosa Barreto v. Portugal*, 334 Eur. Ct. H.R. (ser. A) (1995), para. 23; *Stubbings v. The United Kingdom*, 1996-IV Eur. Ct. H.R. 1488, paras. 66–7.

[17] *Young, James and Webster v. The United Kingdom*, 44 Eur. Ct. H.R. (ser. A) (1980), para. 49; *Plattform 'Ärzte für das Leben' v. Austria*, 139 Eur. Ct. H.R. (ser. A) (1988), para. 32; *Wilson and the National Union of Journalists v. The United Kingdom*, 2002-V Eur. Ct. H.R. 49, paras. 41–2.

the right to life[18] as well as in relation to the prohibition of torture[19] and slavery,[20] the right to freedom and security,[21] the freedom of religion[22] and opinion,[23] and the right to property.[24]

The duty to protect is addressed to all branches of the state. Due to the separation of powers, human rights can only be protected effectively if all branches adopt those protective measures that fall within their sphere of competence.[25] To take the example of the right to life: there is, first, an obligation of the state to secure the right to life by putting in place effective criminal law provisions to deter the commission of offences against a person. Thus, under the European Convention individuals may successfully raise a complaint that a failure to legislate properly violates their human rights. The most well-known case is *X and Y v. The Netherlands* where there was a lacuna in the law which prevented criminal prosecution for the rape of mentally handicapped women.[26] Secondly, there is a positive obligation of the executive authorities to take preventive measures to protect an individual whose life is endangered by criminal acts of others. 'It is common ground that the State's obligation ... extends beyond its primary duty to secure the right to life by putting in place effective criminal-law provisions ... Article 2 of the Convention may also imply in certain well-defined circumstances a positive obligation on the authorities to take preventive operational measures.'[27] The

---

[18] *L. C. B.* v. *The United Kingdom*, 1998-III Eur. Ct. H.R. 1390, para. 36; *Cavelli and Ciglio* v. *Italy*, 2002-I Eur. Ct. H.R. 1, para. 48; *Oneryildiz*, Eur. Ct. H.R., judgment of 18 June 2002, para. 62, upheld by judgment of the Grand Chamber of 30 November 2004; available at http://www.echr.coe.int.

[19] *A* v. *The United Kingdom*, 1998-VI Eur. Ct. H.R. 2692, para. 22; *Assenov and Others* v. *Bulgaria*, 1998-VIII Eur. Ct. H.R. 3242, para. 102; *D. P. and J. C.* v. *The United Kingdom*, Eur. Ct. H.R., judgment of 10 October 2002, para. 109, available at http://www.echr.coe.int.

[20] *X* v. *The Netherlands*, App. No. 9322/81, 32 Eur. Comm'n H.R. Dec. & Rep. 180, 182.

[21] *Nielsen*, 144 Eur. Ct. H.R. (ser. A) (1988), paras. 63, 72–3.

[22] *Otto-Preminger Institut* v. *Austria*, 295-A Eur. Ct. H.R. (ser. A) (1994), para. 47.

[23] *Özgür Gündem* v. *Turkey*, 2000-III Eur. Ct. H.R. 1, para. 43; *VGT Verein gegen Tierfabriken* v. *Switzerland*, 2001-VI Eur. Ct. H.R. 243, paras. 44–7.

[24] Read together with Art. 8 ECHR: *Velosa Barreto* v. *Portugal*, 334 Eur. Ct. H.R. (ser. A) (1995), paras. 23 and 37; Art. 1 Add. Protocol 1: *Oneryildiz*, Eur. Ct. H.R., judgment of 18 June 2002, paras. 144–5, available at http://www.echr.coe.int.

[25] L. Jaeckel, *Schutzpflichten im deutschen und europäischen Recht* (Baden-Baden: Nomos-Verlag-Ges., 2001), 166–7; K. Wiesbrock, *Internationaler Schutz der Menschenrechte vor Verletzungen durch Private* (Berlin: Verlag Spitz, 1999), 160.

[26] *X and Y* v. *The Netherlands*, 91 Eur. Ct. H.R. (ser. A) (1985), para. 23.

[27] *Osman* v. *Turkey*, 1998-VIII Eur. Ct. H.R. 3124, para. 115; *Akkoc* v. *Turkey*, 2000-X Eur. Ct. H.R. 389, para. 78; *Kilic* v. *Turkey*, 2000-III Eur. Ct. H.R. 75, para. 63; *Mahmut Kaya* v. *Turkey*, 2000-III Eur. Ct. H.R. 149, para. 86; *Paul and Audrey Edwards* v. *The United Kingdom*, 2002-II Eur. Ct. H.R. 137, para. 55; *Mastromatteo* v. *Italy*, 2002-VIII Eur. Ct. H.R. 151, paras. 67–8.

European Court of Human Rights has confirmed a duty to protect in cases
in which the authorities ought to have known of a real and immediate risk to
the life of a person emanating from criminal acts of another person. In such
cases the authorities must take measures to avoid that risk. The Court
affirmed the violation of this duty in the case *Akkoc* where a Kurdish teacher
was killed after the police authorities had rejected his request for personal
protection.[28] The extent of the authorities' duty to take preventive measures
depends on the vulnerability of the individuals concerned as well as the
importance of the human rights involved. Thirdly, the duty to protect may
also require proper adjudication. The state's responsibility is engaged if
domestic courts apply national legislation in breach of the Convention to
acts of private parties who enjoy contractual freedom.[29] In addition to these
primary duties to protect, the European Court has developed secondary
duties that require effective procedural measures to secure the substantial
guarantees of the Convention. This includes duties to investigate and to
provide effective remedies. The Court has said on a number of occasions that
positive obligations require an effective independent judicial system which
must include having recourse to criminal law remedies under certain
circumstances.[30]

When developing positive obligations the European Court has
engaged in a dynamic interpretation of the Convention. Positive obligations are based on the substance of the human right concerned and on its
value for a democratic society. In addition, the Court has increasingly
emphasised the interplay between the substance of a particular human
right and the state's general obligation under Art. 1 of the European
Convention to secure 'to everyone within their jurisdiction the rights
and freedoms defined in this Convention'.[31] The Court determines the
scope of the duty to protect in the light of all the circumstances of any
particular case. This leads to a case-by-case evaluation of all circumstances and the Court has even emphasised that it does not consider it
desirable to develop a general theory of positive obligations. The Court's
approach is thus characterised by considerations of equity in individual

---

[28] *Akkoc* v. *Turkey*, 2000-X Eur. Ct. H.R. 389, para. 78.
[29] *Velosa Barreto*, 334 Eur. Ct. H.R. (ser. A) (1995), paras. 23 and 26; *VGT Verein gegen Tierfabriken* v. *Switzerland*, 2001-VI Eur. Ct. H.R. 243, paras. 45–7.
[30] *Vo* v. *France*, Eur. Ct. H.R., judgment of 8 July 2004, para. 90, available at http://www.echr.coe.int.
[31] See *Young, James and Webster* v. *The United Kingdom*, 44 Eur. Ct. H.R. (ser. A) (1980), para. 49; *Gustafsson* v. *Sweden*, 1996-II Eur. Ct. H.R. 637, para. 45.

cases. This case-by-case evaluation may, at times, endanger the uniformity, predictability and legal certainty of its jurisprudence.[32]

II. A difference in quantity or quality?

Michelman considers possible explanations for the described differences between the US and the European constitutional systems. His ultimate conclusion that protection against private violence is also a constitutional principle under the US Constitution, although under-enforced, is not as astonishing as it seems, even in the light of the *DeShaney Case* (1.). Overall, however, the differences in this respect between European and US constitutionalism nevertheless appear to remain of a qualitative rather than a quantitative kind (2.–3.).

1. The protective function as the basic purpose of the state

General constitutional theory confirms that all constitutions presuppose the protective function of the state as its most fundamental purpose. This has been the reasoning of philosophers such as John Locke and William Blackstone.[33] The Virginia Bill of Rights of 1776 proclaims: 'That government is, or ought to be, instituted for the common benefit, protection, and security, of the people, nation, or community; of all the various modes and forms of government that is best, which is capable of producing the greatest degree of happiness and safety.' State purposes serve as a basis for the state's power to restrict human rights. The state is justified in limiting the individual's freedom as enshrined in human rights by laws in the interest of certain State functions which include the function to protect the rights of other members of the community. This purpose to provide safety and security for the members of the community is the basis for the State's entitlement to provide for criminal law and prosecution as well as for the judicial enforcement of civil law in order to protect the life and the property of individuals.[34] The European Convention on Human Rights lists among the possible justifications for an interference with human rights the interests of

---

[32] C. Dröge, *Positive Verpflichtungen*, above, note 13, p. 379; B. Hofstötter, 'European Court of Human Rights: Positive Obligations in *E and others* v. *United Kingdom*' (2004) 2 *International Journal of Constitutional Law*, 525, 527.

[33] G. Robbers, *Sicherheit als Menschenrecht* (Baden-Baden: Nomos, 1987), pp. 46 et seqq.; C. Starck, *Praxis der Verfassungsauslegung* (Baden-Baden: Nomos, 1994), pp. 47 et seqq.

[34] Starck, *Verfassungsauslegung*, above, note 33, pp. 53–4.

public safety, the prevention of disorder or crime, and the protection of the rights and freedoms of others (Paragraphs 2 of Articles 8–11 ECHR). It must be borne in mind, however, that the question whether the state is *justified* in restricting human rights in the interest of the protection of the rights of others is fundamentally different from the question whether an individual is entitled to and can judicially enforce state protection. It is thus an important question whether there is an enforceable constitutional right to protection.

2. The enforceable right to state protection

The European Court has developed positive duties directly from the rights themselves because, for the Convention system, the right of individual complaint is decisive. The European Court has not based positive obligations on a concept of objective principles, although elements of a value-oriented approach can be found where it emphasises the importance of a specific human right for a democratic society.[35] In such contexts, however, the Court does not explicitly refer to the concept of human dignity, or to an understanding of human rights as embodying an objective-value order or to concepts such as the '*ordre public européenne*'[36] or the 'constitutional instrument of European public order'.[37] The Court rather emphasises an approach based on the rights of the individual. The contracting states are obliged to provide a comprehensive protection of human rights which according to the Court includes positive obligations. These guarantees can be enforced by the individual through the complaints procedure.[38] Thus, under the European system every individual in a contracting state can judicially enforce the obligation of the State to provide protection.

---

[35] For an objective-value approach see A. Clapham, *Human Rights in the Private Sphere* (Oxford: Oxford University Press, 1996), pp. 145 et seqq., 240; G. Ress, 'The Duty to Protect and to Ensure Human Rights Under the European Convention on Human Rights', in E. Klein (ed.), *The Duty to Protect and to Ensure Human Rights* (Berlin Verlag Spitz, 2000), pp. 165 et seqq. at pp. 188 et seqq.; Villiger, *Handbuch*, above, note 8, at note 164 et seqq.; against: Dröge, *Positive Verpflichtungen*, above, note 13, pp. 189–92; Jaeckel, *Schutzpflichten*, above, note 25, p. 139; Robbers, *Sicherheit*, above, note 33, p. 25; W. Streuer, *Die positiven Verpflichtungen des Staates* (Baden-Baden: Nomos, 2003), pp. 322 et seqq.; Wiesbrock, *Menschenrechte*, above, note 25, p. 188.

[36] *De Wilde, Ooms and Versyp* v. *Belgium*, 12 Eur. Ct. H.R. (ser. A) (1970), para. 65.

[37] *Loizidou* v. *Turkey*, 310 Eur. Ct. H.R. (ser. A) (1995), para. 75.

[38] Jaeckel, *Schutzpflichten*, above, note 25, at p. 139.

In my view, this contrast to the jurisprudence of the US Supreme Court entails a difference in quality. The development of duties to protect leads to an enlarged sphere of justification for interferences with human rights. Positive obligations significantly influence the balancing process. What used to be a mere expression of the state's purpose to protect the rights of others is now a judicially enforceable right with considerably more weight. The general function of the state to protect its citizens from terrorist threats results in a different balancing process than a person's enforceable right to be protected against a specific terrorist threat.[39] Moreover, in cases in which the duty to protect is compromised by the lack of, or inadequateness of, a legal regulation, enforceable rights have a strong impact on the separation of powers. If the Court holds that a lack of legislation infringes the duty to protect, any ruling on how the positive obligation must be realised directly circumscribes the competences of the political branches.[40] The European approach limits political decision-making and thus attributes political responsibility for framing social conditions to a considerable extent to the courts.[41] This, in turn, reduces democratic accountability for protective functions and it fosters the individual's reluctance to use democratic political means instead of judicial ones to achieve certain aspects of protection.

It should be noted, however, that the European Court of Human Rights has developed different methods in order to take into account the essential place that democratic self-governance and thus political responsibility holds in the Convention system. In cases where the duty to protect would result in new financial obligations, the Court constantly stresses that these matters are for political and not for judicial decision.[42] Where the Court deals with the right to protection against infringements of the right to life it confirms that the state must be free to make operational choices in terms of priorities and resources. The duty to protect must not impose an impossible or disproportionate burden on the authorities. This means that the Court limits the duty to protect

---

[39] O. Lepsius, *The Relationship between Security and Civil Liberties in the Federal Republic of Germany after September 11* (Washington, DC: American Institute for Contemporary German Studies, 2002); also available at http://www.aicgs.org/publications/PDF/lepsiusenglish.pdf., pp. 19–20.

[40] Starck, *Verfassungsauslegung*, above, note 33, p. 83.

[41] Regarding the issue under German law: Starck, *Verfassungsauslegung*, above, note 33, p. 78.

[42] *Osman* v. *The United Kingdom*, 1998-VIII Eur. Ct. H.R. 3124, paras. 115 et seqq.

by requiring a real and immediate risk of which the authorities ought to have known.[43] As far as other human rights are concerned, the Court grants states a margin of appreciation in their choice of methods.[44] The margin of appreciation mitigates the difficulties which arise when international jurisprudence is applied to democratic states under the rule of law. The European Court respects the decisions taken by national democratic institutions to a large extent. The Court emphasises the diversity of valid opinions in democratic societies with respect to general social policy and pays tribute to national policy decisions.[45] The approach is backed by the principles of subsidiarity and of diversity of the contracting States.[46] The Court leaves the primary responsibility to the national authorities and interprets positive obligations restrictively where no common European standard exists. However, the margin of appreciation is itself not unlimited. The Court tries to strike a fair balance between the competing interests of the individual and the community as a whole.[47]

3. The position of the individual in the democratic state

Does an explanation based on the role of the judiciary suffice to explain the divergent approaches of the European and US systems? Is this explanation preferable, as Michelman suggests, since it resists any explanation to use a left–right ideological divergence? As attractive as this interpretation appears to be, it nevertheless leaves the question open why Europe prefers to give courts such an important role in implementing human rights protection notwithstanding the possible influence on the separation of powers.

---

[43] For instance: *Osman* v. *The United Kingdom*, 1998-VIII Eur. Ct. H.R. 3124, para. 116; *Mastromatteo* v. *Italy*, 2002-VIII Eur. Ct. H.R. 151, para. 74.

[44] *Rees* v. *The United Kingdom*, 106 Eur. Ct. H.R. (ser. A) (1986), para. 37; *Johnston* v. *The United Kingdom*, 112 Eur. Ct. H.R. (ser. A) (1986), para. 55; *Plattform 'Ärzte für das Leben'* v. *Austria*, 139 Eur. Ct. H.R. (ser. A) (1988), para. 34; *López Ostra* v. *Spain*, 303-C Eur. Ct. H.R. (ser. A) (1994), para. 51; *Hatton* v. *The United Kingdom*, Eur. Ct. H.R., judgment of 2 October 2001, para. 98, available at http://www.echr.coe.int.

[45] *Hatton* v. *The United Kingdom*, Eur. Ct. H.R., judgment of 2 October 2001, para. 97, available at http://www.echr.coe.int.

[46] Regarding the margin of appreciation see E. Brems, 'The Margin of Appreciation Doctrine in the Case-Law of the ECHR' (1996) 56 *Zeitschrift für ausländisches öffentliches Recht und Völkerrecht*, 240–314.

[47] *Johnston* v. *The United Kingdom*, 112 Eur. Ct. H.R. (ser. A) (1986), para. 55; *Powell and Rayner* v. *The United Kingdom*, 172 Eur. Ct. H.R. (ser. A) (1990), para. 41; *López Ostra* v. *Spain*, 303-C Eur. Ct. H.R. (ser. A) (1994), para. 51.

A. The text of the human rights provisions

As Michelman explains,[48] the texts of the human rights provisions already point in different directions. There are indeed differences in the wording which make the assertion of affirmative duties somewhat easier to justify under the European Convention and the German Constitution than they would be under the US Constitution. In the *Abortion* cases, the German Constitutional Court invoked not only the right to life but also Art. 1 (1) of the *Grundgesetz* which makes it the duty of all state authority not only to 'respect' but also to 'protect' the dignity of human beings.[49] Likewise, the European Court of Human Rights relies on a norm that bridges the gap between negative and positive obligations. The Court finds this norm in Article 1 of the European Convention according to which the State has a general obligation to secure 'to everyone within their jurisdiction the rights and freedoms defined in this Convention'.[50]

B. Historical context and dynamic interpretation

American observers often assume that the historical context explains at least partly why positive obligations are read into human rights in Europe. David Currie suggests that the different social and political climates in which the constitutional texts have been adopted explain differing interpretations because 'James Madison and his friends were not modern social democrats.'[51] Michelman speculates that the European Convention is the 'product of a generation far removed from the height of laissez-faire thinking'.[52] However, a close look at the *travaux préparatoires* of the Convention reveals that the European founding fathers and mothers were not particularly prone to social-democratic ideas. Member States of the Council of Europe in 1950 were consciously going back to the liberal tradition of human rights as negative defensive rights against intrusion by the State. It was indeed the intention of the European founders that the European Convention

---

[48] Michelman, 'Protective functions', in this volume pp. 162 et seqq.

[49] BVerfGE 39, 1 (1975); for an English translation see Donald P. Kommers, *The Constitutional Jurisprudence of the Federal Republic of Germany* (2nd edn, Durham: Duke University Press, 1997), pp. 336–7.

[50] *Young, James and Webster* v. *the United Kingdom*, 44 Eur. Ct. H.R. (ser. A) (1980), para. 49; see Ress, 'Duty to Protect', above, note 35, p. 174.

[51] Currie, 'Constitutional Rights', above, note 14, pp. 871–2.

[52] Michelman, 'Protective functions', in this volume p. 166.

should only protect classical negative rights and only to the same extent as they existed in national constitutions. The contracting states were only willing to accept the intervention of other member states or international institutions in respect to these negative rights.[53]

It is rather the European Court which rejected an originalist approach, in contrast to the US Supreme Court which relied on the intent of the framers in the *DeShaney* case.[54] The European Court uses the so-called dynamic method of interpretation and bases its arguments on the aims and purposes of the Convention. In Europe, it is conventional wisdom that the Court's jurisprudence is a recognition that today major threats to human rights stem from sources other than the state itself. By applying the dynamic interpretation the Court wants to react to changing social circumstances. The Convention is intended to guarantee not rights that are theoretical or illusory but rights that are practical and effective.[55] The European Court aims to guarantee the full effectiveness of the Convention, since for the individuals concerned it makes little difference whether their rights have been violated by the state or another private party.[56]

C. A different understanding of liberty

Are these different interpretations of human rights a question of contemporary constitutional culture or of prevailing political philosophy, or do they reflect a more basic difference in understanding the role of the individual within society?

Like Michelman,[57] Tushnet has proposed that the divergence can be explained by the different degree of commitment to social-democratic norms among different political systems. While the United States would be only rudimentarily committed to such values,[58] the German Constitution, for example, explicitly includes the *Sozialstaat* principle. The Constitution describes the German Federal Republic as 'a democratic and social federal State' and requires that 'the constitutional order of the *Länder* shall conform to the principle of the . . . social

---

[53] K. Partsch, 'Die Rechte und Freiheiten aus der Europäischen Menschenrechtskonvention', in K. Bettermann (ed.), *Die Grundrechte* (1st edn, 3 vols., Berlin, 1966), vol. I, pp. 235 et seqq. at p. 331.

[54] *DeShaney* v. *Winnebago County Department of Social Services*, 489 U.S. 189 (1989).

[55] *Airey* v. *Ireland*, 32 Eur. Ct. H.R. (ser. A) (1979), para. 24.

[56] Hofstötter, 'Positive obligations', above, note 32, 527.

[57] F. Michelman, 'Protective funtions', in this volume p. 170.

[58] Tushnet, 'State Action', above, note 1, 88.

state under the Rule of Law'. In such a state, courts are more prone to impose a duty on the political branches to take active steps to protect constitutional interests. The political theory of the liberal state sees the powerful state as the main threat to freedom while social democracy reacts in part to concerns about the effective social power which market actors can deploy because they control social resources such as property and employment opportunities. This approach holds that the exercise of private social power can endanger freedom as much as the exercise of public power can.[59] In this sense the jurisprudence of the European Court reflects a social-democratic approach to the state.[60]

Ultimately, however, this interpretation is not identical with the left–right divide. Michelman argues that to the left lies the community, to the right the individual, and that consequently European societies heave more to the left, American society heaves more to the right.[61] It is, however, a European experience that the extreme right-wing overemphasises the community, and denies and violates individual liberties and freedoms. Protective functions do not only serve social-democratic concerns in the sense of the left–right divide. They may also be used for essentially conservative causes, as shown by the so-called 'right to security' (*Recht auf Sicherheit*).[62] A right to police protection can even be used to foster a police state. Thus, I would suggest that it is not so much a certain political tendency that encourages a certain interpretation of human rights but a different understanding of the role of the individual in the state and the democratic process.

The United States Constitution reads human rights in the light of a negative understanding of liberty. According to Isaiah Berlin this interpretation of freedom entails the absence of obstacles to possible choices and activities.[63] Starting from a negative concept of freedom, it is the individual himself or herself who must take care that he or she can realise the freedoms protected from governmental interference. This interpretation enabled the US Supreme Court in the *DeShaney* case to underline that the Framers were content to leave the protection of

---

[59] Ibid., 91.

[60] Dröge, 'Positive Verpflichtungen', above, note 13, pp. 215 et seqq.

[61] Michelman, 'Protective funtions', this volume pp. 170 and 178.

[62] J. Isensee, *Das Grundrecht auf Sicherheit: zu den Schutzpflichten des freiheitlichen Verfassungsstaates* (Berlin: de Gruyter, 1983).

[63] I. Berlin, 'Two Concepts of Liberty', in I. Berlin, *Four Essays on Liberty* (Oxford: Oxford University Press, 1990), p. 122.

individuals from each other to the 'democratic political process'[64] in
which the individual can take part. In contrast, the European Court
adopts an understanding of freedom where the individuals sometimes
need the support and protection of the state to realise the freedom they
want to enjoy. In a case regarding the duty to protect against private
interferences with political rallies, the Court stated: 'The genuine and
effective freedom of peaceful assembly cannot be reduced to a mere duty
of the State not to interfere .... but requires positive measures even in
the sphere of relations between individuals'.[65] The Convention starts
from the idea of an effective overall protection of human rights. Viewed
against the background of a dynamic interpretation the Convention is
seen to be based on a positive concept of freedom.[66] This concept leads
to an understanding of the individual that needs the help of state
institutions, including the judiciary, to realise his or her freedoms.
Some read this as a 'holistic understanding ... of human rights'. 'To
rule otherwise would fit uneasily with an enlightened notion of the State,
in a European context.'[67] But perhaps there is indeed some romanticism
connected with such an interpretation of affirmative duties.

[64] *DeShaney* v. *Winnebago County Department of Social Services*, 489 U.S. (1989) 189,
195–6.
[65] *Plattform 'Ärzte für das Leben'* v. *Austria*, 139 Eur. Ct. H.R. (ser. A) (1988), para. 32.
[66] Dröge, *Positive Verpflichtungen*, above, note 13, pp. 215 et seqq.
[67] Hofstötter, 'Positive obligations', above, note 32, 534.

PART V

Adjudication

8

Constitutional adjudication in Europe and the United States: paradoxes and contrasts

MICHEL ROSENFELD*

I. Introduction

Constitutional adjudication is much older and more deeply entrenched in the United States than in Europe.[1] Moreover, constitutional adjudication is *concrete* and *a posteriori* in the United States, whereas it is, to a large extent, *abstract* and, in certain cases, *ex ante* in Europe, suggesting that the former should be inherently less political than the latter.[2] Indeed, in abstract, ex ante review, the constitutional adjudicator tackles laws as they are produced by parliaments, prior to their coming into effect.[3] This gives some European constitutional adjudicators an important policy-making function. Typically, the losing parliamentary minority can challenge the constitutionality of a law it had opposed in the legislature before a constitutional adjudicator who is empowered to strike down the challenged law prior to its actual promulgation,[4] or to condition its promulgation on the adoption of interpretive

---

* I wish to thank Marian Ahumada, Norman Dorsen and Victor Ferreres for their helpful comments and suggestions.

[1] Judicial review of constitutional issues has been implemented continuously in the United States since the Supreme Court's landmark decision in *Marbury* v. *Madison*, 5 U.S. 137 (1803). Constitutional review in Europe, however, is largely a post-WWII phenomenon.

[2] See Louis Favoreu, 'Constitutional Review in Europe', in Louis Henkin and Albert J. Rosenthal (eds.), *Constitutionalism and Rights: the Influence of the U.S. Constitution Abroad* (New York: Columbia University Press, 1990), p. 38. Whereas abstract review is nearly universal in Europe, only in certain countries, such as France and Portugal, is there pervasive use of ex ante review. In some other countries, such as Germany, ex ante review is highly exceptional.

[3] In France, constitutional review can take place only before a law is promulgated. See John Bell, *French Constitutional Law* (Oxford/England and New York: Oxford University Press, 1992), pp. 32–3.

[4] See Alec Stone Sweet, *The Birth of Judicial Politics in France* (New York: Oxford University Press, 1992), p. 48.

197

glosses that limit, alter or expand it.[5] In the United States, on the other hand, judicial review is supposed to be fact driven, meaning that courts are not supposed to decide on the constitutionality of a law in the abstract but only as it applies to particular facts linked to an actual controversy among real adversaries.[6] Two important consequences follow from the American approach: first, constitutional review cannot be triggered in the absence of a concrete controversy;[7] and, second, the factual setting of the relevant controversy tends to anchor constitutional review within a framework that is more conducive to adjudication than to legislation.[8]

Paradoxically, however, American constitutional adjudication has been attacked much more vehemently for being unduly political than its European counterpart.[9] Certainly, the common law tradition has typically afforded broad interpretive latitude to judges whereas the civil law tradition prevalent in Europe has tended to circumscribe the

[5] See Dominique Rousseau, 'The Constitutional Judge: Master or Slave of the Constitution?', in Michel Rosenfeld (ed.), *Constitutionalism, Identity, Difference and Legitimacy: Theoretical Perspectives* (Durham: Duke University Press, 1994) (discussing the French Constitutional Council's use of three techniques of interpretation, namely *limiting interpretation, consulting interpretation* and *guideline interpretation*, to conform otherwise wanting statutes to the constitution).

[6] See U.S. Const. Art. III, § 2 (restricting jurisdiction of federal courts to 'cases' or 'controversies').

[7] See e.g. *Raines* v. *Byrd*, 521 U.S. 811 (1997) (challenge by members of Congress on losing side of legislation granting President a 'line item veto' held not justiciable). The line item veto was later held unconstitutional in *Clinton* v. *New York* 524 U.S. 417 (1998), a case brought by parties who were denied funds by the President's actual use of such veto.

[8] Take, for example, the issue of the constitutionality of affirmative action under a broadly phrased constitutional equality clause. Arguably, in the case of abstract review, the constitutional judge is most likely to focus on issues of principle and policy in a future-oriented exercise not unlike that typically undertaken by the legislator. Imagine, however, that the constitutional challenge is brought by a single mother from a modest background who through diligence and sacrifice would have secured a place in a professional school but for preferential admission of racial minority candidates regardless of socioeconomic status. In that case, the judge's focus is likely to be on whether the plaintiff has suffered an injustice – a backward-looking concern – rather than exclusively on principle or policy. Moreover, if the actual facts before the judge are particularly compelling, they may have a disproportionate effect on the decision. Thus, if a judge rules in the context of the above facts – which we will assume, for the sake of argument, are exceptional rather than typical – that affirmative action is unconstitutional, and if that decision becomes a binding precedent, the resulting constitutional outcome will have been unduly overdetermined by factual contingencies showcased as central when they may be rare and exceptional.

[9] See e.g. Robert Bork, *The Tempting of America: the Political Seduction of the Law* (New York: Touchstone Books, 1990); Mark Tushnet, *Taking the Constitution Away from the Courts* (Princeton: Princeton University Press, 1999).

scope of judicial interpretation rather narrowly. Be that as it may, expansive judicial interpretation of the constitution has fostered far greater criticism in the United States than in Europe, as evinced by the famed 'countermajoritarian' difficulty.[10] More generally, the several differences between American and European constitutional adjudication – and these include the contrasts noted above, plus other distinctive variations, such as exist among the German *Rechtsstaat*, the French *Etat de droit* and the American conception of the rule of law, the American concern with 'originalism', which is lacking in Europe, and the American focus on 'checks and balances', which has no European counterpart – lead to multiple paradoxes.

I propose to examine the most salient among these differences between the American and the European approaches, to assess their breadth and depth, and to inquire whether they are predominantly systemic or contextual in nature. Section 2 compares the respective bases of constitutional adjudication in Europe and the United States. Section 3 focuses on the differences between the *Rechtsstaat, Etat de droit* and 'rule of law' and examines corresponding differences in the respective conceptions of the constitution as law. Section 4 concentrates on the countermajoritarian problem, probes its links to the institutionalisation of checks and balances, and seeks to account for the vast differences between Americans and Europeans on this point. Section 5 deals with issues of constitutional interpretation and contrasts the important role of originalism in the United States with its negligible role in Europe. Finally, Section 6 evaluates the differences examined in the previous sections, in order to determine whether these are predominantly structural or contextual.

II. Civil law and common law constitutional adjudication

Behind the contrast between abstract and concrete review lurks the difference between civil law and common law adjudication, reinforcing the impression that European constitutional review is inherently more political than its American counterpart. Traditionally, civil law adjudication was supposed to be a narrowly circumscribed deductive endeavour; common law adjudication, on the other hand, developed as a more open-ended empirically grounded inductive process. At the time of the

---

[10] See Alexander Bickel, *The Least Dangerous Branch: The Supreme Court at the Bar of Politics* (2nd edn, New Haven: Yale University Press, 1986).

French Revolution, continental judges were largely discredited as the pliable servants of the absolute monarch's arbitrary will.[11] In reaction, in post-revolutionary France the law was codified, and the work of the judge was confined to the application of a legal rule, as crafted by the legislator, to the particular case at issue by means of a syllogism in which the law figures as the major premise and the facts of the case as the minor premise.

Inasmuch as adjudication remained deductive and syllogistic, moreover, the judge's role would seem clearly beyond the realm of politics. Constitutions, however, tend to be less specific than codes and, hence, cannot be subjected to syllogistic reasoning in the same way. Furthermore, since constitutional adjudication is bound to call periodically for judicial invalidation of popular laws, the role of the constitutional adjudicator seems far removed from that of the ordinary civil law judge. The constitutional judge, therefore, must be a different kind of judge – one who, to use Kelsen's expression, functions as a 'negative legislator'.[12]

The constitutional judge as negative legislator may invalidate laws only to the extent that they contravene formal constitutional requirements (e.g. the rules for parliamentary law making) and, therefore, may remain largely apolitical. In contrast, since the Second World War constitutional judges have invalidated laws on substantive as well as formal grounds, thus coming increasingly to resemble positive legislators. For example, when the German Constitutional Court decided, in its 1975 *Abortion I* decision, that the constitutional right to life required the legislator to enact further criminal sanctions against abortion, it acted very much as a positive legislator selecting one among several plausible political choices.[13] In short, in contrast to the statutory adjudication by ordinary judges, which is supposed to be largely apolitical, constitutional adjudication by special judges seems inherently political.

Common law adjudication, on the other hand, seems to strike a middle course between the work of the ordinary judge and that of the constitutional judge. To the extent that it involves an inductive rather than a deductive process, it allows for greater variations than civil law adjudication. Assume, for example, that in a civil law jurisdiction,

---

[11] See R. C. Van Caenegem, *Judges, Legislators and Professors* (Cambridge and New York: Cambridge University Press, 1987), pp. 138–9 and 151–3.

[12] Hans Kelsen, *General Theory of Law and State* (Anders Wedberg, trans., New York: Russel and Russel, 1961), p. 268.

[13] BVerfGE 39, 1.

a statute provides that a landowner is responsible for any damage the owner's domestic animals cause to a neighbour's land. Accordingly, whether such damage is caused by a cow or a cat, a judge would determine liability through a straightforward use of syllogistic reasoning. Imagine, however, a common law judge confronted with damage by a cat in a jurisdiction with a single precedent holding that the owner of a cow is responsible for damage that such cow inflicts on a neighbour's property. That judge may either hold the owner liable by inferring that the cow precedent imposes liability on owners of domestic animals, or not liable by inferring that the cow precedent merely imposes liability on owners of large animals. More generally, so long as relevant precedents allow for more than one result in a case, a judge performs a legislative function in the very act of resolving a dispute – the judge produces a rule or standard applicable to future occurrences that are sufficiently similar to the one in dispute.

When it comes to constitutional adjudication, on the other hand, the common law judge, being bound by precedents, in theory ought to be more constrained than the civil law constitutional judge, who is detached from the ordinary judiciary and under no obligation to treat past constitutional decisions as precedents. Typically, constitutional provisions, such as equality or due process provisions, tend to be general and vague, leaving judges with large margins of interpretive freedom.[14] Since the civil law judge is not constrained by precedent,[15] he or she enjoys full interpretive latitude to extract any plausible legal rule or standard from an applicable constitutional provision. In contrast, a constitutional adjudicator in a common law jurisdiction enjoys less latitude, to the extent that relevant precedents constrain interpretive choices.

Both civil law and common law adjudication thus involve a legal as well as a political component – where 'legal' means the application of a pre-existing rule or standard and 'political' means choosing one from among many plausible principles or policies for the purposes of settling

---

[14] For example, different justices on the US Supreme Court have interpreted the Equal Protection Clause of the US Constitution respectively as broadly allowing and as all but prohibiting race-based affirmative action. See Michel Rosenfeld, *Affirmative Action and Justice; a Philosophical and Constitutional Inquiry* (New Haven: Yale University Press, 1991), pp. 163–215.

[15] As a practical matter, civil law constitutional judges are roughly as constrained as their common law counterparts. Although they are not bound by precedents, they are mindful not to contradict past decisions for reasons of institutional consistency and integrity. Nevertheless, at least in theory, civil law constitutional judges remain free to take a fresh look at constitutional provisions each time they are called upon to interpret them.

a constitutional issue.[16] I have indicated, thus far, how civil law and common law constitutional and non-constitutional adjudication differ in theory in their respective incorporations of law and politics. Before determining how those theoretical differences play out in practice, it is necessary to explore briefly three closely related features from a comparative perspective. These are: the bases of constitutional adjudication; the relevant conception of the rule of law; and the sense in which the constitution is law.

While constitutional review has been entrenched longer in the United States, it is more firmly grounded in France and Germany. The French Constitution empowers the Constitutional Council to determine the constitutionality of laws,[17] and the German Basic Law specifies that the German Constitutional Court is the authoritative interpreter of the constitution.[18] In contrast, the US Constitution is silent on the subject. In *Marbury v. Madison* the US Supreme Court declared that the Constitution is law, and that courts can adjudicate disputes arising under the Constitution in a way that is binding on the parties, but it did not specify whether those interpretations of the Constitution were meant to be authoritative or binding on anyone beyond the actual litigants. Although Supreme Court decisions have been treated generally as authoritative and binding on everyone, including the president of the US and the Congress, there have been periodic and recurring challenges to that notion. In 1987, for example, Edwin Meese, President Reagan's attorney general, argued that while everyone was bound by the US Constitution, Supreme Court decisions produced 'constitutional law' that was not binding on the president or the Congress. In Meese's view, the latter are as authoritative, as interpreters of the Constitution, as the Court, given that all three branches of the federal government are co-equal under the Constitution.[19]

As a consequence of these differences, the question of the authoritativeness of constitutional adjudication is much more politicised in the

---

[16] For Dworkin, policy choices are political while selection and application of principles is essentially a legal task. See Ronald Dworkin, 'The Model of Rules' (1967) 35 *University of Chicago Law Review*, 14. For present purposes, unlike Dworkin, I consider both policy choices and choices among principles as being predominantly political. I offer a justification for my position in section 3. For a more extensive discussion that casts law and politics as different though related, see Michel Rosenfeld, *Just Interpretations: Law Between Ethics and Politics* (Berkeley: University of California Press, 1998), pp. 74–83.

[17] See 1958 French Const. Art. 62 (2).   [18] See German Basic Law, Art. 93.

[19] See Edwin Meese, 'The Law of the Constitution' (1987) 61 *Tulsa Law Review*, 979.

United States than it is in France or Germany.[20] Moreover, although challenges to the authoritativeness of constitutional adjudication tend to arise in response to politically divisive decisions,[21] such challenges are ultimately more profound than those concerning mere interpretive controversies. The issue is not whether the Court gave a wrong interpretation of the constitution, but whether it acted wrongly as the official interpreter of the constitution.

Accordingly, it is not surprising that American constitutional scholars disturbed by the Supreme Court's recent sharp turn to the right should advocate 'taking the constitution away from the courts'.[22] In short, because the US Supreme Court lacks a clear mandate from the Constitution as the authoritative constitutional adjudicator, its occupation of the field is subject to attack as being essentially political. And this may explain, at least in part, why, although common law constitutional adjudication is on its face less political than its civil law counterpart, the US Court appears more vulnerable to attack for being political than the German Court or the French Council.

III. The rule of law and the constitution as law

The more constitutional adjudication is political, the more it would seem to be in tension with the rule of law. In the broadest terms, 'the rule of law and not the rule of men [and women]', to which the aphorism refers,[23] is also not the rule of politics. In other words, the rule of law stands in contrast to arbitrary or unrestrained power and to purely political power; thus, to be legitimate, constitutional adjudication must conform to the rule of law. As will be discussed below, the

---

[20] Constitutional adjudication became more political in France after the 1971 *Associations Law Decision* 71–41 DC. The 1958 Constitution clearly empowered the Council to decide whether it was within the constitutional powers of Parliament to enact the law that was being challenged. In its 1971 decision, however, the Council invalidated a law on *substantive* grounds as violating the constitutional right to freedom of association, thus arguably exceeding its constitutional mandate. See F. L. Morton, 'Judicial Review in France: a Comparative Analysis' (1988) 36 *American Journal of Comparative Law*, 89, at 90–2.

[21] Thus, Meese's 1987 remarks were in the context of Supreme Court decisions on abortion and affirmative action that were squarely contrary to the positions taken on these issues by the Reagan Administration.

[22] See Tushnet, *Taking the Constitution Away*, above, note 9.

[23] See e.g. *Marbury* v. *Madison*, 5 U.S. 137, 163 (1803) (contrasting a 'government of laws' to a government of men).

American conception of the rule of law differs from the German conception of the *Rechtsstaat* and from the French conception of the *Etat de droit*. Because of this, to be consistent with law, constitutional adjudication may have to satisfy different requirements in the United States than it would in France or Germany.

Before focusing on differences, it is necessary to specify, briefly, in what sense the rule of law should be understood as not being political. To be sure, the making of law is political, and democratically enacted laws are political in that they embody the will of the majority. Moreover, a particular political vision or agenda can be furthered through the application and enforcement of certain laws. What ought to remain beyond politics, however, is the law's predictability, applicability, interpretation and enforcement. To return to an example employed above, a parliamentary law imposing liability on the owner of domestic animals for damages that these animals may cause on neighbouring lands represents a political choice and may have emerged after a political debate between representatives of cattle breeders and those of crop growers, with the latter eventually mustering a parliamentary majority. After such a law's enactment, however, and until its repeal, it is as if politics were temporarily frozen. All would be on notice regarding the rights and obligations apportioned by the law; authorities would be charged with enforcing the law generally, regularly and even-handedly, and judges would be charged with interpreting the law according to its terms. The syllogistic model discussed above would presumably provide the best means of ensuring interpretations that were faithful to the law and insulated from further political influences.

1. The German Rechtsstaat

The ideal just sketched above would fare differently according to whether it were set within the framework of the German *Rechtsstaat*, the French *Etat de droit* or the American rule of law. The best fit would be with the German conception of the positivistic *Rechtsstaat*, which emerged with the failure of the bourgeois revolution attempted in Germany in 1848. Frustrated in their efforts to establish a constitutional democracy, the German bourgeoisie settled for a guarantee of state rule through law as opposed to arbitrary or personal rule by the sovereign. In its positivistic embodiment, therefore, *Rechtsstaat* is better translated as 'state rule through law' than as 'rule of law'. By insisting that Germans be ruled through laws and that the adjudicative function be separate from the legislative, the positivistic *Rechtsstaat* comes very close to the ideal invoked above, of law as separate from politics. The *Rechtsstaat*, however, leaves no room for constitutional challenges to legislation and thus sheds no light on constitutional adjudication.

However well the positivistic *Rechtsstaat* may have suited Germany's legal and political reality at the end of the nineteenth century, it no longer fit post-WWII Germany following the adoption of the Basic Law. Some contemporary German scholars have argued that Germany is better described today as a *Verfassungsstaat*, which is to say, 'state rule through the constitution', than as a *Rechtsstaat*.[24] The *Verfassungsstaat* certainly contemplates a legitimate role for constitutional adjudication. But because the *Verfassungsstaat* encompasses not only constitutional rules and standards but also constitutional values such as human dignity (explicitly enshrined in Article 1 of the Basic Law) and because it prescribes not only subjective rights but also an objective order,[25] the German Constitutional Court has assumed an expansive role that casts it, at least in part, as a positive legislator prone to dictating policy.[26] In short, by subjecting an ever-increasing slice of interactions within the polity to constitutional principles and values, the *Verfassungsstaat* tends to constitutionalise the political and to politicise the constitution. Constitutionalisation of the realm of politics is fostered by a shift from purely formal constitutional constraints to predominantly substantive constitutional norms, which then become increasingly pervasive.

---

[24] See, e.g., Ulrich Karpen, 'Rule of Law' in Ulrich Karpen (ed.), *The Constitution of the Federal Republic of Germany* (Baden-Baden: Nomos-Verlag-Ges, 1988), pp. 169, 173 (defining the *Verfassungsstaat* as a state which 'means to organize politics and evaluate goals by applying, executing the constitution').

[25] Roughly speaking, 'subjective rights' are the constitutional rights of a rights holder that constrain the state's legitimate power to legislate. For example, a law that unduly curtails the citizens' free speech rights would have to be struck down as unconstitutional. 'Objective order', on the other hand, refers to the obligation imposed on those responsible for the development of the legal order to shape it according to constitutional values and to orient it in such a way as to extend and complement constitutional rights and obligations. For example, if the constitution prohibits the state from discriminating on the basis of religion, implementation of the objective order may require laws forbidding religious discrimination among private parties and commanding the teaching of religious tolerance in state schools.

[26] See Bernhard Schlink, 'German Constitutional Culture in Transition', in Rosenfeld, *Constitutionalism, Identity, Difference and Legitimacy*, above, note 5, p. 197 (criticising German Constitutional Court for engaging in policy making while seeking to impose an 'objective order').

At one end of the spectrum, the constitution would impose formal
constraints exclusively, thus minimising the opportunities for constitutional adjudication to become political. At the other end of the spectrum, in a constitution such as Germany's – which enshrines human
dignity, as an overriding constitutional value;[27] protects a wide array of
substantive rights, such as free speech and equality rights; and is conceived as having horizontal as well as vertical effects[28] – much of what
would be left to politics in the context of a formal constitution will
assume a constitutional dimension and thus become subject to constitutional adjudication. As the reach of constitutional imperatives
becomes more extensive the realm of ordinary politics is bound to
shrink. For example, where the constitution does not guarantee a right
to a free public education, whether to offer the latter and to increase
taxes to generate revenues for it remains a political question entrusted to
the legislator. In contrast, where the constitution mandates a free public
education, that issue is removed from the realm of ordinary politics, and
the constitutional judge's power may extend to ordering the state to
raise the taxes necessary for it to meet its constitutional obligations
regarding education.[29]

In the context of a broad consensus regarding an expanded constitutional sphere, the increased scope of constitutional adjudication may
become widely accepted as legitimate. This has been the case for a long
time in post-WWII Germany, where profound distrust of politicians as a
consequence of the disastrous politics of the Third Reich has made the
soil particularly fertile for expansive rule by untainted constitutional
judges.[30] Thus, in the case of the *Verfassungsstaat* at its best, constitutionalisation of the political can be regarded as the triumph of rule
according to fundamental values and high principles over rule informed
by narrow or tainted interests. In these circumstances, the constitutional

---

[27] German Basic Law, Art. 1.
[28] 'Vertical' refers to relationships between state and non-state actors while 'horizontal'
refers to relationships among non-state actors. Thus, in an exclusively vertical constitutional order a constitutional prohibition against state employers engaging in sex
discrimination would not extend to private employers. Where the constitutional
order also encompasses horizontal relationships, however, the prohibition in question
would also extend to private employers.
[29] Cf. *Missouri* v. *Jenkins*, 495 U.S. 33 (1990) (ordering state barriers lifted to allow for
raising taxes necessary to achieve constitutionally mandated public school racial
desegregation).
[30] See Ludger Helms, *Institutions and Institutional Change in the Federal Republic of
Germany* (New York: Palgrave, 2000), pp. 87, 95.

judge is likely to achieve a maximum of power and prestige. As the *Verfassungsstaat* expands, however, it seems bound to encounter increasing difficulties in maintaining an adequate level of consensus. Some relatively recent decisions of the German Constitutional Court, such as the *Crucifix II* case[31] and the *Tucholsky II* case,[32] have been very divisive and illustrate the difficulties that confront a powerful constitutional court when national consensus breaks down.[33] More generally, when there is a split over fundamental constitutional values, or over their interpretation, the *Verfassungsstaat* becomes vulnerable to the politicisation of the constitution.

For example, in a polity deeply divided over abortion, with a constitution that, like the German, entrenches human dignity as a fundamental value, some are bound to insist that human dignity requires affording constitutional protection to the foetus, while others are sure to insist that the human dignity of women requires that they have full control over their bodies and, hence, that they be guaranteed a constitutional right to obtain an abortion.

In short, the advent of the *Verfassungsstaat* indicates that disenchantment with politics paves the way for the constitutionalisation of the political, while the great expansion of the realm of the constitutional can lead to numerous splits over constitutional norms and values, thus provoking a politicisation of the constitution. Consistent with this, the *Verfassungsstaat* greatly enhances the role of the constitutional adjudicator, but, by the same token, that very expansion increasingly threatens to weaken the adjudicator's grip on legitimacy.

2. The French Etat de droit

Although the French expression *Etat de droit* is the literal translation of the German expression *Rechtsstaat*,[34] the two are by no means synonymous. Actually, what comes closest to the German *Rechtsstaat* is the

---

[31] BVerfGE 93, 1. The decision produced 'a firestorm of protest' throughout Germany and was widely regarded as a threat to Germany's Christian culture. See Donald P. Kommers, *The Constitutional Jurisprudence of the Federal Republic of Germany* (2nd edn, Durham: Duke University Press, 1997), pp. 482–3.

[32] BVerfGE 93, 266 (criminalisation of statement 'soldiers are murderers' held unconstitutional).

[33] Bavarian officials defied the Court and refused to enforce the *Crucifix II* decision. See Kommers, *Constitutional Jurisprudence*, above, note 31, at p. 483.

[34] See Jacques Chevallier, *L'Etat de droit* (3rd edn, Paris 1999), p. 11.

French *Etat légal*.[35] The main difference between the positivistic *Rechtsstaat* and the *Etat légal* is that whereas both refer to a system of laws made by legislators, only the *Etat légal* requires that the legislators in question be democratically elected. *Etat légal* can thus be translated as 'state rule through democratically enacted laws'.

According to the constitutional vision launched by the French Revolution, law is the product of the legislative majority, while constitutional objectives and constraints are cast as exclusively political. Thus a parliament enacts laws that are conceived as expressing the general will of the polity,[36] and constitutional imperatives, such as those enumerated in the 1789 Declaration of the Rights of Man and the Citizen, are supposed to constrain legislators with respect to the legislative choices they are called upon to make. Consistent with revolutionary France's profound mistrust of judges, the *Etat légal* leaves no room for constitutional adjudication. In fact, it was not until the twentieth century, when state rule through democratically enacted laws came to be viewed as no longer adequate to meet the requirements of constitutional democracy, that exclusive reliance on the *Etat légal* emerged as unsatisfactory.

It was to remedy this deficiency that the *Etat de droit* was invoked to supplement the *Etat légal*. The precise task for the *Etat de droit* was to transform constitutional guarantees that theretofore had been political in nature into legal guarantees. In short, the *Etat de droit* was designed to juridify the constitution, by transforming 'constitution as politics' into 'constitution as law'. Thus, the combination of the *Etat légal* with the *Etat de droit* is closer to the *Verfassungsstaat* than to the *Rechtsstaat*. Unlike the *Verfassungsstaat*, however, the legal regime framed by the *Etat de droit* does not seek to constitutionalise politics; it merely subjects

---

[35] See Michel Rosenfeld, 'The Rule of Law and the Legitimacy of Constitutional Democracy' (2001) 74 *Southern Californian Law Review*, 1330 (explaining that *Etat légal* may be roughly translated as 'democratic state rule through law').

[36] This conception is derived from Rousseau's republican political philosophy. According to Rousseau, democratic legislation by civically minded legislators committed to the common good results in legislation that expresses the polity's 'general will'. See Jean-Jacques Rousseau, *The Social Contract* (Charles Frankel, ed., New York: Hafner Publishing Co., 1947) pp. 14–18. Rousseau's 'general will' is a somewhat mysterious concept that corresponds neither to 'the will of the majority' nor to the 'will of all'. Instead, it amounts to 'the sum of the differences among the individual wills involved' (at p. 26 n.2). For present purposes, suffice it to consider the general will as the expression of the common interests of the members of the polity *qua* citizens (as opposed to *qua bourgeois* or private persons) as articulated in laws supported by a parliamentary majority.

the realm of politics to constitutional constraints that have the force of law. In other words, whereas in the *Verfassungsstaat*, the constitution partially replaces politics as the source of law making, in the *Etat de droit*, politics remains the exclusive source of law making, though the legitimate bounds of political law making are set by the constitution as law.[37]

3. The Anglo-American rule of law

The 'rule of law' imported into the United States from England seems to fall somewhere between the positivistic *Rechtsstaat* and the *Etat de droit* in that it encompasses something more than law solely made by the legislature but not necessarily a set of constitutional constraints with the force of law. To be sure, as already mentioned, in the United States, unlike in France, the Constitution has been considered from the outset to be law.[38] Moreover, the rule of law must equally respect all law, whether it be common law or statutory law, and constitutional law can be regarded as a special kind of statutory law.[39] Yet, at its core, the American rule of law depends neither on statutory law, as the positivistic *Rechtsstaat* does, nor on a written constitution with the force of law, as the *Etat de droit* does.

Stripped to its essentials, the rule of law requires that all interpersonal relationships and conflicts within the polity be subjected to regular, generally applicable rules and standards, and that no person, not even the head of state, be above them. Moreover, these rules and standards must foster predictability and fairness. Also, because it is deeply rooted in the common law, the American rule of law encompasses law making as well as interpreting or deriving the law and applying it. As already pointed out, common law adjudication involves judicial law making because in adjudicating a dispute arising from past events, the common

---

[37] To subject laws to the constitution as law, the *Etat de droit* must institute constitutional adjudication. This did not occur in France until the establishment of the Constitutional Council by the Fifth Republic Constitution of 1958. Moreover, the Constitutional Council, originally set up to insure against legislative usurpation of executive prerogatives, did not act as a full-fledged constitutional tribunal until its 1971 landmark *Associations Law Decision*, above, note 20.

[38] See above, note 1.

[39] Viewed phenomenologically, the constitution plus the whole body of constitutional law generated since *Marbury* v. *Madison* emerge as a complex mix of statutory and common law. Viewed formally, however, the constitution is more akin to a statute than to a set of rules and standards generated by the common law, albeit a special kind of statute elaborated by a constituent assembly rather than an ordinary legislature.

law judge announces (or further specifies) a rule or standard applicable to future events.[40] In other words, understood *functionally*, the rule of law is both a source of law and an approach to existing or evolving law; seen *descriptively*, it includes at present the common law, statutes, and the constitution, and it permeates both law making (whether it be legislative, administrative or judicial) and interpreting the law, as well as applying and enforcing it. Consistent with this, the impact of the rule of law on constitutional adjudication is the product of the effects of the rule of law – as a source of law and a particular approach towards law – on the current American legal regime based on the interplay among the common law, statutes, and the constitution as law or, more precisely, as superior law.

Functionally and methodologically, the rule of law is inextricably intertwined with the common law and its development through judicial law making. In both the rule of law and the common law, the same two key issues are highly problematic: finding and justifying the requisite sources of law; and securing adequate means to foster predictability and fairness, particularly since these objectives are often in tension. As noted above, the principal tools of the common law judge are judicial precedents and the powers of inductive reasoning.[41] The problem concerning the sources of law is ever present in common law adjudication since the sum of existing relevant precedents, combined with the proper use of the tools of inductive reasoning, cannot alone predetermine the outcome of a case in the way that reference to the civil code, combined with application of syllogistic reasoning, is supposed to do in civil law jurisdictions. Returning to the example discussed above, concerning damage caused by a landowner's domestic animal to his neighbour's crop,[42] what accounts for the decision of the judge in the case of the cat – whatever the decision turns out to be – given the precedent concerning the cow, and the powers of inductive reasoning? More fundamentally, can anything account for the decision in the unprecedented case of the cat, absent a political decision? More generally, are all common law adjudications somewhat political and all unprecedented adjudications purely political?

The answer to these questions depends on whether common law adjudication can be ultimately linked to sources of law that are, can be or ought to be commonly shared throughout the polity. For example, if the sources in question are found in natural law, Lockean natural rights,

---

[40] See above, p. 201.   [41] See ibid.   [42] See ibid.

Dworkinian principles, the mores of the polity, or a commonly shared morality,[43] then common law adjudication could be reasonably viewed as interpreting and applying the law rather than making the law, thus minimising its vulnerability to the charge of being unduly political.

On the other hand, in the context of deep ideological splits, ethnic or cultural clashes, or contentious lifestyle differences,[44] the sources of law to which the common law judge must inevitably resort are bound to seem political. These sources may be no more political than those embodied in the laws of the *Rechtsstaat* or of the *Etat légal*. The crucial difference is that in the latter contexts the political dimension is attributable to the legislator, while in context of the common law the political decision seems to rest squarely with the judge. The role of the judge is more crucial to the success of the rule of law than to that of the *Rechtsstaat* or of the *Etat de droit*. To be sure, the rule of law in the sense of acting in conformity with law extends to all branches of government, but the judiciary plays a special role in defining, shaping, interpreting, altering and applying the law. This special judicial role is anchored both in the important role traditionally played by judges and the judicial process under the common law and in the US Constitution's establishment of the judicial branch of the federal government as being co-equal with the executive and legislative branches.[45]

The unique position of judges and of the judicial system in the Anglo-American tradition goes back to feudal England, where legal norms traditionally issued from multiple sources and adjudication became divided among different and often competing institutional actors.[46] Statutory law made by parliament has existed side by side with judge-made common law; courts of law were supplemented by courts of equity;[47] and the responsibilities delegated to the judicial function

---

[43] Legal norms derived from moral norms may have the same contents, but in contrast to moral norms which are meant to govern internal relations, legal norms are applicable to external relations and are enforceable. For further discussion of this distinction, see Rosenfeld, *Just Interpretations*, above, note 16, at pp. 69–74.

[44] See Will Kymlicka, *Multicultural Citizenship* (Oxford and New York: Oxford University Press, 1995), p. 19 (distinguishing between national or ethnic differences and 'lifestyle' differences, such as those advocated by feminists or gay-rights advocates).

[45] See U.S. Const. Arts. I, II, III.

[46] See e.g. Frederick Pollock and Frederic William Maitland, *The History of English Law* (2nd edn, Cambridge: Cambridge University Press, 2 vols. 1923), vol. II, pp. 578–97.

[47] See Fleming James and Geoffrey C. Hazard, *Civil Procedure* (Boston: West Publishing Company, 1985), pp. 14–15.

were apportioned between judges and juries, with the latter serving as a check on the monarchy's judges since the seventeenth century.[48]

Unlike the Continental tradition, where the law is exclusively the product of the legislator, and judges are confined to applying the legislator's law, in the American common law tradition the judge is an independent source of law and a check against the legislator's (unconstitutional) laws. Thus, in both the *Rechtsstaat* and the *Etat légal* law is made by the state through the legislator, and judges serve both of these when interpreting and applying the law. In contrast, judges within the American rule-of-law system at times follow the legislator, at times make law, and at other times strike down the legislator's law or the executive's decrees, thus using the powers of the state against the state itself. In other words, whereas the *Rechtsstaat* and the *Etat légal* and, for that matter, the *Etat de droit* and the *Verfassungsstaat* involve state rule through law, the rule of law is characterised by an interplay between state rule through law and law rule against the state.[49]

4. Substantive law, the role of the judge and predictability

Underlying these contrasts, there is an important conceptual difference. This difference – one with significant repercussions on the conception and justification of constitutional adjudication – is that between the American conception of fundamental rights as essentially 'negative rights' of the citizens against the state and the Continental conception of fundamental rights as essentially 'positive rights'[50] creating citizen entitlements that require affirmative state intervention for their realisation. The American conception is predicated on Locke's theory of inalienable natural rights, which are pre-political

---

[48] See Jack H. Friendenthal, Mary Kay Kane and Arthur R. Miller, *Civil Procedure* (St Paul: West Publishing Company, 1985), p. 472.

[49] From a formal standpoint, even when a judge strikes down a popular law as unconstitutional she is engaged in state rule through law as she is acting as a state official who belongs to one of the branches of government. From a substantive standpoint, however, judges who exercise equity power in the common law tradition to award a remedy unavailable at law, or a judge who strikes down a law for unconstitutionally infringing on a litigant's fundamental rights uses law to protect a member of the polity against (unfair or unconstitutional) state rule.

[50] The distinction between 'negative' and 'positive' rights is analogous to that between negative and positive liberty. See Isaiah Berlin, 'Two Conceptions of Liberty' in his *Four Essays on Liberty* (London and New York: Oxford University Press, 1969), p. 118.

and can be enjoyed by individuals so long as the state does not interfere with their exercise.[51]

For example, the right to free speech is deemed to be innate, and therefore when the state through laws or an arbitrary use of power prevents a citizen from speaking freely, the judge is supposed to side with the citizen against the state and to order the state to cease infringing the citizen's rights. In the Continental tradition, on the other hand, a free speech right is deemed a state-granted right and infringement of that right would be regarded as a state official's failure to comply with state rule through law – in this case constitutional law. Accordingly, a Continental constitutional adjudicator, strictly speaking, would be vindicating state rule through constitutional law against what amounts to state lawless rule rather than taking the side of the citizen against the state.

What this conceptual difference underscores is the contrast between the rule of law as encompassing many different sources and centres of law, often competing with one another, and the *Rechtsstaat* and *Etat de droit* with a single source (or multiple sources aligned in a well established hierarchy) of law. Accordingly, the rule-of-law judge plays a pivotal role in the management and attempted harmonisation of these multiple sources and centres of law, and alternates between imposing the will of the state (as articulated by the legislative majority) on the citizen and protecting the rights of the citizen against the state.

The Continental judge, in contrast, operates in a single hierarchical system of law and is either subordinate to the legislator (the ordinary judge) or operates at the top of the constitutional pyramid as a super-legislator with confined powers delimited by the constitution (the constitutional judge). But whether ordinary judge or constitutional, the Continental judge is always on the side of the state. In order to manage the tensions produced by the juxtaposition of multiple sources and centres of law, the rule-of-law tradition has resorted to constraining devices designed to produce order and unity. These devices come in two pairs, each creating new tensions of its own. These are: (1) predictability and fairness; and (2) procedural and substantive safeguards against unwarranted extensions of state rule through law. Moreover, in the context of the common law these two pairs of constraints are inter-linked, as problems concerning predictability appear to become more

---

[51] See John Locke, *The Second Treatise of Government* (New York: Harlan Davidson, 1982), paras. 4, 6, 44, 123.

manageable if the rule of law is understood as revolving primarily around procedural safeguards.

To the extent that relevant precedents do not dictate a particular outcome in a case at hand, the common law system of adjudication remains sufficiently unpredictable so as to thwart one of the principal objectives of rule through law. Unlike the Continental judge, who follows a previously established rule, the common law judge establishes the applicable rule in the course of deciding a case, and thus the parties to that case cannot know the legal consequences of their acts prior to litigation. Moreover, since it is virtually impossible for many cases to be exactly alike or for any set of relevant precedents to be thoroughly exhaustive, the rule of law based on the common law must always remain somewhat unpredictable.

Common law unpredictability can be mitigated by procedural safeguards or by adherence to certain standards of fairness. These procedural safeguards, often implemented as 'due process' guarantees, have been constitutionalised in the American 'due process clauses'.[52] Due process requires, at a minimum, that cases be decided by impartial judges, that parties have adequate notice and an equal opportunity to present their side of the case, and that trial procedures be designed to maximise the chances of discovering the truth and to minimise the chances of prejudice and oppression. Arguably, because of these safeguards, even if unpredictable, the common law is not akin to the 'rule of men'.[53]

Fairness, on the other hand, can mitigate unpredictability by providing an assurance that justice will be done by the common law adjudicator even if, in most cases, a person cannot know beforehand the precise legal consequences of his acts. Fairness, however, can play this role only where there is a commonly shared sense of justice and equity within the polity, one that provides a reasonably well unified and integrated common law jurisdiction.

Given these conditions and a commonly shared sense of fairness,[54] the problem of unpredictability may be lessened, ensuring that rule through law will conform to the rule of law. Although the common

---

[52] U.S. Const. Amend. V (providing that 'no person shall be deprived of life, liberty, or property, without due process of law'); U.S. Const. Amend. XIV.

[53] See above, note 23.

[54] For purposes of this discussion it is assumed that the sense of fairness involved is not outcome determinative in a large number of cases. Otherwise, the norms of fairness would allow for a syllogistic system of adjudication and precedents would become superfluous.

law tradition is well entrenched in the United States, at present the legal norms issuing from the common law are supplemented by statutory law and the Constitution. As a source of law, the common law has lost much ground to the Constitution and statutes; as a legal approach, however, the common law method of reasoning and interpretation remains pervasive.

Unlike the common law, statutes – like civil code provisions – seem well suited to fostering predictability. Moreover, as a body of law, the Constitution seems more akin to a statute than to norms issuing from the common law. To be sure, constitutional provisions are, for the most part, more general and vaguer than statutory provisions. For example, the constitutional guarantees of 'due process of law' or 'the equal protection of the laws'[55] are much less specific than a statute providing that 'no employee earning hourly wages shall be required to work in excess of forty hours per week'. Nonetheless, constitutional provisions, like statutes, are imposed on judges who must follow them in their decisions and thus are required to do more than merely harmonise a body of judicial decisions, as would a judge operating in a pure common law environment.

A constitutional provision may be, formally, more like a statute than like an evolving juridical norm extracted from a string of relevant precedents. Paradoxically, however, the pervasive use of common law methodology in constitutional adjudication appears to exacerbate the respective tensions between predictability and fairness and between procedural and substantive safeguards. This can be illustrated by focusing briefly on the US Constitution's due process clause. Like a statute, this clause imposes a legal norm on a judge in contrast to due process norms that judges have gradually developed in the course of elaborating the common law.[56] However, in the course of deploying the common law methodology to ascertain the meanings of the due process clause, judges have identified predictability and fairness as essential components of due process, thereby locating the inevitable tension between the two at the very core of constitutional adjudication. Moreover, these judges have also brought the contrast between procedural and substantive safeguards to the forefront of due process jurisprudence – by

---

[55] See U.S. Const. Amend. XIV.

[56] It is interesting in this respect that efforts to establish the meaning of constitutional due process have referred back to the development of due process notions in English common law. See e.g. *Murray's Lessee* v. *Hoboken Land and Improvement Co.*, 59 U.S. 272 (1856) (origins of 'due process' are found in Magna Carta and its meaning is derived from English statutory and common law).

alternating between a purely procedural interpretation of due process and one that is also substantive in nature – but without ever deciding, definitively, on either of these two conceptions.[57]

Leaving to one side whether a purely procedural interpretation of due process is ultimately coherent,[58] the continued, uneasy coexistence of the two conceptions underscores a vexing tension. This tension exists between the less controverted yet probably insufficient 'thin' protection afforded by procedural due process and the highly contested, often profoundly divisive, 'thicker' protection afforded by substantive due process.[59]

In theory at least, common law adjudication need not involve repudiation of precedents, only their refinement and adjustment through further elaborations. Accordingly, gaps in predictability may be merely the result of indeterminacies; the recourse to notions of fairness is meant primarily to reassure the citizenry that the inevitably unpredictable will never be unjust. Constitutional adjudication, on the other hand, while relying on precedents as part of its common law methodology, must ultimately be faithful to the constitutional provision involved rather than to the precedents. As a result, when precedents appear patently unfair or circumstances have changed significantly, the US Supreme Court is empowered – perhaps obligated pursuant to its constitutional function – to overrule precedent, thus putting fairness above predictability.[60]

---

[57] The 'substantive due process' approach was embraced by the US Supreme Court in *Lochner* v. *New York*, 198 U.S. 45 (1905), one of its most criticised opinions, in which the Court held that the Due Process Clause provided constitutional protection to freedom of contract and private property rights. The *Lochner* doctrine was repudiated during the New Deal, see *Nebbia* v. *New York*, 291 U.S. 502 (1934), and the Due Process Clause has since been interpreted as affording exclusively procedural safeguards in cases involving economic relations. See e.g. *Williamson* v. *Lee Optical Co.*, 348 U.S. 483 (1955). However, there has been a revival of substantive due process in the realm of personal privacy and liberty rights. See *Griswold* v. *Connecticut*, 381 U.S. 479 (1965) (marital privacy requires constitutional protection to use contraceptives); see also *Roe* v. *Wade*, 410 U.S. 113 (1973) (abortion rights).

[58] For a philosophical defence of the argument that procedural justice cannot be coherently separated from substantive justice, see Michel Rosenfeld, 'A Pluralist Critique of Contractarian Proceduralism' (1998) 11 *Ratio Juris*, 291.

[59] The fierce debate provoked by the constitutionalisation of abortion rights vividly illustrates this last point. See Laurence Tribe, *Abortion: the Clash of Absolutes* (2nd edn, New York: W. W. Norton and Co., 1992).

[60] The Court elaborated criteria to determine whether to overrule a constitutional precedent in *Planned Parenthood of Southeastern Pennsylvania* v. *Casey*, 505 U.S. 833 (1992).

For example, in its recent decision in *Lawrence v. Texas*,[61] the Supreme Court overruled its 1986 decision in *Bowers v. Hardwick*,[62] which held that the due process clause did not extend constitutional protection to homosexual sex among consenting adults, thus upholding a law that criminalised such conduct. More generally, whenever a constitutional challenge raises a significant question that could entail overruling a constitutional precedent, the Supreme Court faces a choice between predictability and fairness.

American rule of law, like the *Verfassungsstaat*, involves constitutional rule through law, but unlike the *Rechtsstaat* it produces a rule through law where predictability is but one among several, often antagonistic, elements. American rule of law ultimately amounts to a complex, dynamic interplay between competing elements and tendencies. Moreover, it appears, at least initially, that more than the *Rechtsstaat* or the *Etat de droit*, American rule of law depends for its viability on a broad-based consensus regarding extralegal norms, such as fairness and substantive notions of justice and equity. Indeed, if there is a consensus on what constitutes fairness or justice, then the tensions between predictability and fairness, and between procedural and substantive safeguards, seem entirely manageable, and the work of the constitutional adjudicator more legal than political. If, on the contrary, there are profound disagreements over what is fair or just, then the work of the constitutional adjudicator is bound to seem unduly political. Accordingly, at least prima facie, the task of the American constitutional adjudicator seems more delicate and precarious than that of her continental counterpart.

Under all three traditions – that of the *Rechtsstaat* (evolving into the *Verfassungsstaat*), that of the *Etat de droit* and that of the American rule of law – the constitution is conceived as law and constitutional interpretation is conceived as legal interpretation.[63] Based on the preceding comparison of these three traditions, however, it becomes clear that constitutional law is not law in the same sense in all three of them. In all three, constitutional law is superior law, and the constitutional adjudicator's task is to ensure conformity with such superior law. But because the

---

[61] 539 U.S. 558 (2003).   [62] 478 U.S. 186 (1986).

[63] This does not mean, strictly speaking, that all *constitutional* rights and obligations are necessarily *legal* rights and obligations, only that the vast majority are. For example, pursuant to the Political Question Doctrine elaborated by the US Supreme Court, some constitutional guarantees are not legally enforceable. Thus, the Guarantee Clause, U.S. Const. Art. IV, § 4, which guarantees every state a republican form of government, has been held non-justiciable, leaving it up to Congress to define its prescriptions. See *Baker* v. *Carr*, 369 U.S. 186 (1962).

nature and scope of such superior law is different in each of these three traditions, constitutional adjudication is bound to differ among them.

By enshrining constitutional values and by conceiving of the constitution as framing an objective order as well as protecting subjective rights, the German Basic Law juridifies values and policies and endows them with the same force of law as that bestowed on those of its provisions that fit within the customary garb of legal rules and legal standards. As a consequence, the legitimate role of the German constitutional judge includes: invalidating, shaping or reshaping laws to ensure conformity with constitutional values; reshaping, extending or even creating laws in furtherance of the establishment of the objective order prescribed by the Constitution; and, of course, performing the most common and widespread task of constitutional adjudicators, determining whether ordinary laws conform to the law of the Constitution. Just as values and policies are incorporated into German constitutional law, so they seem instilled in American constitutional law, but with one big difference.

In the American context, values and policies cannot be directly linked to the Constitution but, rather, emerge in the broader context of the Constitution as law embedded in the American rule-of-law tradition. Moreover, because of the complexity, tensions and the multiplicity of sources of law characteristic of the rule of law, the place of values and policies is bound to be much more contested and murkier. Compare, for example, the place of human dignity in the German constitutional order with that of human autonomy in the American. Arguably, human autonomy, interpreted as encompassing broad liberty and privacy concerns, has a place in the American constitutional order that is equivalent to human dignity in the German. Evidence of the constitutional importance of human autonomy in the United States abounds. It is found in many places, such as the expansive free speech jurisprudence, and in the varied and extensive due process jurisprudence, in all its facets, from *Lochner* to *Roe* and *Lawrence*. Yet, while human dignity is explicitly grounded in article 1 of the German Basic Law, the sources of human autonomy in America are far from obvious, since it has textual roots in the Constitution,[64] unenumerated rights roots,[65] common law roots[66] and also fairness roots.[67]

---

[64] Thus, free speech rights are explicitly protected by the First Amendment, and privacy rights in part protected by the Third, Fourth and Fifth Amendments. See *Griswold* v. *Connecticut*, 381 U.S. 479 (1965).
[65] Ibid.   [66] See ibid.   [67] See ibid.

As a consequence of these distinctive features, for all that the actual differences between German constitutional law and its American counterpart may not be very significant, it is easy to understand that the legitimacy of the American constitutional adjudicator is much more fragile and contested than that of the German constitutional judge.

In France, the advent – through implementation of the *Etat de droit* – of the constitution as law results from the transformation of the constitution as a set of political constraints into the constitution as a set of legal rules and standards that are to be given priority over the legal rules and standards produced by the Parliament. Thus, prior to the Constitutional Council's landmark 1971 *Associations Law* decision,[68] the 1789 Declaration of the Rights of Man and the Citizen and other sources of fundamental rights amounted to directives to the members of Parliament requesting that they not enact laws curtailing the citizens' constitutional rights and freedoms.[69] What the *Associations Law* decision did was to change the relevant constitutional rights provisions from political directives to hierarchically superior laws. Consequently, the parliamentary law at stake in the *Associations Law* decision was declared unconstitutional because it was contrary to the constitutional prescription that citizens are entitled to freedom of association. In short, the French Constitution has become law, but, at least thus far, law in a narrower sense than the American and German constitutions.

IV. Constitutional adjudication and the countermajoritarian problem

In a democracy, parliamentary law is, by its very nature, majoritarian, and the invalidation of parliamentary laws by constitutional judges who are unelected and unaccountable to the electorate, countermajoritarian. So long as constitutions clearly constrain the realm of majoritarian law making, and constitutional judges routinely enforce these constraints, their countermajoritarian role should not be problematic. Given the previous discussion, it would seem that France, with its tradition of the *Etat légal* in which all law is parliamentary in nature and hence majoritarian, would have the greatest difficulties with countermajoritarian constitutional adjudication.

---

[68] See the 1971 *Associations Law Decision*, above, note 20.
[69] Besides the 1789 declaration, there are other sources of constitutional rights and freedoms, such as the preamble to the 1946 Constitution and 'the fundamental principles recognised by the laws of the Republic'. See Georges Burdeau, Francis Hamon and Michel Troper, *Droit Constitutionnel* (25th edn, Paris: LGDJ/Montrestien, 1997), pp. 704–5.

Yet, surprisingly, it is in the United States, where one of the principal aims of the Constitution's framers was to guard against the 'tyranny of the majority' through a system of constitutional 'checks and balances', that the counter-majoritarian issue has been by far the most contentious.

The American concern with the countermajoritarian difficulty is all the more paradoxical because unlike in the United Kingdom or in France, there is no tradition of parliamentary sovereignty in the United States. Not only is the power of the judiciary equal to that of the legislature, but, as already mentioned, judicial law making has deep roots in the common law. Moreover, judicial countermajoritarianism would seem to fit well within a constitutional system of checks and balances pitting the federal electorate's majority against the various majorities in the several states, and, within the federal level of represen-tation, congressional majorities against the majority represented by the president. Indeed, though countermajoritarian, judicial power provides yet another check on potentially runaway majority powers.

The reason that countermajoritarian constitutional adjudication can be a problem stems from its status as a check that is itself unchecked. Whereas in statutory adjudication the legislator can overcome unwar-ranted judicial interpretations through further legislation,[70] the only available remedy against aberrant or abusive constitutional adjudication is to amend the Constitution, which is extremely difficult in the United States.[71] As those preoccupied by the countermajoritarian difficulty note, the Constitution establishes majoritarian rule as the norm – granted, different majorities may compete against one another or divide the realm of democratic law making among themselves – while making antimajoritarian constitutional constraints the exception.[72] For example, although the US Congress is empowered to regulate commerce among the states,[73] it cannot ban the interstate transportation of books critical of the president as that would violate constitutionally protected free speech rights.[74]

---

[70] For example, the US Congress enacted the Civil Rights Act of 1991 in part to overcome U.S. Supreme Court statutory interpretations with which it disagreed. See Civil Rights Act of 1991, Pub. L. No. 102–166, §§ 2 (2), 3 (3) (explicitly repudiating Court's interpretation in *Wards Cove Packing Co., Inc.* v. *Atonio*, 490 U.S. 642 (1989)).

[71] See U.S. Const. Art V. The most used path to amendment requires a two-thirds vote in each of the houses of Congress followed by ratification by three-quarters of the state legislatures. In sharp contrast, amending the constitution in France or Germany requires a far less onerous process, though the German Basic Law contains some unamendable provisions. See German Basic Law, Art. 79 (3).

[72] See Bork, *Tempting of America*, above, note 9, at pp. 146–7. See U.S. Const. Art. I, § 8, cl 3.

[73] See U.S. Const. Art. I, § 8, cl 3.   [74] See U.S. Const. Amend. I.

In such a clear cut case, even those who emphasise the countermajor-itarian difficulty agree that judicial invalidation of a popular law is entirely appropriate but where the constitutional proscription is not clear, they argue that judges should err on the side of democracy and refrain from striking down laws.[75] Thus, strictly speaking, the counter-majoritarian objection has less to do with unchecked judicial power itself than with the problem of confining that power to a narrow range of clear cases. That restrictive view of the judge's legitimate role, however, runs counter to the habits instilled through the use of the common law methodology. The Constitution sets up a system of democratic law making whereby the appropriate majority through the enactment of statutes can supersede substantive common law rules and standards. The Constitution itself is ultimately akin to a statute, albeit one issuing from a constitutional as opposed to an ordinary legislator, but its many general, broadly phrased provisions, as well as its incorporation of certain common law standards, make it particularly suited to interpre-tation by a common law approach. Thus the countermajoritarian diffi-culty is made more acute because, although the Constitution is set up as a statute, its broad terms and judicial practice seem to conspire to transform it into a special extension of the common law.

Similar difficulties are largely absent in other jurisdictions. In Canada, the countermajoritarian difficulty is largely absent, since the problem of the unchecked check is obviated by section 33 of the Constitution,[76] which in many cases authorises a legislative override of a Supreme Court constitutional ruling.[77] In France and Germany, on the other hand, there seems to be little concern about a countermajor-itarian difficulty, though these two countries, along with the other constitutional democracies in the European Union, confront a far greater 'democratic deficit' than could be conceivably created by the American judiciary.[78] This deficit stems from the lack of democratic accountability of the EU institutions that have law-making powers. It is further exacerbated through decisions of the European Court of Justice, which are binding on the judiciary of the member states and require

---

[75] See Bork, *Tempting of America*, above, note 9, at pp. 264–5.

[76] See Canada Constitution Act of 1982, § 33.

[77] Decisions in certain subject areas, such as freedom of speech, cannot be overridden. In the vast number of permissible subject areas, however, both the federal and the various provincial parliaments have the right to override. See ibid.

[78] See e.g. Joseph H. H. Weiler, 'Does Europe Need a Constitution? Reflections on Demos, Telos and the German Maastricht Decision' (1995) 1 *European Law Journal*, 219.

member states to set aside laws that are inconsistent with Union law as interpreted by the European Court of Justice.[79]

The constitutional adjudicator in France and Germany invalidates popular laws it deems unconstitutional just as the American adjudicator does. But, in addition, the French and German judiciary must subordinate democratically adopted domestic law to democratically deficient Union law as interpreted by a supranational court. Accordingly, one might logically expect that France and Germany would experience a far greater emphasis on the countermajoritarian difficulty than the United States. And yet they do not – at least not when it comes to constitutional adjudication.

Several reasons account for this seeming discrepancy. First, as far as the democratic deficit involving the EU is concerned, it is above all a legislative and administrative deficit and not a judicial one. Thus, while the countermajoritarian problem in the United States lies squarely with judges as constitutional adjudicators, the European judge – whether she be on the Union's Court of Justice or on a member state's constitutional or ordinary court – interprets and applies undemocratic Union law. Accordingly, any countermajoritarian difficulty would much more likely concern the law itself rather than its judicial interpretation.

Second, when the constitutional adjudicator in France or Germany strikes down a law as unconstitutional she frustrates the polity's legislative will just as much as the US Supreme Court when it does the same, but there is a major difference in the European and American situations. Because, as already mentioned, the constitutions of France and Germany are far easier to amend than that of the United States, the effects of judicial invalidation of popular laws are far less drastic.[80] Thus the situation in France and Germany falls somewhere between the state of affairs prevailing in Canada and that of

---

[79] See e.g. Case 26/62, *Van Gend en Loos* v. *Nederlandse Administratie der Belastingen* (1963) ECR 1.

[80] In France, for example, amending the constitution to overcome an invalidation of a law by the Constitutional Council is a smooth process that has often been used. For example, after the Constitutional Council found certain provisions of the European Union Amsterdam Treaty unconstitutional, see 97–394 DC of 31 December 1997, the French Constitution was amended and the Treaty ratified. See Norman Dorsen, Michel Rosenfeld, Andras Sajo and Susanne Baer, *Comparative Constitutionalism: Cases and Materials* (St Paul: West Publishing Company, 2003), p. 65, fn. 1. In contrast, in the United States, while there are calls for constitutional amendments after many controversial Supreme Court decisions, these usually fail. For example, after the Court's decision recognising a right to abortion in *Roe* v. *Wade*, above, note 57, there were many attempts to amend the constitution, but none were successful. See Kathleen Sullivan and Gerald Gunther, *Constitutional Law* (14th edn, New York: Foundation Press, 2001), p. 531. Moreover, although Germany has some unamendable constitutional provisions, see

the United States. In France and Germany, decisions of the constitutional judge cannot be overcome through simple majoritarian means as is possible in Canada, but they can be overcome through regularly achievable super-majoritarian means. Accordingly, constitutional adjudication in France and Germany is often not the final word as it is in the United States, where it confronts nearly insurmountable supermajoritarian hurdles.

Third, because of the civil law tradition and its syllogistic model of adjudication, European constitutional adjudication seems in little danger of proving excessively countermajoritarian. As already mentioned, the countermajoritarian difficulty in the United States stems less from the judicial vindication of antimajoritarian rights than from the danger that judges, nurtured on the broad and open-ended common law approach, will trample on majoritarian laws much more than is constitutionally necessary. From a theoretical standpoint, at least, civil law constitutional adjudicators should be much less likely to exceed their narrow constitutional antimajor-itarian mandate, given their roots in a deductive system of judicial inter-pretation. From a practical standpoint, however, there may be little difference in the degree of discretion available to a common law judge, applying a broadly phrased constitutional provision, and a civil law judge, addressing equally general constitutional provisions. Significantly, how-ever, because of the different traditions involved, criticism of a civil law constitutional judge who appears to have gone too far is not likely to be on countermajoritarian grounds but, rather, on something different, such as the application of 'supraconstitutional' norms.[81] In other words, the accu-sation against the European constitutional judge is not that he has taken law making into his own hands but, instead, that he is applying certain legal norms not explicitly within the constitution as if they were valid supra-constitutional norms, and then deducing from the latter conclusions that may not be derived from the applicable constitutional norms.

V. Constraining the constitutional adjudicator through canons of interpretation: the divide over originalism

One way to counter the dangers of excessive countermajoritarianism is through the imposition of constraints on the constitutional

---

above, note 71, in the case of those provisions any countermajoritarian difficulty would have to be ascribed to the constitution itself rather than to judicial interpretation.

[81] This is an accusation made against the French Constitutional Council. See Louis Favoreu, 'Souveraineté et supraconstitutionnalité' (1993) 67 *Pouvoirs*, 71.

adjudicator. In the United States, 'originalism' has been offered as the solution, which means looking to the original intent of the framers of the Constitution to resolve all interpretive issues that cannot be settled through a reading of the constitutional text.[82] In Europe, however, recourse to originalism is virtually non-existent.[83] This contrast may seem paradoxical on first impression. Would it not be more reasonable to expect greater reliance on original intent in Spain, where the current Constitution is barely twenty-five years old, than in the United States, where the Constitution is almost 220 years old? That is to say, is not the intent of the constitutional legislator more relevant if the latter shares a contemporary perspective with the judges who must interpret the constitution and the citizens who must live with the consequences of those interpretations?

A closer look at the reasons for the importance of originalism in the United States, and at the practical implications of the theoretical controversy over originalism, reveals that the main concern is not with the democratic legitimacy of judicially enforced constitutional constraints, as suggested above. If it were, the constitutional legislator's intent would be relevant because it represented the will of the majority (or of the requisite supermajority, in the case of the constitutional legislator) and because democratic rule through law required that judges refrain from interpreting laws in ways that frustrate the will of the majority. When the constitutional legislator is a contemporary of the constitutional interpreter, that argument may be persuasive, but it seems less so as increasing numbers of generations separate the constitution's framers from its judicial interpreters.[84]

---

[82] See e.g. Bork, *Tempting of America*, above, note 9, at pp. 143–60.

[83] Even though there may be no reference to originalism, some European attacks on constitutional interpretation may be characterised as being originalist in substance even if not in form. For example, the 1971 *Associations Law Decision*, above, note 20, can be criticised as creating an unwarranted expansion of the Constitutional Council's jurisdiction beyond the role reserved for it by de Gaulle's 1958 Constitution, namely to act exclusively as a referee on questions of division of powers between the Parliament and the President. See Stone, *Birth of Judicial Politics*, above, note 4, at p. 48. Nonetheless, in Europe even implicit references to originalism in substance are quite rare.

[84] Consistent with this, the eighteenth-century framers can only be said to express the majority or supermajority will of twenty-first century Americans in the *negative sense* that the latter have not mobilised to replace the 1787 constitution. See e.g., Bork, *Tempting of America*, above, note 9, at pp. 143–60.

The American preoccupation with originalism arises not from a concern over the enduring legitimacy of the Constitution itself but, rather, from a concern over the democratic legitimacy of subjecting majoritarian laws to constitutional review. Indeed, when viewed in the context of the Constitution, strictly speaking, originalism is based on a perception of the Constitution as a quasi-sacred text[85] and as a statute, rather than as an evolving set of broad principles to be elaborated through a common law-style process of accretion. Originalism, it might be argued, is premised on a belief that the framers had quasi-divine attributes that justify deference to their extraordinary wisdom and authority. Moreover, insofar as the Constitution should also be treated as a statute, the judges interpreting it should be bound by its text and the intent of its authors as opposed to having great latitude to mold it in accordance with the broad standards embodied in the common law. Further, these two reasons for embracing originalism are mutually reinforcing. Not only does statutory interpretation require fidelity to the intent of the legislator but the constitutional legislators' extraordinary wisdom makes fidelity to their intent the optimal means of achieving the common good. On the other hand, if, as in Europe, constitutions are not regarded as quasi-sacred texts, and statutory interpretation is not seen to be vulnerable to common law judicial law making, then there seems little need to resort to originalism.

American originalism has competed with many rival theories of constitutional interpretation. All of them attempt to reconcile the Constitution as a superior law, having statute-like properties, with the common law approach and tradition. Each of them also seeks to offer a solution to the countermajoritarian problem. Moreover, since there is a great deal of congruence between the way American and European judges actually go about the task of constitutional interpretation, this raises the question of why there are far greater doubts expressed in the US regarding the legitimacy of judicial interpretation of the Constitution than are heard in Europe.

The American debate goes back to the beginning of constitutional interpretation in the United States.[86] At that time, Supreme Court justices differed over whether the constitution should be subordinated to natural law – or natural rights – principles, or whether it should be

---

[85] See e.g. Sanford Levinson, " 'The Constitution' in American Civil Religion" (1979) *Supreme Court Review*, 123.
[86] See *Calder* v. *Bull*, 3 U.S. 386 (1798).

subjected to a positivistic approach, faithful to its provisions and understood as forming part of a unified and coherent legal code.

The latter view has prevailed and the Constitution has become
firmly entrenched as the highest law of the land.[87] Nevertheless, the
debate among proponents of these two positions has been recast as a
debate over the legitimate means of constitutional interpretation
when the constitutional text is open-ended or is not plainly outcome-
determinative. In such cases, natural law or natural rights notions
have been used to fill textual gaps and to shape the meaning of broadly
phrased, open-ended constitutional provisions. Conversely, textualism
and originalism can be viewed as the interpretive tools of constitutional
positivism. Under the most extreme version of this view, the constitutional
judge is confined to the 'plain meaning' of the text and clear intent of the
constitutional legislator, and if neither of these, individually or in combination, imposes an unequivocal solution to the constitutional problem at
hand, then the judge ought to uphold the majoritarian law.[88]

In the broadest sense, originalism is one of the three principal
approaches to constitutional interpretation elaborated in the shadow
of the countermajoritarian difficulty. The other two approaches may
be characterised, respectively, as the 'principle-based' approach and
the 'process-based' approach. Originalism and the principle-based
approach agree that constitutional adjudication is countermajoritarian
but nonetheless legitimate so long as judges remain within proper
bounds of interpretation. What divides them, however, is that they
carve out a legitimate domain for the constitutional judge very differently. The process-based approach, in contrast, does not regard constitutional adjudication as inherently countermajoritarian but, rather, as
an adjunct to democratic rule, providing a corrective safeguard to
majoritarian processes that have gone astray.

Originalists purport to constrain judges by demanding consistency
with the intent of the framers. Principle-based theorists purport, for
their part, to constrain judges to decide cases according to the dictates of
principles that have been (according to them) enshrined in the
Constitution.[89] On the other hand, according to the most eminent

---

[87] See Sullivan and Gunther, *Constitutional Law*, above, note 8080, at p. 454.
[88] See generally Bork, *Tempting of America*, above, note 9.
[89] See Ronald Dworkin, 'The Forum of Principle' (1981) 51 *New York University Law Review*, 469 (arguing that the US Constitution embodies liberal egalitarian principles).

process-based theory, that of John Hart Ely,[90] judicial interpretation of the US Constitution can be justified, generally, as a means of safeguarding the integrity of the democratic process.

Specifically, Ely argues that most of the Bill of Rights provisions are process based. For example, protection of free speech rights is essential to maintaining an informed electorate, and thus judges in deciding free speech cases are safeguarding the democratic process rather than engaging in policy making. Moreover, if free speech decisions are considered process-enhancing, then equality decisions are deemed to be process-corrective, since racist laws stem from undue prejudice rather than from genuine policy differences.

None of these approaches has dealt successfully with the counter-majoritarian difficulty or with the broader issues concerning the legitimate bounds of constitutional interpretation. This failure is due to both internal and external reasons. From an external standpoint, the principle-based approaches, predicated on morals or public policy, will necessarily diverge from originalist solutions. Finally, the very possibility of a coherent process-based approach has been vigorously challenged.[91] For example, what kind of and how much free speech is necessary to ensure that an electorate be adequately informed so as to best fulfil its democratic function? Should free speech be confined to political speech? To all forms of expression, including pornography, as they may all have political implications? For many, these questions cannot be answered without reference to substantive notions of democracy and of democratic will-formation. And consistent with this, there cannot be a purely process-based understanding of free speech rights.

Internal reasons also prevent these approaches from fostering a consensus on the legitimate bounds of constitutional interpretation. Thus, proponents of principle-based approaches by no means agree on *which* principles should inform constitutional interpretation. For example, the Supreme Court's decisions in *Lochner*,[92] which interpreted the

---

[90] See John Hart Ely, *Democracy and Distrust: a Theory of Judicial Review* (Cambridge, Mass.: Harvard University Press, 1980).

[91] See e.g. Dworkin, 'Forum of Principle', above, note 89, (criticising Ely's theory for depending on one of many theories of democracy, all of which ultimately depend on a substantive political vision); Lawrence H. Tribe, 'The Puzzling Persistence of Process-Based Constitutional Theories' (1980) 89 *Yale Law Journal*, 1063 (arguing that even most procedural rights included in the Bill of Rights, such as those of criminal defendants, only make sense in the context of a broader substantive vision).

[92] *Lochner* v. *New York*, above, note 57.

Fourteenth Amendment's due process clause as enshrining private property and freedom of contract rights, clearly evinces a principle-based approach. But the principles involved are libertarian ones that are, to a large extent, at odds with the liberal egalitarian principles invoked by Dworkin.[93] Similarly, there are deep internal divisions within the originalist camp.[94] Beyond serious questions concerning the actual intent of the framers in light of the paucity of reliable sources concerning their debate, there are several key disagreements with wide-ranging implications. For example, whose original intent? The framers or the ratifiers? Specific intent or general intent?[95] Significantly, it is even claimed that the framers' intent was that their intent be ignored by subsequent generations of constitutional interpreters.[96] There is nothing comparable to the American debate concerning judicial review and constitutional interpretation in continental Europe. Moreover, the case of Germany is particularly striking, as its Constitutional Court is even more activist than the US Supreme Court. As Dieter Grimm, a former justice on the German Constitutional Court, emphasises, ' ... the counter-majoritarian difficulty, the perennial problem of American constitutional law, plays no role in Germany. Criticism of [the German Constitutional Court] usually concerns individual opinions, not the legitimacy of the courts or even that of judicial review in general.'[97] This does not mean that there is no debate in Germany,[98] and there seems to be even more of a debate in France.[99] Nevertheless,

[93] Libertarians oppose any redistribution of wealth whereas liberal egalitarians require some such redistribution. For an account of this contrast in the realm of political philosophy compare Robert Nozick, *Anarchy, State and Utopia* (New York: Basic Books, 1974) with John Rawls, *A Theory of Justice* (Cambridge, Mass.: Belknap Press of Harvard University Press, 1971).

[94] See Paul Brest, 'The Misconceived Quest for the Original Understanding' (1980) 60 *Boston University Law Review*, 204.

[95] For example, the eighteenth-century framers of the Free Speech Clause, see U.S. Const. Amend. I, could not have foreseen the advent of television. Therefore, it may have been their general, but not their specific, intent to protect speech over the airwaves.

[96] See H. Jefferson Powell, 'The Original Understanding of Original Intent' (1985) 98 *Harvard Law Review*, 885 (arguing that while the framers were textualists, they were not originalists; rather, they expected subsequent generations to adapt the Constitution to their own needs).

[97] Dieter Grimm, 'German and American Constitutionalism', address before The American Academy in Berlin (4 May 2003) (text on file with author).

[98] See e.g. Schlink, 'German Constitutional Culture in Transition', above, note 26.

[99] See Rousseau, 'Constitutional Judge', above, note 5, at p. 261.

these debates have nothing of the scope or intensity of the American debate.

For all the differences at the levels of theory and ideology, when it comes to the practice of constitutional adjudication, there are remarkable similarities between the United States and Europe, or at least Germany. Viewed from the standpoint of the types of arguments made in constitutional cases by advocates and by judges in giving reasons for their decisions, the American and German practices are, in most relevant respects, largely similar. A survey of constitutional decisions by the US Supreme Court reveals the use of five kinds of arguments: (1) arguments from the text; (2) arguments from the framers' intent; (3) arguments from constitutional theory; (4) arguments from precedents; and (5) value arguments.[100] In Germany, four kinds of arguments are prevalent: (1) grammatical arguments; (2) historical arguments; (3) systematic arguments; and (4) teleological arguments.[101]

American arguments from the text are equivalent to German grammatical arguments because they both rely on textual analysis. Since the text of the Constitution is rarely determinative in cases involving major constitutional issues,[102] arguments from the text must be combined, in most cases, with other arguments to justify a particular decision. And this is true in both Germany and the United States.

American arguments from the framers' intent have much in common with German historical arguments, though the two are not equivalent. Both of these look to past understandings of the relevant constitutional provisions when called upon to interpret these to resolve a current constitutional challenge. The difference between the two is that arguments from the framers' intent occupy a much higher position in American constitutional interpretation than do historical arguments in German constitutional interpretation. Indeed, whereas arguments from the framers' intent are to be given greater weight than arguments from precedents or value arguments,[103] German historical arguments

---

[100] See Richard H. Fallon Jr., 'A Constructivist Coherence Theory of Constitutional Interpretation' (1987) 100 *Harvard Law Review*, 1189.

[101] See Winfried Brugger, 'Legal Interpretation, Schools of Jurisprudence, and Anthropology: Some Remarks from a German Point of View' (1994) 42 *American Journal of Comparative Law*, 395.

[102] For example, the text of the U.S. Equal Protection Clause neither requires nor forbids racial segregation, see *Plessy* v. *Ferguson*, 163 U.S. 537 (1896), or race-based affirmative action in university admissions, see *Grutter* v. *Bollinger*, 123 S. Ct 2325 (2003).

[103] See generally Fallon, 'Constructivist Coherence Theory', above, note 100, at 1194.

are given no greater weight than any of the other kinds of arguments used in constitutional interpretation. The practical effect of this clear difference is, however, quite limited. This is because arguments from the framers' intent have very rarely been decisive in major American constitutional cases.[104] Arguments from constitutional theory in the United States are essentially equivalent to systematic arguments in Germany. They both place the constitutional text at issue in the case at hand in its broader context within the constitution and interpret it from the premise of the constitution as a systematic and coherent unified whole.

There is also much congruence between American value arguments and German teleological arguments. Teleological arguments are purposive ones, and they foster an interpretation of the Basic Law and its provisions according to the purposes for which constitutional rule was established in Germany. Since, to an important extent, such purposes include the promotion of fundamental values, such as human dignity, teleological arguments often result in interpretations seeking to achieve conformity with a particular value. In the United States, value arguments are those that 'appeal directly to moral, political or social values or policies'.[105] In Dworkinian terms, value arguments are those that are premised on either principle or policy. Thus, if the constitutional judge is confronted with two plausible alternatives, only one of which is morally compelling, then that judge ought to make the available moral value argument decisive.[106]

The principal difference between American value arguments and German teleological arguments is that whereas the values involved in the German context are internal to the Basic Law, those at stake in the American context are, by and large, external to the Constitution. For example, there is no reference to abortion in the US Constitution and arguments for and against abortion rights tend to refer to general moral precepts debated within American society at large rather than clearly embedded in the constitutional text.[107] In Germany, in contrast, though there is also no reference to abortion

---

[104] For example, arguments from the framers' intent do not account for the decisions in such landmark cases as *Plessy v. Ferguson*, 163 U.S. 537 (1896), *Brown v. Board of Education*, 347 U.S. 483 (1954), *Lochner v. New York*, above, note 57, *Griswold v. Connecticut*, above, note 57 or *Roe v. Wade*, above, note 57. It is fair to claim that arguments based on the framers' intent have had scant influence on the vast majority of Supreme Court decisions in leading cases on separation of powers, federalism and fundamental rights.

[105] See Fallon, 'Constructivist Coherence Theory', above, note 100, at 1204.

[106] See e.g. *Griswold v. Connecticut*, above, note 57 (Harlan, J., concurring) (due process interpreted as protecting fundamental value of marital privacy).

[107] See e.g. Tribe, *Abortion*, above, note 59.

in the Basic Law, the Constitutional Court has evaluated claims to a right to abortion in terms of the values of human dignity explicitly constitutionalised in Article 1 of the Basic Law.[108]

The principal difference between the two practices is that arguments from precedents are used in the United States, but not in Germany. On closer inspection, however, even this difference is not all that important. First, although the German Constitutional Court is not bound by precedent, out of a concern for its institutional integrity, it tends to follow its past decisions as if they had precedential value.[109] And, second, although the US Supreme Court tends to follow constitutional precedents, it does not do so slavishly and on many occasions has reversed itself.[110]

In the final analysis, the most relevant practical difference between the United States and Germany, with reference to the legitimacy of constitutional interpretation, derives from the greater weight given to arguments based on the framers' intent than to historical arguments. A difference of another sort stems from the fact that, in the US, the values in value arguments are external to the Constitution, rather than internal, as is the case with German teleological arguments. Of these two differences, the latter seems more important, considering the vast disagreements within the United States over the significance of the framers' intent. Undoubtedly, if a constitution explicitly embraces a value, constitutional interpretation shaped by that value ought to be less subject to contest than constitutional interpretation deriving from contested values external to the constitution. But the difference may not be great. Even if the value of human dignity is constitutionally enshrined, there may still be genuine differences over what its implications ought to be in a particular case.[111] Conversely, there may be a strong consensus in the United States about certain external values, such as fairness, liberty or privacy, even when there is disagreement as to what these require in particular cases. In any event, it does not seem that these two differences, as noted here, can by themselves account for the vast gulf that separates the United States from Germany with respect to the legitimacy of constitutional interpretation.

---

[108] See *Abortion I Case*, above, note 13.   [109] See above, note 15.

[110] For example, as mentioned above, *Lawrence* v. *Texas*, above, note 61, overruled *Bowers* v. *Hardwick*, above note 62, and as mentioned below, *Adarand Constructors Inc.* v. *Peña*, 515 US 200 (1995), overruled *Metro Broadcasting* v. *FCC*, 497 US 547 (1990).

[111] See above, p. 00.

Before further assessing what may account for the differences between European countries, such as France and Germany, and the United States, reference must be made to a last difference that looms large in theory and in tradition, but has come to be minimised in actual practice. That is the difference, discussed at the outset,[112] between the civil law approach to adjudication and that of the common law. Potentially, this difference could be enormous in the context of the legitimacy of constitutional interpretation. If the European constitutional adjudicator were to adhere to the civil law ideal of a purely deductive model of legal interpretation, then American preoccupations with the counter-majoritarian difficulty, and concern over the adoption of illegitimate canons of constitutional interpretation, would be completely irrelevant in Europe. The practice of constitutional interpretation in Europe has increasingly veered away from the deductive model, however, and is today not much different from that employed by American judges.[113] Indeed, as European constitutional judges must apply broad values, like human dignity, or interpret general and open-ended constitutional liberty or equality provisions, they cannot rely on the kind of syllogistic reasoning that may be appropriate in the application of a concrete and detailed provision of the civil code. In short, the more that European constitutional judges must look to history, values and broad principles to resolve constitutional cases, the more their actual work of interpretation is likely to resemble that of their American counterparts.

VI. Assessing the differences between American and European attitudes regarding constitutional adjudication

Based on the preceding analysis, the differences between American and European attitudes towards constitutional adjudication stem, in part, from structural and institutional factors and, in part, from contextual factors. More precisely, the differences derive from contextual factors interacting with structural and institutional ones. Each system of constitutional adjudication discussed above has its own structural and institutional strengths and weaknesses. Crises concerning legitimacy

---

[112] See above, p. 119.
[113] See, e.g., Rousseau, 'Constitutional Judge', above, note 5 (discussing role of the constitutional judge in France); Schlink, 'Constitutional Culture in Transition', above, note 26 (discussing broad powers, including policy-making powers, of the German Constitutional Court).

are most likely to occur when contextual factors exacerbate these weaknesses. Conversely, the greatest sense of legitimacy is likely to prevail when contextual factors reinforce structural and institutional strengths.

If crises in legitimacy were primarily a function of the power wielded by the constitutional adjudicator, problems of legitimacy should loom larger in Germany than in the United States, since the German Constitutional Court clearly surpasses the US Supreme Court in its power and reach.[114] On the other hand, given France's traditional mistrust of judges, and the fact that substantive constitutional adjudication was introduced by fiat of the Constitutional Council rather than by constitutional design,[115] one would expect France to be – institutionally, at least – much more susceptible than the United States to crises of legitimacy regarding constitutional adjudication.

That the crisis in legitimacy is greater in the United States than in either France or Germany is due, above all, to the fact that the United States is currently deeply divided politically. This is evinced by the closeness of the 2000 presidential election and its bitter aftermath, as well as by the prevalence of contentious politics for most of the period since that election.[116] Moreover, this political division within the country came on the heels of a period of controversy within the Supreme Court, resulting in a series of contentious 5–4 decisions.[117] These two trends actually converged in the Court's decision in *Bush* v. *Gore*[118] in which, by what was in effect a 5–4 decision, the Court settled the election in favour of Bush in what many consider an unprincipled, mainly political decision.[119] The current divisions not only revolve around interest-group politics but also around something deeper, namely, what Justice Antonin Scalia has characterised in bitter dissent as a

---

[114] See Grimm, 'German and American Constitutionalism', above, note 97.

[115] See above, note 37.

[116] The one notable exception was a short period following the 11 September 2001 terrorist attacks on New York and Washington. That period ended, however, once the drastic measures adopted to root out terrorism became highly contested as posing a severe threat to fundamental rights and to constitutionally prescribed checks and balances.

[117] See e.g. *United States* v. *Lopez*, 514 U.S. 549 (1995), *Alden* v. *Maine*, 527 U.S. 706 (1999), *Kimel* v. *Florida Bd. of Regents*, 528 U.S. 62 (2000), and U.S. v. *Morrison*, 529 U.S. 598 (2000).

[118] See U.S. Const. Art. I, § 8, cl 3.

[119] See Michel Rosenfeld, '*Bush* v. *Gore*: Three Strikes for the Constitution, the Court and Democracy, But There is Always Next Season', in Arthur Jacobson and Michel Rosenfeld (eds.), *The Longest Night: Polemics and Perspectives on Election* (Berkeley:

Kulturkampf.[120] On one side are feminists, gay activists, environmen-
talists, zealous defenders of abortion rights and affirmative action, and
the like; on the other, religious fundamentalists, defenders of traditional
family values, and vehement opponents of abortion rights and of affirmative action. Because there is often no middle ground between the two
groups, as the vehemence of their mutual antagonism increases it threatens to provoke a split in the country's identity. Furthermore, since most
of these divisive issues end up before the Supreme Court, and since the
Constitution has played a major role in shaping the country's national
identity, constitutional adjudication is at the forefront of the culture
wars and of the struggle over the nation's evolving identity.

This deep division exacerbates the tension between the Constitution
as a species of statutory law and the common law tradition. Indeed,
while this tension may play an important positive role when there is a
consensus on fundamental cultural and societal values, it looms as the
Achilles' heel of the American system of constitutional review when that
consensus breaks down. In times of solid consensus, the common law
tradition and the role of the constitutional adjudicator as mediator
between the state and the citizen can cement a sense of fundamental
fairness even in the face of vigorous differences at the level of interest-
group politics. However, when consensus breaks down, as seems to be
the case at present, the constitutional adjudicator cannot help but take
sides and thus cannot foster harmony, whether he or she stands on the
side of the state or on that of the citizen. For example, when the
constitutional adjudicator strikes down popular laws that outlaw or
restrict abortion or gay rights, he or she will be regarded by some as
protecting citizens against state oppression, but by others as under-
mining the very social fabric of the polity by arbitrary fiat. Moreover,
the fact that the Constitution does not explicitly address these issues
aggravates the problem and contributes to a further erosion of the
legitimacy of constitutional interpretation. To be sure, specific constitutional provisions granting or denying abortion rights or gay rights

---

University of California Press, 2000), p. 111 (distinguishing between 'judicial politics'
that are inevitable and 'plain politics' in which the Court's majority appears to have
engaged as it departed from established positions developed over a long series of
opinions to reach a result that squared with their apparent political leanings). The
decision did have its defenders. But even among these, its virtue lay in its having put an
end to an unsettling and potentially disruptive crisis, not in the soundness of its
constitutional analysis. See e.g. Charles Fried, 'Response to Ronald Dworkin,
A Badly Flawed Election', in Jacobson and Rosenfeld, *Longest Night*, pp. 100–3.

[120] See *Romer* v. *Evans*, 517 U.S. 620, 636 (1996) (Scalia, J. dissenting).

would not be likely to heal the existing divisions over these issues. But they would undoubtedly shift most of the existing frustration and resentment away from the courts.

The differences between the German and American attitudes towards constitutional adjudication are due to a number of factors. As widely noted, German society is more paternalistic and less individualistic than American society, and there is in post-WWII Germany a disenchantment with politics that bolsters the legitimacy of the constitutional judge.[121] There are also two institutional differences between the two countries that account, in some measure, for the greater acceptance of constitutional adjudication in Germany. One such difference, already mentioned, is the relative ease of constitutional amendment in Germany.[122] For example, while affirmative action remains in the United States a highly contentious issue that has yielded a series of closely divided and often contradictory Supreme Court decisions over a twenty-five year period,[123] in Germany the constitutional legitimacy of gender-based affirmative action has been settled through an amendment of the Basic Law.[124]

The second important difference concerns the appointment of judges entrusted with constitutional adjudication. In Germany, appointment requires a two-thirds vote in parliament, which cannot be achieved without a consensus among the major political parties.[125] In the United States, in contrast, appointment of a president's nominee requires a simple majority vote in the Senate. In times of great division, with the Senate almost equally divided among Democrats and Republicans, as is the case now, divisive nominees may squeak by on a strictly partisan basis or become blocked – leaving many vacancies on the federal courts unfilled – or be appointed without Senate confirmation in a recess appointment.[126]

Beyond these institutional differences, and given the great power of the German Constitutional Court, the most important difference between the

---

[121] See Grimm, 'German and American Constitutionalism', above, note 97.

[122] See above, note 71.

[123] See e.g. *Adarand Constructors Inc.* v. *Peña*, above, note 110 (overruling *Metro Broadcasting* v. *FCC*, above, note 110).

[124] See the 1994 amendment to Art. 3 of the German Basic Law.

[125] See Grimm, 'German and American Constitutionalism', above, note 97.

[126] See 'Bush puts Pickering on Appeal Court: Bush Bypasses Democrats who had Blocked Judge' (16 January 2004) (available at http://www.cnn.com/2004/LAW/01/16/bush.pickering.ap/). Blocked Bush nominees have included Texas judge Priscilla Owen,

countries is the far greater consensus in Germany concerning the fundamental values behind, and inherent in, constitutional rule under the guidance of the constitutional adjudicator. It is an attitude encapsulated in the
German citizenry's commitment to 'constitutional patriotism'.[127]

Substantive constitutional adjudication is on much shakier ground in
France than in Germany or the United States. Paradoxically, that may
account, to some degree, for why there is less of a crisis of legitimacy in
France than in the United States. There is a debate in France over whether
the Constitutional Council is a genuine constitutional court,[128] and over
the scope of its legitimate responsibilities. Moreover, this debate is going on
within the Council as well as without.[129] According to one side, the Council
is an extension of the political branches and as such its proper role is
political. According to the other, it is more akin to a court, and its role is
judicial. Another reason why the legitimacy of constitutional adjudication
is a less contentious issue in France than in the United States is that the
French Constitution is easy to amend.[130] A third reason is the prominent
role played by supranational constitutional norms binding France to international tribunals such as the European Court of Human Rights and the

> lawyer Miguel Estrada, California judges Carolyn Kuhl and Janice Rogers Brown. See
> also 'Bush Dumps Clinton Nominees' (20 March 2001) (available at
> http://www.cbsnews.com/stories/2001/03/20/politics/main280123.shtml), listing candi-
> dates whose names were withdrawn from consideration: Bonnie Campbell, Enrique
> Moreno, Kathleen McCree-Lewis (nominated for 6th Circuit), James Duffy (for 9th
> Circuit), North Carolina State Court of Appeals Judge James A. Wynn (for 4th Circuit),
> Helene White (for 6th Circuit), Barry P. Goode of Richmond, Ca. (for 9th Circuit), H.
> Alston Johnson III (for 5th Circuit), and Sarah Wilson (U.S. Court of Claims).

[127] See Grimm, 'German and American Constitutionalism', above, note 97.

[128] See Stone, *Birth of Judicial Politics*, above, note 4, at p. 48 (stating that the government
never considered the Council to be a court). The constitution does not provide for
interaction between the Council and the judicial system and, unlike other continental
constitutional courts, there is no prerequisite of prior judicial service or minimum
requirements of legal training. The 1958 constitution does not mention the Council in
its chapter on 'judicial authority' but rather sets it apart in its own chapter.

[129] For example, Robert Badinter, who was president of the Council from 1986 to 1995,
envisioned it as a full-fledged constitutional court whereas a later president, Yves
Guéna, saw its institutional mission in much narrower terms. See Dorsen et al.
Comparative Constitutionalism, above, note 80, at p. 130.

[130] See the 1958 French Constitution, Art. 89. For example, just as in Germany, France
amended its constitution to make room for gender-based affirmative action. In the
Feminine Quotas Case, 82–146 DC of 18 November 1982, the Constitutional Council
held feminine quotas unconstitutional under Article 3 of the Constitution. In 1999,
Articles 3 and 4 of the Constitution were amended to reverse the 1982 decision. After
that amendment, a law requiring overall parity between the sexes, 50–50, on certain party
election candidate lists was enacted by the Parliament. In its decision 2000–429 DC of 30
May 2000, the Constitutional Council upheld that law with minor exceptions.

European Court of Justice.[131] For example, France was forced to recognise a right of privacy with regard to phone tapping as a consequence of the European Court of Human Rights ruling that it was in violation of privacy rights protected under the European Convention on Human Rights.[132]

Even though such norms represent European or European Union standards and may or may not be supported by a substantial majority of the French citizenry, conflicts over them are unlikely to be focused on the French constitutional adjudicator. Moreover, even if the latter relied on such norms to settle a question under French constitutional law, there would be little incentive to seek a reversal if the norms in question most likely would be imposed eventually by the European courts.

Beyond these relevant institutional differences there seems to be a much broader consensus regarding the contours of fundamental rights in France and Germany – and, for that matter, throughout Western Europe – than in the United States. Perhaps the best example is the wide variation in attitudes towards the death penalty. The abolition of the death penalty throughout Europe has often been initiated 'from above' and, in several cases, as a pre-condition to coveted admission to the Council of Europe or the European Union rather than out of conviction.[133] Nonetheless, there now seems to be a solid consensus throughout Europe against the use of the death penalty. In contrast, the death penalty remains a highly divisive issue within the United States and within the Supreme Court.[134]

---

[131] Technically, the norms involved are treaty-based norms whether they derive from the European Convention on Human Rights or the various treaties among the members of the European Union. From a substantive standpoint, however, many of the treaty-based norms involved have all the attributes of legally enforceable constitutional norms.

[132] See Eur. Court H. R., *Kruslin Judgment* of 24 April 1990, Series A no. 176 A.

[133] See Alkotmánybíróság (Hung. Const. Ct.) Decision 23/1990 (X 31) AB hat (absent a constitutional provision on the subject, the Hungarian Constitutional Court held the death penalty unconstitutional based on generally accepted European standards about the sanctity of life).

[134] The death penalty is in force in thirty-eight of the fifty states. See David W. Moore, 'Public Divided Between Death Penalty and Life Imprisonment Without Parole: Large Majority Supports Death Penalty if No Alternative is Specified', The Gallup Organization, 2 June 2004 (available at http://www.gallup.com/content/ login. aspx?ci=11878). According to the Gallup Poll, over the past twenty years, Americans' support for the death penalty in preference to life imprisonment has fluctuated between a low of 49 per cent and a high of 61 per cent. See also Edward Lazarus, 'A Basic Death Penalty Paradox That Is Tearing the Supreme Court Apart'

VII. Conclusion

Constitutional adjudication currently enjoys less legitimacy in the United States than in Europe as a consequence of an interrelation between structural and institutional factors, on the one hand, and contextual factors, on the other. The prevailing contextual differences ultimately seem more weighty, as the profound divisions over fundamental values found in the United States do not appear to be replicated anywhere in Western Europe. For reasons noted throughout this article, the structural and institutional features prevalent in Germany and, to a somewhat lesser extent, those in force in France seem better suited than their American counterparts to the task of averting the deep divisions prevalent in the United States.

Still, the national and supranational structural and institutional apparatuses currently in place in Europe may not always be able to blunt the effect of dramatic divisions over fundamental values and thus help to avert crises in legitimacy with respect to constitutional adjudication. Resistance to decisions of the German Constitutional Court, such as occurred in Bavaria after the order to remove crucifixes from public elementary school classrooms,[135] may be isolated, as Dieter Grimm emphasises.[136] Nevertheless, one can imagine greater divisions within Germany and other European countries as an increasingly heterogeneous society, in both a secular and religious sense, struggles to maintain harmony in the public sphere. Furthermore, as the European Union expands and adopts its own constitution,[137] it is unclear whether the Continent will move towards greater unity or greater divisions. And, if the latter, whether European constitutional adjudicators or national ones will be perceived as bearing a significant part of the responsibility. In any event, it seems clear that without a workable consensus on fundamental values, it is unlikely that constitutional adjudication will be widely accepted as legitimate.

(4 November 2002) (at http://writ.news.findlaw.com/lazarus/ 20021031.html): 'On the current Court, there is an unbridgeable gap – between those who do not want to look again at the troubling realities of the capital punishment system, and those anxious to pursue the legal conclusions to which those realities point them.'

[135] See *Classroom Crucifix II*, BVerfGE 93, 1.

[136] See Grimm, 'German and American Constitutionalism', above, note 97.

[137] See Thomas Fuller and Katrin Bennhold, 'Leaders Reach Agreement on European Constitution', *New York Times*, 19 June 2004, at A3 (documenting the adoption of the EU's first constitution by European leaders, characterised as the first step in what will prove to be a long and trying process).

Comment

JEFFREY JOWELL

I. Introduction

The United Kingdom, in its island isolation, stands apart from the new and old worlds, yet draws liberally from both. We have still not adopted a written constitution. Nevertheless, despite initial protests to the contrary, the country is today imbued with the notions of constitutionalism which lie comfortably with the ideals framed in Philadelphia in 1776 and 1787, which so influenced the French Declaration of the Rights of Man and the Citizen in 1789. It has even been contended that the 'self-evident truths' adverted to in the US Declaration of Independence 'did not spring Athena-like from Jefferson's brow, but were firmly rooted in a coherent and forceful strand of (radical) British constitutional theory'.[1]

I shall consider the transformation of British public law from the middle of the twentieth century, concentrating on the role of judicial review in this process. Judicial review was until very recently concerned not with review of legislative Acts but with review of powers (mostly discretionary powers) conferred on public officials by the Parliament. Only since 2000 have the UK courts been able to review parliamentary statutes – for conformity with the European Convention on Human Rights.

I shall begin by summarising the development of judicially determined constitutional standards in the UK and, considering its constitutional justification, and then discuss the influences from the USA and Europe (judicial, academic and other) and attitudes to international legal standards.

---

[1] Ian Loveland, *A Special Relationship: American Influences on Public Law in the UK* (Oxford: Loveland, Clarendon Press, 1995), p. 9.

II. Background

According to the seminal work written by Professor Dicey at the end of the nineteenth century,[2] Britain has one cardinal constitutional rule: namely, parliamentary sovereignty or supremacy. This rule is tempered (but not necessarily overridden) by the principle of the rule of law.

In the nineteenth century the courts implicitly employed the rule of law as a principle to constrain the exercise of power. Thus, even where a statute seemingly conferred unlimited power upon public officials the courts read down that power and insisted that, unless expressly stated to the contrary, it was limited by the notion of 'due process'.[3] Due process is an American term. The preferred English term is 'natural justice', or 'the right to a fair hearing'. Even during this period of relatively activist jurisprudence, challenge to legislation itself was, however, never even contemplated by the courts. *Marbury v. Madison*[4] had no place in a system so dominated by the notion of legislative sovereignty.

From about 1914 the courts began to be much more deferential when assessing the lawfulness of discretionary power. Their interpretation of such power was literal. Where Parliament had conferred power on a minister in terms that appeared on their face subjective – 'the minister may' do thus and such; if he 'has reasonable cause to believe' something exists – the courts would not readily imply that such power could be much limited. They were anxious not to challenge the powers needed to prosecute two world wars and (later) the development of a centralised welfare state. Some ringing judicial dissents did suggest that the courts at this time were 'more executive-minded than the executive'.[5]

From the mid-sixties the courts almost abruptly altered their approach to judicial review of discretionary power. Literal interpretation gave way to a purposive approach. 'The minister may' could mean 'the minister must', if such a meaning fitted with the 'objects and purpose' of the statutory scheme. Decisions which on their face did not require any due process or natural justice were struck down for want of a fair hearing.[6]

---

[2] A. V. Dicey, *Lectures Introductory to the Study of the Law of the Constitution* (London: Macmillan, 1886).

[3] *Cooper* v. *Wandsworth Board of Works* (1863) 14 CB(Ns).

[4] 5 U.S. 60 (1803).

[5] *Per* Lord Atkin in *Liversidge v. Anderson* [1942] A.C. 206.

[6] See generally, de Smith, Woolf and Jowell, *Judicial Review of Administrative Action* (London: Sweet and Maxwell, 1995), ch. 1.

By the nineties the courts and the executive were engaged in a turf war. On at least a dozen occasions between 1995 and 1996 the Home Secretary's decisions under discretionary powers were struck down for 'illegality' (being outside of the purpose of the governing legislation) or for procedural unfairness. However, despite their more robust approach to judicial review, English courts were still reluctant to enter into the substantive merits of a decision, granting a wide 'margin of appreciation' to the decision-maker, and confining their intervention to instances where he acted not merely unreasonably in the ordinary sense of that term, but 'so unreasonably that no reasonable decision-maker could so act' (The *Wednesbury* test[7] – a ground of review later referred to as 'irrationality').

The approach of the courts during this time to international human rights instruments was governed by the fact that the UK has a 'dualist' system whereby treaties, to be fully effective, need to be specifically incorporated into domestic law. Where domestic legislation was ambiguous, the courts would presume that the treaty obligation should apply, but it was ruled that the conferment of broad discretionary power on a decision-maker did not qualify as an ambiguous grant of power.[8] In this connection, note that although the UK spearheaded the drafting of the European Convention on Human Rights [ECHR] in 1950, and was the first country to sign it, it did not incorporate it into domestic law until 1998 and therefore the effect of the ECHR was only in international law, as a treaty obligation.

Despite the technicalities of the ECHR as a (then) treaty obligation alone, from the mid-nineties the courts began to recognise the role of fundamental human rights as meriting the lowering of the *Wednesbury* barrier of review. In a number of leading cases they applied more intense scrutiny to decisions in which human rights were involved – such as a ban against gays in the armed forces.[9]

A major alteration of approach then occurred in a series of cases. It began when the courts were faced with a challenge to an interference by a minister with a prisoner's right of access to his lawyer. In that case the court did not engage with the notion of 'irrational' or 'unreasonable' action, or with any margin of appreciation or deference to a substantive decision made under discretionary power. It was simply held that the

---

[7] *Associated Provincial Picture Houses* v. *Wednesbury Corp.* [1948] 1 K.B. 233.
[8] *R* v. *Home Secretary exp. Brind* [1991] 2 A.C. 696.
[9] *R* v. *Ministry of Defence exp. Smith* [1996] Q.B. 517.

prisoner's 'constitutional right' of access to justice had been breached, and that such interference is unlawful in the absence of specific statutory language to the contrary.[10] This case was followed by others, for example, recognising freedom of expression as a constitutional right – despite the absence of a written catalogue of such rights set out in a document with constitutional effect.[11]

In 1998, the new Labour Government enacted the *Human Rights Act*. The effect of that Act is to incorporate into UK law most of the Articles and Protocols of the European Convention on Human Rights ('Convention rights'). It is unlawful for any 'public authority' to contravene Convention rights. 'Public authority' includes the courts but does not include Parliament. Nevertheless, parliamentary legislation (and subordinate legislation) may be reviewed by the courts and declared incompatible with Convention rights. Such a declaration of incompatibility does not invalidate the legislation, and it is then for Parliament to decide whether to amend the offending law, which can be done swiftly by means of executive order rather than a full-blown amendment procedure.

III. Explanations and justifications

What theories or approaches explain or justify the above remarkable developments? Before returning to the approaches under the Human Rights Act, let us consider the role of the courts without the benefit of the guidance of any Convention or other fundamental catalogue of human or constitutional rights. As I have said, for most of the last century the courts deferred to the executive acting under powers conferred by Parliament in broad terms, interpreting such powers literally. What justified the sudden importation of a purposive interpretation, leading to the superimposition of requirements of legality and procedural fairness? Review for substance was less intense, but became more so when human rights were in issue. More boldly still, the courts overtly recognised 'constitutional rights' as implicit in a democracy. What justified these further intellectual leaps?

Analysis of the initial shift in the sixties from literal to purposive interpretation reveals little overt change of approach or method. Purposive interpretation was expressly justified, if at all, by the same reference that had been employed under literal interpretation, namely,

---

[10] *R* v. *Home Secretary exp. Leech* [1994] Q.B. 198.
[11] *R* v. *Home Secretary exp. Simms* [1999] 2 W.L.R. 328.

on the ground that it properly translated the true intention of a (sovereign) Parliament. The imposition of standards of due process was justified merely on the basis of an ungrounded notion of fairness.

Recently a heated academic debate has been raging in the pages of UK law reviews, asking on what basis the imposition of these standards can be justified in a system without a written constitution. One school (the '*ultra vires*' school) argues that in the UK system the only justification is the implied intent of Parliament. The other ('common law') school argues that it lies within the powers of the independent courts to develop these standards in accordance with general standards of justice. The *ultra vires* school counter that such an approach could lead to a *Marbury v. Madison* on British shores, a course which the overriding principle of parliamentary sovereignty forbids. The 'common law' proponents riposte by ridiculing their opponents for inventing 'fairy tales' about Parliament's intent.[12]

In my view the true shift of approach in the early years of the more activist judicial review in the UK can best be understood by viewing it in the full context of later developments, culminating in the recognition of implied constitutional rights in the 1990s. With the benefit of hindsight, we can now see that the changes in approach were not due entirely, as has been suggested, to the personalities of particularly creative, yet ultimately wholly pragmatic, judges. Under the case-by-case development of law under a judge-made, common law system, a different model of democracy was being asserted. Under this model, government was expected to respect human rights, which were integral to and constitutive of democracy and not opposed to it. Despite the ultimate sovereignty of Parliament, the role of the courts was not simply to endorse Parliament's literal instructions. Such instructions should be presumed to be subject to a new, rights-based constitutional order.[13]

A number of questions now present themselves about the relationship between law and public opinion, and about the 'influences' upon judicial approaches in these circumstances. It is at this point that the American and, to a lesser extent, European (or 'other European') influences appear to have had an impact.

[12] The arguments are summarised in P. Craig, 'Constitutional Foundations, the Rule of Law and Supremacy' (2003) *Public Law*, 92.

[13] I have argued this more fully in J. Jowell, 'Judicial Difference and Human Rights. A question of competence', in P. Craig and R. Rawlings (eds.), *Law and Administration in Europe* (2003).

It should be remembered that during the process of 'decolonisation' the UK provided its former colonies with written constitutions and bills of rights, starting with the Indian Constitution, which came into force in 1950. The Warren court's opinions, especially on matters such as segregation, reverberated through the common law world.[14] Without departing from the constraints of appropriate judicial reasoning, that court demonstrated how law could be a force for justice. Indeed, the positivistic distinction between law and morality was under serious consideration in the Hart–Fuller and Hart–Devlin debates.[15] In the USA of the 1960s a 'rights culture' was developing in respect to issues such as claims for welfare benefits and public participation in urban development schemes.[16] On the other side of the Atlantic, under the rubric of traditional if vague formulations such as fairness and natural justice, judges found ways of supporting these and similar claims within the bounds of legal principle, and without straying into the realm of policy.[17]

From 1964 the UK Parliament progressively banned discrimination on the grounds of race, colour, national origin and then sex. The first legislation was heavily influenced by anti-discrimination laws introduced after the Second World War in the States of New York and Massachusetts. These laws were administratively enforced – through state commissions rather than through the criminal law. Britain established similar public boards to assist the implementation of those laws which outlawed discrimination first in public facilities and then in employment, housing and other areas. The prohibition of indirect discrimination in UK law was directly influenced by US Supreme Court decisions.

The English have not always, however, been that hospitable to American notions. In a decision of the Privy Council on appeal from Singapore in 1980, counsel sought the assistance of American case-law, but was met with a rebuff by Lord Diplock, who warned that 'decisions of the Supreme Court of the United States on that country's Bill of Rights, whose phraseology is now nearly 200 years old, are of little help in construing provisions of ... modern Commonwealth constitutions which follow broadly the Westminster model'.[18] This judgment has

---

[14] Especially *Brown* v. *Board of Education* (1954) 347 US 438.
[15] See N. Lacey, *A Life of H. L. A. Hart* (Oxford: Oxford University Press, 2004), chs 8 and 10.
[16] See J. Handler, E. Hollingsworth and H. Erlanger, *Lawyers and Pursuit of Legal Rights* (New York: Academic Press, 1978).
[17] J. Jowell, 'The Legal Control of Administrative Discretion' (1978) *Public Law*, 178.
[18] *Ong Ah Chuan* v *Public Prosecutor* [1981] A.C. 648 at 669.

been cited as a 'rare example of antiquity being regarded with judicial disfavour'.[19]

While English law has not gone as far as American law in the realm of procedural protections to the accused, the American notion of 'due process' is very similar to the English 'natural justice' or 'procedural fairness'. However, English law does not normally extend to the extensive rule-making procedures required of regulatory bodies in the USA. It is interesting to note, however, that in the 1960s and 1970s there was a similar reaction in the USA and UK against the allocation of government 'largesse'. Recipients of government benefits of various kinds demanded welfare 'rights', viewed by Professor Charles Reich of Yale University as 'the new property'.[20] Residents of communities which had been destroyed in favour of 'urban renewal' demanded 'citizen participation'. As a result, both through judicial decisions and legislation, the weakest members of society were extended entitlements that were at least procedural. The work of the eminent American administrative lawyer K. C. Davis, who argued as a matter of principle for constraints on all official discretion, was greatly influential in the UK as well.[21]

In the area of free speech, English law has not adopted the rigorous approach to prior restraint of American law. Reputation may not that easily be sacrificed on the altar of free speech. However, in the case of defamation of a public body, the English courts employed almost as binding precedent the Supreme Court decision in *New York Times v. Sullivan*.[22] In the case of *Derbyshire*,[23] the House of Lords recognised the 'chilling effect' that libel actions against public officials could cause to legitimate criticism of a body which was expected to act in the public interest.

In the area of privacy, however, the English are closer to other European countries. Although no tort of privacy exists in the UK, the law of confidence is used to similar effect although, like the USA, wide exceptions are made for public figures.[24]

European influence on English law started with the ratification of the European Convention in 1951. Although not incorporated into

---

[19] Anthony Lester QC, 'The Overseas Trade in the American Bill of Rights', 88 *Columbia L. Rev.* (1988), 537 at 543.

[20] C. Reich, 'The New Property', 73 *Yale L. J.* (1964), 733.

[21] K.C. Davis, *Discretionary Justice* (1969). See C. Harlow, 'A Special Relationship? American Influences on Judicial Review in England', in I. Loveland, note 1 above.

[22] 376 US 254 (1964).

[23] *Derbyshire C.C.* v. *Times Newspaper Ltd* (1993) A.C. 531.

[24] See D. Anderson in Deakin, Johnston and Markesinis, *Tort Law* (Oxford: Oxford University Press, 2003), p. 721.

domestic law, in 1966 the right of direct petition to the Court of Human Rights at Strasbourg was permitted to British citizens. At least in international law, the primacy of rights over convenience was recognised. In 1972, the UK acceded to the European Community, and was subjected to its jurisprudence of rich principles such as legal certainty, equality and proportionality. Professor Schwarze's book[25] was important in demonstrating that the newly crafted principles of European Law were neither novel nor dangerous, and indeed fitted comfortably with English tradition and practice. A more purposive, 'teleological' approach to statutory interpretation also came into play, influenced in large part by European practice. In the mid-1970s EC Law incorporated the jurisprudence of the European Convention, so the rights under the ECHR had to be applied in all directly-effective EC Law, which even permitted the review of UK statutes by UK courts.[26]

All the above factors may have played their part in the changing approach of the British judiciary towards public power from the mid-1960s. None, however, had as much influence as the lessons of history during the course of the twentieth century; lessons learned from the ideological storms which ushered in totalitarian tyrannies of the left and right in large parts of Europe. It was these tyrannies, some of them initially elected by popular will, which demonstrated conclusively that democracy is not synonymous with majority rule – that parliamentary sovereignty should, in a democracy properly so-called, be constrained by rights – constitutional rights.

IV. The process school and the question of deference

Review under the Human Rights Act is already challenging the courts, and the relationship between the courts, the executive and Parliament, in new ways. In particular, it raises questions about the extent of deference which the courts should accord to Parliament. When the distinguished American Professor Louis Jaffe came to England in 1969 he reflected that the American judge 'would assume a role in the polity far greater than that played by his confrère in Britain'.[27] That can no

---

[25] J. Schwarze, *European Administrative Law* (London: Sweet and Maxwell, 1992).

[26] As held in the case *R* v. *Secretary of State for Transport ex parte* Factortame Ltd [1990] 2 A.C. 85.

[27] L. Jaffe, *English and American Judges as Lawmakers* (Oxford: Clarendon Press, 1969) at 83.

longer be the case, but English judges are still struggling with the extent to which they can challenge Parliament's literal intent. The problem is coloured by the fact that, under the Human Rights Act, parliamentary supremacy seems to have survived by virtue of the fact that the courts may not strike down Acts of Parliament (but may only issue a declaration of incompatibility). It has sometimes been said that because Parliament has the last word, the courts, even when reviewing an Act of Parliament for compatibility with Convention rights, ought still to defer to the superior constitutional status of Parliament.

Such an approach accords with the low degree of scrutiny that the English courts have imposed upon the exercise of administrative discretion over the years. However, the Human Rights Act shifts the courts from administrative law concepts to that of constitutional review.[28] Under the test of proportionality the courts have already accepted that a stricter degree of scrutiny is required. This is because the Act has constitutional significance in itself. Although not entrenched, it is a 'super-statute', which not only sets out a series of rights equivalent to rights of way or social benefits, but it also incorporates a coherent set of civil and political entitlements that are inherent in a new, rights-based conception of democracy for the United Kingdom. Parliament retains the ultimate power to defy the expectations of the new order, but it is for the courts to define them.[29]

Despite the absence of need to defer on *constitutional authority*, the courts may be obliged to defer on grounds of lack of *institutional capacity*. We would not expect the courts to rearrange the rates of taxation or themselves to reallocate funds from one social purpose (say, transport) to another (say, medical assistance to AIDS patients). US thinking will be helpful here. Although the courts in the UK have not often in the past had to confront the issues that have so dominated US constitutional debate over the past half century or so, they can no longer avoid joining the issues engaged in by Hart and Sacks, Wechsler, Bickel and others in the USA.[30] Under the new rights regime the 'counter-majoritarian difficulty' has directly to be confronted. That is not to say that that work or those issues have been unknown in the UK. Many of

---

[28] J. Jowell, 'Beyond the Rule of Law: Towards Constitutional Judicial Review' (2000) *Public Law*, 671.
[29] J. Jowell, above, note 13.
[30] See Harlow, above, note 21 and N. Duxbury, 'Faith in Reason: the Process Tradition in American Jurisprudence' (1993) *Cardozo L. Rev.*, 601.

our leading jurists studied in the United States and there has been a
frequent two-way traffic in scholars, judges and, in particular, legal
philosophers. Even before the Human Rights Act, Professor Fuller's
work on the limits of the adjudicative process in deciding 'polycentric
problems'[31] has been adopted in cases involving the exercise of administrative discretion. Perhaps most noteworthy of all is the fact that
Professor Ronald Dworkin took up the Chair of Jurisprudence at
Oxford in the early 1970s, before moving to University College London
in the late '90s while simultaneously holding a chair at New York
University. Dworkin's theories of adjudication, his concept of the distinction between principle and policy, and his notion of equality and,
perhaps most important, his notion of moral rights against the state,
have greatly guided English thinking.[32]

Finally, we should note a paradox. We have seen that in the mid-
twentieth century it was the Warren court which inspired much of the
jurisprudence of the UK and other jurisdictions. Today we are engaged
in an era of sharing of comparative practice as never before, and also of
reference to growing international legal instruments. English courts
even a decade ago were reluctant to refer to authority outside of the
UK. Now, they freely range over the practice of other countries. In the
UK, the Human Rights Act requires judgments of the European Court of
Human Rights to be taken into account by our courts when assessing the
scope of a Convention right. However, ECHR jurisprudence does not
need to be slavishly followed. Since most issues under the Convention
explore the necessary qualities of a democratic society – expressly or by
implication – we find that this exploration engages a rich comparative
conversation through reference to the case law of a number of countries,
including other European states, Commonwealth countries such as South
Africa and Canada and that of the United States. The paradox is that,
while this was happening, the United States Supreme Court seemed to
turn away from both comparative example and internationally established
standards. But perhaps that is just a temporary phenomenon.

[31] L. Fuller, 'The Forms and Limits of Adjudication' (1978) *Harvard L. Rev*, 353.
[32] E.g. R. Dworkin, *Taking Rights Seriously* (London: Duckworth, 1977); *A Matter of Priniciple* (Cambridge, MA: Harvard University Press, 1986).

Comment

LÁSZLÓ SÓLYOM

University classes on constitutional adjudication usually start with John Marshall and Hans Kelsen. That is, the difference between American and European constitutional review belongs to the elementary knowledge in this field. These differences are of a structural nature (diffuse v. centralised review, concrete case/controversy v. abstract norm control, supreme court v. a separate body outside of the ordinary judicial branch). The structural differences have an impact on the character of constitutional review. Furthermore, they affect the self-understanding of the given court and thereby the role which the constitutional court plays within its political context and in the legal system. The self-understanding of a constitutional court is particularly important because constitutional courts actively shape their own competences and power. Accordingly, *my* first point is the abstract character of European constitutional justice and the consequences thereof. Being the basic difference between US and European constitutional adjudication, this abstractness indicates the limits of any convergence between them. In fact the gap may become even broader and deeper if the abstract norm control acquires a dominant position in Europe, and if the individual constitutional complaint loses its present significance.

My second point is the importance of historical circumstances. First, history may help to explain the paradox of the countermajoritarian difficulty. On grounds of pure theory this difficulty could be expected to prevail in Europe and to be neglected in the United States, but on historical grounds the contrary is true. A second relevant question is whether the great activist and liberal periods of constitutional adjudication were really preconditioned by previous negative historical experience, and, if so, whether such lessons of history really have a lasting influence after over half a century. How can the recent changes in Britain be explained? Is the rise of constitutional adjudication in the seventies

249

and – in particular – again in the nineties still due to the tyrannies formerly experienced elsewhere in Europe?

It is beyond question that the European Convention on Human Rights and Strasbourg case law, and increasingly the European Union, do exercise a homogenising effect on the substance of the jurisprudence of European constitutional courts. In addition, European courts – unlike the US Supreme Court – often work on a comparative basis. Institutions exist which facilitate this practice, such as the Venice Commission and the Conference of the European Constitutional Courts. However, beneath this uniform 'European blue sky' the institutional landscape is rather colourful. There are important states where the constitutional adjudication was not able to break through the doctrine of parliamentary supremacy. Not only in Britain does Parliament have the last say. In France, the *Conseil Constitutionnel* will probably never be emancipated from the Parliament. The efforts of President Badinter who wanted to benefit from the big founding wave of constitutional courts throughout Europe in the nineties were unsuccessful.

Even between the countries with proper constitutional adjudication the relationship between the constitutional court and the legislative is different. Constitutional review spread in Europe in three waves: after the Second World War, then in the seventies and later in the nineties. It is significant that the three generations of the European constitutional courts all came out of a 'system change' or democratic transition, following the fall of authoritarian regimes. More importantly, the three waves of democratisation in Europe did not originate among the people. The regime changes in many of the countries were neither the result of a real revolution, nor popular upheaval. In Germany and Italy, democracy was established under the tutelage of the victors (mainly the USA); the Spanish, the Portuguese and the post-Communist changes were based on negotiations between democratically minded elites who were not democratically legitimised. These European constitutional courts were created out of a deep mistrust in the majoritarian institutions, which had been misused and corrupted during the Nazi, fascist and communist regimes. In this given historical setting the constitutional court judges believed that they represented the essence of democratic change, and that they enjoyed 'revolutionary legitimacy'.

This is the history which explains the self-conscious activism of the leading European courts. Such feelings of a European constitutional court judge may be supported by the abstract competences of the court. If laws are reviewed regardless of concrete case or controversy, that is without any factual basis and lacking an injured personal plaintiff, the only possible determination of unconstitutionality is by way of a formal declaration of a law as being null and void. The conflict of a European constitutional court with the parliament is necessarily open and provocative, and the power of the constitutional court is in no way 'hidden', as Tocqueville noted in 1830 about the power of American judges.

The power of the constitutional court to review and annul legislative acts was included in the new constitutions and became part and parcel of the new democratic structure. The pioneering German Constitutional Court had to fight out its status as a 'constitutional organ' and thereby established itself above all other powers in constitutional matters. It had serious conflicts with the legislature, the president and also with the ordinary courts, but by the seventies constitutional adjudication had already become a traditional and successful means of democratic governance and defending basic rights. In the third wave of democratisation in Europe the existence of a constitutional court was seen as natural and the Council of Europe required that candidates for membership have a strong constitutional court, open to public access.

Under such circumstances the countermajoritarian difficulty was not raised in Europe even in academia. It is a separate issue that clashes between the government and the constitutional court may occur, especially when the court interferes with the economic policy of the state. It is also true that post-communist parliaments, fully aware of their fresh democratic legitimacy, found the limitation of their power hard to bear. But the new political elite soon learned how to push responsibility onto the constitutional court when a decision would be unpopular or would divide the population too deeply. For example, it is not by chance that the abolition of capital punishment has been spelled out by constitutional courts, first in Hungary, then in the Baltic States, in the Ukraine, in Albania and, similarly, in South Africa. In countries where the vast majority is in favour of maintaining the death penalty, no Member of Parliament is willing to introduce such a bill into the House or even to support it. The same is true regarding compensation for lost property which was nationalised or confiscated during Communism. Such problems can never be solved in a manner that satisfies everyone. The final decision remained with the constitutional court.

The German Constitutional Court introduced a seminal novelty which was added to Kelsen's norm control: the protection of individual fundamental rights. This was not a decision of the constituent assembly.

The Basic Law of 1949 entrusted the protection of individual rights to all courts. The 'constitutional complaint' (*Verfassungsbeschwerde*) developed only gradually in the practice of the German Constitutional Court, and was incorporated into the Basic Law only in 1969. Both the protection of individual rights and the unlimited access of citizens to the Constitutional Court in constitutional complaint cases connected the constitutional review directly to the great human rights movement of the second half of the twentieth century and made a comparison with the United States easier. The double function of the constitutional court – the review of laws and protection of individual rights – continued in the second generation. In Spain and Portugal the *amparo* procedure fitted into the tradition of constitutional complaint. The third generation, however, seems to return to Kelsen with the dominance of the abstract norm control. Only four or five out of about thirty new constitutuional courts can review individual cases, that is, decisions of ordinary courts. For the new courts, 'constitutional complaint' typically means the (abstract) review of a law on the occasion of its application in an individual case with the result that the concerned party may have his or her case reopened before the ordinary court after the law has been annulled.

The abstract control of norms has sometimes been developed to extreme forms such as the *actio popularis* in Hungary. Under the Hungarian Constitutional Court Act everybody is entitled to file for the constitutional review of any law or decree and he or she is not required to show any violation of his or her rights or interests. This unlimited standing opened the door for citizens to participate in the constitutional transformation; it brought laws to the Constitutional Court which contradicted governmental interests and which would never have been challenged by ministers or parliamentarians. It almost functioned as a special channel of direct democracy, securing influence of the citizenry upon legislation. But apart from such an unprecedented case, the abstract norm control is today the dominant competence of European constitutional courts.

Besides the abstract norm control, constitutional courts in Europe have further abstract competences which would be unthinkable in the United States. The US Supreme Court had declared already in 1793 that it would not give advisory opinions to the President. In contrast, many third generation constitutional courts in Europe deliver *binding interpretations* of constitutional provisions on the motion of high state organs. Although there is always a concrete and often delicate political issue in the background, the courts keep their opinion in abstract terms. It sounds like a law and has the force of a law. Such opinions usually transgress the border between interpreting and writing the constitution.

Under different names and using various techniques European courts can also oblige the parliament or government to pass a law, the content of which is determined by the constitutional court. This was already the case when the German Constitutional Court declared the mere non-compatibility (*Unvereinbarkeit*) of a law with the Constitution (in contrast to declaring the law null and void), but the institution developed fully in the third generation. Many of the new courts can determine the unconstitutional omission of the legislature to pass an act. The court sets a deadline for passing the law and it usually tells the law maker how to fill the gap. If the court holds existing legislation to be incomplete it may oblige the legislator to amend the law and prescribe how to bring it into harmony with the constitution.

The significance of such competences and techniques lies in the fact that they can be used instead of killing laws to offer cooperation to the legislator. Thus, the parliament is not humiliated by the annihilation of its acts and is ready to follow the advice of the constitutional court in the subsequent legislation. The situation is a paradox. Mitigating conflicts and cooperation help to avoid clashes with the legislator, but at the same time the constitutional court transforms its role from that of a 'negative legislator' (as Kelsen originally called the constitutional court) to that of a positive legislator. European courts go far beyond abstractly formulated tests of constitutionality which are common on both sides of the Atlantic. I am referring not only to the binding interpretation just mentioned. Many new courts put positive rules into the operative part of the decision – and these rules will unquestionably have the force of law.

If anything, such judicial legislation should raise the countermajoritarian difficulty. But – and this is another paradox – European courts have their difficulty not so much with the democratic legislator but rather with the ordinary courts. Problems – in fact rivalry between the constitutional court and the ordinary judiciary – were present from the first moment when the German Court reviewed final judgments of ordinary courts. Quite unexpectedly, the tension continued into the third generation constitutional courts which have no power to revise individual court decisions. Ordinary courts refuse to accept the 'legislation' by constitutional courts; in particular they do not follow the interpretation of the laws as determined by the constitutional court.

It is as if the ordinary courts acted instead of, or on behalf of, the parliament in order to save the democratic majoritarian rule.

Of course, the motives of the ordinary courts are not always of such a democratic nature. It is more a question of prestige: a Supreme Court is not willing to accept a more supreme court. But the question is serious, it is not just about the rank of both court presidents at state celebrations. The uniform interpretation of the constitution is at stake. At present the question is posed whether and how constitutional courts can maintain their monopoly on the interpretation of the constitution. The question arises not only vis-à-vis domestic courts. The relationship with international courts is also far from easy. For the moment, this is a problem that exists only for Europe.

To sum up: if one compares European and US constitutional cases, the standards of constitutionality and scope of protection of fundamental rights may converge in some cases and may differ in others; each case needs an explanation of its own. This is true for free speech, for instance. If, however, the structure of constitutional adjudication is compared, the well-known differences which I have described may be supplemented by two more points. One is the abstract character of European constitutional justice, which shapes their powers. The other is the understanding by European constitutional courts of the role of constitutional review in the political and legal system. This self-understanding is rooted in, and reinforced by, the genesis of the three generations of European constitutional courts.[1]

---

[1] This comment partly draws upon my article, 'The Role of Constitutional Courts in the Transition to Democracy', *International Sociology*, 18 (1) (2003), 133. There is an immense amount of literature on constitutional review in Europe, but less on the third generation courts. Regarding the latter see G. Brunner, 'Entwicklung der polnischen Verfassungsgerichtsbarkeit in rechtsvergleichender Sicht', in G. Brunner and L. Garlicki, *Verfassungsgerichtsbarkeit in Polen* (Baden-Baden: Nomos Verlagsgesellschaft, 1999); H. Schwartz, *The Struggle for Constitutional Justice in Post-Communist Europe* (Chicago: Chicago University Press, 2000); L. Sólyom and G. Brunner, *Constitutional Judiciary in a New Democracy. The Hungarian Constitutional Court* (Ann Arbor: University of Michigan Press, 2000); R. Procházka, *Mission Accomplished. On Founding Constitutional Adjudication in Central Europe* (Budapest, New York: Central European University Press, 2002). C. Dupré: *Importing the Law in Post-Communist Transitions. The Hungarian Constitutional Court and the Right to Human Dignity* (Oxford, Portland: Hart, 2003).

Comment

CÉSAR LANDA

I would like to consider the historical context of constitutional adjudication, in particular in Britain, the United States and Latin America.

Democracy and constitutional adjudication

The concept of democracy as a form of government limited by law is the main origin of constitutional justice. Thus, in the English legal system the old polemic between the *gubernaculum* – absolutism of the monarchy – and *jurisdiction* – liberty of subjects – was resolved in favour of the common law. Nevertheless, after the Glorious Revolution of 1688, Parliament, as the representation of the citizens and their common law, assumed supreme power without being subject to control, as described by Blackstone and Dicey. The British flexible constitutional system, based on conventions that were not laid down in a written constitution, found it impossible to directly control the acts of Parliament because it was not circumscribed in a *rigid constitutional* text (Bryce). However, the judges, as interpreters of common law, developed a certain form of judicial review. They focused on controlling the discretionary power of the public services of the government according to natural justice – as Jowell has explained.

The early British experience directly influenced the constitutional foundation of the United States. The founding fathers of the US Constitution, like Hamilton, reflected in *The Federalist* about the dangers of a government and parliament without limits. The Marshall court then recognised the power of the judicial review of laws in the famous case of *Marbury v. Madison* (1803). Since then, the principle of constitutional supremacy over ordinary legislation, and the possibility to declare a statutory act of Congress unconstitutional in a concrete case, was the rule in the United States. However, this rule was not applied without controversies, as can be seen by the conflict between two currents of thought: judicial activism and self-restraint, which represent different points of view concerning the role of the judiciary and social processes. The first advocates social change by the judiciary under the leadership of judges such as Cardozo and then Warren, the second is more prudent or passive regarding reality and power, with leaders such as Judges Holmes and Frankfurter. The Supreme Court has been somewhere between the critics of non-interpretativists (Ely, Choper) and interpretativists (Bickel, Berger) Ultimately, the Court has flexibly resolved the challenges of social, economic and political modernisation through a creative jurisprudence.

Constitutional justice in Europe had other origins due to the erratic development of the rule of law. Thus, almost every European state passed its own constitution during the nineteenth century, according to which the parliament was the first power of the state and statutory law an instrument of liberty, without yet permitting the judicial review of statutes. When the liberal state fell into crisis, the necessity arose to assure the rationality and the supremacy of the constitution through a constitutional tribunal, as Kelsen proposed and realised in the 1920 Austrian Constitution. However, this fresh idea was rejected by Schmitt because the judicialisation of politics, according to him, was a utopian idea that would lead to the politicisation of justice. Indeed, the first experiences of constitutional tribunals in Austria and then in Czechoslovakia and Spain were overtaken by totalitarian regimes and their ideology – Nazi–fascist and communist – which concentrated all power in the leader or in the party without any mechanisms of control.

After the Holocaust and the Second World War, the renewed democratic regimes in Germany, Italy and, to a certain extent, in France, established the constitutional tribunal as defender and supreme interpreter of the constitution. Later, many other countries in Eastern Europe and Latin America, which passed from dictatorship or communist regimes to democratic governance, adopted constitutional jurisdiction in their new constitutions.

Constitutional adjudication in the UK

By adopting the Human Rights Act of 1998 the United Kingdom has challenged its historical constitutional law in several respects: implementing the decisions of the European Court of Human Rights, the British judges approach the role of judicial policy makers. The judges, as defenders of the *superstatute* of human rights, are supposed to interpret the intentions of Parliament in the light of the decisions of the European Court of Human Rights. This creates an ambiguous status for the courts, because the adjudication lacks precise boundaries but must at the same time assure the predictability of the fundamental rights of citizens.

It is clear that the global wave to protect human rights has not only reinforced the role of the international adjudicatory system on human rights but also the debate on human liberties as ideology, inevitably reopening debates over the position of the treaties on the national sources of law and the question of the organisation and the effectiveness of national courts. However, we must remember what Blackstone said: international law is part of the law of the land.

In a modern constitutional government, fundamental rights are the measure of the quality of the democratic regime. It is, however, also important to mark boundaries for judicial activism. Three criteria are important: self-restraint, fundamental rights and the freedom of the legislator.

Constitutional adjudication in the USA

Michel Rosenfeld has demonstrated the link between constitutional review and democracy, in particular the intermediary role which judges play. Controlling the excesses of government does not mean assuming an antimajoritarian position when constitutional values or rights are injured. Because, as Madison said, 'if angels were to govern, neither external nor internal controls on governments would be necessary' (*The Federalist* no. 51). Therefore, the judges do not replace the opposing parties, but they aid the implementation of the constitution and democracy through judicial interpretation.

It is only possible to understand the role of adjudication in the framework of a given political government system. This means that adjudication is linked to three essential characteristics of modern constitutional democracy: limiting the powers of government, adherence to the rule of law and protection of fundamental rights. Nevertheless, the view has been expressed by Rosenfeld that the common law constitutional adjudication is legitimate in the context of a core of commonly shared values, and the current crisis is due to profound splits within the increasingly pluralistic American polity. It should, however, not be forgotten that the social and political fragmentation in a modern society enriches the adjudication when there is a balance between the majoritarian and minoritarian goals, because it is the pluralistic society itself which is protected in the constitution.

Thus, the idea of national and international open society means: democratic consensus, pluralism and toleration, and human rights. This idea is contained in a constitution which is open to the influence of international treaties. Thus, constitutional interpretation is not only a technique, but also requires a constitutional theory that helps the solution of constitutional conflicts, avoids the false politicisation of constitutional justice, and remains within the framework of the international treaties that formulate the idea of modern constitutionalism.

Thus, strengthening constitutional adjudication requires a democratic consensus on defending the values of the constitution and treaties, as they are embodied in the limitation of the government by law. Moreover, the negative and positive human rights are the two faces of Janus; one is the condition of the other. There are no true liberties without social rights and it is impossible to recognise social rights without respecting liberties. This means that the 'political questions' about social rights could help to re-evaluate constitutional jurisdiction in an era of new global challenges to the state and society.

Only rational constitutional adjudication in a humanitarian spirit can control the excesses of political power, and can possibly integrate majority and minority interests. Rational constitutional adjudication can offer an ethical regeneration of the political controversies but it must avoid excessively interfering in social and political issues, since this only produces the politicisation of justice, instead of the judicialisation of the political.

Constitutional adjudication in Latin America

The contemporary constitutional situation in Latin America must be studied in light of the conflict between democracy and authoritarian constitutionalism. This is because instability has been a historical constant which produced not only pendulum swings between democracy and authoritarian regimes, but also a permanent mixture of both regimes. The instability of the Latin American constitutional regimes is enhanced by a traditional positivist idea of the law, sometimes called 'formalist' and sometimes 'voluntarist'. The failure of positivism and of its kind of democratic constitutionalism is the background for the rise of constitutional adjudication. Thus, the development of constitutional jurisdiction in the Latin American countries with their weak democracies requires re-thinking the foundations of constitutional law. On one hand, modern constitutional justice cannot function efficiently under the old and formal *jus positivum* which is entrenched in this region, and on the other hand, the new social and political values of the open society must be reflected in the decisions of any constitutional court. It is therefore important to find the roots of the constitutional system in contemporary history in order to understand the legal problems of such simultaneously traditional and modern states, which are partly integrated in the universal culture of the democratic and constitutional state.

Latin America is experiencing the democratic transformation as a gap between the protection of fundamental rights and the *raison d'Etat*. This means that the idea of the law as an expression of popular sovereignty, *vox populi vox dei*, coexists with the idea of the law as an expression of the power of the Republic's President, *auctoritas non veritas facit legem*. Strengthening constitutional adjudication in Latin America requires a democratic consensus on the defence of the constitution and its values, that is the limitation of the government by constitution, and on the protection of fundamental rights.

In practice, the situation of constitutional adjudication is complicated. Sometimes the courts are impotent to annul an unconstitutional statute in the face of the presidentialist governments. Such situations mainly occur in highly political situations, such as the re-election of former Peruvian President Fujimori or the monetary control of the Argentine *corralito*. In these cases, the constitutional courts could not protect the Constitution or they played a timid role as guardian of fundamental rights. Also, the constitutional courts displayed a poverty of arguments and submitted positivist interpretations of the Constitution. Finally, the judges reproduced the political conflict in legal language among themselves, duplicating the political confrontation between the government and opposition.

In general terms, constitutional adjudication in Latin America is linked proportionately to the stability or instability of the government. The possibilities to develop constitutional adjudication depend, in the final analysis, on the strengthening of the economical and political democracy and on renewing constitutional thinking.

PART VI

Democracy and international influences

9

Democracy and international influences

LECH GARLICKI

I. Introductory remarks

My intention is to address the structural dimension of 'democracy', i.e. the question, how to make the organs of the state capable of reflecting the principle of 'rule by the People'. Such a question cannot be discussed in abstract terms, but must be related to a particular historical and geographical setting. The evolution of constitutionalism in post-Communist Europe in the 1990s, in which I had the privilege to participate, seems to meet this requirement.

The term 'international influences' can be understood in different ways. In particular, 'international influences' can be associated with attempts of the outside world to impose certain solutions upon the constitution-drafting process in a particular country. Short of military intervention and/or economic pressure, the most civilised way of imposing certain standards upon national processes of constitution drafting is to 'universalise' these standards by expressing them in the norms of international law. Such norms, if vested with sufficient binding authority, can pre-define the content of national constitutions leaving to the framers of a particular constitution no alternative but to reproduce them in the text of the constitution. In consequence, the choices reserved for the sovereign decisions at the national level may become rather limited. If 'international influences' develop in such a direction, it would inevitably lead to a conflict between democracy (or, rather, national sovereignty) and international law. Professor Rubenfeld's concern[1] seems quite legitimate from this perspective.

I am not sure, however, whether such a 'coercive' perception of 'international influences' could be applied to the realities of constitution-drafting processes in Central and Eastern Europe, in particular in the

---

[1] Jed Rubenfeld, 'The two world orders', this volume, p. 278.

first half of the 1990s. First of all, the existing body of universally binding international law was (and still is) limited in its scope and was oriented mainly towards the protection of human rights. All 'new democracies' aspired to join the Council of Europe and all of them had to accept the authority of the European Convention on Human Rights and the jurisdiction of the European Court of Human Rights. In consequence, national constitutions had no alternative but to conform to the European Convention in structuring rights and liberties in their texts. But the Convention deals mostly with personal and political rights and, even in this area, leaves several important matters, like abortion, to the national legislatures. Therefore, it was not difficult 'to surrender' to the Convention standards and requirements: it is worth remembering that it was precisely the establishment of political and personal freedoms that the democratic opposition has always fought for. More leeway has been left to the member countries in regard to social and economic rights as well as to other problems unique to post-Communist societies, such as economic reform, property restitution, lustration, etc.

Secondly, there are few binding norms of international law that relate to the organisational dimension of the state. Most of them deal with the procedural assurance and implementation of individual rights and liberties by public authorities and, therefore, are connected to the administration of justice and to democratic elections. The Council of Europe and its Venice Commission have been rather careful in elaborating generally applicable standards of the organisation of government. Although the developments in all new (as well as in some 'old') democracies are regularly monitored at the Council of Europe level, such monitoring results mainly in political action and does not enter the 'coercive' dimension of international law.

Finally, the same applies to the role of the Council of Europe, and in particular the Venice Commission, in assisting new democracies in their processes of constitution writing. While there have been examples of rather intensive involvement of these bodies in the drafting of some new constitutional documents in the recent years, the picture in the early nineties was quite different. The Venice Commission was still in the initial stage of its existence and the political elites as well as legal experts in countries like Poland or Hungary were capable of addressing most problems without detailed foreign assistance. This picture may have changed later on, in particular with regard to countries or territories which required foreign intervention to solve internal political problems (as in the cases of Bosnia-Herzegovina or Kosovo).

Therefore, it would be very difficult to prove that the processes of constitution drafting in Central and Eastern Europe in the beginning of the 1990s have been dominated by 'international influences', i.e. by standards and requirements imposed by foreign powers and/or European institutions, and to prove that this domination has reached an extent which was incompatible with the sovereignty of these countries. But, at the same time, national constitution writing could not remain isolated from the outside world and, in particular, from the patterns and models offered by those countries whose politics and economy successfully emerged from the earlier crisis. Since the main goal of the process of democratic transformation in Central and Eastern Europe was to re-integrate those countries into the Western world, it was quite obvious that constitutional institutions of Western democracies would be regarded as an attractive inspiration by the drafters of new constitutions.

In this perspective, 'international influences' can be associated with attempts of the new democracies to identify and to follow solutions which had already proven their effectiveness in the developed democracies. While there was some 'wishful thinking' in the belief that what has been successful elsewhere would – by definition – fit the political and social situation of the post-Communist countries, the opening towards Western constitutional institutions constituted one of the most visible features of the constitution writing in the 1990s. Therefore, it was the 'inspirational' rather than a 'coercive' function of international influences that really mattered in Central and Eastern Europe in the relevant time.

In consequence, there was no contradiction between 'democracy' (understood as a process of decision-making by legitimate representative bodies within a country) and 'international influences' (understood as a pool of information inspiring national drafters in shaping national constitutions). This 'inspirational function' was particularly visible in regard to the constitutional principles of the organisation of the state, because international law did not intervene in this area. At the same time, there were several problems concerning the distribution of power, the role of representative institutions, and the position of the executive branch, which were crucial to the 'democracy' (understood as such organisation of government which guarantees the fair expression of the 'will of the People') and which had to be solved in the new constitutions. The drafters, while constantly looking at the institutions of other countries, had to decide which of them would be the best for both the interest of their country and the implementation of their political ideas. Thus, in taking such decisions, it was, at first, necessary to define whether there were any universally recognised standards in a respective area, secondly, what were the 'typical solutions' adopted in the developed democracies, in particular in Europe and in the United States, and, finally, which of these solutions, if any, should be preferred in the drafting of the new constitution.

The separation of powers represents the most general principle upon which the organisation of the state is structured in a modern democracy. In other words, the structure of government presupposes the distinct existence of the Legislative, Executive and Judicial branches of government.

Already at this level of abstraction, contradictions began to be visible. On the one hand, the etymology of the word 'democracy' suggests that the primary role within the state should be attributed to the branch most closely connected to the people and that some decisions should be left to the people itself. At the same time, however, the idea of the separation of powers requires a certain balance among all three branches of government, independently of their popular legitimacy.

In this respect, three questions seem to merit attention:

- What is the relation between 'direct' and 'representative' democracy?
- What is the relation between the Legislative and Executive, i.e. between the 'political' branches of government?
- What is the role of the Judicial branch, in particular regarding constitutional adjudication?

Each of these questions had to be addressed by the drafters of the new constitutions in Central and Eastern Europe. No comprehensive answers were provided for any of them in international law. That was why the drafters had to find their own solutions and, therefore, they had to consider:

- What (if any) are the universally recognised standards that could be regarded as conditions *sine qua non* for a modern democratic government?
- How has American (US) constitutionalism addressed the problem?
- How has the problem been solved by the 'traditional' West European democracies?
- How should it be solved in the 'new democracies' that emerged in Europe after 1989?

II. Referenda and parliaments

From a theoretical perspective, referenda as well as other procedures of 'direct democracy' represent the pinnacle of the 'rule by the People'. It opens to the electorate a possibility of taking the most important decisions without delegating this power to representative bodies. However, from a political (or practical) perspective, the problem becomes more complicated, particularly if a popular referendum is used to bypass the parliamentary procedures. Therefore, discussions among proponents and opponents of referendum procedures have continued for many decades and no universally accepted solutions have emerged as yet.

The American constitutionalism does not offer any clear suggestion in this respect. While, in the US, there is no possibility of conducting a referendum on a national level, different states adopt different approaches to the 'direct democracy' procedures. A relatively broad array of constitutional amendments and legislative decisions may be adopted via a referendum at least in some states. Nevertheless, it would be rather difficult to define any general pattern and to find 'a typical solution' which could influence constitutional developments in Europe.

In Europe itself no widespread tradition of popular referenda has ever existed. While some countries (in particular Switzerland) have willingly applied referendum procedures since the end of the nineteenth century, in other traditional democracies more emphasis has been attached to representative bodies, primarily national parliaments. Before the Second World War, there were few, if any, examples of national referenda in major democracies of Western Europe. At the same time, experience of 'plebiscites' organised, for example, in Nazi Germany delivered a warning rather than encouragement.

The situation seemed to remain unchanged after the War. While some new constitutions, such as the 1946 French Constitution, and/or constitutional amendments (Ireland, Austria) have been approved or disapproved in national referenda, and while some new constitutions provided for other forms of referendum as well, no wide-spread practice of referenda developed over the first twenty-five years. Only in the Fifth French Republic did the procedure of national referendum acquire real importance. At the same time, however, at least some of the referenda held in France in the 1960s have been used to bypass the parliament and to take decisions which otherwise would not have been adopted in the National Assembly.

The situation began to change in the 1970s. In some countries the first enlargement of the European Community was confirmed by referenda, particularly in the UK, and new democratic constitutions in Greece, Portugal and Spain provided for referendum procedures. In Italy the practice of 'abrogative referenda' began to gain ground. In the next two decades, the ratification process of the Maastricht Treaty (France, Ireland, Denmark) and subsequent enlargements of the EU have delivered several new examples of referenda held in the countries of Western Europe. Step by step, the idea that some important decisions could and should be taken directly by the electorate has been accepted by the political elite in most countries, including in the UK. At the same time, most referenda held in Western Europe have been conducted upon decisions of respective national parliaments. In some cases, parliaments possessed a discretion to decide whether a referendum should take place at all, in other cases it was the constitution itself which required a popular vote on certain matters. In most cases parliaments (and not the Executive branch) set the date of the referendum and formulated question(s) to be submitted to the electorate. Thus, it would be difficult to analyse these referenda in the traditional perspective that regarded the referendum as a tool of communication between the Head of State and the electorate, bypassing the parliament, and, therefore, being anti-parliamentary in its nature. More and more often, referenda have been held not with an intention to produce a decision that would not have been adopted by the parliament, but in order to confirm a decision already approved by the parliament, but so politically important that the parliament preferred to delegate the ultimate responsibility to the electorate. In consequence, the co-deciding and thus supplementary role of referenda became more visible than the competitive role.

The message sent from Western Europe to the new European democracies was twofold. On the one hand, the referendum could be regarded as a 'typical' procedure, known to most West European constitutions, practically applied in several countries and, generally speaking, free from traditional anti-parliamentary – or even anti-democratic – connotations. On the other hand, the referendum could not be regarded as an indispensable component of democratic government: some important countries of Western Europe (in particular, Germany on the federal level) do not provide for any referendum-like procedures.

The 'new democracies' had to interpret this message in the light of their own experience. Referenda were not unknown under the Soviet-oriented 'constitutionalism', but, like parliamentary elections, the results of such referenda were usually determined in advance. In some cases, referenda were used to confirm the Soviet occupation such as in the Baltic states in 1940, in others, to legitimise the new system of government, such as in Bulgaria and Poland in 1946. Later, the referendum was used mostly to confirm new constitutions. No common pattern, however, has ever emerged, since it was obvious that such referenda have never offered a real choice to the voters.

The practice of the Soviet times did not, however, compromise the idea of the referendum as such. Thus, when the process of transformation began in 1989, several countries of Central and Eastern Europe resorted to referendum procedures. The lack of developed political parties and the lack of trust in politicians and representative institutions made the referendum an attractive form of public participation. At the same time, new democracies had to take some political decisions of such magnitude that their parliaments have not always felt ready or sufficiently legitimised to bear the full responsibility. In effect, the referendum became a universally accepted procedure: in all new constitutions, provisions for different forms of referendum on the national as well as on the local level were adopted. Between 1989 and 1997 there were twenty-eight national referenda held in the countries of Central and Eastern Europe. In nine of them, the question of independence was submitted to the electorate, in ten others the electorate was invited to confirm new constitutions or to decide some basic questions of the new constitutional order (Hungary). At the beginning of the twenty-first century, the problem of EU enlargement, and in some countries the problem of accession to NATO, gave rise to a new wave of national referenda (Slovenia, Slovakia, Lithuania, Hungary, Poland). At the same time, there have not been many examples of referenda dealing with more 'routine' problems. However, three examples of 'privatisation' referenda held at the beginning of the 1990s in Poland, Lithuania and Slovakia could not be regarded as clearly successful. While the referendum became universally recognised as a component of the democratic constitution and while some kind of consensus emerged that a referendum constitutes a preferable way of taking the most important constitutional or political decisions, there is also a broad consensus that the responsibility for governing the country is vested in parliament and cannot be too often delegated to the electorate. In this respect, the influences of the West European experience are quite visible.

In most cases, the above-mentioned referenda played a co-decisive and therefore supplementary role and could not be regarded as tools to bypass the national parliaments. Some referenda had preceded the first democratic elections, most others were held to confirm decisions already taken, or at least endorsed, by the respective parliament. At the same time, however, there have been some more controversial examples of referenda. In some of the post-Soviet republics in Asia, referenda were held to prolong the term of office of the incumbent president. In 1996, the president of Belarus used a referendum for approval of a constitutional amendment limiting the powers of the parliament and curtailing the independence of the constitutional court. In 1993, President Yeltsin, after having dissolved the parliament and having partly suspended the existing constitution, submitted his new constitution to a national referendum. While similar examples could have been found in an earlier constitutional history of Western Europe as well, they proved that, also in the modern world, referenda may have different faces and, sometimes, their competitive role may gain a clear priority.

III. Separation of powers and the political branches of government

The modern theory of state (as well as several international documents) emphasises the requirement that the state must be organised in a manner respecting the 'democratic principle'. At the same time, unlike as in the area of human rights, there are only few detailed and rigid standards imposed on national governments in regard to the organisation of the state.

It is commonly recognised that the structure of the central government should be based upon the separation of powers principle, i.e. that the three branches of government should remain distinct in their organisation and functions. It is, however, notable that while the general idea of separation of powers has been accepted by almost all democratic countries around the world, and while there is a certain uniformity in its application to the position and functions of the judicial branch, the understanding of this principle remains very different in different countries.

It is universally recognised that the judicial branch should be separated from the political branches of government. From a functional perspective, this means that the 'administration of justice' may be exercised only by the judicial bodies, at least in the final instances. From a structural perspective, this means that both the courts and the judges must be vested with a considerable degree of independence.

All above-mentioned consequences result from several international instruments – human rights treaties as well as separate regulations concerning the administration of justice – imposing numerous relatively detailed requirements on the national governments.

Less uniformity can be found with respect to the structure of the political branches of government. The separation of powers principle presupposes the distinct existence of the Legislative and Executive. Furthermore, it is universally recognised that the existence of a parliament constitutes a *sine qua non* prerequisite of a democratic government. At least two other requirements concerning the Legislative branch seem to have equally universal character: the parliament must be a representative body, meaning that it must be a product of democratic elections (in this respect the 'structural' perspective overlaps with the universally recognised consequences of the right to vote) and the parliament must be a real body, meaning that it must be vested with powers allowing it to play an adequate role in the process of government, in particular in the area of law making. At the same time, there are no detailed standards as to the organisation of parliament (unicameralism v. bicameralism), its procedure, its functions and its powers. A relatively wide margin of appreciation is left here to the national constitutions.

This margin is considerably broader with respect to the Executive branch. In the history of modern constitutionalism several versions of the organisation and functions of the Executive branch have emerged. Some countries adopted a presidential version of government, other countries developed different versions of the parliamentary system, still other countries opted for mixed systems, trying – in a more or less successful manner – to combine parliamentary and presidential concepts of government. At the same time, it would be very difficult to determine any universally recognised standards, *conditiones sine qua non*, of a democratic government, in regard to the organisation, structure and powers of the Executive branch. While we could agree that every 'democratic constitution' must provide for the existence of a 'real' parliament and must guarantee independence and separateness of the Judicial branch, universal and binding standards of the modern constitutionalism and international law end here. It allows national authorities more freedom to shape their own constitutional solutions, and – in the process of constitution drafting – it offers more choices between already existing models and versions of the organisation of the Executive branch.

The American tradition of constitutionalism has always been associated with the presidential system of government. The US Constitution has always been regarded as a 'model' of a democratic presidentialism. Its concepts have been followed in most other countries of both Americas, Canada remaining the most notable exception. These concepts have also played an important role in the development of European constitutionalism. Since most of the European constitutions are later in date than the US Constitution, the latter has always influenced – positively or negatively – the process of constitution drafting in other countries. The authors of the new constitutions have been aware of the undisputed success of the presidential system of government in the United States. At the same time, however, they also have been aware that some other countries were less fortunate with their imitations of US presidentialism, and that the establishment of a strong presidency often led to the degradation of the role of parliament as the democratic representation.

West European constitutionalism has traditionally developed along the lines of the parliamentary system. The US version of presidentialism seemed too dangerous for emerging national parliaments, and, for obvious reasons, it could not be applied within a monarchical structure of government. While several constitutions in the nineteenth century reserved a rather strong position for the Executive branch – the development of German constitutionalism being the best example – the influences of US constitutionalism have never played a decisive role.

The parliamentary system combined the structural division of the Executive branch (the head of state v. the prime minister/the cabinet) and the strong position of the parliament whose confidence was essential for the formation of the cabinet, as well as for its survival. Without entering into the differences between the British and French versions of the parliamentary system, it seems possible to conclude that the European constitutionalism of the nineteenth century developed a mature concept of parliamentary government. While parliamentary government had found real application in only a few countries, in political thought it was associated with democratic organisation of the state. Consequently, when – after the First World War – new independent countries began to emerge in Europe, the parliamentary system – usually in the version developed in the French Third Republic – constituted the main source of inspiration for drafters of the new constitutions.

None of the 'new democracies' accepted the US model of presidential government. Several countries adopted a 'pure' version of parliamentarism, sometimes going far beyond the model of the French Third Republic (like the 1921 Constitution of Poland). Even those countries that chose a popular election of the president and offered more powers to the head of state – in particular Germany and Austria – retained the principle of parliamentary responsibility of the cabinet. At the same time, most democracies – old and new – adopted proportional electoral systems that, in several countries, resulted in an excessive fragmentation of parliaments.

There is no need to enter into historical presentations. Generally speaking, the inter-war period was not extremely successful for European constitutionalism. Most countries on the Continent experienced problems with the formation of stable parliamentary majorities; in consequence, the operation of the parliamentary system appeared rather difficult. These problems emerged with particular pertinence in the 'new democracies': out of a dozen post-war democratic constitutions, only the Czechoslovak one survived until 1939. While the real reasons for the collapse of the inter-war democracies were situated outside the realm of constitutional law, it has been noticed that some constitutional law institutions were contributing to the inability of parliaments to exercise their function in an effective way. Hence, as early as the 1920s, the first attempts were made to 'rationalise' the traditional shape of the parliamentary system, in particular to prevent excessive fragmentation of parliaments and to protect the cabinet against 'negative majorities'.

The grim recollection of the inter-war crisis of parliamentary government in most European countries has clearly influenced the processes of constitution drafting after WWII. It should be noted that, notwithstanding the growing influence of the US constitutional concepts, the presidential model of government has not been regarded as attractive for 'new' or 'renewed' democracies on the Continent. Almost all post-war constitutions restored the parliamentary system, sometimes with 'rationalising' modifications, as in the case of the 1949 German Basic Law. Also in the subsequent constitutional developments, the presidential system has remained rather unpopular. While the most advanced step toward presidentialism seemed to have been made by the French Fifth Republic, a certain 're-parliamentarisation' of the system became visible already in the 1970s, when France successfully experienced the first period of 'cohabitation'. A similar evolution, gradually confirmed by constitutional amendments, took place in Finland, where the strong presidency finally disappeared in the course of the last decade. Finally, out of the three 'new democracies' that emerged in Western

Europe in the 1970s, only Portugal initially adopted certain institutions typical of the presidential system.

The message sent from Western Europe to the post-Communist countries was threefold. First of all, almost all West European constitutions adopted a parliamentary system of government, and rejected the US presidential alternative. Secondly, several countries have modified the traditional version of parliamentarism, introducing different 'rationalising' mechanisms. Since such 'rationalisation' was meant to exclude an excessive fragmentation of parliaments, it could be seen as a constitutional check on democracy. Finally, unlike the institutions of the inter-war period, the post-war constitutional institutions have worked rather successfully in most West European countries.

The 'new democracies' appeared quite receptive in accepting this message. It should be noted that some of them (e.g. Czechoslovakia, Lithuania, Poland) had their own tradition of pre-war constitutionalism, when, at least initially, a parliamentary system of government had been adopted. Not without importance was also the doctrine of the 'socialist constitutionalism' which had always emphasised the role of the parliament as the supreme organ of the state. While the political reality of the Communist countries has never allowed any significance to parliaments, the idea that the parliament should occupy the leading position within the state was well rooted in the minds of the political elite. At the same time, new democracies had to confront several difficult, political and economic problems. Their civil societies and their party systems still had to develop, and their parliamentarians still had much to learn. In effect, popular opinion was sometimes inclined to trust more in individual leaders than in the elected representatives.

Nevertheless, most of the new constitutions adopted the parliamentary system of government, in particular the concept that parliamentary approval and support is necessary for the formation and operation of the cabinet. In this respect, experience of West European democracies constituted the most obvious source of inspiration. None of the new democracies has openly opted for the US-style presidential system. At the same time, however, in several countries, there has been a visible trend to construct mixed systems of government and to grant broad powers to the President of the Republic. In some countries, it finally led to the establishment of quasi-presidential systems of government. Quite often this development was accompanied by human rights violations and the elimination of democracy (e.g. in some post-Soviet countries in Asia or in Belarus). On the other hand, such negative evaluation could hardly apply to the case of Russia, where the 1993 Constitution adopted several concepts typical of presidentialism.

The parliamentary system became typical for those Central European countries which once belonged to the Soviet bloc, as well as for the three Baltic countries. It should be noted that the same group of countries seems to be quite successful in their internal transformation as well as with respect to the accession to the European structures. In most of these countries it is rather the Prime Minister than the President of the Republic who controls the Executive branch. In all countries cabinets must enjoy confidence and support of the parliamentary majority, and in Hungary, the Czech Republic, Estonia, Latvia and Albania – but not in Bulgaria, Croatia, Macedonia, Poland, Romania, Slovenia and Slovakia – the President of the Republic is elected by the parliament. At the same time, the concepts of 'rationalised parliamentarism' appear to be quite attractive for most countries of Central Europe. Thus, when the parliament becomes unable to produce a stable majority, different 'reserve solutions' are provided for. Usually, it is the President of the Republic who may then act as an arbiter. Some constitutions (Hungary, Poland) contain provisions protecting the cabinet against 'negative majorities' in parliament, the so-called 'constructive vote of non-confidence', some others allow the dissolution of parliament only if it is unable to fulfil its constitutional functions. Most of the electoral systems adopt the proportional vote; at the same time, however, electoral thresholds (*Sperrklauseln*) bar small parties from the parliament. Also in this respect, the West European experience, in particular the experience of countries having their own record of totalitarian regimes, rather than the US experience, constituted an important source of inspiration.

IV. Constitutional adjudication and the role of the judicial branch

From a theoretical perspective it seems clear that the modern constitution, being 'the supreme law of the land', must be protected against violations by any branch of government. Not entering into the history of judicial review, it is possible to note that nowadays, in almost all democratic countries of the world, the judicial branch has become entrusted with the task of protecting the constitution. Since the review of constitutionality of parliamentary legislation constitutes the core of this task, the question of whether courts and judges are sufficiently legitimised to invalidate statutes adopted by a representative and democratically elected legislature inevitably arises. This question is often discussed as a possible contradiction between parliamentarism and constitutionalism, or between democracy and the rule of law. Not even trying to repeat all arguments submitted by proponents and opponents of the judicial review of legislation, it seems necessary to note that:

— while the judicial review of the constitutionality of parliamentary statutes represents a solution typical of almost all modern democracies, there are undoubtedly democratic countries (e.g. the UK or the Netherlands) which decided not to follow this idea. Therefore, it would be difficult to regard the existence of such judicial review as a *conditio sine qua non* for modern constitutionalism;

— traditionally, the idea of judicial review of legislation contrasted sharply with the concept that a law adopted by the parliament should be inviolable since it represents the 'will of the People'. In the last fifty years, this concept has constantly eroded due to the development of international human rights law and, in Europe, due to the development of supranational institutions. In consequence, national parliaments in Europe must respect not only their national constitutions, but also international treaties and the law of the EU. There are international and supranational courts vested with powers to review the conformity of national legislation with the above-mentioned instruments. Finally, the national courts also have to enforce these instruments, even if it results in a refusal to apply national legislation. Thus, parliamentary legislation is no longer immune to judicial review;

— the judicial review of legislation cannot be squeezed into the Kelsenian concept of 'negative legislature'. Since constitutional adjudication presupposes a constant process of judicial interpretation of both the Constitution and the statutes, it transforms the Court into a 'positive legislature', in particular in regard to the development of the Constitution.

The US constitutional tradition has been, almost from the beginning, based on the concept of judicial review. Three short remarks seem sufficient in this respect:

1. the US system of judicial review has always had a 'deconcentrated' or 'diffuse' nature, i.e. the power of judicial review belonged to all courts and all judges; in the political reality, the US Supreme Court occupies a particularly powerful position;

2. the US system of judicial review had already reached a mature stage by the end of the nineteenth century and allowed the 1787

Constitution to survive for more than 200 years. Therefore, the US experience could not be ignored in the constitution drafting process elsewhere, since the overwhelming majority of other countries have adopted their current constitutions within the last sixty-five years;

3. for at least sixty-five years, constitutional case law in the US has been oriented, to a considerable extent, towards the protection of individual rights. Therefore, the US experience appeared particularly attractive for those countries who had some record of totalitarian rule and violation of human rights.

The Western European tradition of constitutionalism was originally rather hostile towards the idea of judicial review. In the nineteenth century, only few constitutions provided for some limited forms of judicial review, and also in the 'legal doctrine' the opponents of judicial review formed a clear majority. While in countries like Greece and Norway the Supreme Courts arrogated the power to review constitutionality of parliamentary legislation, most European countries have not been ready to grant such powers to the judicial branch. The lack of trust in the judiciary and fear of *un gouvernement des juges* did not disappear after the First World War. Even if some new constitutions (Austria, Czechoslovakia, and Spain) established procedures permitting the review of the constitutionality of parliamentary legislation, in none of these countries were the reviewing powers granted to the 'regular' courts. Instead, and in clear rejection of the US concept of judicial review, special quasi-judicial bodies were created: namely, the constitutional courts. It should be noted that none of the inter-war constitutional courts ever managed to play an important role in the process of government. The understanding of the constitution as a primarily political document still dominated in Europe and sporadic attempts of some supreme courts to decide constitutional questions could not change the general picture.

The time for a real change came with the end of the Second World War. The sad lessons of the collapse of the inter-war constitutionalism and the new emphasis on protection of human rights resulted in the acceptance of the juridical function of national constitutions. In all post-totalitarian countries the judicial branch was vested with powers to adjudicate constitutional questions, including the review of parliamentary legislation. At the same time, however, the Austrian concept of a separate constitutional court appeared to be more attractive than the US system of judicial review. Constitutional courts could be staffed with new judges, not compromised under the old regime. Therefore, constitutional courts seemed to be better suited for the review of legislation. At the same time, the 'democratic argument' questioning the constitutional courts' legitimacy to nullify parliamentary decisions was no longer convincing since the parliaments had failed in their duties before.

Already by the end of the 1950s it had become clear that the experiment with establishing constitutional courts in the defeated countries had been quite successful. In all three countries the constitutional courts managed to establish an independent position and began to develop constitutional case law, oriented – at least in part – towards the protection of individual rights. At the same time, two European jurisdictions, the European Court of Human Rights and the Court of Justice, joined the club. Finally, the Constitution of the French Fifth Republic created the *Conseil Constitutionnel*. While the *Conseil Constitutionnel* was not conceived to be a 'regular' constitutional court, its creation meant that France abandoned its traditionally negative attitude towards constitutional adjudication. No reminder is needed that two decades later the case law of the *Conseil Constitutionnel* had developed in a direction quite similar to other constitutional courts. It was not astonishing that other Western European countries followed, sometimes immediately establishing a 'regular' constitutional court (Spain), sometimes gradually developing in this direction (Belgium), sometimes adopting mixed systems of constitutional adjudication (Portugal and Greece). In effect, notwithstanding continuous discussions among scholars and the sporadic attacks of some politicians, the existence of constitutional courts became an obvious component of modern Continental Western European constitutions. While it was clear that the very concept of the constitutional court makes it a check on a democratically elected legislature, a priority was given to other values, in particular to the role of the constitution as the 'supreme law of the land'. In this respect, Europe followed the US developments. At the same time, however, most Western European countries preferred to establish a separate constitutional court.

The message sent from Western Europe to the post-Communist countries was twofold. Firstly, constitutions must be regarded as legal instruments and, therefore, they must provide for procedures protecting their superiority within the system of legal norms. Secondly, the institution of a constitutional court seems to constitute the most suitable form for the protection of the constitution.

The 'new democracies' had no hesitation in following this message. While there had been no significant tradition of judicial review in this region – save for the Czechoslovak Constitutional Court before the Second World War, constitutional courts in the communist Yugoslavia, and the Constitutional Court in Poland since 1985 – all constitutions adopted or amended in the 1990s provided for procedures of constitutional adjudication, in particular procedures of review of parliamentary statutes. Almost all new constitutions adopted the Western European model of a separate constitutional court; it seemed quite obvious that the existing judicial institutions, due to their links to the past, would be neither able nor legitimated to exercise the power of judicial review. Only Estonia – due to its close ties with the Nordic legal culture – decided to grant the power of judicial review to the Supreme Court. Most of the new constitutions tried to follow the German version of constitutional jurisdiction, including the procedure of individual complaint. It should be kept in mind that several constitutions 'borrowed' from Germany the idea of the *Rechtsstaat* as well as other general concepts in regard to fundamental rights. The influence of the French model surfaced in particular in Romania and, later on, in Kazakhstan. It is noteworthy that within ten years, several constitutional courts have established their independence and begun to play a substantial role in their countries' progress.

But not every country has been so successful. As was recently observed by Herman Schwartz:

> An independent and vigorous constitutional court is the child of liberal democracy, and without that king of polity, a constitutional court cannot function effectively. The evidence for this is abundant. In Belarus and Kazakhstan, constitutional courts' judges' efforts to assert their independence ... met strong resistance: the court was abolished entirely in Kazakhstan, and in Belarus, defiance was followed by the forced resignation of judges ... In Russia, the Constitutional Court was put out of business for a year and half, when President Yeltsin resorted to forcible overthrow of the constitutional order ...

The question whether constitutional courts are sufficiently legitimised to act as a check upon a democratically elected parliament and/ or a democratically elected president has been discussed in all 'new democracies'. While no universal answer has been found, as yet, it did not stop the development of constitutional adjudication. It seems that, in the political dimension, it has been recognised that neither constitutionalism, nor the rule of law, nor democracy can be regarded as isolated values, and that their harmonisation appears necessary.

10

The two world orders

JED RUBENFELD

What is the source of America's growing unilateralism? The easy answer is self-interest: we act unilaterally to the extent that we see unilateralism as serving our interests. But the answer prompts a more searching question: Why do so many Americans view unilateralism this way, given the hostility it provokes, the costs it imposes, and the considerable risks it entails? Americans sometimes seem unilateralist almost by instinct, as if it were a matter of principle. Might it be?

It will not do to trace contemporary US unilateralism to the eighteenth-century doctrine of isolationism, for unilateralism is a very different phenomenon. An isolationist country withdraws from the world, even when others call on it to become involved; a unilateralist country feels free to project itself – its power, its economy, its culture – throughout the world, even when others call on it to stop. Although there may still be a thread of isolationism in the United States today, unilateralism, the far more dominant trend, cannot usefully be derived from it.

The search for an explanation should begin instead at the end of the Second World War. In 1945, when victory was at hand and his own death only days away, Franklin Roosevelt wrote that the world's task was to ensure 'the end of the beginning of wars'. So Roosevelt called for a new system of international law and multilateral governance that would be designed to stop future wars before they began. Hence, the irony of America's current position: more than any other country, the United States is responsible for the creation of the international legal system it now resists.

The decisive period to understand, then, runs roughly from the end of the war to the present, years that witnessed the birth of a new international legal order, if not, as widely reported, the death of the Westphalian nation-state. America's leadership in the new internationalism was, at the beginning, so strong that one might be tempted to see today's US unilateralism as a stunning about-face, an aberration even, which may yet subside before too much damage is done. But the hope that the United States will rediscover the multilateralism it once championed assumes that America and Europe were engaged in a common internationalist project after the Second World War. Was that in fact the case?

It is undoubtedly true that, after the war, Americans followed the path Roosevelt had charted and led Europe and the world towards an unprecedented internationalism. We were the driving force behind the United Nations, the primary drafters of the initial international human rights conventions, the champions of developing an enforceable system of international law. Indeed, America pressed on Europe the very idea of European union – with France the primary locus of resistance. At the same time, America promoted a new constitutionalism throughout Europe and the world, a constitutionalism in which fundamental rights, as well as protections for minorities, were laid down as part of the world's basic law, beyond the reach of ordinary political processes.

How then did the United States move from its post-war position of leadership in the new international order to its present position of outlier?

The Cold War played an essential role in the change, fracturing the new international order before it had taken root. At the same time, the Cold War also had the effect of keeping the Atlantic alliance intact for many decades by suppressing divisions that would show themselves in full force only after 1989. When, in the 1990s, the United States emerged as the last superpower standing, it became much easier for the forces of European union to move ahead and for the buried divisions between America and its European allies to be made apparent. The most fundamental of those divisions had been the most invisible: from the start, the post-war boom in international and constitutional law had had different meanings in America and Europe – because the war itself meant different things in America and Europe.

At the risk of overgeneralisation, we might say that for Europeans (that is, for those Europeans not joined to the Axis cause), the Second World War, in which almost 60 million people perished, exemplified the horrors of nationalism. Specifically and significantly, it exemplified the horrors of popular nationalism. Nazism and fascism were manifestations, however perverse, of popular sovereignty. Adolf Hitler and Benito Mussolini rose to power initially through elections and democratic processes. Both claimed to speak for the people, not only before they assumed dictatorial powers but afterwards, too, and both were broadly popular, as were their nationalism, militarism, repression and, in Hitler's case, genocidal objectives. From the post-war European point of view, the Allies' victory was a victory against nationalism, against popular sovereignty, against democratic excess.

The American experience of victory could not have differed more starkly. For Americans, winning the war was a victory for nationalism – that is to say, for our nation and our kind of nationalism. It was a victory for popular sovereignty (our popular sovereignty) and, most fundamentally, a victory for democracy (our democracy). Yes, the war held a lesson for Americans about the dangers of democracy, but the lesson was that the nations of Continental Europe had proven themselves incapable of handling democracy when left to their own devices. If Europe was to develop democratically, it would need American tutelage. If Europe was to overcome its nationalist pathologies, it might have to become a United States of Europe. Certain European countries might even need to have democratic institutions imposed upon them, although it would be best if they adopted those institutions themselves, or at least persuaded themselves that they had done so.

These contrasting lessons shaped the divergent European and American experiences of the post-war boom in international political institutions and international law. For Europeans, the fundamental point of international law was to address the catastrophic problem of nationalism – to check national sovereignty, emphatically including national popular sovereignty. This remains the dominant European view today. The United Nations, the emerging European Union, and international law in general are expressly understood in Europe as constraints on nationalism and national sovereignty, the perils of which were made plain by the war. They are also understood, although more covertly, as restraints on democracy, at least in the sense that they place increasing power in the hands of international actors (bureaucrats, technocrats, diplomats, and judges) at a considerable remove from popular politics and popular will.

In America, the post-war internationalism had a very different meaning. Here, the point of international law could not ultimately be anti-democratic or anti-nationalist because the Allies' victory had been a victory for democracy (American democracy) and for the nation (the American nation). America in the post-war period could not embrace an anti-nationalist, anti-democratic international order as Europe did. It needed a counter story to tell itself about its role in promoting the new international order.

The counter story was as follows: when founding the United Nations, writing the first conventions on international rights, creating constitutions for Germany and Japan, and promoting a United States of Europe, Americans were bestowing the gifts of American liberty, prosperity and law, particularly American constitutional law, on the rest of the world. The 'new' international human rights were to be nothing other than the fundamental guarantees made famous by the US Constitution. Wasn't America light years ahead of continental Europe in the ways of democracy? International law would be, basically, American law made applicable to other nations, and the business of the new internationalism would be to transmit American principles to the rest of the world. So of course America could be the most enthusiastic supporter of the new international order. Why would it not support the project of making the world more American?

In the American imagination, then, the internationalism and multilateralism we promoted were for the rest of the world, not for us. What Europe would recognise as international law was law we already had. The notion that US practices – such as capital punishment – held constitutional by our courts under our Bill of Rights might be said to violate international law was, from this point of view, not a conceptual possibility. Our willingness to promote and sign on to international law would be second to none – except when it came to any conventions that might require a change in US domestic law or policy. The principal organs of US foreign policy, including the State Department and, famously, the Senate, emphatically resisted the idea that international law could be a means of changing internal US law. In the 1950s, the United States refused to join any of the major human rights and anti-genocide conventions. The rest of the world might need an American-modelled constitution, but we already had one.

In part, this exceptionalist attitude reflected American triumphalism in the wake of the war; in part, it expressed American know-nothing parochialism; and, in part, it placated southern fears that US participation in international rights agreements could loosen the chokehold in which American blacks were held. But it reflected something more fundamental as well: a conception of constitutional democracy that had been reaffirmed by the war. It was impossible for Americans to see the new international constitutionalism as Europeans saw it – a constraint on democratic nationalism – for that would have contradicted America's basic understanding of constitutional democracy.

It is essential here to distinguish between two conceptions of constitutionalism. The first views the fundamental tenets of constitutional law as expressing universal, liberal, Enlightenment principles, whose authority is superior to that of all national politics, including national democratic politics. This universal authority, residing in a normative domain above politics and nation-states, is what allows constitutional law, interpreted by unelected judges, to countermand all governmental actions, including laws enacted by democratically elected legislators. From this perspective, it is reasonable for international organisations and courts to frame constitutions, establish international human rights laws, interpret these constitutions and laws, and, in general, create a system of international law to govern nation-states. I call this view 'international constitutionalism'.

Let me make the abstract picture more concrete. The Council of Europe – the first post-war organisation of European states, and the progenitor of today's European Union – has a quasi-judicial branch, called the Commission on Democracy through Law (also called the Venice Commission), on which I have served for several years as the US representative or observer. One of my first duties was to assist a committee participating in the drafting of constitutional frame-work legislation for Kosovo. The committee consisted of distinguished jurists and constitutionalists from all over Europe. We met in Paris and Venice, and the proceedings were professional and expert in every respect. But though the committee had visited Kosovo for three days, it had no Kosovar members. Uncertain as to whether their absence was deliberate, I made inquiries among the committee members. It was indeed intentional: the decision not to include Kosovars at this stage in the process had apparently been made by UN authorities. The framing of constitutional law was a delicate business, I was told, and to have involved Kosovars in the process would have impeded the committee's work and mired it in political in-fighting.

Might it therefore be desirable, I asked, to draft an explicitly transitional document, on the model of the interim South African constitution, one that created institutions through which local drafting and ratification of a permanent charter could later take place? No, was the committee's answer. We were drafting constitutional law, and constitutional law is not meant to be transitional.

The committee's attitude perfectly exemplified international constitutionalism, which is the dominant constitutional worldview in Europe. From this viewpoint, it is not particularly important for a constitution to be the product of a national participatory political process. What matters is that the constitution recognise human rights, protect minorities, establish the rule of law, and set up stable, democratic political institutions, preferably of a parliamentary variety, in which the chief executive is not directly elected by the people. National ratification of a new constitution might be instrumentally valuable, but having a committee of expert foreign jurists draw up a constitution would be perfectly satisfactory in principle. Having that constitution imposed on the society by an occupying power would be awkward, but so long as the occupying power was recognised as valid under international law, and so long as the constitution took, imposing it by force would be entirely acceptable.

The alternative to international constitutionalism is American, or democratic, national constitutionalism. It holds that a nation's constitution ought to be made through that nation's democratic process, because the business of the constitution is to express the polity's most basic legal and political commitments. These commitments will include fundamental rights that majorities are not free to violate, but the counter-majoritarian rights are not therefore counterdemocratic. Rather, they are democratic because they represent the nation's self-given law, enacted through a democratic constitutional politics. Over time, from this perspective, constitutional law is supposed to evolve and grow in a fashion that continues to express national interpretations and reinterpretations of the polity's fundamental commitments.

In American constitutionalism, the work of democratically drafting and ratifying a constitution is only the beginning. Just as important, if not more so, is the question of who interprets the constitution. In the American view, constitutional law must somehow remain the nation's self-given law, even as it is reworked through judicial interpretation and reinterpretation, and this requires interpretation by national courts. By contrast, in international constitutionalism, interpretation by a body of international jurists is, in principle, not only satisfactory but superior to local interpretation, which invariably involves constitutional law in partisan and ideological political disputes.

The overtly political nature of American constitutional law stuns Europeans; indeed it is one of the features of the American system at the root of the differences between American and European constitutionalism. Claims about 'American realism' are often exaggerated, but there is undoubtedly in the United States a greater understanding than in Europe that all law, including judge-made law (i.e. judicial decisions), and even judge-made constitutional law, is a political product. From an American point of view, if the law is to be democratic, the law and the courts that interpret it must retain strong connections to the nation's democratic political system. By contrast, the processes through which

EU law has emerged so far betray a disconnection with, and even a disrespect for, democratic processes that would be unacceptable as a basis for constitutional transformation in the United States.

Americans at bottom do not believe in the claims made for a non-political, neutral constitutional law. They know that judges' values inevitably inform constitutional law. Europeans tend to have a different understanding. To be sure, there was for a long time, and perhaps still is, a European tradition of distrust of judges, especially constitutional judges, shared by left-wing and right-wing European political thinkers. Yet this scepticism about 'government by judiciary' coexisted with a belief in the possibility of an expert, neutral bureaucratic rationality and a dogmatic, apolitical legal reason. The result was a deeply ambiguous attitude toward judicial review and constitutional law. Before the Second World War, Europe had some constitutional courts, but these courts had almost no power to strike down laws on the ground that individuals' rights had been violated.

Post-war European constitutionalism has shed this equivocation. European constitutionalism today invests courts with full jurisdiction over individual rights, without fully acknowledging that judicial decisions about the meaning of constitutional rights are fundamentally political in character. On the contrary, what makes the new European constitutionalism cohere, and gives European constitutional courts their claim to legitimacy, is the ideology of universal or 'international' human rights, which owe their existence to no particular nation's constitution, or which, if they derive from a national constitution, possess nonetheless a kind of supranational character, rendering them peculiarly fit for interpretation by international juridical experts. In America, by contrast, it would be nothing short of scandalous to suggest that US constitutional questions had to be decided by an international tribunal claiming supremacy over our legal system.

From the American perspective, national constitutional courts are an essential feature of constitutional law, and it is critical that constitutional interpretation remain interwoven with the nation's processes of democratic self-governance. This is done in various ways: through a politically charged judicial nomination mechanism; through judges' membership in the national polity and the nation's particular political and legal culture; through the always-open possibility of amendment; and, perhaps most important but least understood, through periodic but decisive contests between the judicial and political branches. The most famous twentieth-century example was the confrontation between

Franklin Roosevelt and the Supreme Court of the 1930s, which repeatedly struck down New Deal legislation – a battle Roosevelt won only after proposing to appoint six additional justices to the court. Such clashes are too often portrayed as moments of institutional peril to be avoided at all costs. In reality, they play a crucial role in maintaining the judiciary's connections to a nation's long-term democratic development. The ideal is not to make constitutional courts responsive to popular will at any given moment, but to make sure that constitutional law remains answerable to the nation's project of political self-determination over time.

To summarise: international constitutionalism contemplates a constitutional order embodying universal principles that derive their authority from sources outside national democratic processes and that constrain national self-government. American or democratic national constitutionalism, by contrast, regards constitutional law as the embodiment of a particular nation's democratically self-given legal and political commitments. At any particular moment, these commitments operate as checks and constraints on national democratic will. But constitutional law is emphatically not anti-democratic. Rather, it aims at democracy over time. Hence, it requires that a nation's constitutional law be made and interpreted by that nation's citizens, legislators, and judges.

Let me give three illustrations – in turn, historical, theoretical and practical – that make plain the contrast between American and European conceptions of constitutionalism. In 1789, the popular assembly of France promulgated the Declaration of the Rights of Man. The document spoke in the language of universal rights. The rights of man were at issue, not merely the rights of Frenchmen. That same year, the US Congress promulgated the Bill of Rights, which, far from proclaiming universal law, originally applied only to the federal government and not to the state governments. Thus, the First Amendment forbade national religious establishments but not religious establishments in the states. The US Constitution did not speak in the language of universal rights. It spoke in the language of popular sovereignty: 'We the People of the United States . . . do ordain and establish . . . .' American constitutional law was understood from the outset to be part of the project of popular self-government, as opposed to an external force checking that project. The American language of constitutional rights, properly understood, does not claim the authority of universal law. It claims, rather, the authority of democracy.

A second illustration of the contrast between the two types of constitutionalism makes the point at the level of theory. Contemporary American constitutional theorists are unendingly concerned with the so-called countermajoritarian difficulty: because constitutional law allows unelected judges to override the outcomes of the majoritarian democratic process, it is potentially in conflict with democracy. European constitutionalists used to share this obsession, but since 1945, and particularly with the recent explosion of 'international human rights' law, the countermajoritarian difficulty rarely figures in European thinking any more. The reason is that Europeans have embraced international constitutionalism, according to which the whole point of constitutional law is to check democracy. For Americans, constitutional law cannot merely check democracy. It must answer to democracy – have its source and basis in a democratic constitutional politics and always, somehow, be part of politics, even though it can invalidate the outcomes of the democratic process at any given moment.

The third contrast is more practical. It involves the question of whether there must be one order of human rights applicable to all nations. In the European view, human rights transcend national politics and ought, at least ideally, to be uniform throughout the world. For example, European nations – or at least European governments – now see capital punishment as a human rights violation. Accordingly, European diplomats and politicians not only excoriate the United States for allowing the death penalty but even call for our expulsion from international organisations such as the Council of Europe. The American view holds that democratic nations can sometimes differ on matters of fundamental rights. For example, freedom of speech is stronger in America than in many other nations; an individual has the constitutional right in the United States to make statements in favour of Nazism that might land the person in jail in Germany. Yet the United States does not demand that Germany change its law on this point or risk expulsion from international organisations. Again, in America today, it is a bedrock principle of constitutional freedom that there be no established church at any level of government. But the American position does not require every nation with an established church – such as England or Italy – to disestablish.

For Europeans, a great marker of successful constitutional development is international consensus and uniformity. They point to such consensus as if agreement throughout the 'international community' were itself a source of legal validation and authority. The more consensus there is on a constitutional principle throughout the international community, the greater the strength of that principle. Americans do not share this view. We have learned to see our own constitutional judgments as worth defending even during periods when most of the nations of Europe scorned or violated them. For Americans, a democratic nation's constitutional law is supposed to reflect that nation's fundamental legal and political commitments. Consensus in the 'international community' is not the compelling source of legal or constitutional authority that it is made out to be in the European perspective.

Whether out of hubris or principle, or both, the United States has not understood its support for international law and institutions to imply a surrender of its own commitment to self-government. As the international system became more powerful, and international law diverged from US law, the United States inevitably began to show unilateralist tendencies – not simply out of self-interest but because the United States is committed to democratic self-government. The continental European democracies, with their monarchical histories, their lingering aristocratic cultures, and their tendency to favour centralised, bureaucratic governance, have always been considerably less democratic than the American democracy. It is not surprising, then, that in forging the European Union they should be so tolerant of what Europeans casually refer to as the Union's 'democratic deficit'.

Three specific developments over the past decade helped press the United States toward unilateralism: the 1999 military intervention in Kosovo; a growing scepticism about international law, including the concern that international law might be used as a vehicle for anti-Americanism; and the events of 11 September 2001. Each merits additional consideration.

For many in the United States, the Kosovo intervention stands today as a unilateralist precedent. Because the UN Security Council never approved the use of force in Kosovo, international lawyers regarded the US-led bombing as plainly illegal. But this asserted illegality has not caused Americans to regret the intervention. On the contrary, it has reinforced the view that events in the former Yugoslavia represented an appalling failure on the part of the international law system, the United Nations and, in particular, the nations of Europe. From the American perspective, if the UN-centred international law system could not bring itself to authorise the use of force in Kosovo, then that system was incapable of discharging the responsibility that is an essential corollary of authority.

The United States had no compelling territorial, imperial or economic interests in Kosovo. The intervention sought rather, at least in the American account, to prevent manifest, grotesque, genocidal crimes. And if the United Nations did not respond to the most blatant, wanton and massive of human rights violations in Kosovo, how could it be trusted to respond to less demonstrable but perhaps more dangerous threats elsewhere?

Kosovo is a doubly significant precedent because it illustrates how Americans do not quite recognise the UN Charter as law. American society is notorious for turning political questions into legal ones. Yet Americans, including American lawyers, were and are largely uninterested in the Kosovo bombing's asserted illegality under the UN Charter. The same broad indifference would emerge again when internationalists claimed that the war in Iraq was illegal.

To be sure, some American international-law specialists are interested in these issues, but they are often perceived by the rest of the US legal world to be speaking a foreign language, or not so much a language as a kind of gibberish lacking the basic grammar – the grammar of enforceability – that alone gives legal language a claim to meaning. Kosovo symbolises not merely an exceptional, exigent circumstance in which the United States was justified in going outside the UN framework, but rather an entire attitude about that framework, according to which the UN system, while pretending to be a legal system, is really not a legal system. And what, in this view, is the United Nations really about? The several possible answers to the question are not attractive: hot air, a corrupt bureaucracy, an institution that acts as if it embodied world democracy when in reality its delegates represent illegitimate and oppressive autocracies, an invidious wonderland where Libya can be elected president of a human rights commission.

A second spur to US unilateralism has been a growing scepticism about the agenda the 'international legal community' has been pursuing. The scepticism is partly due to the proliferation of human rights conventions that are systematically violated by many of the states subscribing to them. A good example is the convention banning discrimination against women, which the United States has been almost alone in refusing to ratify. But what is one to make of the fact that the signatory nations include Saudi Arabia and other states not exactly famous for respecting women's equality?

A deeper reason for the scepticism lies in the indications that international law may be used as a vehicle for anti-American resentments.

A case in point is the position taken by the 'international community' with respect to the continuing use of capital punishment in some American jurisdictions. Most Americans, whatever their view of capital punishment, can respect the moral arguments that condemn the death penalty. But what many Americans have trouble respecting or understanding is the concerted effort to condemn the United States as a human rights violator because of the death penalty and to expel the United States from international organisations on that ground. When the international community throws down the gauntlet over the death penalty in America while merely clearing its throat about the slaughter in Yugoslavia, Americans can hardly be blamed if they see a sign that an anti-American agenda can be expected to find expression in international law.

This is not a purely speculative concern. Given that the US-led military interventions in Kosovo and Iraq were probably in violation of international law, might US officers therefore be liable to criminal prosecution in international courts? No, say the international lawyers. Americans need not fear criminal repercussions because international law 'clearly' distinguishes between *jus ad bellum*, the law that determines whether the use of military force is legal, and *jus in bello*, the law that determines whether particular acts undertaken during armed hostilities are criminal. But academic certainty about the 'clear' meaning of law has never been a reliable predictor of how the law will actually be interpreted by courts. How can Americans be certain that the international law system will not embrace the perfectly reasonable logic under which an unlawful bombing becomes a criminal act, especially when Americans have acted unilaterally? This possibility may help explain US resistance to the International Criminal Court.

The events of 11 September 2001 had obvious implications for US unilateralism. There was a critical period in the weeks following the massacre when a renewed US multilateralism in the prosecution of the war against terrorism seemed a distinct possibility. Americans were stunned by the prevalence and intensity of anti-American sentiments expressed all over the world. Even Europeans who condemned the attacks frequently suggested, implicitly and explicitly, that the United States had it coming, that the motives behind the attack were understandable, and that the massacre, though reprehensible, might have a salutary effect on US policy. A period of soul-searching followed in the United States. It lasted maybe a month and ended with a characteristically American reaction: to hell with them.

So began the rhetoric that continues to escalate today. The White House took increasingly belligerent positions, which elicited new denunciations of our bullying, and the denunciations spurred Americans to feel more and more that they would have to fight this world war on their own. The fighting in Afghanistan hardened that resolve. For whatever reason, the European nations, with the exception of Great Britain, contributed almost nothing to the war, and instead issued repeated warnings that the war might be illegal, that the bombings could be considered war crimes if too many civilians died, and that the fight, in any case, would be unwinnable once the opposition took to the mountains. Did we win? That remains to be seen. But the American experience of the Afghan campaign was of an overwhelming, unexpectedly swift victory – achieved essentially without the help of the international community. And this made possible the war in Iraq.

Because of that war, US unilateralism is now identified in many people's minds with US military aggression and the occupation of Iraq. I am not arguing here either for or against the Iraq War; the case for US unilateralism does not turn on the justifiability of that war. The fundamental question is this: Which of two visions of world order will the United States use its vast power to advance? Since the Second World War, much of 'old' Europe has been pursuing an anti-national, anti-democratic world constitutionalism that, for all its idealism and achievements, is irreconcilable with America's commitment to democratic self-government.

There is, among international lawyers, a hazy notion that the emergence of the international community in the world of law and politics is itself a democratic development. The unfortunate reality, however, is that international law is a threat to democracy and to the hopes of democratic politics all over the world. For some, that may be a reason to support internationalism; for others, a reason to oppose it. Either way, the fundamental conflicts between democracy and international law must be recognised.

The United Nations and the other institutions of international law take world government as their ideal. In theory, there is no necessary conflict between democracy and the ideal of a world government. A world government could be perfectly democratic – if there were world democracy. But at present, there is no world democracy, and, as a consequence, international governance organisations are, at present, necessarily and irremediably anti-democratic.

The anti-democratic qualities of the United Nations, the International Monetary Fund (IMF), and other international governance organisations – their centralisation, their opacity, their remoteness from popular or representative politics, their elitism, their unaccountability – are well known. Internationalists counter this criticism by pointing to the growing influence of 'nongovernmental organisations' (NGOs) in international law circles, as if these equally unaccountable, self-appointed, unrepresentative organisations somehow spoke for world public opinion. But the fundamentally anti-democratic nature of international governance is not merely a small hole that NGOs might plug. World government in the absence of world democracy is necessarily technocratic, bureaucratic, diplomatic – everything but democratic.

Nor are international organisations undemocratic only in themselves; they undermine the hopes and vitality of democratic politics elsewhere. The point is familiar to every nation in Latin America that has seen its internal policies dictated by IMF or World Bank directives. To an increasing extent, democratic politics throughout the developing world is being displaced by a relentless demand for competitiveness and growth, which are authoritatively interpreted by international organs to require the implementation of designated social, political and economic policies. So far, these have had rather mixed success in delivering competitiveness and growth, though they have contributed to several national catastrophes, as in Argentina.

The irony is that the United States remains the world's greatest champion of internationalism in economic affairs. Weaker countries correctly perceive US-led marketisation programmes as deeply undercutting their own ability to decide for themselves what their social and economic policies should be. To be sure, the United States does not exactly force economic policy on other countries. Ruling elites agree to the emasculation of their countries' politics in order to get their hands on the money. But the result is the same: democracy is hollowed out.

So all the talk of US unilateralism needs an important qualification. The United States plays utterly contradictory roles on the international stage: it champions multilateralism on the economic front, because worldwide free trade and marketisation are perceived to serve US interests, and resists it elsewhere. But if a commitment to democracy is what underlies America's growing unilateralism today on matters of war, criminal law, human rights, and the environment, that commitment is violated wherever US-led international economic organisations cripple the possibilities of democracy under the guise of free-trade principles and loan conditionality.

The American and French revolutions tied democracy to the ideal of a self-determining nation. If the European Union should successfully forge itself into a democratic mega-nation, it would be another example of this linkage, not a counterexample. Two hundred years later, there remains no realistic prospect of world democracy, and if there were such a prospect, the United States would resist it, because world decision-making would very likely be unfriendly to America. But though the United States would be no friend of world democracy, it ought to be a friend to a world of democracies, of self-governing nation-states, each a democracy in its own politics. For now, the hopes of democratic politics are tied to the fortunes of the nation-state.

Europeans tend to neglect or minimise the damage that universal constitutionalism does to the prospects for variation, experimentation and radical change opened up by national democracy. So long as democracy is allied with national self-government rather than with world governance, it remains an experimental ideal, dedicated to the possibility of variation, perhaps radical variation, among peoples with different values and different objectives. Democratic national constitu-tionalism may be parochial within a given nation, but it is cosmopolitan across nations. Democratic peoples are permitted, even expected, to take different paths. They are permitted, even expected, to go to hell in their own way.

That is what the ideology of international human rights and of a global market will not allow. Both press for uniformity among nations on some of the most basic questions of politics. Both, therefore, stand against democracy.

The response from the Right will be that a market economy is a pre-condition of a flourishing democracy, so international free trade and lending institutions cannot be called anti-democratic. Rejecting the Right's claim to the transcendental democratic necessity of the IMF or the World Trade Organization, the Left will reply that the existence of a capitalist economy and the particular form it should take are matters for independent nations to decide for themselves. But the Left, for its part, will insist that international human rights, the abolition of the death penalty, and environmental protections are necessary preconditions of democracy. To which the Right will reply that these are matters for independent nations to decide for themselves.

Claims that any particular multilateral order, whether humanitarian or economic, is a necessary condition of democracy should be received with extreme scepticism. We all tend to sympathise with such claims when they are made on behalf of policies we support, but to see through the same claims when they are on behalf of policies we oppose. To be sure, in some cases of national crisis and political breakdown, international governance has brought about stability and democratisation. And for the many nations incapable at present of sustaining flourishing democratic politics, international law offers the hope of economic and political reforms these nations cannot achieve on their own. But every time a functioning, self-determining nation surrenders itself to the tender mercies of international economic or political regimes, it pays a price. The idea that men and women can be their own governors is sacrificed, and democracy suffers a loss.

The justification of unilateralism outlined here is not intended to condone American disdain for the views of other nations. On the contrary, America should always show a decent respect for the opinions of the rest of mankind, and America would be a far safer, healthier place if it could win back some of the support and affection it has lost. Unilateralism does not set its teeth against international cooperation or coalition building. What sets its teeth on edge is the shift that occurs when such cooperation takes the form of binding agreements administered, interpreted and enforced by multilateral bodies – the shift, in other words, from international cooperation to international law. America's commitment to democratic self-government gives the United States good reason to be sceptical about – indeed, to resist – international legal regimes structured, as they now are, around anti-nationalist and anti-democratic principles.

The unilateralism I am defending is not a licence for aggressive US militarism. It is commanded by the aspirations of democracy and would violate its own essential principles if it were to become an engine of empire. But the great and unsettling fact of twenty-first-century global governance is that America is doomed to become something like a world policeman. With the development of small, uncontainable nuclear technologies, and with the inability of the United Nations to do the job, the United States will be in the business of using force abroad against real or feared criminal activity to a far greater extent than ever before.

This new American role will be deeply dangerous, to other nations and to our own, not least because American presidents may be tempted to use the role of the world's law enforcer as a justification for a new American militarism that has the United States constantly waging or preparing for war. If the United States is going to act unilaterally abroad, it is imperative that in our domestic politics we retain mechanisms for combating presidential overreaching.

Since 11 September 2001, the White House has flirted with a dangerous double unilateralism, joining the president's willingness to act without international consent abroad to an effort to bypass Congress and the judiciary at home. In December 2001, without congressional approval, the president announced the withdrawal of the United States from an important missile treaty with Russia. In early 2002, the White House began claiming a presidential power to deem any individual, including an American citizen arrested on American soil, an 'enemy combatant' and on that basis to imprison him indefinitely, with no judicial review. Later that year, the president came close to asserting a power to make war on Iraq without express congressional authorisation.

This double unilateralism, which leaves presidential power altogether unchecked, is a great danger. If we are to be unilateralists abroad, we have a special responsibility – to ourselves and to the world – to maintain and reinvigorate the vital checks and balances of American constitutionalism at home.

Comment

ARMIN VON BOGDANDY

As Lech Garlicki convincingly shows, the European democracies are engaged in an international discourse on how to organise and exercise public power. This discourse has not, contrary to what our American colleague Jed Rubenfeld asserts, ended up in one single form of European constitutionalism, and in particular not in one single model regarding how to relate courts and political institutions – as any comparison between Sweden, the Netherlands, Great Britain, Switzerland, Germany or France easily proves. One common European trait is, however, the rejection of the US-American constitutional model. As Lech Garlicki skilfully portrays, even the new democracies have mostly modelled their constitutions along the lines of Western European examples. For most Europeans, it is beyond question that these international influences have not worked to the detriment of democracy.

Only one specific international influence on democracy is developed in Rubenfeld's paper: the influence of international law and international institutions on national democracy. The thrust of the argument is to present the respective European openness as a democratic deficiency whereas the US-American resistance is praised as living up to the democratic ideal. Some European scholars – though not myself – will argue that the constitutions of most European states are not nearly as open and deferential to international law as Rubenfeld asserts. Nevertheless – as many examples reported by Rubenfeld prove – European states are far more willing to subscribe to and to fulfil international obligations.

He puts forward three arguments as to why international law endangers and cripples national democracy. I share all of these well-known opinions. There is little room to argue that international law making and international jurisprudence do not fulfil the prerequisites and procedures of an established democracy. Moreover, if democracy is understood – as Rubenfeld seems to understand it – as the auto-determination of a people conceived as a self-sufficient macro-subject, international law must be considered as a substantial threat, the extent and impact of which should be limited to the level of absolute necessity. From such a perspective, any self-respecting polity is normatively required to mini- mise the influence of international law on itself.

However, there is a different understanding of democracy available which leads to utterly different results. This is an understanding many Europeans will embrace as a civilising and normative advancement. It is based on an understanding of democracy not as the auto-determination of a macro-subject, but as a number of procedures which give a say to those affected. From this angle, a self-respecting democratic polity is one which attempts to provide for the necessary avenues of participation for affected individuals.

In an interdependent world, many decisions of the authorities of one polity substantially affect individuals living abroad who often do not have standing in domestic procedures. This situation is one of the undemo- cratic features of globalisation: more and more 'domestic' decisions are having a transnational impact with ever greater significance.

There is almost no remedy in the domestic democratic process. It is the nature of the domestic political process that the interests of the polity's citizens enjoy a priority over those of foreigners. Even when the process does not aim at hurting non-citizens, domestic interests tend to be favoured and foreign interests are relegated to the fringe. International law, with all its deficiencies, is so far the only instrument to provide some level of say for foreign persons affected by the adoption of measures of another polity. A state open to international law is therefore not limiting its democratic life, but rather realises a new dimension of it.

The same result can be achieved from the perspective of sovereignty. Traditionally, sovereignty is nothing but power. The core of the con- ventional understanding of sovereignty is for an entity to be able to decide freely and to assert its will against the unwilling. In Europe, however, a different concept of sovereignty is taking hold, namely the fundamental normative insight that sovereignty entails responsibility for those affected by the measures taken. So far, this dimension has been based mainly on national fundamental rights which impose duties on the state to protect core interests of the individuals within its territory. The idea, applied to the external side of sovereignty in an interdepen- dent world, entails some constitutional responsibility for people living outside the polity as well. Hence, the search for international coopera- tion can be construed as an adequate constitutional understanding of a responsible sovereign state in an interdependent world. To create and respect international law in an increasingly interdependent world is not a limitation to democratic sovereignty, but a most valuable tool for living up to the principle of democratic sovereignty. This idea informs Article 3 para. 4 of the EU Constitutional Treaty.

With all its limitations, international law provides the only avenue to give life to the democratic principle in an interdependent world. This argument does not provide democratic legitimacy to international human rights which limit public power with respect to the citizen. However, our American colleague overestimates the relevance of the Strasbourg jurisprudence for the domestic political process and neglects the doctrine of the margin of appreciation. Furthermore, it should be recalled that the Strasbourg jurisprudence does not enjoy direct effect in most domestic legal orders. If it is nevertheless followed by national courts – which is not always the case – it is because it presents convincing legal arguments. That, however, might be difficult to understand if the legal process is considered as being political to the extent our American colleague appears to believe.

The crude legal positivism our colleague portrays as the European standard can – unfortunately – indeed be found in some pieces of bad legal scholarship. But most European lawyers are far more enlightened. Nevertheless legal theory convincingly shows that there is still a world of legal argument apart from politics and neglecting it means misunderstanding the law as it is practised in Europe. In any event, the impact of the European Court of Human Rights does not rest on a sweeping constitutional decision, but on the persuasiveness of its judgments.

The argument by our American colleague is tainted by a further problem. Let me call it the 'Carl Schmitt Fallacy'. Perhaps some important representatives of the American intellectual establishment are – as Martti Koskenniemi has recently argued – late disciples of the 'old' Europe, in particular of Carl Schmitt as an advocate of a political order that Europe as it is today has – hopefully – overcome. Carl Schmitt ridiculed the Weimar Republic by comparing and delegitimising the reality of the Weimar political process against an ideal of parliamentarianism. In a similar vein, in Rubenfeld's paper the reality of the international legal process is pitted against an idealised US-American democracy. This idealisation is reminiscent of Carl Schmitt in a further way. Schmitt's basic understanding of democracy is that of the identity of ruled and rulers, amalgamated in a homogeneous 'we'. 'We' is a very important word in Rubenfeld's piece in which all internal differences have disappeared. And that 'we' is forged above all – as with Schmitt – by enmity: anti-Americanism is a crucial part in Rubenfeld's argument. Moreover, for Schmitt, legal scholarship has to be part of political struggle in order to be meaningful. Rubenfeld's partisanship appears to follow that path: it might explain his style.

With Schmitt and related understandings we will achieve nothing except to justify hegemonic politics in a rather illiberal setting. It closes all avenues of development of the international system to more democratic features and recommends involution. It is not surprising that such an understanding is not attractive to Europeans.

Larry Siedentop in his seminal book on 'Democracy in Europe' asserts that the United States had supported European integration for one specific reason: because the liberal East Coast establishment saw – according to Siedentop – a shift of political gravity in the country to the West with a much more populist approach. The liberal establishment supported European integration – again according to Siedentop – in order to strengthen a new international actor who might bear the torch of freedom and liberty when a populist United States is incapable of fulfilling that role.

Siedentop wrote a great book, but he is nevertheless – to my mind – wrong on almost all accounts. I hope that this is also the case regarding his vision of the US-American future. Rubenfeld's basic outlook presents an utterly dire prospect. US-American democracy would – in his vision – pose a threat to international law. But most people consider international law essential to building a decent world.

Comment

YASUAKI ONUMA

Professor Rubenfeld's contribution is most challenging, aggressive and stimulating and I admire it very much. I would also like to point out that there are many points on which I find myself in agreement with his view. For example, Rubenfeld emphasises the significance of the different perceptions held by Europeans and Americans. Some of the points which he referred to, such as the perception of the Second World War, I found very persuasive.

However, I tend to disagree with him in many other respects. I cannot, in particular, agree with him with respect to most of the points that he characterises as American exceptionalism. In dealing with this issue, I believe that we should look back to the very first days of the establishment of the United States. Even during the period of so-called isolationism, we could discern many of the features which Rubenfeld describes, for example, when he talks about transmitting American principles to the rest of the world. I think this started at the very beginning of the US republic. In fact, even during the period when the US followed so-called isolationist policies, it was actively engaged in interventions in foreign nations, including Asian nations, but most actively in Latin American nations.

The Monroe Doctrine may have been a defensive and 'isolationist' principle vis-à-vis European powers which were more powerful than the US at that time and which were perceived by the Americans as wicked, illegitimate and corrupted regimes. But at the same time, the Monroe Doctrine was a manifestation of the US-American will that Latin America should be within the US's sphere of influence: Europeans, do not touch them. This was already apparent in the nineteenth century, well before the Second World War. The US has been constantly engaged in interventions in the domestic affairs of Latin American nations, most conspicuously in Caribbean nations. For Caribbean nations, the fundamental principles of international law such as independence and sovereign equality have meant almost nothing in their relations with the US. So if you concentrate your attention on just the post-war period, you would lose sight of the whole of US history, which has this interventionist aspect.

Rubenfeld refers to two kinds of constitutionalism. I find this difficult to understand. I certainly understand that the idea of democracy, which emphasises the importance of local and participatory decision-making and includes the voices of the 'grass roots', is regarded by Americans as a foundational concept of constitutionalism. However, this does not necessarily mean that the US has been reluctant to impose this or similar ideas on foreign nations when the US thinks that this is appropriate. The case of Japan is a typical example. Our constitution was provided by the US occupation forces and we substantially had no other choice but to accept it.

The belief in grass roots popular democracy is one thing. The problem whether the US has been aggressive or reluctant in disseminating and propagating this idea is quite another. The fact that the Americans have committed themselves to this version of democracy does not necessarily mean the US has been reluctant to disseminate or propagate this idea to the outside world. In fact, this proselytising zeal has been a characteristic feature of the United States, deeply associated with a sense of righteousness to establish an ideal society on earth, separated from a 'corrupted and oppressive' Europe. This was the myth of the foundation of the American republic and this spirit has been maintained throughout the history of the United States. I have regarded this spirit – the genuine, even naïve, pursuit of establishing an ideal society on earth and the desire to share this ideal with other people – as a charming and attractive aspect of the United States. But on the other hand, as we all know, it has the danger of self-righteousness, arrogance and a preachy attitude which have appalled a large number of people all over the world.

I have been engaged in the study of comparing three major regional normative systems of the pre-modern period: Euro-centric, Islamo-centric and Sino-centric. There are and have been, of course, many other great regional systems, including Indo-centric and some others, but I have concentrated on these three major civilisations or regional systems. I have found interesting common characteristic features of major powers that have played a critical role in human history, such as the Roman Empire, the Han Dynasty, the Chin Dynasty, the Ottoman Empire, etc. While achieving great things in respective regions, they were all egocentric, universalistic and obsessed with a superiority complex. However, apart from these common features, they differed sharply in their ways of disseminating their ideas, cultures or civilisations. In the case of Islamo-centric civilisations, most dynasties were very aggressive and proselytising. So were a number of Christian kingdoms during the Middle Ages in Europe. France in the nineteenth and twentieth centuries was also eager to proselytise its ideas to other peoples. Chinese dynasties, however, were not proselytising at all. They regarded themselves as the only civilised nation in the world. We non-Chinese were all regarded as barbarians. We Japanese were 'Eastern barbarians', you Europeans were 'Southern barbarians'. However, the Chinese did not want to proselytise their ideas or civilisation to the outside world. They restricted themselves to inviting 'barbarians' to visit their empire and make tribute to the emperor for which they would in return provide the visiting 'barbarian' with huge amounts of goods, letters, and political, administrative and legal ideas among other things.

In this way, in human history there are types of empires or central powers with a proselytising zeal and those without. The United States apparently belongs to the former. In this respect, I have trouble with Rubenfeld's analysis of constitutionalism, because his explanation sharply contradicts the explanation which I have just provided. I have been a human rights activist for more than thirty years, and have encountered a large number of American people, who were far more interventionist, far more proselytising than their European counterparts. Analyses such as the one provided by Rubenfeld do not, in my view, explain this proselytising and preachy aspect of the United States.

Let me turn to the problem of the relationship between international law and democracy. Here, Rubenfeld points out three problematic features of international law. First, the problem of treaty creation. Rubenfeld points out the democratic deficit in the process of creating treaties. However, if you observe the constitutional systems of 190 nations in the present world, then you would have a very different impression. In my understanding, most nations have made serious efforts to institutionalise democratic checking-mechanisms in the process of ratification of treaties and they have succeeded in checking the treaty-making process at least to a certain extent. If Rubenfeld analyses these 190 nations and still argues that their practice is wanting, then his dissatisfaction is due to his peculiar understanding of democracy based on his US-centric way of thinking. It is this peculiar version of democracy which makes it difficult for him to understand democratic procedures taken not only by European countries but also by other nations of the world.

Another issue is the problem of international courts. A specific agreement is needed for a nation to be subjected to the jurisdiction of an international court. Without this agreement no international court can have jurisdiction over sovereign states. Therefore, the fundamental requirement of democracy, that is, that the agreement of those who should be subject to the binding decision must be secured, is satisfied.

And, finally, the problem of world government without world democracy. Here, I share some of Rubenfeld's criticisms. As I previously mentioned, I have been a human rights activist for more than thirty years, and I have encountered a number of NGOs, some of whom are incredibly self-righteous, preachy, interventionist, self-appointed teachers. They have nothing to do with the principle of democracy. I quite agree with Rubenfeld in this respect. On the other hand, I have fought with the Japanese government and some other governments for the human rights of a number of victims, and I firmly believe in the power of NGOs and the media in the dynamic process of liberal democracy. They may not fall within the formal, static category of democracy, but if you view liberal democracy as a dynamic process of representing voices, aspirations, expectations, grudges and animosities of various kinds of people, including various kinds of minorities that cannot be properly represented in the parliament, then you can see that the combination of NGOs, media institutions, scholars, lawyers and ordinary citizens is an essential component of democracy.

Recently, an American lady asked me whether I thought that the war in Iraq marked the decline of the United States as an empire. 'Well', I answered, 'Yes and No.' Yes, if following administrations of the United States pursue similar policies and if the American population as a whole does not learn the lesson from history that every empire which ignores the critical importance of legitimacy has eventually declined. One of the critical sources of power is the support, or at least the acquiescence, of those who are subject to power. This is the lesson that the Americans should learn from the war in Iraq. However, having lived altogether three years in the United States, I firmly believe in the diversity and fairness of the US society. So let me conclude my remarks with the hope that my answer would be 'No' and the US population as a whole will learn important lessons from the war and will seek legitimacy not only in terms of Rubenfeld's version of democracy, but in terms of democracy, constitutionalism and international law as perceived by most people outside the United States.

INDEX